WOMEN IN SCOTLAND
*c.*1100–*c.*1750

WOMEN IN SCOTLAND
*c.*1100–*c.*1750

Edited by
Elizabeth Ewan and Maureen M. Meikle

TUCKWELL PRESS

First published in Great Britain in 1999 by
Tuckwell Press Ltd
The Mill House
Phantassie
East Linton
EH40 3DG

The publication of this book has been assisted by a grant from the Scouloudi
Foundation in association with the Institute of Historical Research

ISBN 1 86232 046 2

British Library Cataloguing in Publication Data
A Catalogue record for this book is available
on request from the British Library

Typeset by Hewer Text Ltd, Edinburgh
Printed and bound by Cromwell Press, Trowbridge, Wiltshire

To the Women of Scotland – past, present and future.
May their voices be heard.

Table of Contents

List of Illustrations

1. The Prioress Anna of the nunnery at Iona as depicted upon her tombstone.
2. Eleanor, fourth daughter of James I.
3. Margery Bowes or Margaret Stewart, wife of John Knox.
4. Dame Jean or Jonet Scott, Lady Ferniehirst, shown as a widow in 1593.
5. Anna of Denmark, consort of James VI and I.
6. The family of Sir William Dick of Braid.
7. Washer women of Dundee, as depicted by John Slezer in 1678.
8a. Esther Inglis, calligrapher, printer and embroiderer of bookbindings.
8b. Title pages of Bibles printed by Agnes Campbell in 1707.

(Part title illustrations)

1. Iona nun (detail).
   H. D. Graham, *Antiquities of Iona* (1850)

2. Lady Grisel Baillie's crewel work.
   The Household Book of Lady Grisell Baillie, 1692–1733
   ed. R. Scott-Moncrieff (Scottish History Society, 1911)

3. Henrietta Stewart, 6th Countess of Huntly, with George Gordon, 6th Earl.
   The Scottish National Portrait Gallery

4. Woman with a basket (detail).
   J. Slezer, 'Ruins of Dryburgh', *Theatrum Scotiæ* (1874), plate 33. By permission of Special Collections, University of Guelph Library.

5. A Scotch Woman.
   J. Speed, *The Kingdome of Scotland* (1652)

6. A Highland Woman.
   J. Speed, *The Kingdome of Scotland* (1652)

Foreword

On 18 May 1996 the Scottish History Department of the University of Edinburgh, in conjunction with the Scottish Women's History Network, held a highly successful day conference entitled *Women in Scotland c.1100–c.1750*. It was exciting to hear a series of papers based on the latest research, all the more so because relatively little on that subject had appeared in print. Twenty years ago, feminists were publishing vehement and often entertaining polemics deploring sexual stereotyping and the plight of women condemned to lives of domestic drudgery. In order to achieve social change, inspired enthusiasts often use lively rhetoric to alert others to wrongs which need to be righted but, in drawing urgent attention to sexual inequalities, most feminist writers had no time to undertake historical research and when they did allude to the situation in centuries gone by, they often gave the impression that women had consistently been held down by the law and by their husbands, forced into a submissive, secondary role which they were unable to challenge.

Anyone who looks at the records soon discovers that this was far from being so, and indeed most people have vague recollections of stories heard in childhood about Black Agnes of Dunbar defending her castle or Flora MacDonald taking Bonnie Prince Charlie across the sea to Skye. Amusing as these tales may be, they are largely anecdotal and most of them derive from one small section of society, the aristocracy. For any more scientific study, what was needed was fundamental documentary research of the kind which takes time, expert knowledge and, above all else, patience. The evidence exists, but it is fragmentary, scattered and requires painstaking investigation over a period of months and years before it can be gathered together and conclusions can be drawn.

Fortunately, scholars have not been deterred by these difficulties and in the past few years we have begun to see the results of their work. Now, this splendid volume of conference papers, with additional essays by other experts, gives us a comprehensive view of the feminine situation, based on archival sources ranging from Court of Session records to Middle Scots poetry. Here we can discover how women really lived and what they really thought, whether they were twelfth-century nuns or late-medieval brewers, widows or wives of ministers of the kirk. Their attitudes, their experiences, the way people perceived them and the manner in which they perceived themselves are examined and assessed, to fascinating effect.

In 1983, when I was completing my own contribution to Scottish women's studies, I longed for information like this. Sixteen years later, it is therefore a particular pleasure to contribute the Foreword to this book.

Rosalind K. Marshall

Acknowledgements

We would like to thank all our contributors for taking part in this project and for giving us such a rich variety of papers. Thanks are also due to our anonymous referees who gave excellent guidance. The conference on which this book is based would not have been possible without the official help of Professor Michael Lynch and the Department of Scottish History at the University of Edinburgh and the support of the Scottish Women's History Network. Ruth Grant and Sharon Adams deserve a special mention for co-ordinating the entire conference preparations and administration whilst the editors were busy elsewhere. Their efficiency ensured a smooth-running event that was greatly enjoyed by speakers, session chairs and audience alike. The conference sessions were expertly chaired by Dr Jane Dawson, Dr Rosalind Marshall, Mr David Sellar and Professor Geoffrey Barrow. Dr Stana Nenadic's closing comments were incisive and encouraging to all involved in researching medieval and early modern Scotswomen.

Post-conference thanks are due to Dr Rosalind Marshall and the staff of the Scottish National Portrait Gallery for helping us acquire illustrations for the book. By agreeing to write the Foreword for the book, Dr Marshall gave the project a most welcome bonus. For agreeing to publish an unusual collection of Scottish essays, we are very grateful to John and Val Tuckwell of Tuckwell Press, who have also extended hospitality to us on several occasions.

We would like to point out that the project could not have gone ahead so quickly without the assistance of e-mail, as one editor and many of our contributors live in North America. If only the same could be said of Scotrail! They took Elizabeth on an extra journey to North Berwick in the summer of 1996, whilst Maureen was waiting for her to alight at Longniddry. The train door refused to open at the station, so Maureen chased the train to North Berwick, via Drem, to try and rescue Elizabeth. Every time the train was in sight, the traffic intervened. We eventually met back at Longniddry and proceeded to visit the Tuckwells as planned.

The University of Guelph and its Archives have assisted the book's production, as has the University of Sunderland. Elizabeth would like specifically to acknowledge the assistance of the Social Sciences and Humanities Research Council of Canada and the International Social Sciences Institute at the University of Edinburgh. She also thanks Jean and

Marjorie Ewan for their Edinburgh hospitality and Kris Inwood for moral and intellectual support. Maureen would like to thank her parents Roy and Davina Meikle for all their support over many years and their ever-welcoming hospitality at Gullane.

Timeline

This timeline is selective and meant to illustrate the events mentioned in the essays in this collection. It is not a detailed outline of Scottish history.

1058–93	Reign of Malcolm III and St Margaret
1113–4	Matilda princess of Scotland marries Henry I of England
1107–24	Reign of Alexander I
1124–53	Reign of David I
1136–53	David supports his niece Empress Matilda against Stephen in England, takes over much of Northern England
1153–65	Reign of Malcolm IV
1157	Henry II of England recovers English lands from Scotland
1160–4	Malcolm IV subdues Galloway, Argyll and Somerled, ancestor of the Lords of the Isles
1165–1214	Reign of William I 'the Lion'
1214–49	Reign of Alexander II, marries 1221 Joan of England, 1239 Marie de Coucy
1249	Alexander II dies on expedition to subdue Western Isles
1249–86	Reign of Alexander III, marries 1251 Margaret of England, 1285 Yolande de Dreux
1263–6	Alexander ends Norse control of Western Isles, ceded to Scotland in 1266
1286–90	Margaret, Maid of Norway, granddaughter of Alexander III, recognised as queen, dies on way to Scotland in 1290
1291–2	Edward I of England, asked to rule on nearest heir to throne, chooses John Balliol
1295	Balliol makes alliance with France
1296	Edward I invades Scotland and deposes John, claims direct rule over Scotland
1296–1328	First War of Independence
1306	Robert Bruce claims Scottish throne
1328	England recognises Scottish independence
1329–71	Reign of David II
1332–41	Second War of Independence
1371–90	Reign of Robert II, first king of Stewart dynasty
1390–1406	Reign of Robert III
1406–1424	Prince James captured by English and imprisoned to 1424, Robert III dies 1406. James marries Joan Beaufort 1424
1424–37	James I returns to Scotland, personal reign
1436	James commits to French alliance, marries daughter to Dauphin
1437–60	Reign of James II

1449	James II marries Mary of Gueldres
1460–88	Reign of James III
1468	James III marries Margaret of Denmark, Orkney and Shetland pledged for her dowry, come into Scottish possession
1488–1513	Reign of James IV
late 15th C/	flourishing of Scots poetry – William Dunbar, Robert
16th C	Henryson, David Lindsay, Gavin Douglas, Alexander Scott
1493	Final forfeiture of Lordship of the Isles
1503	Marriage of James IV and Margaret Tudor of England
1507–8	First printing press established in Edinburgh
1512	Renewal of Auld Alliance with France
1513	Battle of Flodden against English – James IV and leading nobles killed
1513–15	Regency of Margaret Tudor for James V
1513–28	Minority of James V – struggle for power between factions
1521	Major, *History of Greater Britain*
1527	Boece, *History of Scotland*
1532	Establishment of College of Justice as central court in Edinburgh
1530–40s	Growth of Protestantism
1537	James V marries Madeleine of France
1538	James V marries Mary of Guise-Lorraine
1542	Scots defeated by English at Solway Moss, James V dies, infant Mary succeeds
1554–60	Regency of Mary of Guise
1558	Mary Queen of Scots marries Dauphin of France
1559–60	Protestant Reformation established, Kirk Sessions established
1561–7	Widowed Mary returns to Scotland and rules as Catholic queen
1563	Legislation against witchcraft and adultery
1566	Prince James born, Mary's second husband Darnley murdered
1567	Mary deposed, James accedes as James VI
1568–87	Mary imprisoned in England, factional fighting for power over James VI
1568	Bannatyne Manuscript
1579–83	Sir James Balfour, *Practicks*
1580s	Maitland Folio
1581	Presbyteries established, influence of Andrew Melville on church
1589	James VI marries Anna of Denmark
1590	Beginning of Catholic missions to Scotland
1592	Spanish Blanks – letters by Catholic earl of Huntly to king of Spain
1603	James VI succeeds to English throne (Union of the Crowns)
1609	Statutes of Iona and other royal efforts to 'civilise' Gaelic society
1610	Restoration of bishops
1625	Accession of Charles I

early 17th C	Rise to power of Campbells of Argyll
1637	Attempt by Charles I to impose new prayer book on Scottish church
1638–49	National Covenant to defend Presbyterian church, Scots join war in England against Charles I
1644–5	Royalist campaign led by Montrose and Alasdair MacColla
1650–9	Cromwellian occupation of Scotland
1660	Restoration of Charles II
1662	Restoration of Episcopacy
1680s	Persecution of Covenanters defending Presbyterian church
1685	Accession of James VII
1688–9	deposition of James VII, accession of William of Orange and Mary
1690	Establishment of Presbyterianism
1696–1700	Famine, Dutch and French wars
1695–8	Darien scheme to found Scottish trading colony in Americas fails disastrously
1707	Parliamentary Union with England
1715	First Jacobite Rising to restore James VIII, defeated at Battle of Sheriffmuir
1730s	Decline of kirk session discipline
mid 18th C	Scottish Enlightenment begins
1745–6	Second Jacobite rising, defeated at Battle of Culloden
1746	Punitive measures taken against Gaelic society and culture
c.1750	Beginning of industrialisation

INTRODUCTION:

A Monstrous Regiment of Women?

_____ *Elizabeth Ewan and Maureen M. Meikle*

This book is not about Mary Queen of Scots. Much – and, some believe, too much – has been written on her already. It is ironic that in a country with one of the most famous female historical figures in the world, little has been written on other women. Mary's *bête noire*, John Knox, wrote passionately about the 'Monstrous Regiment of Women'.[1] Knox was referring to the 'regiment' or rule of queens such as Mary's mother, Mary of Guise. This book is about the 'regiment' or group of Scottish women *c.*1100–*c.*1750, few of whom occupy a prominent role in existing histories of Scotland. We hope that this collection of essays will go some way towards making such women more visible in Scottish history and encourage others to undertake more research into their lives.

When Margaret MacCurtain and Mary O'Dowd co-edited a very interesting collection of essays on early modern Irishwomen it prompted Scottish comparisons.[2] In spite of the destruction of the National Archives in 1922, the contributors to the Irish volume were able to begin restoring early modern women to their rightful place in history. Reading through these papers, one could only wonder about women in medieval and early modern Scotland. They had received little attention from historians, yet Scottish sources are undoubtedly richer for the period 1100–1750. Independently from each other, Elizabeth Ewan and Maureen Meikle were thinking that it would be a good idea to produce a Scottish version of MacCurtain and O'Dowd, ideally launched with a one-day conference in Edinburgh. Both had a teaching and research interest in women's history and wanted to know more about Scotswomen from all social strata. It was time to challenge some existing Scottish historians to think 'gender' and stop them belittling women's role in Scotland's medieval and early modern past. Dauvit Broun gave us our first opportunity to voice these opinions in review articles for *The Innes Review*.[3]

From the outset, *Women in Scotland c.1100–c.1750* was an international project as Maureen was in Missouri, U.S.A and shortly afterwards moved to Sunderland, England, whilst Elizabeth works in Guelph, Canada. Early in 1995 Ruth Grant and Sharon Adams agreed to be the local contacts for a one-day conference as they were both postgraduate students in the Department of Scottish History at the University of Edinburgh. The conference was held in May 1996. The Scottish Women's History Network were happy to co-sponsor the event with the Department of Scottish History. One hundred and forty people attended the conference to hear nine very interesting papers with lively discussion sessions. Interest was widespread, with speakers and delegates from several countries.

Participants at the conference were encouraged to submit their papers for consideration in a refereed collection of essays. Other contributions were requested from a wide range of researchers. The book did not seek to encompass all aspects of women's lives from *c.* 1100 to *c.*1750. The sparse coverage of the fourteenth century was unintentional. In the end, with the help of referees, twenty papers were selected and loosely arranged under the themes of religion, literature, legal history, the economy, politics and the family. This book is the result.

Women's history has developed fairly late in Scotland in comparison with other western countries. The reasons for this are complex,[4] but one cause may be the emphasis on Scottish political history in the last fifty years. As the Empire declined, historians in the constituent parts of the British Isles began to focus more on the history of their own countries, separate from that of the United Kingdom.[5] In Scotland, this development was furthered by the disappointment of the 1979 referendum on devolution with its promise of political change. Paradoxically this led to a renaissance of other aspects of Scottish identity, including music, literature, art and history. Because the focus was on identity, political history took pride of place, especially for the period before 1707 when Scotland still had its own parliament.

The social history that has occupied such a prominent place in the historiography of many countries since the 1960s and 1970s did not enjoy the same growth in Scotland. This was in spite of the pioneering efforts of historians such as Harry Graham, Eunice Murray,[6] and Christopher Smout, whose landmark *History of the Scottish People 1560–1830* appeared in 1969.[7] Social history emphasised the stories of those beyond the elite who occupied centre stage in traditional histories. Combined with new questions and issues arising from the women's movement of the 1960s and 1970s, this led to a new interest in women's past. In Scotland, however, few addressed the topic, with the exception of Rosalind Marshall whose doctoral research on Anne Duchess of Hamilton resulted in *The Days of Duchess Anne* in 1973, and Elspeth King whose pioneering look at the Scottish women's suffrage movement appeared in 1978.[8]

In the early 1980s two major works appeared which advanced our understanding of Scotswomen. Christina Larner's classic study of the Scottish witch-hunt, *Enemies of God* (1981),[9] raised many fascinating questions about the role of gender in the witch-hunt and the position of women in early modern Scotland. Some of her theories such as the 'criminalization of women' after 1560 and 'witch-hunting as woman-hunting' are still very influential on historians writing today. Rosalind Marshall's important survey *Virgins and Viragos: A History of Women in Scotland 1080–1980* (1983),[10] was a novel attempt to look at women from medieval to modern times. Reflecting the material available in largely printed records and her own research, she had to focus mainly on elite women, but her work raised awareness that Scottish women had also played a role in the nation's history.

A series of demographic studies, stimulated by Flinn's *Population History of Scotland* (1977),[11] began to lay the groundwork for studies of population and family in the 1980s and these shed further light on women's lives. The works of Ian Whyte, Rab Houston, Rosalind Mitchison and Leah Leneman, among others, demonstrated the high mobility of rural women, patterns of marriage and female economic activity. Houston and Whyte's edited collection *Scottish Society 1500–1800* (1989)[12] included an essay giving an overview of women's economic and social position during this period. Mitchison and Leneman's *Sexuality and Social Control: Scotland 1680–1780* (1989)[13] examined illegitimacy and irregular marriage, areas which by their very nature involved women.

A turning-point for women's history in Scotland was marked by the 1990 publication of the essay collection, *The World is Ill-Divided* edited by Eleanor Gordon and Esther Breitenbach, followed by their 1992 collection *Out of Bounds*.[14] These two volumes stimulated new research into nineteenth- and twentieth-century women's history and also raised the possibility of looking at women further back in time.[15] The challenge was met more quickly by modern historians than those working on medieval and early modern Scotland. Nevertheless, in the last two years, monographs focusing on women in the early modern period have appeared, including Elizabeth Sanderson's pioneering *Women and Work in Eighteenth-century Edinburgh* (1996)[16] and Deborah Symond's *Weep Not for Me* (1997)[17] on infanticide. Elspeth King has also surveyed the history of Glasgow women from medieval to modern times.[18] A political study of *The Heiresses of Buccleuch*,[19] and a study of women in the 1745 rising, *Damn' Rebel Bitches*, appeared in 1997.[20] Several articles have appeared in journals, both well-known ones and those not so easily accessible.[21] There are other findings in as yet unpublished doctoral work.

One advantage of the relatively late development of Scottish women's history is that researchers are able to make use of findings, approaches, and theories developed by scholars in other countries. This exposure to such comparative work is heightened by the tendency of scholars to present papers at international conferences on women's history as well as at conferences focusing on Scotland. In the last few years papers on

Scottish women before 1750 have been presented at the Leeds and
Kalamazoo International Medieval Congresses, Sixteenth-Century Stu-
dies Conferences, an Exeter conference on 'Women, Trade and Business',
and the North American Conference on British Studies amongst others. In
Scotland, the first conference on medieval women was held in 1991 by the
Scottish Medievalists. Since then, there have been several day-conferences
organised by the Scottish Women's History Network. In 1996 the
Edinburgh conference mentioned above was organised as well as an
Aberdeen meeting that examined women's history from both Scottish and
international perspectives, and brought together scholars from Scandi-
navia, Europe, England, Ireland and North America.[22]

There is still a long way to go. General histories of Scotland have little
to say about women.[23] Even the most recent collection of primary sources
for Scottish history after 1707 has only a few documents on women from
the years before 1830 and gender does not appear as a separate category
until the section dealing with the later period.[24] Literary scholars have
been ahead of historians, both in research and in publishing primary
sources.[25] This led to an embarrassing experience for one of the editors at
a 1995 conference session on images of women in medieval Scottish
literature. When a speaker asked what was the historical experience of
women at this time, she had to reply that we didn't yet know.

This volume, by presenting a large number of short essays, indicates the
great variety of potential topics and approaches. We have intentionally
asked for contributions from both younger and more senior researchers,
those working specifically on women and those considering them as part
of a different project. We have indicated elsewhere[26] some of the directions which future research could take, but we consider the ultimate goal
to be a Scottish history where the contributions of both women and men
are considered as a matter of course.

Because most historical sources have been written or constructed by
men, scholars of women's history have had to dig deep, range far and
wide through a variety of sources, and read between the lines to
reconstruct the worlds of women in the past. Many of the essays in this
collection demonstrate the value of an interdisciplinary approach. We
have purposely not given titles to the different sections, because so many
of the papers cross disciplinary and topical boundaries. As well as formal
historical records, our contributors have used literary sources, archaeological evidence, sculpture, painting and manuscript illumination, contemporary narrative sources, letters and diaries, oral tradition and
folklore.

The collection begins with an examination of women's piety in the
Middle Ages. Andrew McDonald makes use of a great range of sources,
archaeological, documentary, architectural and sculptural, to indicate

just how much can be learned about the founders of twelfth- and thirteenth-century female monastic houses, especially those of native aristocratic families. He discusses the role of women in such foundations, a role often hidden by conventional phrasing in legal documents, and suggests how much more can be discovered about these houses by further research in existing documents. He also places Scottish female monasticism from the twelfth century firmly in a European context, while suggesting the survival of earlier Celtic characteristics. His interdisciplinary approach is continued by Audrey-Beth Fitch who uses a similarly wide range of sources to examine the types of messages which late medieval lay women received about their spiritual strengths and weaknesses, especially in the area of sexuality. Again the importance of European influences is brought out, in the devotion to female saints from the Continent. Her paper raises questions about the impact of native female saints and their images on Scottish women.

The images of female piety from the late medieval period can be compared to those from the reformed church after 1560, discussed in David Mullan's essay. Here the influence of English as well as European Protestant theology on Scottish religious writers is convincingly demonstrated. The gendered nature of theological writing is examined. The negative image of women's sexuality continues from pre-Reformation days, but there are also more positive characterisations of women's spiritual strength and piety, reflected in the actions women took to support those ministers who belonged to what they regarded as the true kirk. One wonders if the ministers' wives discussed in Ian and Kathleen Whyte's paper were equally supportive of their husbands. Mullan also refers briefly to a fascinating early example of Scottish female writing, the spiritual diary of Mistress Rutherford, of which he will shortly be producing a published version.[27]

Very little has survived of the words of women from before 1560, but as Priscilla Bawcutt's and Bridget Henisch's essay on three of the daughters of James I shows, women did compose poems and other works. Unfortunately, nothing survives of the poetry of Margaret, sent from Scotland at an early age to become the wife of the Dauphin of France. One wonders if her literary talents were encouraged by becoming part of the same court in which the writer Christine de Pizan (mentioned at the beginning of Mullan's paper) had earned her living. Her sisters Isabel and Eleanor seem to have inherited the Stewart love of books, and Eleanor is an important figure in German literature for her sponsorship or possibly her actual translation of a major work of German literature, *Pontus und Sidonia*. The princesses followed in the European tradition of female patronage of literature.

Moving from the experiences of Scottish women in Europe back to

Scotland, the next two papers examine the content of Scottish poems and songs. Evelyn Newlyn examines the nature of female imagery in male-authored poems in two manuscript collections, the Bannatyne and Maitland Manuscripts, of the sixteenth century. She shows the strong misogynistic tradition that is a noted feature of writing in this period. Again, the concern with the danger of women's sexuality comes to the fore. These male poems can be compared with the songs of Gaelic women examined by Anne Frater. Frater demonstrates how women in their song-writing could both accept and rebel against their inferior status in Gaelic society. The beautiful poetry, here presented in both the Gaelic original and in English translation, brings us the authentic voice of individual women from the period and in some cases provides us with a female reaction to the political events of the day. The subject of women's songs, this time from the work-song tradition, is brought up again in the paper of Domhnall Uilleam Stiùbhart.

The role of women at the Scottish Court is detailed in the papers by Andrea Thomas, Maureen Meikle and Ruth Grant. Interference at the later British Court is noted by Karl von den Steinen. Thomas skilfully depicts both the powerful and the meek at the Scottish Court of James V against the stereotypical poetic background also noted by Newlyn. The comparisons of three queens consort are revealing. Similarly intriguing correspondence between Dame Jean Scott as facutrix to her husband, Sir Thomas Ker of Ferniehirst, and Mary, Queen of Scots is long overdue for exposure. Grant precisely points out the importance of this to national and international politics. Equally revealing are the antics of the countess of Arran, who appears really to have worn the trousers (kilt?) in her marriage to Scotland's one-time political leader. As a powerful woman she was ridiculed and typically accused of witchcraft to try and precipitate her fall from grace. Anna of Denmark, consort of James VI, was both gregarious and shrewd. Meikle has shown that Anna knew well the value of jewels and how to raise money by them. By taking good advice, and acting upon it, Anna nearly brought the royal coffers of Scotland into order during the chaotic 1590s.

According to von den Steinen, a century later elite women were still able to play political gambits. The aristocratic sisters, the duchess of Atholl and the countess of Panmure, involved themselves with politics at a critical time in British history. Against the background of the Darien fiasco, the Union of 1707 and the '15 rebellion these sisters were heavily involved with all the political intrigues of the day, both in Edinburgh and London.

Elizabeth Ewan, Alistair Mann and Helen Dingwall have all looked at different aspects of women's contribution to the economy. All adult women were expected to know how to brew ale. However, the role of the female brewers in the urban economy, as highlighted by Ewan, is revealing. There were both professional and part-time brewsters supplying a regular demand for household use and for sale. Many were wives, others were servants supplementing their wages. They honed their marketing techniques within a localised area, with shrewd observation of supply and demand. Sadly, this activity was never going to be a high profile business. When the brewing trade became more professional in the sixteenth century, women became marginalised.

Discussion of women involved with the book trade may appear to be incongruous. Nevertheless, Mann clearly shows how women were part of this relatively deregulated craft. Based in the burghs, skilled book women ranged from widows in charge of a publishing house to printers, booksellers and embroiderers of fine book bindings. Agnes Campbell, the royal printer, even had the audacity to publish a counterfeit Bible in 1707, though a more usual female achievement was the embroidered bindings greatly treasured by their elite owners. Although they may have represented only ten per cent of all Scottish book traders, women definitely made their mark in this crafts-based sector of the economy.

Dingwall's paper proves that women were still a vital part of the economy in the late seventeenth century and had not been relegated to the shadows as the Clark thesis once alleged. Despite changing socio-economic conditions, women's role in the economy as either unskilled or skilled workers was sustained. Restoration Edinburgh had a greater female than male population – 3,000 of whom were servants. Others were traders, retailers and merchants in their own right, rather than acting for their husbands. Textiles were commonly traded or processed by women and they were known to be moneylenders as well in a pre-banking era. However, the expanding Edinburgh professions mostly excluded women with the exception of education, where single women taught at the lower end of the scale.

Studies of women's legal position have recently moved from emphasising their second-class status in the formal law codes to stressing their ways of getting around legal restrictions.[28] There are examples of both approaches in the essays by John Finlay and Winifred Coutts. Using the Court of Session papers in the Scottish Record Office, Finlay shows how active some women could be in pleading their cases before the Lords of Council, the precursor to the Court of Session established as Scotland's central court in the 1530s. Coutts discusses women's formal legal position in more detail, but demonstrates, as Amy Erickson has for post-Reformation England,[29] how limitations on women's legal rights were overcome by marriage contracts and testaments.

In post-Reformation Scotland, women faced the courts of a newly-Protestant nation, sometimes with lethal results in the case of the Scottish witch-hunt. Michael Graham examines the ways in which women were treated by the kirk sessions, local parish church courts, especially in the area of moral discipline. This was set against a pervading sense of public order linked to the enforcement of the Reformation which women may have found repressive. However, Graham's examination of the surviving records for the period 1560–1600 suggests that although women were more likely to be called before the court to answer for sexual misbehaviour (as their pregnancies made such behaviour visible), the courts were remarkably even-handed in dealing with men and women. Women also used the courts to defend their family honour in a manner akin to their English sisters, recently highlighted by the work of Laura Gowing.[30] The one area where women suffered the penalties of the law disproportionately was in charges of witchcraft. Eighty-five per cent of those charged were women, a ratio of women to men similar to many other areas of Europe. Historians are now beginning to examine the role of gender in Scottish witch-hunting to show how sexual immorality was often equated with witchcraft. Scotland had one of the most severe witch-hunts in Europe and this has attracted research into one of the few areas of Scottish history that openly involved women of all social strata. This has set the background for more detailed local studies of the phenomenon that are beginning to emerge.[31]

Although underrated, no one can really deny the importance of the female sex to the procreation and rearing of humankind. It was in this central role that most Scotswomen contributed to past societies. Women and the family appear in many of these papers from the elite down to the subservient. Meikle, Thomas and von den Steinen demonstrate how royal and elite women's marriages were often political arrangements. They were expected to produce heirs to perpetuate dynasties, but sometimes could manipulate the marriages of their own offspring in turn. Marriage customs varied from region to region, with the marriages of young St. Kildans highlighted by Stiùbhart being very different to those of the Highland women mentioned by Roxanne Reddington-Wilde, who married at a more usual age for Western Europe. Scottish ministers took particular care in their choice of a bride, as the paper by the Whytes suggests. Ministers' wives are a neglected area of research and this contribution goes some way to amending this situation. The legal aspect of marriage again contrasts the customs of the Gàidhealtachd and Lowland Scotland. The strict legal contracts drawn up for dowers and tochers in the Lowlands contrast with the more relaxed divorces possible under Gaelic law, as Coutts and Stiùbhart demonstrate. Sadly, by the eighteenth century the older Gaelic customs were being swept away in favour of the Lowland lifestyle being adopted by the clan elite. The unique place of widows in society is reinforced by the examples given in von den Steinen's and Reddington-

Wilde's papers, where they could exert considerable power within their families.

The threat of death in childbirth was ever present in Scotland as elsewhere. The fascinating details about North-Eastern wet-nurses unearthed by Gordon Desbrisay will certainly fill rather large gaps in our knowledge of this female employment in Scotland. That unmarried pregnant girls were held back from the wrath of the Kirk Session by ministers and Aberdeen retailers seeking a wet-nurse for their own children is a startling revelation. These women did penance for their fornication many months later. By way of contrast, Frater and Stiùbhart prove that the illegitimate children of clan chiefs and their lower-caste mothers were not shamed or discriminated against. The fact of their existence was regarded as a source of pride.

As can be seen from the discussion above, there are many approaches to women's history and not all of our contributors agree with one another in their view of the past. For example, some lay more stress on women's agency, others on the factors which disadvantaged women. Far from being a problem, this indicates the flourishing nature of the field, as scholars begin to enter the debate about different interpretations of the past. It also provides a good base for student discussion. We have tried to design the book so that it can be used effectively in schools and universities, as well as by the general reader, and to introduce some of the issues raised by women's history. Through such ongoing debate the study of the past is advanced.

Several new findings for both women's history and Scottish history have emerged from the work undertaken for this book. Women's participation in the legal sphere shows them to have been much more active than previously assumed. Some women even acted as procurators in the courts for others, a development possibly unique to Scotland. The link between illegitimacy rates and the ready availability of wet-nurses found in Aberdeen appears not to have been recognised in most studies of illegitimacy and wet-nursing outside Scotland. Just as ballads have increasingly been recognised as an important source for the lives of lowland women, so female songs are revealed as a major new source of material for the history of Gàidhealtachd society. The multiplicity of sources for the piety of medieval women, both religious and lay, disproves the assertion that almost nothing can be found out about medieval female religious houses. The contribution of women, especially domestic servants, to the urban economy is shown to be far more pervasive than thought. This suggests the importance of looking at internal trade as well as export trade when considering the fortunes of towns. New suggestions are made about the importance of kinship ties for women, an important issue in Scotland where kinship has loomed large in the historical discussion. The centrality of ideas on gender in literary works, theological discussion and discipline imposed by the church is demonstrated. In court politics, women's role is shown to be far more influential than traditionally assumed, especially when 'political power' is not defined strictly in terms of holding office.

This collection is by no means the final word on women in medieval and early modern Scotland. There are many important areas to which we have not been able to give attention, due to constraints of time, space and the research that is actually taking place. Much more work is needed on women of the Gàidhealtachd – most research on Scottish women has been on women of the Scots-speaking areas. We have not been able to include material on Scandinavian women and we deliberately restricted the number of contributions on elite and royal women, though there is some fascinating work being done in this area.[32] Supposedly straightforward questions about why many Scotswomen kept their name after marriage, whereas their English sisters could not, merit further investigation.[33] More work also needs to be done on women's role in the rural economy, along the lines suggested by Alex Gibson and Christopher Smout in their recent *Prices, Food and Wages in Early Modern Scotland*.[34] Christopher Whatley's recent essay on the contribution of women to the industrial revolution is a model of this type of research.[35] Experiences of marriage and motherhood, sexuality, both heterosexual and homosexual and women's roles in popular culture, are topics which historians have only recently started to consider. The impact of gender has only begun to be explored in this collection. Gender ideology affected men as well as women, and in order to arrive at a clearer picture of Scottish society as a whole, this needs to be taken into account.

Rather than provide a printed bibliography, we have created an on-line bibliography on the World Wide Web at http://www.uoguelph.ca/~eewan that will be frequently updated. This will supplement the bibliographic material available in the essays. Readers are encouraged to submit suggestions for additions to Elizabeth Ewan at Dept of History, University of Guelph, Guelph, Ontario, Canada N1G 2W1 or e-mail eewan@uoguelph.ca. Through this process and the research that we hope this book will encourage, a co-operative effort can be made in recovering the history of both the women and men of Scotland's past.

NOTES

1. John Knox, 'The First Blast of the Trumpet Against the Monstrous Regiment of Women' in *The Works of John Knox*, ed. D. Laing, vol. 4 (Edinburgh, 1895), 349–422.

2. *Women in Early Modern Ireland,* (Edinburgh, 1991). Maureen would like to thank Dr Margaret Mackay for showing her a copy of this book. Little did Maggie know what she had started!

3. M. M. Meikle, 'The World of Women: Recent Medieval and Early Modern Publications', *The Innes Review* [*IR*], 45 (1994), 71–77. E. Ewan, 'Women's history in Scotland: towards an agenda', *IR*, 46 (1995), 155–64.

4. Joy Hendry, 'Snug in the Asylum of Taciturnity: Women's History in Scotland' in I. Donnachie & C. Whatley, eds. *The Manufacture of Scottish History* (Edinburgh, 1992); Esther Breitenbach, ' "Curiously Rare?" Scottish Women of Interest or the Suppression of the Female in the Construction of National Identity', *Scottish Affairs,* 18 (Winter, 1997); E. Ewan, 'A Realm of One's Own: The Place of Medieval and Early Modern Women in Scottish History' in T. Brotherstone et al, eds. *Gendering Scottish History; an international approach* (Glasgow, forthcoming 1999).

5. D. Cannadine, 'British History as a "new subject": Politics, perspectives and prospects' in A. Grant & K. Stringer, eds. *Uniting the Kingdom? the making of British History* (London, 1995), 13–16; John Stevenson, 'Writing Scotland's History in the Twentieth Century: Thoughts from across the Border', *Scottish Historical Review* [*SHR*], 76 (1997), 112–4.

6. H. Graham, *The Social Life of Scotland in the Eighteenth Century* (2 vols, London, 1899) and *A Group of Scottish Women* (London, 1908); E. Murray, *Scottish Women in Bygone Days* (London, 1930), *A Gallery of Scottish Women* (1935) and *Scottish Homespun* (London, 1947). For more detail on these books see Ewan, 'A Realm of One's Own'.

7. T. C. Smout, *A History of the Scottish People, 1560–1830* (London, 1969).

8. R. K. Marshall, *The Days of Duchess Anne: life in the household of the Duchess of Hamilton, 1656–1716* (London, 1973); E. King, *The History of the Scottish Women's Suffrage Movement* (Glasgow, 1978).

9. C. Larner, *Enemies of God: the witch-hunt in Scotland* (London, 1981).

10. R. K. Marshall, *Virgins and Viragos: a history of women in Scotland from 1080 to 1980* (London, 1983).

11. M. W. Flinn ed. *Scottish Population History, From the Seventeenth Century to the 1930's* (Cambridge, 1977).

12. R. A. Houston & I. D. Whyte, eds. *Scottish Society 1500–1800* (Cambridge, 1989).

13. R. Mitchison & L. Leneman, *Sexuality and Social Control: Scotland 1680–1780* (Oxford, 1989).

14. E. Breitenbach & E. Gordon, eds. *The World is Ill-Divided. Women's work in Scotland in the nineteenth and early twentieth centuries* (Edinburgh, 1990); E. Gordon & E. Breitenbach, eds. *Out of Bounds. Women in Scottish Society* (Edinburgh, 1992).

15. For the state of research in various periods see 'Whither Scottish History?' *SHR,* 73 (1994). Social history figures more prominently in modern times.

16. E. Sanderson, *Women and Work in Eighteenth-Century Edinburgh* (London, 1996).

17. D. Symonds, *Weep Not For Me. Women, Ballads and Infanticide in Early Modern Scotland* (University Park, Penn., 1997).

18. E. King, *The Hidden History of Glasgow's Women* (Edinburgh, 1993).

19. M. Lee, *The Heiresses of Buccleuch: marriage, money and politics in seventeenth-century Britain* (East Linton, 1996).
20. Maggie Craig, *Damn' Rebel Bitches: The Women of the '45* (Edinburgh, 1997).
21. For example, *Etudes Ecossaises; Journal of the Canadian Historical Association.*
22. Brotherstone, *Gendering Scottish History.*
23. Cf. Michael Lynch's *Scotland: a New History* (London, 1992).
24. A. Cooke, et al *Modern Scottish History, 1707 to the Present,* vol. 5, Major Documents (East Linton, 1998)
25. For example, Catherine Kerrigan, ed. *An Anthology of Scottish Women Poets* (Edinburgh, 1991); D. Gifford & D. McMillan, eds. *A History of Scottish Women's Writing* (Edinburgh, 1997); J. C. Watson, *Gaelic Songs of Mary MacLeod* (Scottish Gaelic Texts Society, 1965).
26. See note 3.
27. Scottish History Society, forthcoming.
28. J. Kermode & G. Walker, eds. *Women, Crime and the Courts in Early Modern England* (London, 1994); E. Ewan, 'Scottish Portias: Women in the Courts in Medieval Towns' *Journal of the Canadian Historical Association,* new ser. 3 (1992).
29. A. L. Erickson, *Women and Property in Early Modern England* (London, 1993).
30. L. Gowing, *Domestic Dangers. Women, Words and Sex in Early Modern London* (Oxford, 1996).
31. Cf. Stuart MacDonald, 'Threats to a Godly Society. A Witch-Hunt in Fife, Scotland 1560–1710' (unpublished PhD thesis, University of Guelph, 1997); J. Goodare, 'Women and the Witch-hunt in Scotland', *Social History 23/3* (1998), 288–308.
32. Cf. Fiona Downie, '"Sche is but a Womman": the queen and princess in Scotland, 1424–63' (unpublished PhD thesis, University of Aberdeen, 1998).
33. *The Lawes Resolutions of Women's Rights* (1632), quoted in N. H. Keeble, ed. *The Cultural Identity of Seventeenth-Century Woman* (London, 1994), 146.
34. A. J. S. Gibson & T. C. Smout, eds. *Prices, Food and Wages in Early Modern Scotland, 1550–1780* (Cambridge, 1995).
35. C. A. Whatley, 'Women and the economic transformation of Scotland c.1740–1830' *Scottish Economic and Social History,* 14 (1994).

PART ONE

'The Fayth of Women is worthie
to be observed and imitated . . .'

The Foundation and Patronage of Nunneries by Native Elites In Twelfth- and Early Thirteenth-Century Scotland

_____ *R. Andrew McDonald*

IN THE CENTURY between about 1140 and 1240, at least eleven Bene-dictine, Cistercian, or Augustinian nunneries were founded in Scotland: Lincluden (Benedictine); Berwick, Coldstream, Eccles, Elcho, Hadding-ton, Manuel, North Berwick and Abbey St Bathans (Cistercian); Iona and Perth (Augustinian).[1] Geographically, their distribution was centred in the east with only two located in the west and southwest. In general, the growth of nunneries reflects the transformation of religious life taking place in the twelfth-century kingdom, while at the same time mirroring the widening opportunities for religious women that characterises the twelfth century across western Europe. Although the Scottish foundations pale in comparison with both the number of monasteries established for men in the same kingdom and with the contemporary growth of nun-neries in other regions of Britain (notably Ireland and England), the subject of Scottish nunneries has been too much neglected.

English nunneries have received significantly more study than their Scottish counterparts.[2] In part this is because communities of religious women in Scotland were neither as large nor as numerous as those in England, and, as with almost all monastic foundations of the native Scottish nobility, they are particularly poorly served with documentary evidence: only one cartulary survives, that of Coldstream.[3] Moreover, because so many were located between the Forth and the Tay, they suffered greatly during the Anglo-Scottish conflicts of the early fourteenth century onward. Many had already disappeared before the Reformation, and there are few significant architectural remains.[4] Indeed, so scanty is the evidence for communities of religious women that one authority, referring to Eileen Power's study of English nunneries, remarked that, 'no comparable account of the contemporary Scottish nunneries has been attempted nor indeed is it possible . . .'[5] In light of Roberta Gilchrist's recent stimulating work on 'gender archaeology', however, it is doubtful whether such a statement will remain valid for much longer, and systematic archaeological investigation and new methodological ap-proaches might well greatly enhance our knowledge of Scottish nun-neries.[6] Nevertheless, I will concentrate here on one particular (and largely traditional) aspect of the nunneries: their foundation and patronage by members of the native Scottish élite. Such a focus is dictated by two principal factors: first, the fact that, of the eleven nunneries founded in our period, no fewer than five were founded by native nobles not of the royal Canmore dynasty; and second, while the patterns of this dynasty's religious patronage are well-known, patronage of religious houses by native élites remains a virtually untapped subject.[7]

Scotland before the time of King Malcolm III (1058–93) and Queen Margaret possessed none of the monastic institutions so typical of the rest of western Europe. Monasteries, hermits, and other communities of religious there were, but the *Rule* of St Benedict appears to have been unknown before about 1070, when Margaret brought Benedictine monks to Dunfermline. The continuity of this community through the troubled 1090s is difficult to trace, however, and it was really the early twelfth century which saw the Benedictines and other reformed religious orders established in the country under the patronage of the royal family, Anglo-Norman settlers, and native magnates. The first Augustinian community was planted at Scone c.1120 while the first Cistercian monastery was Melrose, founded in 1136 by David I (1124–53), and this order eventually had eleven monasteries in Scotland. Although there is some evidence for communities of religious women in the early middle ages, it is doubtful whether any continued into the twelfth century. In c.1136, David I founded a nunnery at Berwick-on-Tweed, and later in the twelfth century, other members of the royal family established nunneries at Manuel (Malcolm IV, 1153–65), and Haddington (Ada, countess of Northumberland). It is generally acknowledged that the re-introduction of communities of religious women in Scotland (as with religious houses for men) owed much to royal initiative,[8] but this is not the whole story.

One of the most significant contrasts between the Norman conquest of England and the process whereby Scotland was Normanized in the twelfth century is that Scotland did not experience a tenurial revolution, and a dynamic and powerful native aristocracy was left firmly intact. In the west and southwest, regions little affected by initial Norman infiltration, powerful native dynasties ruled largely autonomous territories that were peripheral to the Scottish kingdom itself. In the east, the pre-eminent native dynasty was the earls of Fife, descended from royal stock, who enjoyed the privilege of inaugurating the Scottish kings. Another powerful but more recently established family was that of the earls of Lothian. Of Anglo-Saxon stock, they were exiles from the Norman conquest of England, settled in Lothian by King Malcolm III.[9] Both these families were closely connected to the royal family, and were among its most dedicated supporters; both were also active patrons of the new religious orders making their way into Scotland from c.1120 onward.

Despite being the premier earls in the country, the earls of Fife are not particularly distinguished as founders of monasteries. Earl Malcolm I (1204–c.1228) founded a Cistercian monastery at Culross in 1217–18, but the earls of Fife also patronised at least one house of religious women: the Cistercian nunnery at North Berwick. This was a large house, holding a number of parish churches, but only conventual buildings, much fragmented, remain.[10] There is little doubt that this nunnery owed its origin to Earl Duncan I (1136–54), for he is mentioned in the charter of his successor, Earl Duncan II (1154–1204), as having made a donation to the nuns there.[11] The seventeenth-century antiquarian, Dalrymple, reported that he had seen a charter of King David confirming Earl Duncan's grant.[12] Other writers attribute North Berwick to Malcolm I, Duncan II's successor as earl of Fife, but this cannot be correct.[13] While Malcolm did grant a charter to the nunnery c.1199, the evidence is overwhelmingly against him as the founder.[14] Like most of the other nunneries in question here, North Berwick's date of origin is difficult to pinpoint. While c.1150 is usually favoured,[15] some scholars have attempted to push the foundation back to c.1136;[16] lacking a foundation charter, the matter cannot be settled with certainty. If an earlier date is accepted, however, North Berwick would become one of the earliest monasteries for women founded by any Scottish noble, whether native or Anglo-Norman.

It is also of interest that in conjunction with the nunnery two hospitals were endowed, the *terram hospitalem de Norberwich et terram hospitalem de Ardros*,[17] on the north and south ends of the ferry across the Forth at North Berwick and Ardross. These hospitals appear to have been granted to the nuns before 1177 and probably erected by Earl Duncan I, for the poor people who used the ferry.[18] This was the period when the shrine of St. Andrew was drawing large numbers of pilgrims, and these hospitals may have been erected for their use.[19] About the same time, Robert, bishop of St Andrews, built a hospital at St Andrews to receive pilgrims, perhaps providing an inspiration for Duncan's foundations.[20] In an English context, the association of a nunnery with a hospital was not unusual: 'the line between hospital and nunnery is by no means clear'.[21] At Bury the nuns seem to have cared for the poor as well as the saint and the abbey, while those at St Albans were housed in and around the almonry.[22]

The earls of Lothian were more prominent as patrons of communities of religious women, and it is notable that the women of this dynasty seem to have played a significant role in the establishment of several nunneries. Without doubt the Cistercian priory of Coldstream was their most important foundation; it is attributed to Earl Gospatrick III (1138–66) or his wife, Deirdre.[23] Since the earl's wife figures prominently in the foundation charter, as well as others, it seems possible that she played an important role in creating the nunnery at Coldstream; Sally Thompson has suggested that where a nunnery was established by a husband and wife, the role of the wife can be subsequently obscured.[24] It is impossible to determine from whence the nuns came. The nineteenth-century historian and antiquarian, Chalmers, probably following the earlier antiquarian, Spottiswoode, believed they came from 'Witehou' in England, and, although the charter does mention the 'sisters of Witehou', this is generally regarded as the place where the nunnery was established.[25] Coldstream was generously endowed by several earls of Lothian, suggesting a strong family link with this monastery.[26]

Attempting to date the community's origin is difficult; it certainly existed by 1166, when Earl Gospatrick died.[27] Since the foundation charter was confirmed by Richard, bishop of St Andrews,[28] a narrower dating can be suggested. Richard was not consecrated until March 1165.[29] Thus, the establishment of the nunnery may lie between 28 March 1165 and the death of Gospatrick III in 1166, although too much reliance should not be placed upon such a narrow set of dates since the founding of a religious house could be a long, drawn-out process.[30]

Gospatrick III was also probably responsible for the establishment of the Cistercian nunnery at Eccles in Berwickshire, about six miles north-east of Kelso, where only a few ruins remain.[31] The *Chronicle of Melrose* stated that, 'in the year 1156, a convent of nuns came for the second time to Eccles'.[32] Other dates suggested by later writers included 1154 and 1155.[33] This entry is interesting because it emphasised that Gospatrick's foundation was really a re-establishment of an older house or the revitalisation of an already existing community. This may provide a rare glimpse into the choice of site for the new foundation. Lawrie has suggested that there had been an old religious community here that was re-established, and the memory of this old house led the chronicler to state that it was the second foundation.[34] The place-name itself supports the chronicle: Eccles implies the existence of an early British church, possibly from as early as the seventh century.[35] There were a number of such early monasteries in the area of the Scottish border, some of which, like Coldingham, had their genesis in the seventh century. Other early sites included St Abbs Head, Old Melrose, and Abercorn, among others.[36] Thus, Eccles as an early ecclesiastical site that was either refounded or reformed in the twelfth century should not be ruled out; the significance of this will be discussed below.

Although the founder of Eccles is sometimes identified as David I,[37] this cannot be tenable if a date of 1154–56 is accepted: David died in 1153. The association of this house with David I may be an attempt to add to that monarch's reputation as a patron of religious houses. Further evidence for Earl Gospatrick III as the founder is the fact that he and his wife were said to have been buried there, and the burial of Earl Patrick in 1232 is also suggestive of the association of Eccles with the family of Gospatrick – it was surely intended as their family mausoleum.[38]

A third nunnery associated with the earls of Lothian is Abbey St Bathans in Berwickshire, the ruins of which have almost entirely disappeared.[39] Spottiswoode stated that the founder had been one of the countesses of March in the reign of William I (1165–1214).[40] By implication the candidates are: Ada, the natural daughter of William I who married Earl Patrick in 1184 and died c.1200;[41] Christiana, who married the same earl by 1214;[42] and Euphemia, the wife of Earl Patrick, countess from 1232 to 1267.[43] If the statement that St Bathans was founded in the reign of William I is accepted then the last candidate may be ruled out. Like Eccles, this house was probably founded on a much older site. The *New Statistical Account*, admittedly a poor source, stated that the twelfth- or thirteenth-century nunnery was founded on the site of a seventh-century church dedicated to St Baithen, the cousin of St Columba.[44]

Since no evidence exists to suggest what the mother-houses of these nunneries were, a number of suggestions may be offered based upon the connections of the earls of Lothian. These nobles were prominent in the court of the Scottish kings, and their foundations may owe something to royal inspiration. However, it is appropriate to look across the border for some inspiration, since the earls of Lothian were important cross-border barons holding large estates in England as well as in Scotland.[45] Northern England was home, in the mid-twelfth century, to many monastic communities: in Yorkshire alone between 1100 and 1215 some twenty-four houses of nuns and numerous houses for men were established.[46] Probably the earls of Lothian had knowledge of, and perhaps even connections with, some of these, including the Benedictine nunnery at Newcastle, apparently refounded c.1135 by either Henry I or David I, or the Cistercian nuns at Holystone, also recorded in the time of David I.[47] So, there existed in close proximity to the earls' lands at least two early nunneries founded by monarchs with whom they had the closest of relations. Several monasteries for men also existed which may have provided inspiration for the Dunbar monasteries, and even closer links can be postulated with two of these. Juliana, sister of Gospatrick III, was given in marriage to Ranulf de Merlay, lord of Morpeth, by Henry I.[48] In 1138 she and her husband founded the Cistercian abbey of Newminster and were eventually buried there.[49] Another equally important foundation was that of Kirkham priory. This house of Augustinian canons had been founded c.1122 by Walter Espec, but it was endowed with the land of Titlington which Gospatrick I or II had granted to him.[50] Thus, family, political, and social connections provide yet another clue for the inspiration behind the foundation of some early Scottish nunneries.

Between about 1140 and 1235 the large region of Galloway, in the south-west, remained a semi-autonomous province ruled by its native lords descended from the formidable Fergus of Galloway (d. 1161). The Lords of Galloway were monastic patrons on a scale equalled only by the Canmore dynasty and the rulers of the Isles descended from Somerled,[51] but of their many foundations, only one was a nunnery: Lincluden. Uhtred (d. 1174), the son of Fergus, is reputed to have brought Benedictine nuns here, to a site located on the river Cairn above its junction with the Nith; interestingly, this was the only Benedictine nunnery in Scotland.[52] Sadly, there is virtually no contemporary evidence for this house, and its history is murky indeed; no physical remains survive, the earlier nunnery having been replaced by a collegiate church by the 3rd earl of Douglas, in the early fifteenth century.[53] The antiquarian Spottiswoode placed its foundation date during the reign of Malcolm IV.[54] This would suggest a date between 1161, when Fergus died, and 1165, when Malcolm IV died.[55] Various charters indicate that Uhtred was, like his father, a generous benefactor of the church in general, and, given the role of the Lords of Galloway as religious patrons, it would hardly be surprising if Uhtred were responsible for endowing a nunnery in what was rapidly becoming a family tradition.[56]

In the Hebrides and Argyll, the descendants of the mighty Somerled (d.1164) were instrumental in introducing the Benedictines, Cistercians, and Augustinians. Ranald, son of Somerled, (d.c.1210), brought Benedictine monks to refound the ancient abbey on Iona, settled Cistercians at Saddell, and founded an Augustinian nunnery on Iona, the pretty pink granite ruins of which still attract visitors today; it has been called, 'one of the best-preserved examples in the British Isles of the smaller medieval nunnery'.[57] Surviving architectural features show that building was in progress during the early thirteenth century, and since Ranald may have died around 1210 this, as well as a seventeenth-century tradition, suggests he was responsible for bringing nuns to Iona.[58] The community here was said by the seventeenth-century Book of Clanranald to have been black, or Benedictine, nuns,[59] but a papal mandate of 1421/2 referred to the monasterii sancte Marie de Hy-insula ordinis Sancti Augustini: the Iona nunnery was home to Augustinian canonesses.[60] The first prioress was Ranald's sister, Bethag or Beatrice. The Book of Clanranald stated that 'Bethag, daughter of Somerled, was a religious woman'; the History of the MacDonalds said she was a 'prioress of Icollumkill'.[61] The inscription of her grave was preserved until the nineteenth century: it read Behag niin Shorle vic Ilvrid Priorissa, 'Bethag, daughter of Somhairle, son of Gille-Brigde, Prioress'.[62] It has even been suggested that Bethag may have been the first owner of the so-called Iona Psalter, now in the National Library of Scotland, which was written and illuminated in Oxford in the thirteenth century and which was commissioned by an Augustinian canoness with a special interest in Iona saints.[63] As with virtually all Scottish nunneries, this community has little recorded history. It was evidently home to only a few canonesses, and possessed modest endowments of land in and around Mull, including Staoineig on Iona itself.[64]

These nunneries, founded by members of the native Scottish élite, prove to be an engaging group. Above all, they prompt the question of why there seems to have been such a predilection toward creating religious houses for women among the native magnates? Of course, the larger context is vitally important: the mid-twelfth century witnessed a 'spontaneous growth of female establishments'[65] across Europe, many of which followed the Cistercian way of life although they were not formally admitted into that order until 1213. This would suggest that most if not all of the foundations discussed here were not 'official' Cistercian nunneries.[66] Indeed, in Scotland, as compared to England and Ireland, a very high proportion of nunneries followed the Cistercian way of life.[67]

Many motives could prompt the establishment of a monastery, including piety, and political, social, or economic considerations, but it is well to bear in mind that 'no neat lines separated personal and spiritual needs'.[68] Piety as a motivating factor must not be discounted, although lacking foundation charters and other documents it is difficult to know what accounted for these religious communities for women. Gospatrick III's foundation charter for Coldstream made no mention of his motives, but later donations by Earl Patrick contain the standard *pro anima* ('for souls') clause, as does a grant of Duncan of Fife for North Berwick.[69] Other motives are more speculative, but at least one nunnery, Lincluden, might well owe its origins to politics: Uhtred, son of Fergus of Galloway, was notably open to foreign influences, including feudalism, and the establishment of a nunnery at Lincluden should probably be viewed in the context of opening up Galloway to the foreign influences spreading through Scotland.[70] The foundation and patronage of churches and monasteries also had a status aspect to it – in the case of the native magnates it was a matter of not only 'keeping up with the Canmores' but also of displaying their wealth, status, and power[71] to the Anglo-Normans who settled in Scotland in the twelfth century and created monastic foundations of their own, such as Dryburgh Abbey.

Perhaps more importantly we should ask whether Scottish noble-women played any role in establishing these nunneries. It is a well-known phenomenon of female monasticism that many houses for women had female founders, although their role was often obscured:

> The erroneous designation of a man as founder comes from the tendency of medieval writers to expect a man to be the moving

spirit in any important undertaking. Even if a woman conceived the idea of founding a nunnery, supplied much of the endowment, and carried forward the plans, male monastic writers would be apt to name her husband as central to the process.[72]

We have already noted that Deirdre, wife of Earl Gospatrick III, figures prominently in early documents relating to Coldstream, while a countess of Lothian was responsible for St Bathans, and it is probably no coincidence that Ranald's sister, Bethag, was the first prioress of Iona. Given the conclusions of Johnson and Thompson, it seems likely that these Scottish noblewomen played a significant role in establishing these nunneries, although the patchy nature of the evidence is especially frustrating here. As Thompson has pointed out, however, the very lack of evidence and surviving documentation for English nunneries is often suggestive of a long, drawn-out process whereby houses of women grew up slowly around particularly revered anchoresses.[73] It is possible this might account for the foundation of some of the Scottish houses. Since Eccles and St Bathans were both founded on the site of older ecclesiastical establishments, this might mean that they grew up around an anchoress or a group of recluses there, not unlike Flamstead priory in Hertfordshire,[74] and were remodelled in the twelfth century.[75] But can the popularity of nunneries in general explain the proliferation of Scottish houses for women? The tendency for native families to found and endow monasteries in this relatively remote area of Christendom may also owe something to the tradition in Celtic Christianity of women saints and anchorites, and, although Iona was the only nunnery founded in the Highlands, perhaps these nunneries reflect Celtic undercurrents in Scottish monastic life.[76] It may be significant that the twelfth century saw many ancient nunneries either revived or refounded in Ireland as well.[77]

Roberta Gilchrist has argued that in England the foundation of nunneries occurred as a 'delayed response' movement by members of the lesser nobility and gentry; that women played a prominent role in these foundations; and that they were closely connected with local and family concerns.[78] It is difficult to draw such firm conclusions from the Scottish evidence, but it seems unlikely that the foundation of nunneries represents a secondary response or was primarily a product of the lesser nobility. Not only did the foundation of nunneries take place within the same chronological parameters as the establishment of male houses, but the earls of Lothian and Fife were at the topmost levels of society, as were the rulers of Argyll and Galloway with their regal or semi-regal status. In other respects, however, Scottish nunneries do seem to conform to Gilchrist's model. It is likely that some, at least, had female founders, and several displayed close family and local connections, illustrated by the role of Eccles as a family mausoleum for the Lothian earls.

In the end, given the paucity of sources, it is difficult to say why there was such a proclivity among the native nobility for establishing communities of religious women in the twelfth and thirteenth centuries. Many of these conclusions are necessarily tentative, and it is hoped that further investigation, and fresh methodological approaches like those of Gilchrist, will shed more light upon this dark corner of medieval ecclesiastical and women's history. It would appear, however, that wider patterns, characteristic of western Europe as a whole, were also evident in Scotland: we must not lose sight of the general upsurge of communities for religious women in the twelfth century, and there is evidence that some Scottish nunneries were founded by noblewomen whose roles were subsequently obscured. On the other hand, there may be factors that were more peculiar to Scotland, and possibly strands of continuity with earlier Celtic establishments underlay the foundation of several nunneries. One thing seems certain: the foundation of nunneries was not restricted to the royal family, and native dynasties played a key role in widening opportunities for religious women in the twelfth and thirteenth centuries.

NOTES

1. There are other doubtful foundations not included in this figure of eleven: statistics from I. B. Cowan and D.E. Easson, *Medieval Religious Houses: Scotland* 2nd edn (London, 1976), 143–151. Only one nunnery was founded after the mid-thirteenth century (St Evoca), and only three Dominican and Franciscan nunneries in the fifteenth and sixteenth centuries: ibid, 152–54.
2. E. Power, *Medieval English Nunneries c. 1275 to 1535* (Cambridge, 1922, repr. New York, 1964); S. Thompson, *Women Religious. The Founding of English Nunneries After the Conquest* (Oxford, 1991). See also R. Gilchrist, *Gender and Material Culture. The archaeology of religious women* (London, 1994) and *Contemplation and Action: The Other Monasticism* (London, 1995).
3. See R. A. McDonald, 'Scoto-Norse Kings and the Reformed Religious Orders,' *Albion*, 27/2 (1995), 190–191; D. E. Easson, 'The Nunneries of Medieval Scotland,' *Transactions of the Scottish Ecclesiological Society, 13/ 2* (1940–41), 22. See also S. Thompson, 'Why English Nunneries Had No History: A Study of the Problems of the English Nunneries Founded after the Conquest,' in J. A. Nichols and L. T. Shank eds. *Distant Echoes: Medieval Religious Women* (2 vols, Kalamazoo, 1984), i, 131–149.
4. See, for example, Easson, 'Nunneries,' 28; *New Statistical Account of Scotland* (15 vols, London and Edinburgh, 1845), ii, 57, 109; *Chartulary of the Cistercian Priory of Coldstream* (Grampian Club, 1879), xiii-xiv. See

also D. McRoberts, 'Material Destruction Caused by the Scottish Reformation,' in D. McRoberts ed. *Essays on the Scottish Reformation* (Glasgow,
1962), 424–25.

5. Easson, 'Scottish Nunneries', 22.

6. Gilchrist, *Gender and Material Culture*, passim; on the excavation of Elcho
nunnery, see A. G. Reid and D. M. Lye, *Pitmiddle Village & Elcho Nunnery*
(Dundee, 1988).

7. G. W. S. Barrow, 'The Royal House and the Religious Orders,' and
'Benedictines, Tironensians, and Cistercians,' in *The Kingdom of the Scots:
Government, Church and Society from the Eleventh to the Fourteenth
Century* (London, 1973); McDonald, 'Scoto-Norse Kings and the Reformed
Religious Orders,' passim; K. J. Stringer 'Reform Monasticism and Celtic
Scotland: Galloway, c. 1140–1235,' in E. J. Cowan and R. A. McDonald
eds. *Alba: Celtic Scotland in the Medieval Era* (East Linton, forthcoming).
See also B. T. Hudson, 'Gaelic Princes and Gregorian Reform,' in B. T.
Hudson and V. Ziegler eds. *Crossed Paths: Methodological Approaches to
the Celtic Aspect of the European Middle Ages* (Lanham, Maryland, 1991),
61–82.

8. Easson, 'Nunneries,' 22; J. Burton, *Monastic and Religious Orders in Britain
1000–1300* (Cambridge, 1994), 95.

9. J. Bannerman, 'MacDuff of Fife,' in A. Grant and K. Stringer eds. *Medieval
Scotland: Crown, Lordship and Community. Essays Presented to G. W. S.
Barrow* (Edinburgh, 1993). See also J. C. Hodgson, *History of Northumberland* (15 vols, Newcastle-Upon-Tyne, 1893–1940), vii, 14–61. Despite their
common designation as 'earls of Dunbar,' until 1182 these nobles were
referred to as earls 'of Lothian'.

10. D. B. Swan, 'The Monastery of North Berwick,' *Lothian Transactions of the
East Lothian Antiquarian and Field Naturalists' Society*, 1, pt. 2 (1926–27),
59; Royal Commission on Ancient and Historical Monuments [RCAHMS],
Inventory of Monuments and Constructions in the County of East Lothian
(Edinburgh, 1924), no. 104.

11. *Carte Monialium de Northberwick*, ed. C. Innes (Bannatyne Club, 1842),
no.3.

12. J. Dalrymple, *Collections Concerning the Scottish History Preceding the
Death of King David the First* (Edinburgh, 1705), 268–9.

13. John Major, *A History of Greater Britain as well England as Scotland*,
ed. and trans. A. Constable (Scottish History Society, 1892), 179; J.
Spottiswoode, *An Account of All the Religious Houses that were in
Scotland at the Time of the Reformation*, in R. Keith, *An Historical
Catalogue of the Scottish Bishops Down to the Year 1688* (Edinburgh,
1824), 463.

14. 'Charter by Malcolm, son of Earl Duncan, to the Nuns of North Berwick,' in
Scottish History Society Miscellany [*SHS Misc.*] iv, 308–9, 333–337.

15. See *SHS Misc.*, iv, 334.

16. Swan, 'Monastery of North Berwick,' 57; see also *Annals of the Reigns of
Malcolm and William Kings of Scotland A.D. 1153–1214*, ed. A. C. Lawrie
(Glasgow, 1910) 15.

17. *SHS Misc.*, iv, 308–9.

18. *Northberwick*, no. 3; Swan, 'North Berwick', 57; see also G. Law, 'The Earl's Ferry,' *Scottish Historical Review*, 2 (1905), 21.

19. See D. McRoberts, 'The Glorious House of St Andrew', *Innes Review*, 25 (1974), 130.

20. *Liber Cartarum Prioratus Sancti Andree in Scotia* (Bannatyne Club, 1841) [*St A. Lib*] 122–123; see also N. F. Shead, 'Hospitals in the Twelfth and Thirteenth Centuries', in P. McNeill and R. Nicholson eds. *An Historical Atlas of Scotland* (St Andrews, 1975), 47–48.

21. Thompson, 'Why English Nunneries Had No History', 143. See also J. Durkan, 'Care of the Poor: Pre-Reformation Hospitals,' in McRoberts ed. *Essays on the Scottish Reformation*, 119.

22. Thompson, 'Why English Nunneries Had No History', 143.

23. *Coldstream Chartulary*, p.6 no 8; *Joannis de Fordun Scotichronicon cum Supplementis et Contunuatione Walteri Bower*, ed. W. Goodall (Edinburgh, 1759) [*Chron. Bower*],ii, 541.

24. *Coldstream Chartulary*, p.6 no 8. On p.8 no 11 *Derder Comitissa* appears as the first witness; Thompson, *Women Religious*, 177.

25. G. Chalmers, *Caledonia; or, a Historical and Topographical Account of North Britain From the Most Ancient to the Present Times* (4 vols, London, 1807–24), ii, 342; Spottiswoode, 461; *Coldstream Chartulary*, no 8. See Cowan & Easson, *Religious Houses*, 122, where this suggestion is refuted. There is no Witehou or Whitehow in D. Knowles and R. N. Hadcock, *Religious Houses, England and Wales* 2nd edn (London, 1971), index.

26. *Coldstream Chartulary*, p.18 no.26, pp 12–13 nos.17, 18. On one instance of family benefaction see J. C. Ward, 'Fashions in Monastic Endowment: The Foundations of the Clare Family, 1066–1314,' *Journal of Ecclesiastical History*, 32 (1981), 432.

27. Lawrie, *Annals*, 108–109; *Early Sources of Scottish History 500 to 1286* ed. A. O. Anderson (Edinburgh, 1922, repr. 1990) ii, 264.

28. *Coldstream Chartulary*, Appendix i, p. 46.

29. *Fasti Ecclesiae Scoticanae Medii Aevi ad Annum 1638* ed. D. E. R. Watt (Scottish Record Society, 1969), 291.

30. See V. H. Galbraith, 'Monastic Foundation Charters of the Eleventh and Twelfth Centuries,' *Cambridge Historical Journal*, 4/3 (1934), 5–22.

31. Hodgson, *History of Northumberland*, vii, 44; Spottiswoode, 461; Lawrie, *Annals*, 19; RCAHMS, *Inventory of Monuments and Constructions in the County of Berwick*, rev. edn (Edinburgh, 1915), no. 138.

32. Anderson, *Early Sources*, ii, 232, 698. See also *Chronica Magistri Rogeri de Houedene*, ed. T. Arnold (4 vols, Rolls Series, 1868–71), i, 215.

33. Spottiswoode, 461; Chalmers, *Caledonia*, i, 680.

34. Lawrie, *Annals*, 19 n; see also C. N. L. Brooke, *The Monastic World 1100–1300* (London, 1974), 168.

35. K. Cameron, 'Eccles in English Place Names', in M. W. Barley and R. P. C. Hanson eds. *Christianity in Britain, 300–700* (Leicester, 1968), 87–92; W. F. H. Nicholaisen, *Scottish Place-Names* (London, 1976, repr. 1986), 172.

36. J. and H. Taylor, 'Pre-Norman Churches of the Border', in N. Chadwick ed. *Celt and Saxon: Studies in the Early British Border* (Cambridge, 1963), 212, 220–224.

37. See Cowan & Easson, *Religious Houses*, 146.
38. Hodgson, *History of Northumberland*, vii, 44; Anderson, *Early Sources*, ii, 486.
39. RCAHMS, *Berwick*, no. 1.
40. Spottiswoode, 460.
41. Lawrie, *Annals*, 251; Anderson, *Early Sources*, ii, 307.
42. Cowan & Easson, *Religious Houses*, 148.
43. Cowan & Easson, *Religious Houses*, 148; *Chron. Bower*, ii, 541.
44. *New Statistical Account*, ii, 106–107; see also J. Robson, *The Churches and Churchyards of Berwickshire* (Kelso, 1896), 1; S. Taylor, 'Seventh-century Iona abbots in Scottish place-names', *Innes Review*, 48/1 (Spring, 1997), 50–55.
45. Accordingly, Waldeve founded Harehope hospital in Northumberland after *circa* 1178: see Knowles & Hadcock, *Religious Houses, England*, 362.
46. J. E. Burton, *The Yorkshire Nunneries of the Twelfth and Thirteenth Centuries* Borthwick Papers vol. 56. (York, 1979), 1; F. A. Mullin, *A History of the Work of the Cistercians in Yorkshire (1131–1300)* (Washington, 1932), passim.
47. See Knowles & Hadcock, *Religious Houses, England and Wales*, 263, 280.
48. *Chartularium Abbathiae de Novo Monasterio* ed. J. T. Fowler (Surtees Society, 1878 for 1876), 268–9.
49. Ibid, 1–2 and 269–270. See also Knowles & Hadcock, *Religious Houses, England and Wales*, 123.
50. Knowles & Hadcock, *Religious Houses, England and Wales*, 162; L. Butler and Givens-Wilson, *Medieval Monasteries of Great Britain* (London, 1979), 272. On Titlington see Hodgson, *History of Northumberland*, vii, 29–31 and xiv, 448; see also *The Scots Peerage* ed. Sir J. Balfour Paul (Edinburgh, 1904–14), iii, 246–7.
51. McDonald, 'Scoto-Norse Kings,' passim.
52. Spottiswoode, 459; *New Statistical Account*, iv, 232; A. S. Morton, 'Glenluce Abbey,' *Transactions of the Dumfries and Galloway Natural History and Antiquarian Society*, 3rd ser, 21 (1936–38), 228.
53. RCAHMS, *Inventory of Monuments and Constructions in Galloway* (2 vols, Edinburgh, 1915), ii, no. 431.
54. Spottiswoode, 459.
55. Morton, 'Glenluce Abbey,' suggested a date of 1161.
56. *Liber Cartarum Sancte Crucis* (Bannatyne Club, 1840), 24, 39, 61.
57. J. G. Dunbar and I. Fisher, *Iona* (Edinburgh, 1988), 8.
58. Seventeenth-century tradition: *Book of Clanranald*, in A. Cameron, *Reliquiae Celticae: Texts Papers and Studies in Gaelic Literature and Philology*, eds A. MacBain and J. Kennedy (2 vols, Inverness, 1894), i, 157; architectural evidence: RCAHMS, *Argyll – An Inventory of the Monuments* (Edinburgh, 1971–95), iv, 178. See also the illustration of the Prioress Anna in this volume.
59. *Clanranald Book*, 157.
60. *Highland Papers* ed. J. R. N. Macphail (4 vols, Scottish History Society, 1914–34) iv, 175–6; see also Cowan & Easson, *Religious Houses*, 151; RCAHMS, *Argyll*, iv, 178.

61. *Clanranald*, 157; *History of the MacDonalds*, in *Highland Papers*, i, 11.
62. K. Steer and J. Bannerman, *Late Medieval Monumental Sculpture in the West Highlands* (Edinburgh, 1977), 90; A. and A. MacDonald, *The Clan Donald* (3 vols, Inverness, 1896–1904), i, 520; see also Martin Martin, *A Description of the Western Islands of Scotland circa 1695* (Stirling, 1934, reprint of 1703 edition), 290–1, for the appearance of the slab in 1695.
63. See RCAHMS, *Argyll*, iv, 178 and notes.
64. See note 5.
65. L. J. Lekai, *The Cistercians: Ideals and Reality* (Canterbury, 1977), 349.
66. See Burton, *Yorkshire Nunneries*, 8; Thompson, *Women Religious*, 94–98; also valuable is R. de Ganck, 'The Integration of Nuns in the Cistercian Order Particularly in Belgium', *Citeaux* 25 (1984), 235–47.
67. Gilchrist, *Gender and Material Culture*, 61.
68. P. D. Johnson, *Equal in Monastic Profession. Religious Women in Medieval France* (Chicago and London, 1991), 34.
69. *Coldstream Chartulary*, p.1 no 1; *North Berwick*, p.4 no 3.
70. McDonald, 'Scoto-Norse Kings,' 216.
71. C. Brooke, 'Princes and Kings as Patrons of Monasteries', in *Il Monachesimo e la Fiforma Ecclesiastica (1049–1122)*, Settimana internazionale di studio, 4th, Passo della Mendola, 1968, *Miscellanea Del Centro Di Studi Medioevali* VI (Milan, 1971), 125–44.
72. Johnson, *Equal in Monastic Profession*, 36–7.
73. See Thompson, 'Why English Nunneries Had No History', 141–142; *Women Religious*, ch. 2.
74. Thomson, 'Why English Nunneries Had No History', 143–144.
75. As at St Neots (Huntingdonshire) and Stoke-by-Clare (Suffolk): Ward, 'Fashions in Monastic Endowment', 451.
76. See N. Hunt, 'Notes on the History of Benedictine and Cistercian Nuns in Britain,' *Cistercian Studies*, 8 (1973), 165. Despite the title the article is concerned only with English establishments.
77. A. Gwynn and R. N. Hadcock, *Medieval Religious Houses, Ireland* (London, 1970), 20–46.
78. Gilchrist, *Gender and Material Culture*, 41–49.

CHAPTER TWO

Power Through Purity:
The Virgin Martyrs and Women's
Salvation in Pre-Reformation Scotland

Audrey-Beth Fitch

IN LATE MEDIEVAL Scotland the key to success in the afterlife was gaining sufficient spiritual worth to move quickly from the fires of purgatory to the joys of heaven. The church offered women role models to help them achieve this spiritual worthiness. Jesus himself was the greatest role model for Christians, and male saints could also provide direction, but the Blessed Virgin Mary and the virgin martyrs were considered women's best exemplars. Contemporary understanding of women's nature derived from Aristotelian biology.[1] Scottish theologians held Eve to account for the Fall and humanity's sinfulness[2] and associated her female descendants with matter, the senses and a lack of moral strength, shame or self-respect.[3] In the poem *The Twa Mariit Wemen and the Wedo*, William Dunbar (c.1460–1514) created female characters who equated 'love' and 'nature' with sexual appetite rather than with constancy and loyalty.[4] Women were believed to be preoccupied with matters of the body and in particular with sexual intercourse.[5] Sir David Lindsay (?1486–1555) pointed out sourly that pilgrimage had made 'mony ane hure' of 'gud' wives and daughters who had been overtaken by raging lust once away from home.[6] The stories of courageous virgin martyrs showed women how to overcome their apparent weak nature and resist sexual temptation through a strong personal bond with Jesus, the 'undefiled Lamb' of the Gaelic *Book of Lismore*.[7] The more closely contemporary women followed in the footsteps of the virgin martyrs in their bodily chastity and physical suffering, the more they honoured Jesus in his sexual purity and suffering love.

There is strong evidence of devotion to saints in medieval Scotland, and of devotion to virgin martyrs in particular. In the early 1540's Perth burgess Robert Lambe accused a friar of lying about the need to pray to saints to attain salvation, and was set upon by the crowd, particularly by the women.[8] Saintly martyrdom was considered the ultimate expression of love for God; the virgin martyrs' fierce defence of their sexual purity in the face of torture made them valuable intercessors for humanity and honourable guides to chaste behaviour.[9] Lindsay confirmed that lay people, 'imprudent . . . Ignorant and blynd', worshipped saintly images in church and made pilgrimages to shrines to offer prayers and make offerings, 'To thame aye babland on our beidis, / That thay wald help ws in our neidis'.[10]

As the late medieval period saw increasing emphasis on the saving power of Mary and Jesus, devotion to virgin martyrs was expressed primarily through donations to existing foundations. In honour of the virgin martyrs, Scots made money offerings, donated images, ornaments, vestments and annual rents, and occasionally founded chaplainries and obits.[11] There are references to virgin martyrs in a variety of calendars, litanies, legends of the saints[12] and prayer books;[13] stories about Saints Margaret of Antioch, Barbara, Agatha, Agnes, Apollonia and Lucy would have been told in church on their feast days. Based on surviving evidence, devotion to virgin martyrs appears to have been greatest in the central belt, particularly in the east, and the older saintly cults had the greatest number of dedications. For example, St Katherine of Alexandria was popular for centuries up to the Reformation, but the wave of enthusiasm for St Barbara did not occur until the sixteenth century. Devotion to St Katherine had a wide geographical distribution. She was honoured from Irvine in the west to Leith in the east, and Aberdeen and Inverness in the north.[14] Glasgow Cathedral claimed to have a portion of her tomb as a relic, and the oil from her tomb was believed to have curative properties.[15]

Late medieval devotion emphasised visual imagery, so women's understanding of the virgin martyrs was formed partly through processions, carvings and paintings on tombs, shrines, altars, rood screens, bosses, corbels, altar linens and vestments, statues at altars and along interior and exterior walls, and to a lesser degree, the visual imagery of liturgical and devotional works. Although most of the visual evidence for the pre-Reformation cult of saints in Scotland has been destroyed, inventories of libraries and churches reveal a world rich in visual imagery.[16] Virgin martyrs invariably were presented alongside the tools of their torture. For example, St Apollonia had her teeth torn out before being killed so was depicted holding her teeth; predictably, she was looked to for assistance with tooth problems.[17] These symbols of saintly torture reminded women how difficult it was to defend their sexual purity, yet how important this battle was to salvation. Processions and plays reminded lay people of the general religious truths expressed in saints' *vitae*. Sir Richard Maitland of Lethington claimed that processions were an 'outward' expression of Scots' devotion to God,[18] and the carrying of saints' images in feast day processions continued up to the Reformation. For example, it is possible that the 'St Barball's Castle' in the Dundee Corpus Christi procession represented the tower in which St Barbara was immured by her father. Copies of de Voragine's *Golden Legend* often showed her standing next to this tower.[19] There is no surviving Scottish evidence of plays based on the life of a virgin martyr, although there is German evidence for such plays. There is, however, proof that scenes of torture appeared in some Scottish plays,[20] and it is likely that plays or 'tableaux vivants' included virgin martyr figures, perhaps scenes from their torture. Likely venues for these scenes were the 'clerk plays' referred to by Anna Jean Mill, who believed that the Ayr clerk plays of 1534–5 and 1541 had biblical or hagiographical themes.[21] Devotional and liturgical books were full of saintly imagery. Many of these books were illustrated with woodcuts which helped the laity to understand the text and offered spiritual guidance even to the illiterate.[22] The prayer book of Robert Blackadder (d.1508) had an illustration on almost every page, including images of Saints Barbara, Margaret and Katherine.[23] The latter saint was depicted holding a wheel, the text referring to her as a beloved virgin and advocate with God in (our) struggle.

St Katherine was a popular subject for visual representation. In the college of St Salvator in St Andrews there was an image of St Katherine above St Michael's altar, 'newly painted' by the provost, according to the inventory of 1450,[24] and the executors of Hector Boece (d.1536), principal of Aberdeen, built an altar dedicated to her in King's College, Aberdeen. The King's College altar had a 'table', possibly a triptych, which depicted St Katherine along with St Barbara and the Blessed Virgin Mary, thereby visually associating the two virgin martyrs with Mary, supreme intercessor next to Jesus.[25] St Katherine was linked to Jesus' passion and salvation in a painting in Fowlis Easter collegiate church, Angus. The saint stands to the right of Jesus in his moment of greatest power and glory after his defeat of Satan in hell and triumphal rise into heaven. She holds a wheel at her side, and grasps with both hands the hilt of a large sword that she thrusts firmly down through the head of the emperor who had lusted after her.[26] The wheel represents the wheeled torture device which God shattered before it could be used on her, and the sword was the one with which she was eventually beheaded.[27] This painting reminded the female viewer that preservation of sexual purity involved great sacrifice and commitment, but brought women closer to Jesus and salvation.

Stories about the virgin martyrs were found in such works as Jacobus de Voragine's *Golden Legend*, also known as the *Legends of the Saints*. It was a lay rendition of the Lectionary which the clergy used to produce feast day readings about the lives and deeds of the saints.[28] *Legends of the Saints* were owned by clerics from Caithness, to Glasgow, to St Andrews in the east, several of the copies being used by more than one cleric. Copies were also possessed by ecclesiastical institutions such as St Mungo's Cathedral in Glasgow.[29] Scotland even had its own vernacular *Legends of the Saints* (c.1400). Although it drew heavily upon the

Golden Legend, it was written by several Lowland Scots authors who made its saintly heroes familiar and relevant to a Scottish audience.[30]

The stories of the virgin martyrs proved that women, too, could celebrate reason over passion, love of the spirit and heaven over love of the body and the world, and could thereby gain God's acceptance. The *vita* of St Katherine turned the accepted understanding of women's natures on its head since the saint categorically used reason to refute the arguments of the pagan philosophers whom the pagan emperor had sent to undermine her commitment to Christianity.[31] All of the virgin martyrs rejected their sexual nature in return for the crown of martyrdom; the crown which encircled their heads in church imagery reminded contemporary women of the holiness and status that came with complete commitment to sexual purity.[32]

A growing body of literature in the vernaculars of the British Isles explained how women could become 'good women'. Despite their formulaic and exaggerated nature, vernacular stories of the virgin martyrs were intended to set women on the right track in recognising, avoiding, and fighting against sexual temptation. The author of the English life of St Margaret enjoined 'widows and the married, and especially maidens' to listen carefully, so that they could learn how to overcome the devil and be confirmed in their Christian faith, and the *Ancrene Wisse*, a guide for female recluses, invited its readers to read saints' lives, especially the vernacular life of St Margaret.[33] The Middle English tract *Hali Meidenhad* made available to clergy and lay women the *vitae* of Saints Katherine, Juliana and Cecilia, and a Lowland Scots contributor to the *Lives of the Saints* believed he was aiding in lay religious education by writing in the 'ynglis townge'.[34]

The stories of the virgin martyrs ran along broadly similar lines, the main theme being the connection between sexual purity and devotion to Jesus. By resisting sexual temptation, the virgin martyr gained God's favour.[35] Whereas male saints could overcome sexual temptation by transcending the body, women overcame it primarily by mortifying the body.[36] Virginity accompanied by physical suffering brought the highest spiritual reward. Scottish legends, like many English ones, emphasised the physical sufferings of the virgin martyrs and their triumph over the devil as part of an overall emphasis on 'matters of the flesh'. Elizabeth Robertson attributes this emphasis in Middle English devotional works to the intended female audience; women needed the strongest reminders to resist sexual sinfulness, since they had an inherently sinful nature.[37] Scottish virgin martyr tales included a detailed description of the tortures endured by the saint, interspersed with conversation between the saint and her torturer, who was often a powerful official within the pagan Roman state who had wanted her as a wife or concubine. In these conversations the torturer offered the virgin martyr goddess status (St Katherine), marriage (Saints Margaret, Agnes, Agatha), or at the very least an end to the torture, but the saint protested vehemently against such temptations, declaring her love for Jesus and scorning her torturer's overtures. In St Margaret of Antioch's *vita*, the saint claimed: 'No dearer wish have I . . . than to die for Christ, Who condemned Himself to death for me! . . . This torture of my flesh is the salvation of my soul'.[38]

St Margaret had to suffer physically to prove her love for Jesus; she triumphed symbolically over women's sexual nature by overwhelming the devil in the privacy of her prison cell between bouts of torture.[39] In her *vita* in the Scottish *Legends of the Saints*, the devil was particularly ashamed of being defeated by a woman, for his first human victim, Eve, had been a woman who had been morally weak. Before she let him go, St Margaret grabbed him by the hair and slammed her foot onto his neck, at which point he cowered, calling her 'haly margaret' and 'godis maydine dere'. The Scottish *vita* emphasised her purity of body and spirit through starkly contrasting images of lightness (cleanness) and darkness (filth). The manly devil was darker than soot, and the dungeon in which she met the devil was 'myrk and depe'. St Margaret, on the other hand, was described as a 'maydine clene', clear white through virginity and clean of all 'fleschly delyt'. She harboured no lechery, had given alms, fasted and prayed to overcome temptation, and looked forward to an eternally happy future in a 'clere court' surrounded by 'haly madinis'.[40]

St Margaret's story suggested that women could triumph over powerful sexual threats, whether they were posed by their morally weak nature ('brukil'), like Eve, or by powerful men like the devil or Margaret's torturer Olybrius, who had transformed his sexual frustration into a determination to punish her for her Christian beliefs. The latter story emphasised that women must fight sexual temptation in order to be truly worthy, St Margaret asking God to bring the devil to her so that she might overcome him. The author of *Hali Meidenhad* reminded women that 'no one is crowned except for whoever fights truly in that fight [physical desire instigated by the devil], and with a hard struggle overcomes herself . . . you will not be crowned unless you are attacked'.[41] Thus readers were assured that, far from being a cause for despair, sexual temptation was a gateway to God's love and the bliss of heaven. Further, the extreme youth and sheltered noble upbringing of most of the virgin martyrs demonstrated that even the most vulnerable women could achieve spiritual acceptability if they put their minds to it. In de Voragine's *Golden Legend*, the story of St Agnes' martyrdom was the catalyst for the conversion and martyrdom of St Lucy, a paradigm for contemporary women who wished to achieve sexual purity and *imitatio Christi*, and needed role models to do so.[42]

Believing that women's nature led them to experience life through the body rather than the spirit, men wrote stories about virgin martyrs to provide models of acceptable female experiential spirituality. Jesus was humanised to a great degree,[43] the virgin martyrs rejecting the love of men in exchange for the love of Jesus. In late medieval Scotland this humanising of Jesus was in full swing, Jesus being described as brother, friend and Son of Mary, rather than Son of God the Judge. The notion of Jesus as lover had roots in the *Song of Songs*. The call of the bridegroom (Jesus) to his 'bride, . . . my love, my dove, my undefiled' (Mary) had its echo in the stories of the virgin martyrs. St Agnes called Jesus her lover and her betrothed, and St Katherine claimed to be the 'spouse to Christ. He is my glory, He is my love, He is my sweetness and my delight', preferring the beautiful Jesus to her torturer who was 'ignoble and deformed'. Jesus spoke to St Katherine in similar imagery as he welcomed her into heaven: 'Come, My beloved, My spouse, behold the door of Heaven is opened to thee . . .'[44]

The image of the devout and chaste woman as bride of Christ was reinforced in Robert's Henryson's allegorical poem *The Bludy Serk*. The princess in the poem represented the human soul, but served equally well as a metaphor for women's ideal nature. In the poem the princess was spirited away from her father's (God's) kingdom by a great lion (the devil), and cast into a deep, dark dungeon (hell), where the threat of sexual and physical danger was implicit. There she was kept in darkness, hunger, cold and thirst, shut off from the sight of the earth above, much as a soul in hell was shut off from God and heaven.[45] Finally her father found a champion to fight on her behalf, a great knight (Jesus), who fought and defeated the lion, and released her from prison. However, the knight's fight to rescue the princess had left him mortally wounded, and the princess was distraught at the prospect of losing her greatest love. The knight told her that she could prove her devotion to him by never marrying, and by keeping his bloody tunic ('serk') with her and thinking of him as she looked on it. She made a vow to do this, and after his death refused to marry, spending the rest of her days devoted to his memory, praying for him and thinking about the great love he had borne her.[46]

This tale was written with great emotional appeal, encouraging women to identify with the princess, her great fear in the dungeon, her dread and anticipation as the battle raged between the knight and the lion, her joy at being released and united with her loving knight, her terrible sense of pain and loss as she watched him die, and her grief after his death. Women's devotion to Jesus meant remaining chaste and ever vigilant against being 'kidnapped' by the devil and temptation, and feeling gratitude for Jesus' sacrifice on the Cross, which had freed them from eternal death in hell. They were invited to use devotional objects as a focus for meditation and emotional union with Jesus, just as the princess had used her knight's 'bludy serk'.

Women had three options open to them if they wished to have a good chance of being accepted into heaven: virginity, chaste widowhood, or spiritual purity within marriage. Their best option was to espouse complete sexual purity as 'virgins' or 'maidens'. On 10 November, 1524, notary public Gavin Ros reported that Jonet Carnis, daughter and co-heir of the late Henry Carnis of Dalkeith, had 'chosen for herself the state of religion, and offered herself ready to enter the monastery of nuns or of profession of Haddingtoun, as it may please God or seem expedient for the time'.[47] Of course there was nothing to stop a woman from taking a vow of chastity without entering a convent, contemporary documents distinguishing between 'vows of chastity' and 'vows of religion'.[48]

Contemporary literature often advocated virginity. In the second tale of *The Thre Prestis of Peblis how thai tald thar talis* (*c.*1484–8), the king, wishing to seduce a burgess' daughter, sent his fool to act as go-between. Instead of encouraging the girl to sleep with the king, the fool, the mouthpiece of the author, encouraged her to preserve her virginity. He advised her to be guided by the life experiences of St Margaret and St Katherine, reminding her that the virginity of such saints had brought them a holy crown from God and a heavenly life of great joy and pleasure.[49] Thus reminded of her duty to God and the rewards offered virgins in heaven, the burgess' daughter followed in the footsteps of the virgin martyrs and humbly agreed to do God's will. In the poem *The Dreme of Schir David Lindesay* (1526?), Lindsay described the nine orders of heaven, affirming that virgins had high status. Mary, the 'Quene of Quenis', was next to the throne of Jesus, accompanied by 'Ladyis of delyte. / Sweit was the sang of those blyssit Virginnis: / No mortall man thare solace may indyte'.[50] All commentators agreed that, apart from Mary, virgins had the highest status and happiness amongst women, particularly virgin martyrs.[51] This idea was reflected in a full page woodcut in the *Acts of the Parliaments* printed in 1541. The heaven depicted by the woodcut contained far more virgins than chaste widows and married women, although the very presence of the latter categories encouraged wives and widows to keep up their struggle for chastity.[52]

Despite the legends of the virgin martyrs, and the advice given by contemporary writers and preachers, most women did not remain life-long virgins. As Bishop of Dunkeld Gavin Douglas (1474–1522) noted sadly in *The Palice of Honour*, there were precious few women of 'chaist and trew virginitie' riding to the palace alongside Diana, the epitome of 'chaistitie'.[53] Nevertheless, listening to the stories of the virgin martyrs could benefit less single-minded women. The virgin martyrs' example of assertive womanhood could inspire Scottish women to uphold high moral standards even when they chose ordinary lives that included marriage.

Chaste widowhood was the second-best option for women, less well rewarded than virginity, but still acceptable. Coupled with good works, chastity could improve a widow's spiritual standing greatly by the time of her death. A woman who voluntarily chose chaste widowhood was Catherine Sinclair, widow of William, first lord Seton. She lived in the 'preistis chalmeris' of the parish church of Seton, built an aisle on the south side of the church, located her tomb within it, and appointed a priest to care for her soul perpetually.[54] Other women chose to enter convents after being widowed, such as the ladies of Seton, Glenbervie and Bass who founded the Dominican convent of St Catherine of Siena near Edinburgh in 1517;[55] contemporaries declared that the women of this convent expressed devotion to God through a strictly chaste lifestyle.[56] The laity who enriched such religious foundations built in sanctions to punish unchaste sisters, since the efficacy of their prayers for souls depended to a large degree on their sexual purity. Donor James Fotheringham authorised the town council of Dundee in 1502 to set aside any sisters of the Greyfriars who 'fell away from the perfection and rule of their profession or lapsed into a wicked and suspected manner of living'.[57]

Finally, married women could undertake a form of sexual purity by remaining utterly faithful to their husbands, and by concentrating their minds on spiritual matters rather than the pleasures of the marriage bed. They could even give up sexual activity within marriage, modelling themselves on a variety of women saints.[58] According to Gavin Douglas, married women could gauge whether their devotion to worldly pleasures was excessive by asking themselves if they loved any creature more than God. If they answered in the affirmative, theirs was a wrongful love, more likely to be 'fowle delyte' than a 'leful . . . kyndly passioun'.[59]

Several married women in late medieval Scotland managed to combine marriage with devotion to God. For example, Marion Scrimgeour and her husband Robert Arbuthnott of Arbuthnott together received a plenary indulgence in return for supporting a crusade (1480), joined the confraternities of the Franciscans and St John of Jerusalem (1487), and obtained a portable altar (1490).[60] Queens were expected to set an example of chaste marriage and widowhood, drawing strong criticism if they did not. John Major (1467–1550) and Robert Lindsay of Pitscottie (c.1532–80) were extremely critical of Mary of Gueldres (d.1463), widow of James II, because she forsook chastity in favour of a liaison with the married Adam Hepburn, heir to the lord of Hailes.[61] Eighty years later, in an oration welcoming Mary of Guise to Scotland, Sir David Lindsay warned her to 'fear God, and reverence and obey hir husband, and keip hir awin body cleine according to Godis will and commandementis'.[62] In an earlier poem, *The Dreme of Schir David Lyndesay*, the author described the pains of hell suffered by noble and royal women who had not repented of their sexual sins.[63]

Whatever their situation, women were enjoined to pursue chastity faithfully, not merely to assume 'a sanctis liknes' or the public image of a 'haly wif'. In *The Twa Mariit Wemen and the Wedo*, Dunbar chided court women who thought nothing of taking lovers whilst pretending love and loyalty to their husbands, or feigning grief as widows whilst laughing secretly and ogling men in church over the top of their devotional books. Indeed, Dunbar's poem wryly ascribed some of women's enjoyment of saints' lives to the friars' success at flattering the ladies in the telling.[64] Women who had sexual relations outwith marriage were on a fast road to hellfire; repentance was their only hope.[65] Yet even the worst sexual offenders could be saved if they turned away from sin, carried out the seven deeds of mercy, eschewed the seven deadly sins, and lived chastely in devotion to God. As Gavin Douglas remarked reassuringly, even evil people could be made saints through virtue.[66] Scottish women's best hope was to model themselves on the virgin martyrs, who had rejected the overt sexuality of Eve, followed the lead of the Blessed Virgin Mary in embracing sexual purity, and suffered physically in *imitatio Christi*. For the virgin martyrs, physical suffering in defence of sexual purity had been a pathway to God's favour and heaven's bliss. Their stories could help women turn love for men into love for God, and by defending their own sexual purity, find assurance of salvation.

NOTES

1. Edwin Mullins, *The Painted Witch. Female Body: Male Art. How Western Artists Have Viewed the Sexuality of Women* (London, 1985), 18–9.
2. 'A salutation of the blest wounds of our Saviour' (from British Library, Arundel MS 285) in J. A.W. Bennett, *Devotional Pieces in Verse and Prose* (Scottish Text Society, 1955), 244. See also Jacobus de Voragine 'The Purification of the Blessed Virgin Mary', *The Golden Legend of Jacobus de Voragine* eds. Granger Ryan and Helmut Ripperger (New York, 1969), 150.
3. Robert Henryson, 'The Tale of Orpheus and Erudices his Quene' in *Poems* ed. Charles Elliott, 2nd edn (Oxford, 1974), ll. 438–46, pp 120–1.
4. Priscilla Bawcutt, *Dunbar the Makar* (Oxford, 1992), 333.
5. Elizabeth Robertson, *Early English Devotional Prose and the Female Audience* (Knoxville, 1990), 33–5,37–8,41.
6. Sir David Lindsay, 'The Monarche', ('Ane Dialogue betuix Experience and ane Courteour, Off the Miserabyll Estait of the World'), *The Works of Sir*

David Lindsay of the Mount 1490–1555 (4 vols, Scottish Text Society, 1931), i, ll.2661–76, p.278 and ll.2693–2700, p.279.

7. *Lives of Saints from the Book of Lismore*, ed. and trans. Whitley Stokes (Oxford, 1890), 182.

8. John Foxe, *Actes and Monumentes,* in *The Works of John Knox* ed. David Laing, Appendix V, (6 vols, Wodrow Society, 1846), i, 523.

9. Scottish Record Office [SRO], RH12/24, fo 1. fragment of a common of the saints (St Agatha). Cf. John Hamilton, *The Catechism set forth by Archbishop Hamilton Printed at St. Andrews – 1551 together with The Two-Penny Faith 1559,* ed. Alex F. Mitchell (Edinburgh, 1882), fos clxxxxvi-vii.

10. Lindsay, 'The Monarche', i, ll. 2280–3, 2287, 2291–2, 2295–6, 2306–8, 2313–20, 2366, 2375–6, 2379–80, 2397, pp 267–70.

11. For example, *Accounts of the Lord High Treasurer of Scotland* eds T. Dickson and J. B. Paul (12 vols, Edinburgh, 1877–1916), iv, 179, 180, 190 (offerings); SRO, GD1/413/1, p.105, Haddington burgh court statute of 1545; *Annals of Banff* ed. William Cramond (2 vols, Spalding Club, 1891), i, 244–5 (vestments and ornaments); SRO, RH2/8/46, Dundee burgh and head court book, pp. 89–90; SRO, GD76/13, GD76/16, GD79/4/23, GD76/13, mortifications of annual rents; *Cartularium Ecclesiae Sancti Nicholai Aberdonensis* ed. James Cooper (2 vols, New Spalding Club, 1892), ii, 97–9, 147–8; SRO GD76/39, GD76/49 and GD243/23/2, obit foundations; James S. Marshall, 'The Birth of a Parish Church', *Records of the Scottish Church History Society,* 21 (1983),73; SRO, GD79/22 confirmation of foundation to St Barbara (Perth).

12. A copy of de Voragine, *Legenda Sanctorum* (Lyons, 1554) was owned by John Greenlaw of Haddington, vicar of Keith Humbie (d.1566).

13. National Library of Scotland [NLS], ACC. 11218/7, Mary of Guise's Prayer Book; NLS, MS10270, Dean [James] Brown's Prayer Book; NLS, MS 10271, Blackadder's Prayer Book. See also addition of SS Barbara and Appolonia to Perth Psalter in the sixteenth century, NLS, MS 652.

14. SRO, GD79/4/74 (Inverness); *Charters and Other Documents Relating to the Royal Burgh of Stirling A.D. 1124–1705* ed. Robert Renwick (Glasgow, 1884), 76–9; *The Annals of Banff,* i, 244–5; Edinburgh University Library, Laing Charters, no. 191; Marshall, 'Parish Church', 71 (Leith); *Epistolare in usum Ecclesiae Cathedralis Aberdonensis* ed. Bruce McEwen (Edinburgh, 1924), 103; *Registrum Episcopatus Brechinensis* eds. C. Innes and P. Chalmers (2 vols, Bannatyne Club, 1856), i, 210–2.

15. John Dowden ed. 'The Inventory of Ornaments, Jewels, Relicks, Vestments, Service Books, etc. Belonging to the Cathedral Church of Glasgow in 1432, Illustrated from Various Sources, and more Particularly from the Inventories of the Cathedral of Aberdeen', *Proceedings of the Society of Antiquaries of Scotland,* 33 (Edinburgh, 1898–9), 298,303.

16. Carlos M. N. Eire, *War Against the Idols. The Reformation of Worship from Erasmus to Calvin* (Cambridge, 1986), 315. See also Robert Whiting, *The Blind Devotion of the People. Popular Religion and the English Reformation* (Cambridge, 1989), 3.

17. Lindsay, 'The Monarche', i, l. 2365, p.269.

18. Sir Richard Maitland of Lethington, 'Of the Wynning of Calice' (1558), *The*

Poems of Sir Richard Maitland of Lethingtoun, Knight, ed. Joseph Bain (Maitland Club, 1830), 10.

19. James Murray Mackinlay, *Ancient Church Dedications in Scotland. Scriptural Dedications* (2 vols, Edinburgh, 1910), i, 471; de Voragine, *Legenda Sanctorum* (1554), fo 167v, and, for example, de Voragine, *Legenda Sanctorum* (Lyons, 1487), n.p.

20. Merry Wiesner, 'Women's Response to the Reformation', in R. Po-Chia Hsia ed. *The German People and the Reformation* (Ithaca, 1988), 154, and Anna Jean Mill, *Medieval Plays in Scotland* (Edinburgh, 1927), 69 (Perth play of St Erasmus, with payments to 'cord-drawer' and tormentors).

21. Mill, *Medieval Plays*, 75.

22. Miriam Chrisman, *Lay Culture, Learned Culture. Books and Social Change in Strasbourg, 1480–1599* (New Haven, 1982), 103–6. Cf. British Library Arundel MS 285, a Scottish devotional work which has 17 woodcuts.

23. NLS, Blackadder's Prayer Book, MS 10271, fos 98r-v, 99r-v.

24. 'Register of Vestments, Jewels, and Books for the Choir, etc., Belonging to the College of St Salvator in the University of St Andrews, circa A.D. MCCCCL', eds. A. Macdonald and James Dennistoun in *Miscellany of the Maitland Club* (4 vols, Maitland Club, 1843), iii, 204.

25. Francis C. Eeles, *King's College Chapel Aberdeen. Its Fittings, Ornaments and Ceremonial in the Sixteenth Century* (Edinburgh, 1956), 37.

26. Fowlis Easter Church, Angus.

27. de Voragine, 'Saint Catherine', *Golden Legend*, 713.

28. de Voragine, *Golden Legend*, viii and *Legends of the Saints*, xxxii.

29. John Durkan and Anthony Ross, *Early Scottish Libraries* (Glasgow, 1961), 63, 67, 70–1, 84, 96, 105, 126, 135, 138–9, 147, 158, 162.

30. *Legends of the Saints* ed. Metcalfe, i, pp xxiii,xxv-xxxii.

31. de Voragine, 'Saint Catherine', *Golden Legend*, 709–12 and 'Katerine' *Legends of the Saints*, ed. Metcalfe, ii, ll. 217–20, p.448. Cf. de Voragine, Legenda Sanctorum (1554) fo 167v (St Barbara).

32. See paintings of St Katherine crowned in Fowlis Easter Church and image of heaven with a tier of crowned virgins in *The New Acts and Constitutionis of parliament made be Iames the Fift kyng of Scottis, 1540* (Edinburgh, 1541), fo 27v.

33. Robertson, *Early English Devotional Prose*, 94, citing 'Hali Meidenhad' and 'Ancrene Wisse'.

34. 'Egipciane', *Legends of the Saints*, l. 1471, p.338.

35. Millett and Wogan-Browne, *Medieval English Prose*, xv.

36. Robertson, *Early English Devotional Prose*, 40.

37. Ibid. 97.

38. de Voragine, 'Saint Margaret', *Golden Legend*, 352.

39. Ibid. 352–3.

40. 'Margaret', *Legends of the Saints*, ii, ll. 48–55, p.48, l. 212, p.53, ll. 252–3, p.54, ll. 429–31, p.59, ll. 437,446–54, p.60, ll. 495–503, p.61, l. 543, p.62, and NLS, Blackadder's Prayer Book, MS 10271, fo 99r.

41. Millett and Wogan-Browne, 'Hali Meidenhad' ('A Letter on Virginity'), *Medieval English Prose*, 43.

42. de Voragine, citing St Ambrose, in 'Saint Agnes', *Golden Legend*, 113.

43. Robertson, *Early English Devotional Prose,* 41.
44. de Voragine, 'Saint Agnes', *Golden Legend,* 110–1, and de Voragine, 'Saint Catherine', ibid. 712–4.
45. Lindsay, 'The Monarche', ll. 6006–7, p.376. William of Touris referred to hell as a dark dungeon, in William of Touris, 'The Contemplacioun of Synnaris', *The Asloan Manuscript. A Miscellany in Prose and Verse, ed.* W.A. Craigie (2 vols, Scottish Text Society, 1923–5), ii, 228.
46. Robert Henryson, 'The Bludy Serk', *The Bannatyne Manuscript (1568),* ed. James Barclay Murdoch (4 vols, Hunterian Club, 1896), iv, ll. 1–120, pp 942–6. Cf. 'Ancrene Wisse', with soul as a lady with a knightly lover, in Millett and Wogan-Browne, *Medieval English Prose,* xvii.
47. *Protocol Book of Gavin Ros, N.P.* eds. John Anderson and Francis J. Grant (Scottish Record Society, 1908), i, no.736.
48. Cf. SRO, GD103/2/46, transumpt of papal indulgence (1502).
49. *The Thre Prestis of Peblis how thai tald thar talis* ed. T. D. Robb (Scottish Text Society, 1920), ll.837–44, p.39.
50. Lindsay, 'The Dreme of Schir David Lyndesay', *Works,* i, ll. 554–6, p.20.
51. For example, Millett and Wogan-Browne, 'Hali Meidenhad', *Medieval English Prose,* 21.
52. *New Acts and Constitutionis of parliament,* fo 27v.
53. Douglas, 'The Palice of Honour' (Bannatyne Club, 1827), 8.
54. George Seton, *A History of the Family of Seton* (2 vols, Edinburgh, 1896), ii, 772–3.
55. I. B. Cowan and D.E. Easson eds. *Medieval Religious Houses: Scotland,* 2nd edn (London, 1976), 152.
56. Letter of James V to Pope Clement VII (1532), in *The Letters of James V* eds. R. K. Hannay and D. Hay (Edinburgh, 1954), 232–3; Sir David Lindsay, cited in David McRoberts, 'Material Destruction Caused by the Scottish Reformation', in David McRoberts ed. *Essays on the Scottish Reformation 1513–1625* (Glasgow, 1962), 419; Sir David Lindsay in 'Ane Satyre of the Thrie Estatis' (1552), cited in Carol Edington, *Court and Culture in Renaissance Scotland: Sir David Lindsay of the Mount* (Amherst, 1994), 221.
57. William Moir Bryce, *The Scottish Grey Friars* (2 vols, Edinburgh, 1909), i, 396.
58. Cf. Dyan Elliott, *Spiritual Marriage. Sexual Abstinence in Medieval Wedlock* (Princeton, 1993), 195–6,216.
59. Douglas, 'Prologue of the Fourth Book', *The Aeneid of Virgil Translated into Scottish Verse by Gawin Douglas Bishop of Dunkeld,* ed. George Dundas (2 vols, Bannatyne Club, 1839), ll. 9–10,24–5, p.179.
60. SRO, RH1/2/284, pp 1–2, plenary indulgence granted to Robert Arbuthnott of Arbuthnott and Marion Scrymgeour (1480); Bryce, *Scottish Grey Friars,* ii, 263–4; SRO, RH1/2/294, grant of portable altar to Robert Arbuthnott of Arbuthnott (1490).
61. John Major, *A History of Greater Britain as Well as England as Scotland (1521),* ed. and trans. Archibald Constable (Scottish History Society, 1892), 388; Robert Lindsay of Pitscottie, *The Cronicles of Scotland* (2 vols, Edinburgh, 1814), i, 169–70.

62. Pitscottie, citing Sir David Lindsay, in *Cronicles*, ii, 376, and Lindsay's comments on queens as subjected beings, in Lindsay, 'The Monarche', i, ll. 1064–76, p. 230.

63. Lindsay, 'The Dreme', i, ll: 267–8,271, p.12.

64. Dunbar, 'The Tua Mariit Wemen and the Wedo', *The Poems of William Dunbar* ed. William Mackay Mackenzie (Edinburgh, 1932), ll. 410–417, p.94 and ll. 422–35, 451–75, pp 95–6; 'The Freiris of Berwik', ibid. ll. 32–4, p.183. For authorship of 'Freris', see Bawcutt, *Dunbar the Makar*, 10.

65. Millett and Wogan-Browne, 'Hali Meidenhad', *Medieval English Prose*, 19,21; Bawcutt, *Dunbar the Makar*, 335.

66. Douglas, 'The Palice of Honour', ll. 1990–2007, p. 125. Cf. John of Ireland's 'Of Penance and Confession', in *Asloan Manuscript*, i, 75.

CHAPTER THREE

Women in Scottish Divinity, c.1590–c.1640

David G. Mullan

IN THE TWO generations before the National Covenant, Scottish divines produced a substantial body of material, including catechisms, biblical expositions, treatises, sermons, and poems. Some of the material was published in London and became part of the larger British market for divinity, while English works were marketed and sometimes even printed in Scotland. Clearly the Borders did not generally mark a disruption in the theological continuum of the island. Thus, to a considerable degree, Scottish theology and piety are to be seen not as indigenous plants, but as part of an international Reformed theological culture. It is no surprise to find that what Scottish divines had to say about women is not unique, and that modern scholarship about women in seventeenth-century English religion is commonly transferable to Scotland.

Women make frequent appearances in Scottish divinity. Scottish divines, like their English counterparts, were interested first and foremost in the salvation of human souls; hence their prevailing interest with 'practical divinity', the stuff of life, including male and female experience. This chapter will survey what Scottish divinity of the time had to say about women, what it shows us about the place of women in the life of religion, and how important feminine imagery was to the articulation of the Christian message.

A bound volume in the Laing manuscripts at the University of Edinburgh contains a copy of a printed catechism along with some sheets of handwritten material from the 1640s. A few of these leaves are devoted to women, including some playful verses, but there is another sheet that raises one's interest to a higher level. It is entitled 'The praise of women' and begins its series of statements thus:

1. Women were the first cause of dwelling together in townes, villages, freedomes & congregations.
2. Women were the first inventars of letters & art of wrytting . . .
3. Thei were the first inbringers & ordainers of lawes, & statutes, politick, civill & morall.[1]

These and other statements may have come straight from Christine de Pizan's _Book of the City of Ladies_, written c.1405.[2] How did the student have access to her work? Was it discussed in a lecture, of which these are the 'dictates,' _i.e._ lecture notes? Whatever the answers, Christine's advanced notions about her sex were not definitive of woman's place in

Scotland. As elsewhere, women were viewed according to traditional assumptions about the content of the Bible, with a good dose of Aristotle mixed in, pointing toward an inherent inferiority. John Weemes wrote rather predictably that as Christ is the head of the church, man, 'the more excellent sexe,' has lordship over the woman, 'the infirmer sex'.[3] He noted that man was more gifted than she, thus 'he should instruct and teach her', while she should respond with 'subjection, obedience, and reverence', to be done 'cherefully, readily and constantly'.[4] Archibald Simson's prayer for a woman in labour expressed the theology of gender that lurked within the masculine theological mind:

> . . . And because this paine of mine hath come to all Women, by the transgressions of Eva the first Woman, let me remember that sinne is the mother of these pangues, forasmuch as all have sinned, and must be partakers of their sorrowes. O Lord, I confesse I have sinned with the rest of my Sexe, and I am now punished with them, as thou gavest out sentence against them all. But, Lord, I pray thee, for Jesus sake, who was the Seede of the Woman, that thou wouldest loose the bandes of my sinne.[5]

Female inferiority meant that while it would be thought a compliment to speak of women as having 'masculine mynds', or, in Mary's case, bearing up in the face of Christ's death 'with a manly countenance', it was a means of denigration to refer to a man in feminine terms. In 1619 Walter Balcanquhall complained of 'female foolish Rhetorick' at the synod of Dort.[6]

Despite the almost casual and unthinking fashion in which divines referred to the innate and immutable inferiority of women, they were still dogged by ambivalence. As Mary Maples Dunn has written, 'Puritans certainly brought in their baggage a sense of the inferiority of women; but belief in female equality before the Lord also made it uncertain what role women would play in a new religious order'.[7] Subjection was woven into a draft of the wedding ceremony. A woman was to be her husband's helper and 'to give subjection and obedience to him in the Lord'.[8] Underwritten by divine law, natural law, and conscience, she must respond with 'subjection and obedience', according to Robert Rollock who was referring only to a wife's behaviour toward her husband. In a striking analogy to contemporary political divinity which denied absolute power to any earthly potentate, so a wife's duty to her human head is circumscribed by 'lawfull, honest, agreeable to the will of the Lord'.[9] Lindsay wrote that a woman must not behave so as to please her husband if it meant offending God, and Wariston was upset that he had compelled his first wife to do something which was both sinful in itself and contrary to her will.[10]

Weemes avowed that there were no grounds for a man to despise his wife and he specifically rebuked men who held high conceits of themselves in contrast to their women.[11] Wariston's diary again illustrates the point. The morning after their wedding night he and his bride made a 'paction'. He promised 'never to gloume nor glunche on hir befor folks, and shoe vouing never to disobey me in any compagnie'.[12] The mode was certainly conventional, but there was an undeniable concern to maintain mutual dignity and respect. Rollock emphasised that a husband has obligations to his wife. If he has the greater honour, so he must bear the greater burden. The key was to deal with his wife according to 'a sanctified affection', defined in terms of Christ's love for the church, and he was unsparing in his criticism of men who tyrannised over their wives as if 'it were over a dog or cat'.[13] He utterly rejected the use of physical force: 'Is it lawful for a man to strike his own flesh? wil not every one that heares or sees that, say: the man is mad, and worse then a brute beast'? Robert Baillie alleged that Robert Browne, the eponymous separatist pioneer, beat his wife implying that it was a suitable failing for a schismatic.[14]

However weak they might be, women were quite capable of subverting the morals of the stronger sex, and thus they were exhorted to be careful of their behaviour and appearance. Archibald Simson blamed Bathsheba for David's fall into adultery and upheld her as a type of 'many Women in our dayes, shamelessly haunting such places where they may give occasion to men to lust after them'.[15] In England Thomas Heywood warned women 'to strive that the beauty of your minds may still exceed that of your bodies, because the first apprehends a noble divinity, the last is subject to all frailty'.[16] Simson concurred saying nothing compared to virtue, natural colour, obedience, love, 'by which she purchaseth credit with her Husband, and is famous with men'.[17]

The kirk evinced a striking attachment to the feminine in its theological and devotional discourse. Labour in childbirth was a metaphor for both 'the suddenness of the pains of hell' and for the appearance of the new person, the person of faith.[18] Maternal love could serve as a fit metaphor for the relation between minister and parish: 'The Mother seekes the well of her childe, and not his goods, nor honour: so seeke thou the well of thy flocke, and not their goods, nor honour, and *let thy affection be motherlie*'.[19]

'Church' had a lengthy history as a feminine noun, no less in Scotland than elsewhere.[20] James Melville wrote two laments about his beloved kirk, 'a Queen of great renowne' whose fame was known throughout Europe; she therefore appealed to King James as the son of her womb.[21] James Inglis wrote to Robert Boyd in 1611: 'The Kirk of this land *her* case is very lamentable . . . We that should be *her* watchmen to cry in *her* streets for *her* wakening and on *her* watch towers to the Lord by night and day, to have compassion and heal *her* wounds - we are fast asleep'.[22] William Cowper stated that the Bible uses five figures to describe the relationship of the Christians with Christ: 'First, by a marriage, wherein Christ is the Husband, and we the Spouse'.[23] A recusant woman included in her confession of new faith, undoubtedly with a minister all but moving the pen for her, a similar expression:

> And if the Bride, and new married woman forsake, and leave her fathers house to follow her husband: if she leave the sport and pastime of her youth, to goe about her houswifrie, and to conforme her selfe unto her husband: why should not I alas! forsake that which displeaseth thee, to be agreeable unto thy Son Jesus Christ, which in so great mercie hath wedded me?[24]

At death, wrote David Lindsay of Leith, the soul, 'being happily presented a chast virgine, well decked and trimmed with the ornaments of thy glorious husband Jesus, before thy glorious husband Jesus, shalt have that marriage now contracted with him, solemnized and perfectly consummated . . .'[25] The Song of Solomon was seminal in this use of language, and James Baillie described the book as Spirit-directed love songs to the church.[26] Forbes of Corse described the Holy Spirit as a wedding gift given by Christ to the church. However, if such language could elevate the church as the bride of Christ, the feminine could also turn harlot.[27] Alexander Hume, the Edinburgh schoolmaster, wrote of the church as Christ's spouse but also as having become, under Roman influence, the 'skarlet whore', while John Murray, echoing Hosea, wrote: 'Oh how is the sometimes faithfull nation going on to become an harlot'.[28]

It is typical to find preachers appealing to the examples of godly women. With reference to Rahab the harlot in Hebrews 11:31 David Dickson preached 'that the Fayth of Women is worthie to bee observed, and imitated, even as well as Mens Fayth'.[29] George Gillespie praised Esther for her willingness to jeopardise her life rather than submit to wrong.[30] Lindsay wrote in praise of aged Anna, 'that religious old widow', who served God constantly with prayers and fasts; one should follow her example. Wariston himself provides a lay witness to homiletical references to Biblical women in the pulpits of Edinburgh.[31]

This willingness to exemplify women carried on beyond the Bible, and indeed beyond the Christian tradition. Lindsay spoke well of a female slave martyred in Lyon in 177: 'Were that Martyr Blandina living to this day, sure I am she would say, albeit there be many men in the world now, yet there be wonderous few Christians in the world now'.[32] Abernethy referred to a pagan woman in his treatment of the mortification of 'burning lust'. Hypatia was an Alexandrian philosopher and mathematician, born in 370 and murdered by Christian monks in 415.[33] The author wrote: 'Hypatia (famous because of her erudition and publike teaching) perceiving one of her disciples, for her love, languishing to the death: after many assayed remedies without effect; at last she devised a way to divert his imagination with a filthy spectacle of her self'.[34] In identifying forerunners of puritanism David Calderwood listed Lydia, the widow of Sarepta, Hildegard, and Elizabeth the German.[35]

The most interesting Biblical story in this context is the coming of women to Jesus's tomb where they become the first to learn of the resurrection. Rollock wrote that the Lord

> will have his disciples to sit down in the school of women, to learn of them that glorious resurrection, he will make them to be fools (citing 1 Corinthians 1:27 and 3:18), that they may be made wise, and he will have the women to be their teachers.[36]

He did not suggest therefore that women might continue to teach, and in fact another minister commented on the woman of Samaria in John 4, that she, 'being but a woman, yet being reproved of her adulteries, & instructed by Christ; I will not say preached, but *saith* to her neighbours . . .'[37] Rutherford allowed that when Mary Magdalene was directed from the tomb to report what she had seen there, 'she is made the first preacher of Christ's rising from the dead', but there the matter ends.[38] Charles Ferme wrote that in Romans 16:1, Phoebe was a deaconess. Actually, the Greek the term is 'deacon', with no feminine counterpart, but Ferme saw her in traditional terms. Her role is thus defined in concert with I Timothy as she is turned into a hospitable widow.[39] On Romans 16:3 he noted that Prisca appeared before Aquila: 'so Priscilla, an eminent female, surpassed her husband in the business of the gospel' and even helped her husband to instruct Apollo. Ferme drew no conclusions and women gained no public role in religious life.[40] James Melville allowed that mothers will sometimes pray *en famille*, but that was the full extent and Rutherford held the Christian man of the house responsible for directing the religious life of the family.[41] Several divines thought baptism by women a scandal, an absurdity generated by Rome's false notion of the necessity of baptism for salvation.[42]

Women did, nevertheless, carve out a public role in religious life, if sometimes in a protesting and even riotous fashion.[43] In 1584, when two of Edinburgh's ministers were under threat and took flight to England, their wives wrote a feisty letter on their behalf. At Easter 1622, 'sindrie of the base sort, and some wemen, not of the best, did sit' rather than kneel. William Annand was attacked by women after his Glasgow synod sermon on behalf of the liturgy.[44] When Lord Binning noted that 'many citizens of this towne' were absent from kneeling communion preferring to attend elsewhere, women were prominent.[45] On 31 October 1637 the Rev. Gavin Young of Ruthwall wrote the earl of Annandale that two weeks earlier there had been a gathering in Edinburgh at which a Supplication against the service book was subscribed by eight hundred persons. 'Such was the tumult of the wemen and basse peple that the Bishop of Galloway . . . was violentlie (set) upon . . .' Henry Guthry noted the inclusion of women in the conspiracy to disrupt the introduction of the prayer book in July 1637.[46] Mob activity could also support Catholic religion for in 1628 Adam Simson of New Abbey, along with his wife and others, were abused by a group of women.[47] But this is surely not the whole of the story. While guided generally and ultimately by male spiritual mentors, as will be seen in the spiritual autobiography of Mistress Rutherford (see below) and Wariston's diary, Christian women had a real impact on other women and on men through their spiritual counsel.

Two contemporary circumstances bear relating. A minister portrayed Jean Livingston, awaiting execution for plotting the murder of her abusive husband, as moved by the Holy Spirit to edify others. Culprit and minister were agreed that this grace had a wider purpose, that God 'has set her up to be a preacher of mercy and repentance to us all', her words 'as memorials of the great and marvelouse grace of God, which we have seen in her'.[48] At the time of the National Covenant Margaret Mitchel came to a degree of prominence, or notoriety. Wariston, whose diary records most of what we know of her, first heard of her from the Reverend Henry Rollock in September 1638. She was given to ecstatic fits in which she spoke about 'the greatnes, goodnes, and glorious excellency of King Jesus; it was admirable to hear and seie the varietie of hir expressions and conceptions on that subject, with the continuat bensel and conbined concurrence of al the faculties of hir saule and affections of hir heart', and Wariston took her utterances as favourable omens of the current enterprise, appreciating her positive impact upon some wavering noblemen.[49] Both were, however, remarkable circumstances that do not define the role of women in religious life.

A Scottish Catholic priest wrote that 'East Laudiane knawis the love and fidelitie of ane of thair Ministers towards his wyf, wha worriet hir before he passit to his preaching'.[50] Scottish divines were mainly married men and fathers and they made no apology for a married clergy, or their deep affection for their 'bedfellows'. William Guild maintained the lawfulness of marriage for clergy and Weemes asserted that virginity is not preferable to marriage.[51] Puritan morality dictated that pre-marital chastity should be succeeded by a faithful and loving relationship, where the man ought 'to delight himselfe with his wife'.[52] On his wedding night, with his bride already in bed, Wariston 'thanked the Lord heartily for the keaping thy (*i.e.* his soul's) body until that hour from outward pollution of lust quhrto thou haist bein so oft and so sairly tempted'. Wariston, in many respects hardly distinguishable from the clergy, referred to his deceased and greatly missed first wife as 'my uther half', now in heaven. Before wedding his second spouse he became troubled by 'the inordinat excesse of my affection to hir, quhilk disturbed and diverted my devotion in privat religious exercises'. He feared that he was falling into idolatry, and consequently the young couple 'resolved to temper our affections and set them cheifly on the giver and not on the gift'.[53]

Pastors' wives were themselves commonly daughters of manses, and it is not rare to find appreciative comments about them, both for their tender care and their religious achievement.[54] John Row married Griselle, daughter of David Ferguson, minister at Dunfermline. She was 'a verie comlie and beautifull young woman, so shee proved a verie virtuous and godlie person, fitt to be such a minister's wife'.[55] John Livingston wrote later in life, 'In June 1635, the Lord graciously pleased to bless me with my wife, who how well accomplished every way, and how faithfull an yoke-fellow, I desire to leave to the memory of others'.[56] Josias Welsh related how his wife prophesied, while he was in London, that the ejected Irish ministers would be restored, but only briefly. 'He said he was offended then at her peremptory words; but knowing her otherwise to be most modest, he now perceived she knew more of the mind of God than they did'.[57] A friend recommended Robert Boyd's widow to Boyd's friend Dr George Sibbald of Leith: 'she hath given proof of her sincere love, humble and submissive subjection to her husband, and her godly care about the education of her children'.[58] Given this level of mutual affection that emerges often enough in the literature, the closeness of husband and wife might be used to illuminate the reluctance of body and soul to separate. On the other hand, the recusant might be portrayed as an unwilling wife.[59]

Scholars have long commented upon the relations between women and their male pastors, and recently Louise Yeoman has written that one might think 'that the typical picture of a radical Scots parish was one of the minister, as almost the only activist male, surrounded by a group of enthusiastic parish ladies'.[60] Of course she is well aware of the role of men also, but her point is well made and the phenomenon is best observed in Samuel Rutherford's famous *Letters*.[61] David Mathew described Rutherford's relationship with Lady Kenmure as 'one of those spiritual intimacies which were becoming a pattern for a Presbyterian lady of quality'.[62] His was not the only instance as parallels may be seen in the careers of other Presbyterian ministers such as Livingston and Robert Boyd. As Mathew noted there is no reason to suggest any scandalous behaviour, though in the case of William Murray one relationship went too far too soon and more or less terminated his career in the church.[63]

Such mutual dependencies, which included financial support, even for publication of banned tracts, were noted at the time and drew some disparaging comments.[64] The Catholic John Hamilton asked:

> What folie is it that women, wha can not sew, cairde, nor spin
> without thay lerne the same of uther skilful wemen, suld usurpe to
> reid, and interpret the Bible, and apply the texts thairof as thair
> licht, vaine, and unconstant spirits inventis? I wald exhort thame to
> remark that thair first mother Eva, for melling hir self with maters
> of religion, presumand to interpret the command of God
> concerning the eating of the forbidden Aple, procurit be hir
> doctrine a curs of God to hir and al woman kynd . . .[65]

In Henry Leslie's preface to Wentworth we find that Covenanters appeal mainly to women, since 'they allow them to be at least quarter-masters with their husbands'.[66]

Robert Boyd commented on the people he had known and respected, including a number of women. His cousin Lady Kelwood was 'a virtuouse and wise gentlewoman'.[67] Elizabeth Melville, daughter of Sir James Melville of Halhill, wife of John Colville of Culross and close friend of the circle of godly ministers was a religious poet and a piously imperious mother.[68] Alexander Hume dedicated his *Hymnes and sacred songs* (Edinburgh, 1599) to her. He saw in her speech, behaviour, and piety 'infallible signes of Sanctification'.

In addition to the death row conversion of Jean Livingston and the confession of an elderly aristocratic convert, there are available to the historian a couple of other more substantial records of women's religious experiences. Bessie Clarksone's struggle for faith was thought worthy of publication, though its lack of satisfactory resolution must have deprived it of the desired impact.[69] Of greatest interest for historians may be a manuscript spiritual autobiography of a young woman known to us only as Mistress Rutherford. It covers the years *c.*1615–30, from early adolescence to early adulthood.[70] She supplies us with a catalogue of the religious concerns of her time, and along the way gives some insight into the life of a young woman living on the edges of landed society. This includes attendance at a girl's school in Edinburgh run by Betty Aird (a daughter of an Edinburgh minister), her anxiety over the prospects of marriage and her relationship with prominent Presbyterian ministers in Scotland and in Ireland.

All these works indicate that women were not considered unworthy objects of pastoral care. Women were taught the same religion as men, they were encouraged to enter into the same experience of faith. Charles

Ferme commented on Romans 16 that 'to be the daughter of God in Christ, and through partnership in the common faith, the sister of believers', is the common vocation of a Christian female, concurring well with what Susan Felch has described in an essay on John Knox as 'ungendered Christian godliness'.[71] Women were not excluded from pastoral exhortations. Preachers addressed themselves explicitly to both men and women. The two sexes shared the same corrupt nature, needed the same salvation and both had souls and consciences. Elect men and women belonged to the one church.[72] Sermons and devotional material made explicit references to women. Zachary Boyd commented, by way of stirring his hearers out of dreaded security: 'Many of our weemen if they can say, I am neither whoore nor theefe think that all is well'.[73]

Scottish divinity tried to take women seriously, and to a considerable extent succeeded. If men were the highest authority in the home, they were not to be tyrants or even disciplinarians over their wives, and preachers were emphatic in inculcating marital affection as well as fidelity. Genderless individual piety elevated women to an equal status with men, but as in other areas of public life, divines were prisoners of their culture, and apart from questions of public disorder flowing from traditional notions of kinship, they generally shied away from social reformism. Still, whatever the particulars, it remains that a study of the divinity of the period reveals some interesting facets of female role and experience in early seventeenth-century Scotland.

NOTES

1. Edinburgh University Library [EUL], Laing Manuscripts, La.III.607, (unfoliated), bound in J. Adamson, *Stoicheiosis eliquiorum dei, sive methodus religionis christianae catechetica* (Edinburgh, 1627).
2. Christine de Pizan, *The Book of the City of Ladies*, trans. E. J. Richards (London, 1983), 70 ff.
3. J. Weemes, *An exposition of the second table of the morall law* (London, 1636), 16; Weemes, *Workes*, ii, *Containing an exposition of the morall law, or ten commandements of almightie God* (London, 1636), Aaa3r.
4. J. Weemes, *The portraiture of the image of God in man*, 3rd edn (London, 1636), 15; Weemes, *Second table*, 20. See also (James Melville), *A spirituall propine of a pastour to his people* (Edinburgh, (1598)), 46; P. Mack, *Visionary Women: Ecstatic Prophecy in Seventeenth-Century England* (Berkeley, 1992), 24–5.
5. A. Simson, *Heptameron, the seven dayes* (St Andrews, 1621), 169–70. See also J. Sibbald, *Diverse select sermons* (Aberdeen, 1658), 101, and P. Crawford, *Women and Religion in England 1500–1720* (London, 1993), 6.
6. W. K. Tweedie, ed. *Select Biographies*, (2 vols, Wodrow Society, 1845–7), i, 58; D. Calderwood, *The History of the Kirk of Scotland* (8 vols, Wodrow

Society, 1842–9), vii, 343; A. Simson, *Christes testament unfolded* (Edinburgh, 1620), 74; *Dr. Balcanquals letters from the synod of Dort* (London, 1659), 7.

7. M. M. Dunn, 'Saints and Sisters: Congregational and Quaker Women in the Early Colonial Period,' *American Quarterly*, 30 (1978), 583–4. See also A. Porterfield, *Female Piety in Puritan New England* (New York, 1992), 10.
8. 'A Scottish Liturgy of the reign of James VI,' ed. G. Donaldson, Scottish History Society [SHS], *Miscellany*, x (1965), 113.
9. R. Rollock, *Lectures upon the epistles of Paul to the Colossians* (London, 1603), 341–2.
10. D. Lindsay (Leith), *The godly mans journey to heaven* (London, 1625), 259; *Diary of Sir Archibald Johnston of Wariston 1632–1639*, ed. G. M. Paul (SHS, 1911), 19.
11. Weemes, *Second table*, 23; G. Wakefield, *Puritan Devotion: Its place in the development of Christian piety* (London, 1957), 56–7.
12. *Wariston's Diary*, 10.
13. Rollock, *Colossians*, 346.
14. Rollock, *Colossians*, 347; R. Baillie, *A dissuasive from the errours of the time* (London, 1645), 14; R. K. Marshall, *Virgins and Viragos* (London, 1983), 100.
15. A. Simson, *A sacred septenarie* (London, 1638), 200.
16. T. Heywood, *Gynaikeion* (1624), in N. H. Keeble, ed. *The Cultural Identity of Seventeenth-Century Woman* (London, 1994), 61.
17. Simson, *Heptameron*, 123.
18. R. Rollock, *Lectures upon the first and second epistles of Paul to the Thessalonians* (Edinburgh, 1606), 240; J. Baillie, *Spiritual marriage: or, the union betweene Christ and his church* (London, 1627), 45.
19. Rollock, *Thessalonians*, 62. Emphasis added.
20. Porterfield, *Female Piety*, 3.
21. J. Melville, *Black bastel* (Edinburgh, 1634), idem, *Ad serenissimum Jacobum Primum Britanniarum monarcham, Ecclesiae Scoticanae libellus supplex* (London, 1645), 46. See also *Spirituall propine*, 11. Cf. (D. Calderwood), *The speach of the Kirk of Scotland to her beloved children* (n.p. 1620), 21, and (idem), *An epistle to a Christian brother* (n.p. 1624), 2.
22. R. Wodrow, *Collections upon the Lives of the Reformers and most eminent Ministers of the Church of Scotland*, (2 vols, Maitland Club, 1834–48), ii/1, 101, emphasis added.
23. W. Cowper, *The workes* (London, 1623), 21.
24. *The confession and conversion of the right honorable, most illustrious, and elect lady, my lady countess of Livingston* (Edinburgh, 1629), 28–9.
25. Lindsay, *Godly mans journey*, 602.
26. J. Baillie, *Spiritual marriage*, 36.
27. Scottish Record Office, CH 12/18/6, John Forbes of Corse, Diary, 4. Crawford, *Women and Religion*, 15–6.
28. A. Hume (Edinburgh), *A diduction of the true and catholik meaning of our Saviour his words, this is my bodie* (Edinburgh, 1602), A3r-v; (John Murray), *A dialogue betwixt Cosmophilus and Theophilus anent the urging*

of new ceremonies upon the Kirke of Scotland (n.p. 1620), 43. Cf. Rutherford, *Quaint Sermons*, 174.

29. D. Dickson, *A short explanation of the epistle of Paul to the Hebrews* (Aberdeen, 1635), 274.

30. (George Gillespie), *A dispute against the English-popish ceremonies, obtruded upon the church of Scotland* (n.p. 1637), C1r.

31. Lindsay, *Godly mans journey*, 347; *Wariston's Diary*, 144, 248.

32. Lindsay, *Godly mans journey*, 585.

33. Margaret Alic, *Hypatia's Heritage: A History of Women in Science from Antiquity through the Nineteenth Century* (Boston, 1986), 41–6.

34. Abernethy, *Christian and heavenly treatise*, 444.

35. Calderwood, *Pastor and prelate*, 37.

36. *Select Works of Robert Rollock*, ed. W. M. Gunn (2 vols, Wodrow Society, 1849, 1844), ii, 335.

37. D. Black, *An exposition uppon the thirtie two Psalme* (Edinburgh, 1600), 9. Emphasis added.

38. Rutherford, *Quaint Sermons*, 67.

39. C. Ferme, *A Logical Analysis of the Epistle to the Romans*, trans. W. Skae (Wodrow Society, 1850), 363. Originally published in Latin (1651).

40. Cf. D. L. Parish, 'The Power of Female Pieties: Women as Spiritual Authorities and Religious Role Models in Seventeenth-Century England,' *Journal of Religious History*, 17/1 (1992), 33.

41. Melville, *Spirituall propine*, 18; Rutherford, *Quaint Sermons*, 164.

42. John Welsh, *A reply against M Gilbert Browne priest* (Edinburgh, 1602), 220. See A Laurence, *Women in England 1500–1760: A Social History* (New York, 1994), 200; Crawford, *Women and Religion*, 56; G. W. Sprott and T. Leishman, eds. *The Book of Common Order of the Church of Scotland* (Edinburgh, 1868), 135; 'John Knox's "Order of Baptism"' in J. D. C. Fisher, ed. *Christian Initiation: The Reformation Period. Some early reformed rites of baptism and confirmation and other contemporary documents* (London, 1970), 119; J. Malcolm, *Commentarius in Apostolurum Acta* (Middelburgh, 1615), 211; (David Calderwood), *Perth Assembly* (n.p. 1619), 98, (idem), *The pastor and the prelate: or reformation and conformitie shortly compared* (n.p. 1628), 15.

43. J. Anderson, *The Ladies of the Covenant* (Glasgow, 1859), xv ff.

44. Calderwood, *History*, iv, 126; *Original Letters relating to the Ecclesiastical Affairs of Scotland*, ed. D. Laing (2 vols, Edinburgh, 1851), ii, 712; R. Baillie, *Letters and Journals*, (3 vols, Bannatyne Club, 1841–2), i, 20–1.

45. Calderwood, *History*, vii, 359–60, cited in I. B. Cowan, 'The Five Articles of Perth,' in *Reformation and Revolution*, ed. Duncan Shaw (Edinburgh, 1967), 176.

46. Historical Manuscripts Commission, *Laing Manuscripts* (2 vols, London, 1914–25), i, 198–9; H. Guthry, *Memoirs* (London, 1702), 20.

47. *The Register of the Privy Council of Scotland*, eds. J. Burton, et al (Edinburgh, 1877–), ii, 285–6, 579–80; *Fasti Ecclesiae Scoticanae*, ed. H. Scott (8 vols, Edinburgh, 1915–61), ii, 293.

48. *A Memorial of the Conversion of Jean Livingston, Lady Waristoun, with an Account of her carriage at her Execution, July 1600*, xi, in C. K. Sharpe, ed.

Lady Margaret Cunninghame, Lady Waristoun (Edinburgh, 1827). See K. M. Brown, 'The Laird, his Daughter, her Husband and the Minister: Unravelling a Popular Ballad,' in R. Mason and N. MacDougall, eds. *People and Power in Scotland* (Edinburgh, 1992), 104–25.

49. *Wariston's Diary*, 384–5, 393. See also J. Gordon, *History of Scots Affairs, from 1637 to 1641*, (3 vols, Spalding Club, 1841), i, 131–2.

50. J. Hamilton, *A facile traictise* (Louvain, 1600), in *Catholic Tractates of the Sixteenth Century 1573–1600*, ed. Thomas Graves Law (Scottish Text Society, 1901), 240.

51. W. Guild, *A compend of the controversies of religion* (Edinburgh, 1627), 90; Weemes, *Portraiture*, 281; Simson, *Christes testament*, 89; *Collections upon the Lives of the Reformers and Most Eminent Ministers of the Church of Scotland [Biog. Colls.]* (2 vols, Maitland Club, 1834–48), ii/1, 152; *Select Biographies*, i, 334; D. C. MacNicol, *Master Robert Bruce: Minister in the Kirk of Edinburgh* (Edinburgh, 1907), 244; D. Dalrymple, *Memorials and Letters relating to the History of Britain in the Reign of Charles the First*, 2nd edition (2 vols, Glasgow, 1766), ii, 75.

52. Weemes, *Second table*, 186. Cf. Diane Willen, 'Godly Women in Early Modern England: Puritanism and Gender,' *Journal of Ecclesiastical History*, 43 (1992), 565.

53. *Wariston's Diary*, 10, 28 & 200.

54. Rollock, *Works*, i, pp. lxxxi-lxxxii; Marshall, *Virgins and Viragos*, 65. See also I & K. Whyte in this volume.

55. John Row, *History of the Kirk of Scotland*, ed. D. Laing (Wodrow Society, 1842), 472.

56. *Select Biographies*, i, 150.

57. Patrick Adair, *A True Narrative of the Rise and Progress of the Presbyterian Church in Ireland (1623–1670)*, ed. W. D. Killen (Belfast, 1866), 38.

58. *Biog. Colls.*, ii/1, 243–4.

59. Simson, *Christes testament*, M3r; Simson, *Heptameron*, 98.

60. L. A. Yeoman, 'Heart-work: emotion, empowerment and authority in covenanting times,' (University of St Andrews, PhD thesis, 1991), 255. Cf. Willen, 'Godly Women,' 570–1.

61. A. T. Innes, *Studies in Scottish History chiefly Ecclesiastical* (London, 1892), 5; J. K. Cameron, 'The Piety of Samuel Rutherford (c.1621–1661): A neglected feature of seventeenth century Scottish Calvinism,' *Nederlands Archief voor Kerkeschiedenis*, 65 (1985), 155; J. Coffey, 'Samuel Rutherford (c.1600–61) and the British Revolutions' (University of Cambridge, PhD thesis, 1994), 110 ff.

62. D. Mathew, *Scotland under Charles I* (London, 1955), 38.

63. *Ecclesiastical Records: Selections from the Synod of Fife*, ed. C. Baxter (Abbotsford Club, 1837), 100–1.

64. Calderwood, *History*, vii, 426.

65. Hamilton, *Facile traictise*, 226.

66. Henry Leslie, *A treatise of the authority of the church* (London, 1639), preface.

67. *Biog. Colls.*, ii/1, 264 ff.

68. E. Melville, *Ane godlie dreame, compylit in Scottish metre* (Edinburgh,

1603). See also *Select Biographies*, i, 349–70 and EUL, Laing Mss La.III.347.

69. (William Livingston), *The conflict in conscience of a dear Christian, named Bessie Clarksone* (Edinburgh, 1631). See note 24.

70. EUL, Laing Mss La.III.263: Wodrow Octavo 33, no. 6. I am editing this document for publication in the SHS, *Miscellany*, xiii. See D. Mullan, 'Mistress Rutherford's Narrative: A Scottish Puritan Autobiography', *Bunyan Studies*, 7 (1977), 13–37.

71. Ferme, *Logical Analysis*, 363; S. Felch, 'The Rhetoric of Biblical Authority: John Knox and the Question of Women,' *Sixteenth Century Journal*, 26 (1995), 822.

72. R. Rollock, *Certaine sermons upon severall places of the epistles of Paul* (Edinburgh, 1599), 7; idem, *Select Works*, i, 302; J. Welsh, *Forty-eight Select Sermons* (Glasgow, (1771)), 218; Z. Boyd, *Two sermons, for those who are able to come to the table of the Lord* (Edinburgh, 1629), 62; Rollock, *Colossians*, 124; W. Wishart, *An exposition of the Lord's prayer* (Edinburgh, 1633), 449; Lindsay, *Godly mans journey*, 278; J. Howesoun, *A short exposition of the 20. and 21. verses of the third chapter of the First Epistle of S. John* (Edinburgh, 1600), D5v; D. Dickson, *Therapeutica sacra, shewing briefly the method of healing the diseases of the conscience* (Edinburgh, 1664), 2.

73. Z. Boyd, *Balme of Gilead*, 49.

PART TWO

'In her great anguish she composed the song . . .
and sung it as a lullaby to her babe'

Scots Abroad in the Fifteenth Century: The Princesses Margaret, Isabella and Eleanor

_____ *Priscilla Bawcutt and Bridget Henisch*

MANY YEARS AGO Annie I. Dunlop devoted a pioneering article to the medieval Scotsmen who travelled widely in Europe as diplomats, soldiers, students, priests and merchants.[1] Nothing is said there of Scottish women, however, apart from a passing reference to the 'matrimonial adventures' of the six daughters of James I: Margaret, Isabella, Joan, Eleanor, Mary and Annabella. For most historians this is indeed the chief importance of these women: they figure as pawns in the intricate diplomatic manoeuvres first of their father, and then of their ambitious brother James II, whose treatment of them was governed largely by 'political cynicism and the prospect of financial advantage'.[2] Only a little is known of Mary, who in 1444 married Wolfaert van Borselen, son of the Lord of Veere in Zeeland, or of Joan and Annabella, who were sent abroad, in the hope of prestigious foreign alliances, but eventually, in the late 1450s, were married to Scottish noblemen, Joan to James Douglas, newly created earl of Morton, and Annabella to George, master of Huntly. The lives of Margaret, Isabella, and Eleanor, however, are much better documented, largely in Continental rather than Scottish records, because of their marriages, respectively, to the dauphin of France, the duke of Brittany, and the archduke of Austria-Tyrol. Such marriages – like that of James II himself to Mary of Guelders – were designed to enhance Scotland's standing in European politics. Yet these princesses have interest and importance in their own right, not simply because of their dynastic alliances. What is more, all three were involved in literary activity, whether as readers, book-collectors, patrons, and possibly, indeed, as authors; although differing greatly from each other in character, they illustrate the varied cultural opportunities available to privileged women in the fifteenth century.

MARGARET (1424–1445)

The eldest child of James I and Joan Beaufort, Margaret was betrothed at an early age to the dauphin, who later reigned as Louis XI. The match was a piece of power politics: Charles VII, the father of Louis, wished to

ensure Scottish assistance in his war with England, and James hoped for
financial aid from the French king and to acquire territory in France, in
particular the county of Saintonge. Margaret sailed for France in March
1436: little is known of her parents' feelings towards her, although they
are said to have shed tears and shown some anxiety concerning her
dangerous voyage at such a 'tender age'.[3] Margaret's escort included
some of the greatest Scottish nobles, and she was welcomed in France
with much pomp and pageantry: as she entered Poitiers, for instance, a
child dressed as an angel crowned her with a wreath of flowers. A
miniature in the *Chroniques de Charles VII* (Bibliothèque Nationale,
MS fr. 2691) depicts her entry on horseback into Tours, where she was
married on 25 June 1436.[4] In this image the princess looks small and frail,
but there are contemporary testimonies to her beauty, including that of
the poet Martin le Franc: 'C'est une estoile clere et fine / Mise en ce monde
à parement'.[5]

Margaret spent the rest of her short life at the French court, chiefly in
the household of the queen. She seems to have seen little of the dauphin,
whose aversion to her was notorious and remarked on by several
contemporaries. Malicious rumours are said to have circulated about
her conduct, spread by a Breton, Jamet de Tillay. She is reported to have
regretted ever coming to France, and to have exclaimed on her death bed:
'Fy de la vie de ce monde, et ne m'en parlez plus'.[6] Her life may sound
brief, pathetic and loveless, yet in fact Charles VII and his queen treated
her kindly, and at her death there was a great outpouring of grief. She was
far from being a nonentity, and made a remarkable impression on
contemporaries, exciting far more interest than Louis' second wife,
Charlotte of Savoy, of whom little is reported except for Philippe
Commynes' double-edged remark that she 'was not one of those women
in whom a man would take great pleasure but in all a very good lady'.[7]

Walter Bower praised the literary and musical skills of James I, who is
the reputed author of *The Kingis Quair*, the first and finest of Scottish
medieval love poems.[8] Margaret perhaps inherited an aptitude for poetry
from her father. She is said to have devoted much time to writing
rondeaux and ballades, sometimes producing as many as twelve in
one day. Her doctors later criticised this indulgence in verse-making as
excessive, and suggested that 'poetical overwork' might have contributed
to her death.[9] Unfortunately nothing survives of her poetry; after her
death Louis is said to have ordered that all her papers – 'toutes les lettres
et tous les vers' – should be destroyed.[10] According to W. M. Bryce, a
copy of Pierre de Nesson's *Paraphrase sur Job* has as frontispiece a
miniature of Margaret, 'wearing the Franciscan cord' (see the discussion
of Isabella below). Bryce suggests that Margaret was erroneously believed
to be the work's author, but this seems unlikely. Her possession of this

sombre meditation on death by a then famous fifteenth-century French poet testifies chiefly to her piety. It is unfortunate that the whereabouts of the manuscript are now unknown.[11]

There is no doubt, however, that Margaret was at the centre of a small circle at the French court which took delight in verse-making, along with music and dancing, as a social pastime. One of her ladies-in-waiting, Jeanne de Filleul, wrote verse that has been preserved.[12] Another and more considerable poet in her circle was Hugh, vicomte de Blosseville, a close friend of Charles d'Orléans, whose imprisonment he shared in England. Several of Blosseville's poems survive, including allegorical debates and rondeaux, one of which addresses Margaret in its opening line as 'Celle pour qui je porte l"M"'.[13] Long after her death the sixteenth-century chronicler Jean Bouchet told a famous but apocryphal story that Margaret so admired the poet Alain Chartier that she placed a kiss upon his lips as he lay sleeping. Chartier died before Margaret journeyed to France, and on the one occasion that he visited Scotland, in 1428, she was only four years old. Yet the anecdote is significant, and testifies to Margaret's contemporary image: she was a young woman who 'fort aymoit les orateurs de la langue vulgaire', but was characterised by daring, slightly unorthodox behaviour.[14]

Several French poets mourned Margaret's untimely death. Blosseville celebrated her in a ballade, full of courtly hyperbole, that proclaims her superior to the fairest and most virtuous women of antiquity, and employs the refrain as a prayer: 'Je requier Dieu qu'il en veuille avoir l'ame'.[15] Another poem is inscribed in a book of hours belonging to her sister Isabella, and represents the dying dauphine as bidding farewell to all her kindred, including the dauphin, 'son loial mari', and also 'mon pere, roy d'Escosse'.[16] This poem has sometimes been attributed to Isabella herself, but is more likely to have been copied by (or for) her, since the reference to James I as if he were still alive in 1445 could hardly have been made by anyone in close touch with Scottish affairs, let alone by Isabella. The poem belongs to a well-established literary tradition, in which such 'congés', or 'farewells', are placed in the mouth of the person whose death is being mourned.

The longest and most ornate of the elegies for Margaret has been discovered comparatively recently: an anonymous *Complainte pour la mort de Madame Marguerite d'Escosse, daulphine de Viennoys* (Bibliothèque de l'Arsenal, MS 3523).[17] Its most interesting feature is the highly symmetrical structure: the complaint, or lament, consists of eighteen stanzas, and is matched by a second section, of the same number of stanzas. This contains the reply of Reason, who voices orthodox sentiments about death's inevitability and the consolation of religion. A very free translation of this poem was made into Scots, and is preserved in the

Liber Pluscardensis. The chronicler says that the original was written by the dauphin himself, which seems unlikely in view of his coldness towards Margaret, and that it was placed as an epitaph upon her tomb, which was indeed a common practice. The chronicler says also that the translation was made at the command of James II.[18]

All these poems are accomplished but impersonal expressions of public mourning. A more intimate and poignant sense of grief is communicated by the chronicler himself, an as yet unidentified Scotsman who had spent several years at the French court and knew Margaret well:

> Alas that I should have to write what I sadly relate about her death . . . I who write this saw her every day, for the space of nine years, alive and enjoying herself in the company of the king and queen of France. But then . . . I saw her, within the space of eight days, first in good health and then dead and disembowelled and laid in a tomb at the corner of the high altar, in the cathedral church of Châlons.[19]

Margaret, however, wished to be buried in the abbey church at Thouars (near Poitiers), where she had founded a chapel, and her body was removed there in 1479.

ISABELLA (?1427–c.1495)

Not much has survived to shed light on the personality of Isabella, who married Francis, duke of Brittany in 1442. From a diplomatic report to her prospective father-in-law, it may be inferred that she was a well brought-up young lady, schooled to silence and submission, when she set sail for Brittany.[20] But she was more fortunate than Margaret, and was granted blessings not often accorded to medieval princesses: a long life, and a combination of character and circumstances that enabled her to resist all the pressure, from her brother James II, to return to Scotland after her husband died in 1450, and exchange the independence of widowhood for the dubious pleasures of a second marriage.[21] As a result she enjoyed the luxury of time to develop her own tastes, and the freedom to indulge them.

Like other great ladies of her period, Isabella was devout, and from the evidence of the books she collected it is possible to trace the pattern of her piety. Four books of hours associated with her name still survive. One magnificent example (Fitzwilliam Museum, Cambridge, MS 62), may have been inherited by Isabella from her husband's first wife, Yolande of Anjou, who died in 1440.[22] Another (Bibliothèque Nationale, Paris, MS lat. N. A. 588) was probably commissioned by Isabella, while a third

(Bibliothèque Nationale, Paris, MS lat. 1369) was certainly made for her.[23] These three have long been linked with the duchess, but the presence of a fourth book in the Gulbenkian Museum in Lisbon (simply identified on a postcard reproduction as 'Hours of Isabel Duchess of Brittany') suggests that others from her library may still await discovery.

Having been lucky enough to inherit a splendid book, Isabella in turn presented treasures to her daughters, Marguerite (d.1469) and Marie (d.1506). The book of hours made for Isabella (Bibliothèque Nationale, Paris, MS lat. 1369) probably passed to Marie, while Marguerite received two 'armoyées aux armes de la duchesse ysabeau', of which one may have been Fitzwilliam MS 62.

Besides commissioning at least one book of hours, Isabella directed another book to be made for her. A note in the manuscript (BN. MS fr. 958) gives the date, 1464, the scribe, Jehan Hubert, and the information that 'Ysabeau . . . fist faire ce livre'.[24] The book was a copy of the *Somme le Roi*, that thirteenth-century manual on the articles of faith, the seven sins and the seven virtues, which was one of the building blocks of lay devotion in the later Middle Ages. The book of hours definitely made for Isabella (Bibliothèque Nationale, Paris, MS lat. 1369) also contains much educational material organised in the same simple, schematic way.[25] This manuscript and two of Isabella's books of hours can be dated from internal evidence to some time after her husband's death, and it seems likely that they were purchased or commissioned by her authority alone.

The Fitzwilliam book of hours may have helped to draw another kind of spiritual guide to Isabella's notice, because its borders are decorated with hundreds of tiny scenes from a devotional entertainment cast in the form of an allegorical romance, Deguileville's *Pélerinage de la vie humaine*, c.1350. This book was immensely popular among aristocratic readers, and it is not implausible that Isabella was one of these.[26]

Four formal portraits of the duchess appear in the pages of her books. In each she wears a dress patterned with her heraldic arms, the ermine of Brittany and lion of Scotland, and in each she is protected by her spiritual supporters. In Fitzwilliam MS 62 she is presented to the Virgin and Child by St Katherine of Alexandria, but in the others it is St Francis who stands behind her. He is also the figure who guards her in a fifth portrait, where she kneels in a family group on a page of the Missal of the Carmelites of Nantes (Princeton University Library, Garrett MS 40). The Carmelite community in Nantes enjoyed the patronage of the dukes of Brittany, and the Missal contains a long series of their portraits. Francis I appears with his children and two wives, Yolande and Isabella.[27]

Isabella was linked to the Carmelites by her marriage, but her personal sympathies seem to have lain with the Franciscans. St Francis was the patron saint of the duke, so it is possible that he was adopted by Isabella

in turn as a mark of affection for her husband, but there is one extra clue
that she had her own special devotion to the saint. The portrait which is in
her copy of *Somme le roi* shows her in magnificent heraldic dress, but
round her waist appears a plain, knotted cord.[28] This was the badge worn
by members of the laity who wished to follow a spiritual regime, even
while they continued to live in the secular world. Although Isabella is
always pictured as a great lady, and although her will reveals that she had
many rich possessions to bequeath, the girdle is a sign that she consciously
tried to obey the Order's rules, even while carrying out the duties of her
high estate. Nevertheless, with that endearing medieval fondness for
display as well as devotion, one daughter, Marguerite, thought it appropriate in 1469 to leave Isabella a special legacy, a fine gold chain, knotted
in imitation of the Franciscan cord.[29]

The choice of St Katherine of Alexandria as guardian of the duchess in
Fitzwilliam MS 62 may indicate an interest in education, because
Katherine was famous for her learning, but whether Isabella could
actually write as well as read is open to question. The fact that her name
'Ysabeau' is written, perhaps in her own hand, on the margin of six pages
in another book of hours (Bibliothèque Nationale, Paris, MS lat. 1369) is
no proof of real fluency. (On the poem in this MS, see above, p.47)

As a book collector, Isabella is linked through a tissue of family ties, to
her sisters and to other women patrons in France and England. The
Fitzwilliam hours may have been made originally for Yolanda of Aragon,
and passed first to her daughter and then to Isabella. Through her mother,
Joan Beaufort, Isabella was related to the Beaufort family in England,
which included during Isabella's lifetime two women remarkable for their
piety and their libraries: Cecily Neville, duchess of York and mother of
Edward IV, and lady Margaret Beaufort, mother of Henry VII.[30]

Isabella was not a strikingly original figure. In both piety and patronage she could be matched by others in her world. Her life is of interest,
nevertheless, because it provides precious evidence of the tastes of one
particular woman, shaped by current fashions in devotion. Beneath the
splendid trappings and ceremonial routine appropriate for her rank,
Isabella attempted an internal pilgrimage as a private soul, a day by
day progress on a path to spiritual enlightenment.

ELEANOR (?1433–1480)

Eleanor passed her childhood in Scotland, chiefly in Linlithgow; but in
1445, shortly after their mother's death, she and her sister Joan were
invited to France by Isabella, and arrived there in August only a few days
after the death of their sister Margaret.[31] Eleanor spent the next three

years at the French court, under the charge of Jeanne de Tucé. James II had wished her to marry the dauphin, but this and other marriage proposals were abortive. In 1447 Sigmund, archduke of Tyrol, sent an embassy to Charles VII to ask for her hand, and on 8 September 1448 she married him by proxy.

Little is known of Eleanor in the early years of the marriage, but in the mid-1450s she was appointed regent while Sigmund was out of the country. She was involved in the notorious and long-running dispute between Sigmund and Nicholas of Cusa, who had been appointed bishop of Brixen, and attempted to reform discipline at the Benedictine convent there. Eleanor was given her own seals, and was actively involved in raising money, guns, and mercenary soldiers. Throughout her marriage she was an intrepid traveller, and in 1465 made visits to several warm springs, such as those at Wildbad Gastein. She enjoyed hunting and chivalric sports, and in 1467 witnessed Sigmund tourneying at Basel.[32]

No contemporary portrait of Eleanor survives, and the sixteenth-century heraldic representations of her are vivid but unflattering, showing a plump, sturdy woman.[33] Such an image tallies with what is known of her life. She emerges as a strong and extremely independent woman, 'well able to run a separate household and to look after the administration of scattered properties in difficult terrain and difficult political circum-stances'.[34] Nothing certain is known of Eleanor's education, but she was clearly a cultivated woman, who was literate in several languages. She conducted correspondence in German, Latin, French and Scots; many letters to her are extant in the State Archive at Innsbruck, and a few of her own autograph letters survive, written in German and French.[35]

Sigmund's court has a reputation for learning, and Eleanor seems to have shared with him a love of books. The household accounts contain entries for the purchase, copying and binding of books; there is a reference to a '*vocabulari*' and another to a *spectacel*, or entertainment, which one of the trumpeters had written for Eleanor.[36] It was a custom at that time for nobles to exchange books as gifts: in 1454 Eleanor presented to duke John of Bavaria a *hefftel*, a small volume which unfortunately is untitled. Perhaps even more significant, in view of Eleanor's own literary tastes, was the gift to her in 1478 by duke Albrecht of Bavaria of a *buch des lancilot*. The story of Lancelot was then immensely popular, parti-cularly among women: the Scottish *Lancelot of the Laik* seems to have been composed about this time.[37]

After Sigmund's death in 1496 his library passed to Maximilian or was dispersed, and only a few books can now definitely be traced to the ownership of Eleanor and Sigmund. One interesting example is a psalter (Austrian National Library, MS 1852), which bears both the Austrian and the Scottish coats of arms.[38] Eleanor also possessed an early Italian incunable, an edition of St Jerome's *Epistolae* printed in Rome c.1467, which she presented to the collegiate church of Augustinian canons at Neustift, near Brixen. Each volume of this work has the contemporary inscription: 'Iste liber est Monasterii S. Marie virginis ad grans (grams?) alias ad Novam cellam dicti, donatus eidem ab illustrissima domina Elienor de Scocia domina ac principe huius terre'. Alasdair Cherry considers this 'possibly the earliest recorded Scottish provenance in a printed book'.[39] It has been suggested also that the fine manuscript of Virgil, now in Edinburgh University Library (MS 195), may have belonged to Eleanor: 'the initials 'P' and 'L' beside the Scottish royal arms in the volume are thought to stand for "Principissa Leonora"'.[40]

In 1473 a translation of Boccaccio's *De claris mulieribus* was dedicated to Eleanor. The author, the humanist Heinrich Steinhöwel (1412–78), followed the precedent of Boccaccio himself, who had dedicated his work 'not to a prince but to some illustrious lady'. Steinhöwel also imitated Boccaccio in an apology for including evil women as well as virtuous ones, but he included a fulsome tribute to Eleanor herself as the 'crowning representative of all women'.[41] Steinhöwel followed this work with other translations – of Aesop and the *Speculum vitae humanae* – both of which he dedicated to Sigmund.

Eleanor's great claim to literary fame rests upon *Pontus und Sidonia*, a landmark in the history of German prose literature. It was first printed in 1483, three years after her death, and the title states that Eleanor translated (*getransferiert*) and made (*gemacht*) the work out of French into German, for the pleasure of her prince and lord Sigmund, and as a testimony of her love.[42] Eleanor's authorship of this work has been traditionally accepted for centuries, but in recent years some doubt has been expressed as to whether she was personally responsible for the translation.[43] Women translators were indeed rare in the Middle Ages, but Eleanor has an interesting precedent in Elizabeth von Nassau-Saarbrucken (1397–1456), who translated French *chansons de geste* into German prose.[44] Late medieval English women, such as Eleanor Hull (born c.1394) and Lady Margaret Beaufort (1443–1509), were more obviously pious in their choice of texts, translating prayers and devotional works, such as part of *The Imitation of Christ*.[45] Only experts in German medieval language and literature can discuss this question authoritatively. But perhaps, as A. M. Stewart suggests, we should regard Eleanor as 'a supervising patron rather than as a translator in the modern sense'.[46]

The appeal of the French *Ponthus et Sidoine* to Eleanor, whatever her degree of involvement in its translation, is not difficult to explain. A chivalric romance, full of marvellous exploits, jousts and tournaments, it has much in common with the Scottish *Clariodus* (also a translation from a French prose romance) and with Malory's *Morte d'Arthur*. What is more, the work combined an exciting story with excellent morality; it celebrates the virtues of faithfulness and loyalty in love. During the fifteenth century the romance had an enormous vogue, particularly among aristocrats; one finely illustrated copy of the French work was owned by Margaret of Anjou, whose wedding to Henry VI had been attended by Eleanor's sister Margaret. Eleanor's translation was reprinted several times, and long retained its popularity in Germany; it was still being read in the eighteenth century, long after the story was forgotten elsewhere.[47]

This brief article does not claim to be definitive, although it is firmly based on different types of evidence – pictorial, bibliographical, literary and historical. What it offers is an introduction to a fascinating subject, which deserves further and much fuller investigation. In recent years there has been an 'explosion' of interest in the varied cultural activities of medieval women.[48] Little has been written as yet, however, about this aspect of the lives of medieval Scotswomen, perhaps because the evidence is considered scanty or non-existent. If so, the cultural interests and activities of these three princesses, who travelled 'furth of the realm', should surely receive much greater recognition.

NOTES

1. Annie Dunlop, 'Scots Abroad in the Fifteenth Century', *Historical Association Pamphlet*, no. 124 (London, 1942).
2. Norman Macdougall, *James III: a Political Study* (Edinburgh, 1982), 49, n.27 and 43–4. See also A. I. Dunlop, *The Life and Times of Bishop Kennedy, Bishop of St Andrews* (Edinburgh, 1950), especially 147–8, 179–82, 185–7; R. Nicholson, *Scotland: The Later Middle Ages* (Edinburgh, 1974; 1989), especially 347–8; Christine McGladdery, *James II* (Edinburgh, 1990), 42–6.
3. Louis A. Barbé, *Margaret of Scotland and the Dauphin Louis* (London, 1917), 71–2, 76. See also Pierre Champion, *Louis XI* (2 vols, Paris, 1927); Paul Kendall, *Louis XI* (London, 1971).
4. Barbé, *Margaret of Scotland*, 83–113. For reproductions, see Barbé, frontispiece; Alastair Cherry, *Princes, Poets and Patrons: the Stuarts and Scotland* (Edinburgh, 1987), plate facing p. 28.
5. Quoted in Barbé, *Margaret of Scotland*, 95.
6. Champion, *Louis XI*, i, 182.
7. Quoted by Kendall, *Louis XI*, 123.
8. Walter Bower, *Scotichronicon*, eds. D. E. R. Watt et al (9 vols, Aberdeen and Edinburgh, 1987–97), Book xvi, 28–30; James I of Scotland, *The Kingis Quair*, ed. J. Norton-Smith (Leiden, 1981).
9. Barbé, *Margaret of Scotland*, 122.

10. Gaston du Fresne de Beaucourt, *Histoire de Charles VII* (Paris, 1888), iv, 189; Barbé, *Margaret of Scotland*, 121–2.
11. William Moir Bryce, *The Scottish Grey Friars* (2 vols, Edinburgh, 1909), i, 51–2. A. Piaget and E. Droz, *Pierre de Nesson et ses oeuvres* (Paris, 1925), list manuscripts of the *Paraphrase sur Job*, but do not discuss their provenance.
12. Gaston Raynaud ed. *Rondeaux et autres poésies du XVe siècle* (Paris, 1889), no. lxxxvii; also pp. xv-xvi.
13. Raynaud, *Rondeaux*, no. lxxxii; also pp. viii-x.
14. A. M. Stewart, 'Alain Chartier et l'Ecosse' in J. J. Blanchot and C. Graf eds. *Actes du 2e Colloque de langue et de littérature écossaises* (Strasbourg, 1978), 148–61.
15. Raynaud, *Rondeaux*, no. cxxvi.
16. A slightly inaccurate text of the poem is printed in Barbé, *Margaret of Scotland*, 173–4. Fiona Downie informs us that a correct text is published in J. Trevedy, 'Trois Duchesses douairières de Bretagne' in *Bulletin Archéologique de l'Association Bretonne*, 27 (1909), 49.
17. The poem is unpublished, except in the doctoral dissertation of Claude Thiry, 'Recherches sur la déploration funèbre française à la prérenaissance' (Liège, 1973).
18. On the Scottish poem and its relation to the French one, see P. Bawcutt, 'A Medieval Scottish Elegy and its French Original', *Scottish Literary Journal*, 15/1 (1988), 5–13.
19. See *Liber Pluscardensis*, XI. viii, ed. Felix J. H. Skene (Historians of Scotland, Edinburgh, 1877–80), I, 382–88.
20. Louis Barbé, 'A Stuart Duchess of Brittany' in *Sidelights on the History, Industries and Social Life of Scotland* (London, 1919), 1–45 [4–5]
21. Barbé, 'A Stuart Duchess', 20–40; Dunlop, *Bishop Kennedy*, 147–8,179–81.
22. John Harthan, *Books of Hours and their Owners* (London, 1977), 33, 116–17.
23. M. R. Toynbee, 'The Portraiture of Isabella Stuart, Duchess of Brittany (c.1427–after 1494)' *Burlington Magazine*, 88 (1946), 300–06.
24. Unsigned note in *Scottish Historical Review*, 4 (1907), 488; Toynbee, 'Portraiture', 305.
25. V. Leroquais, *Les Livres d'heures manuscrits de la bibliothèque nationale* (Paris, 1927), i, 185–89.
26. Cf. R. Tuve, *Allegorical Imagery: Some Medieval Books and their Posterity* (Princeton, 1966), 192–5, n. 26; D. Pearsall, *John Lydgate* (London, 1970), 172–3.
27. J. Plummer, *The Last Flowering: French Painting in Manuscripts 1420–1530* (New York and London, 1982), 23–4.
28. Cf. Toynbee, 'Portraiture', 305.
29. Barbé, 'A Stuart Duchess', 44.
30. Cf. W. A. Pantin, 'Instructions for a Devout and Literate Layman' in J. J. G. Alexander and M. T. Gibson eds. *Medieval Learning and Literature* (Oxford, 1976), 407; N. Orme, *From Childhood to Chivalry: the Education of the English Kings and Aristocracy, 1066–1530* (London, 1984), 161.
31. On Eleanor's life, see Beaucourt, *Histoire de Charles VII*, iv, 365–70; Margarete Köfler and Silvia Caramelle, *Die Beiden Frauen des Erzherzogs*

Sigmund von Österreich-Tirol (Innsbruck, 1982), 15–114. We are much indebted to A. M. Stewart of Aberdeen University for the loan of this book, and for his valuable article 'The Austrian Connection c.1450–1483: Eleonora and the Intertextuality of *Pontus und Sidonia*' in J. D. McClure and M. R. G. Spiller eds. *Bryght Lanternis: Essays on the Language and Literature of Medieval and Renaissance Scotland* (Aberdeen, 1989), 129–49.

32. Köfler, *Beiden Frauen*, 15–89; D. Hay, *Europe in the Fourteenth and Fifteenth Centuries* (London, 1970), 319–20.

33. See the portrait of her in this volume.

34. Stewart, 'Austrian Connection', 139.

35. The correspondence is preserved in the Innsbruck Landesregierungsarchiv für Tirol. See Köfler, *Beiden Frauen*, 89–92 who prints a letter from Eleanor to Sigmund; Stewart, 'Austrian Connection', 135–6 prints a letter to her in Scots from James, lord Hamilton.

36. Köfler, *Beiden Frauen*, 97.

37. Köfler, *Beiden Frauen*, 98; C. Meale '. . . "Alle the Bokes that I haue of Latyn, Englisch and Frensch": Laywomen and their Books in Late Medieval England', in *Women and Literature in Britain 1150–1500* (Cambridge, 1993), 128–58 [139]; *Lancelot of the Laik* ed. M. M. Gray (Scottish Text Society, 1912).

38. Köfler, *Beiden Frauen*, 98.

39. This book is in private possession, and we are grateful to Alasdair Cherry for sending a transcript of the inscription; see also his *Princes and Patrons*, 18.

40. Cherry, *Princes and Patrons*, 18; *Treasures from Scottish Libraries: Catalogue of an Exhibition held in the Library of Trinity College, Dublin* (Edinburgh, 1964), no. 41.

41. Köfler, *Beiden Frauen*, 94–5.

42. Stewart, 'Austrian Connection' (see note 31), 138–42. On the origins and great popularity of this romance, see F. J. Mather's edition of the English version: 'King Ponthus and the Fair Sidone: A Prose Romance Translated from the French about the Year 1450', *Proceedings of the Modern Languages Association*, 12 (1897), iv–lxvii [Introduction]; 1–150 [Text].

43. Reinhard Hahn, '*Von frantzosischer zungen in teütsch*': das literarische Leben am Innsbrucker Hof des späteren 15. Jahrhunderts und der Prosaroman '*Pontus und Sidonia (A)*' (Frankfurt, 1990). We are indebted to Klaus Bitterling for bringing this work to our attention.

44. Stewart, 'Austrian Connection', 136.

45. See *Women's Writing in Middle English*, ed. Alexandra Barratt (London, 1992).

46. Stewart, 'Austrian Connection', 136.

47. Cf. Mather, 'King Ponthus', xli–xliv. The National Library of Scotland possesses a copy of the 1548 Augsburg edition (FB.m.500).

48. Cf. June H. McCash ed. *The Cultural Patronage of Medieval Women* (Athens, Ga., 1996), ix. See also Susan G. Bell, 'Medieval Women Book Owners: Arbiters of Lay Piety and Ambassadors of Culture', *Signs*, 7 (1981–2), 742–68; Jane H. M. Taylor and L. Smith eds. *Women and the Book: Assessing the Visual Evidence* (London, 1996).

CHAPTER FIVE

Images of Women in Sixteenth-Century Scottish Literary Manuscripts[1]

_____ *Evelyn S. Newlyn*

IN SCOTTISH POETRY from the sixteenth century, women are generally portrayed in iconic or stereotypic images that seem for the most part to be of male creation. Some promising new scholarship may alter this perception,[2] but, as currently known, Scots literature of this period lacks a significant corpus of works definitely written by women. Thus, while many poems include or even focus upon women, rare indeed are voices consciously based in and speaking for women's experiences, values, and epistemology, rather than voices unconsciously, or consciously, based in and furthering the prevailing culture of male experiences, values, and epistemology.[3] Moreover, since contemporary social and literary circumstances may suggest that probably few anonymous poems can be confidently said to have been written by women, representations of the female in sixteenth-century Scots manuscripts seem largely the products of male poets.

Literature is, however, a product not only of the individual poet, but also of the cultural matrix. Late medieval poetry, accordingly, reflects, reifies, and helps to create images of women; to degrees that are varyingly obvious, these images support and continue the culture's existing social and political arrangements, in particular the location and disposition of power between the sexes.[4] This poetry, then, as most literature, illustrates but also advances the culture's dominant ideology.

In serving such ends, the poetry casts women for the most part in accord with traditional polarities as idealised love object or personification of virtue, or conversely as evil wife, unkind mistress, or the unmarried but sexual woman who may appear, for example, as an abandoned maiden or a prostitute. Poems containing negative and satiric portrayals of women are fairly obvious in their political ends. As they allege women individually and as a sex to be inherently flawed in character, such poems help to justify the limited roles for women in society and the culture's generalised misogyny. However, poetry containing ostensibly positive portrayals of women often serves the same ends. Poems presenting women iconically as idealised love object or personified virtue, seemingly generated by a positive attitude toward women, often prove on closer analysis to confine 'good' women to rigidly restricted positions that forbid and preclude female agency. Thus, whether based upon models of the impossibly good or the unredeemably bad woman, these poems convey how women are meant or not meant to be, and how men are to think and behave toward women, that is, convey to both sexes the gender roles they are to fill. While the term 'gender' seems in this period not to refer to individual roles accorded by sex, something like the concept of 'gender' seems to have been known.[5] In transmitting such politically didactic information, these poems assist the enforcement of gender roles essential to the system of male dominance.

This essay discusses eight poems that illustrate these processes and that are representative of verse containing images of women as icons or stereotypes. These poems are found in two principal late Middle Scots manuscript anthologies, the Maitland Folio Manuscript and the Bannatyne Manuscript.[6] The Maitland Folio Manuscript has a focus on poems by its compiler, Richard Maitland, but also contains poems by other authors. George Bannatyne's literary compendium, much larger in scale with nearly 400 poems, includes work by Scottish writers and by writers from England and elsewhere whose verse was put into Middle Scots.

One iconic type of poem found in these manuscripts concerns the idealised love object, a lady declared to be possessed of all beauty and goodness. Such poems are not, of course, peculiar to Scottish literature, but are common in English and European literature as well.[7] This content would seem to reflect a positive assessment of women or at least of the particular woman objectified. However, such poems often embed another popular if somewhat conflicting image, and treat the woman additionally as the 'unkind mistress'. Such 'love' poems as a result contain strongly manipulative rhetoric to coerce the lady into showing 'mercy' or 'grace' to the would-be lover. The lover's avowals of the lady's superiority and his submission to her are therefore undercut by his veiled or overt threats if she does not respond as he desires. The content and frequency of this manipulative language in poetry addressed to the desired female illustrates the ambiguity of the perspective that professes to hold women preeminent but at the same time unequivocally asserts male authority. One of the Bannatyne Manuscript's poems that idealises the lady while concealing a knife among the flowers is poem number 263, which is anonymous and unique to the Bannatyne Manuscript.[8] The first stanzas reflect the influence of courtly love: the narrator/lover details the lady's excellence, cites his own inadequacies, and expounds upon his devotion. His lady, 'the gudliest / That ever formit wes be dame nature', stands superlative to all other women (ll.17–18). In accord with the catalogue of female beauty, the lover praises her gold hair, her 'beriall brycht' eyes, and her heavenly 'hew' (ll.25,33). Declaring his abject servitude, he professes his heart's enthrallment to this woman who will ever be his

sovereign. In a consummate statement of her qualities, the lover pronounces the lady 'of womanheid the rich mirror' (ll.17–18).

While certainly seeming approbatory, these pronouncements serve a
contravening function, the creation between the two of a synthetic sexual
hierarchy with female dominance. This purportedly unequal relationship
is a necessary context for the would-be lover's later demands. Establishing this false hierarchy makes possible the pressure the lover subsequently
applies to the lady who, because of her alleged position of superiority, is
required by courtesy to show 'mercy' or 'grace' to her subject. The lover's
declarations of his shortcomings and his proclamations of utter devotion
are thus disclosed as major techniques that help create the imbalance
postulated in such poetry between the exalted lady and the inferior lover.

That the lover may have a purpose other than adoration is first
suggested halfway through the poem, when the lover notes suggestively
that because of her he has joy but also says 'allace'. The fourth and fifth
stanzas follow this pattern, offering extravagant dedication and praise
but then, in a line or two at the end of each stanza, betraying the lover's
real insistence when he forcefully asserts his need for 'mercy'. Toward the
end of the sixth stanza the lover ceases to use the third person and directly
addresses the lady, at which time his peremptory nature and his real
purpose emerge most distinctly.

In the course of this apostrophe the lover recites his wishes and the
reasons why the lady must acquiesce to them. His manipulative and
menacing rhetoric divulges both his willingness to compel and the lady's
inferior and vulnerable status. Although the lover first asserts mildly that
no 'medisoneir' but she can save him, he then directs a series of increasingly severe, if not unusual, threats against her if she does not have mercy
on his 'grevois pane' (ll.45, 49). His life is wholly under her control, he
argues, and if she does not accede to his desire he will be slain; then she
will be accused of his death, be shamed forever, and, moreover, thereby
'do grit Injure' to the deity (l.53). This last is not, however, the most
alarming result the lover predicts. In the final line of the poem, the lover
pronounces the final dreadful consequence of the lady's lack of compliance: her failure to show mercy, he tells her, will indicate 'grit lak vnto
your womanhed' (l.56).

The reference to the lady's 'womanhed' in the lover's ultimate threat
echoes his use of the term in his ultimate compliment, and links the
poem's two parts. The poem thus circles back to its beginning by
positioning the lady's gendered status, her 'womanhood', as key element
in both the lover's praise and his intimidation. A favourable attitude
toward the lady and the determination that she is correctly gendered are
thus predicated upon her compliance with male desire. Hence, although
purportedly about love, the poem demonstrates quite decidedly the

pragmatic nature of the lover's exaltation of the lady, since the lover's apostrophe demonstrates his real object to be not the articulation of his love and submission to the lady, but rather coercion of the lady into submission to his desire. Moreover, because of the gravity of the retaliations that are in the lover's power and the precariousness of her status, the lady cannot be said to possess real agency. While such poems idealise the female and seem to demonstrate male worship of women, they also delineate society's structures of power and the role of literature in maintaining those structures.[9]

Another type of poem appearing at its surface to advocate for the female sex portrays women as the image of all virtues. Bannatyne includes several such poems in his miscellany, including number 245 by Robert Henryson which offers a variation on the conventions of such poems.[10] This poem, unique to the Bannatyne Manuscript, is titled in a colophon as 'the garmont of gud ladeis'. The narrator begins by declaring that if the lady will love him and follow his guidance he will make for her 'ane garmond gudliest' (l.3). This garment actually consists of many items of female clothing that the narrator proposes to give the lady and that will bring to her all the qualities an excellent woman should have. Such a state of virtue, clearly, is not inherent in the lady but available to her through male guidance, in keeping with much Biblical *dicta*.[11] Before she can become this paragon, however, the lady must meet the would-be lover's conditions, that she love him and submit herself to his governance.

Drawing upon the organisation of the traditional catalogue of female beauty, the would-be lover starts at the top of her head and works down, listing the garments he will give her for each part of her body and the virtues they will entail. Her hood will be of 'he Honour . . ./ garneist with gouernance', so that 'no demyng suld hir deir'; this hood will ensure that her ethos, mental deliberations, and subsequent conduct will cause no consideration or comment that could injure her (ll.6–7). Her 'sark', in keeping with its location on her body, will be made of chastity mixed with 'schame and dreid' (l.11); her 'kirtill' is similarly meant to make certain that her body and her sexual self are properly assigned and disposed:

> Hir kirtill suld be of clene constance
> Lasit with lesum Lufe
> The mailyeis (eyelets) of continnwance
> for nevir to remvfe (ll.13–16)]

Other clothing such as her gown, belt, mantle, sleeves, and shoes, will bring her such qualities as goodliness, kindness, humility, hope, and stability so that she will not slide into sin.

Whether the lady will attire herself in these garments is uncertain, the narrator's use of the subjunctive at the poem's beginning and end indicating some doubt. At the poem's ending he says that 'Wald scho put on this garmond gay', that is, *if* she will take this clothing, she will wear nothing else half as becoming; this reiteration echoes his opening avowal that 'Wald' the lady love him best he will make for her these virtue-bringing clothes. This language implies that the lady has some self-determination enabling her to decide if she will be guided by him. However, the narrator makes clear that in order to possess these desirable qualities the lady must put herself into his charge and, as he states, 'wirk eftir my will'. Her self-determination may permit her to choose against him, but she will thereby choose against virtue.

The system of virtue he offers thus necessitates that the lady commit herself and her sexuality to one man in marriage. The kirtle he will give her, we remember, is held together specifically by 'lesum' (lawful) love, the eyelets of continence meant to prevent removal. While these indications of the sexual confinement of a woman are couched in relatively mild terms, they nonetheless evoke the chastity belt, a garment similarly designed both to contain sexual activity and to prevent removal.[12] The lady can indeed be the embodiment of virtue, but only if she accepts the role established for women in patriarchy. Like poetry portraying women as idealised love objects, these poems that accord to women all virtue make that state contingent upon resignation to male control.

The popular image of the evil wife is pivotal in a *chanson de mal marie*, poem thirty-one by Richard Maitland, entitled 'The Folye of ane auld Man'.[13] This warning to older men who marry younger women constitutes a good example of the adaptability and ubiquity of the stereotype of the evil wife and the conventions of that image. Although stating at the outset that its focus is men's 'foly', the poem accomplishes its intent not just by noting such elements of men's foolishness as their 'vane consait' and their blindness, but by developing a substantial portrait of women as lustful, superficial, and materialistic.[14] Foremost in this misogynous portrayal, and vividly conveyed through Maitland's metaphors for the female, is the reduction of woman to her sexual and reproductive dimensions.

The influence of Chaucer's 'Merchant's Tale' (pp. 153–68) is conspicuous in the names of May and January, in the attribution of 'blindness' to the man past fifty who marries a young woman, and in the particularising of January's characterization as a man engaged, like Chaucer's Merchant, in international business. Also alluding to Chaucer's tale is a brief but striking scene when the narrator describes a result of the May-January marriage: 'Ane auld gray beird on ane quhyt mouthe to lay / In to ane bed, it is ane petuous sycht / The ane cryis help, the vther wantis mycht' (ll.19–21). Although this bed scene might conceivably generate in the reader sympathy for May, the narrator quickly cuts off such response by shifting attention immediately to the husband, whose worldly experience can not prevent his losing 'his geir' and impoverishing himself. In contrast to Chaucer's more balanced exposition, which permits some sympathy for the young wife of an older man, Maitland's poem prompts the reader to a judgmental perspective toward her.

In poems elaborating the stereotype of the evil wife, her sexuality is often a defining characteristic. This poem begins by warning that since a young woman's blood 'is in ane rage' she will despise the husband who cannot 'serwe hir appetyte' (ll.5–6). The statement implies not just women's lasciviousness, but their superficiality, since they are moved by sexual desire rather than by virtues or larger considerations.[15] The contempt expressed for women and their sexuality is further adduced in Maitland's punning admonition that older men should prefer 'morall telis' (tales) rather than 'talis' (tails); although the pun may equate body and text, the metaphor 'tails' reduces women to a body part and confirms the poem's general condemnation of all women (ll.8–9). The extrapolation from young women to all women is also evident in the assertion that besides being lustful and shallow, wives are materialistic and wasteful, causing husbands to impoverish and ruin themselves.[16] The poem's warning force thus relies not just on iterating that older men are sexually inadequate but on reiterating generalised misogynist statements.

In addition to using the obscene metaphor 'tails', Maitland also discusses women as part of a song, as a ship, and as farmland. The poem employs the first of these metaphors to discuss the marriage's fundamental difficulty, unequal sexual energy: May and January fail to agree 'vpone ane sang' because that song lacks the 'tribbill' (treble) that 'sould be swng abwne' (ll.13–14). Since the 'tribbill' undoubtedly refers to the penis which is unable to be 'above' and is not therefore dominant, this metaphor manifests both the primacy of the penis and masculine anxiety over its potency. The discussion of woman metaphorically as ship further attests the danger of phallic inadequacy; the older man who marries is said to get into a leaking boat when there is also not a 'steif mast' (l.28). Finally, women are discussed as land and the penis, predictably, as a plough. Here we see most clearly the harm accruing to the older man who marries. Because his farm field requires 'grit Laubor', fertilising, and ploughing, it presents to the husband an unrealisable challenge (l.29). The husband lacks 'grayth for to manure the land' as well as 'seid', and lack of seed makes him grow tired of tilling (ll.30–31). As a result of the husband's inability, the field is open to any man who comes along, observes the unused land, 'yokis his pleuch', and tills (ll. 31–33).

Although in other contexts the association of women with the earth can carry positive connotations, woman as land is here both lustful and lumpish; she demands more tilling, fertilising, and planting than the lawful owner can give, yet she also simply waits, available to whoever passes by. The consequence of her demands and availability is shame for the husband, but not as the poem first suggests because of his own 'grit folye' in marrying a young woman, but because her demanding sexuality threatens the husband, and because her overt promiscuity broadcasts his sexual insufficiency. Reducing the wife to her sexuality and demonstrating a lustful woman's ability to injure and topple male sexual ascendancy, the poem actively promulgates the stereotype of the evil wife. Images of the woman who does not marry but is nonetheless sexual are also prevalent in sixteenth-century literature; a group of poems Bannatyne clustered together, and which are found only in the Bannatyne Manuscript, aptly illustrates the culture's contradictory attitudes towards such women.[17] As a group these poems seem to suggest a progression in Bannatyne's mind that accords with late medieval thinking about what we now call 'gender'.[18] Bannatyne offers first poem 185, by Alexander Scott, cynically advising men how to deceive women and accomplish their desires. Then Bannatyne presents three poems, 186, 187, and 188, probably by Robert Sempill,[19] about prostitutes or women sexually available to men. Bannatyne then positions an anonymous poem (189), about an abandoned maiden who attempts abortion. This cluster ends with another poem by Alexander Scott (190), that virulently castigates women for their sexuality. The poems about three prostitutes and an abandoned and pregnant maiden are thus framed by Scott's two works, one poem advising men on how to be sexual with women, and the other denouncing women for being sexual with men. In addition to conveying something of Bannatyne's own attitudes, this cluster of poems certifies the hypocrisy of a society that constructs women as sexual objects which men should try to overcome, but that then condemns women for being the target of male desire.

The narrator of the first of these poems enjoins men in the opening stanza to 'lat be the frennessy of luve' because of women's 'natur course & strynd' (186, ll. 1–5). This abjuration of women is not the narrator's real intention, however, since he devotes six of the seven eight-line stanzas to counselling men on mastering women, instructing men how to conceal yet advance their true ends, to beguile and delude, or, in sum, to be 'Sobir in thair sicht . . . Bot feckill of intent' (ll. 10–11). The general contempt for the female sex visible in such injunctions is also evident in the narrator's assumptions about women. He presumes unmarried women, though initially requiring considerable attentions, to be shallow and essentially malleable; they will respond to soft words and outward performance and, having once surrendered, are entirely compliant. The narrator adopts the language of a siege to assure men: 'Wyn anis the Entres & the hous is yowris' (l.48). He assumes a widow, however, to be more easily attained because of her sexual deprivation. His instruction is therefore succinct: 'as for a weddow wirk weill on hir wame / I knaw no craft sall cause hir lufe yow bettir' (ll. 55–6). Unquestionably, the goal is sexual conquest, the only difficulty anticipated not female virtue, but the man's cynical employment of the right approach and technique.

After this poem advising men how to conquer women sexually, Bannatyne offers three poems focusing on prostitutes, two of which poems are discussed here as representative.[20] The first of these poems about 'slicht wemen' compares 'Margret' to a ship, 'a littill fleming berge' (186; l.1). Although she displays some discernment in refusing to take on certain landsmen, she is available to other sorts of men, especially seamen with strength, experience, and endurance. In the development of this metaphor of Margret as ship, obscene allusions chronicle her abilities and her shortcomings; she will readily sail all the winter night, but the narrator cautions that 'gif scho lekkis' then skilful men are needed 'To stop hir hoilis' (ll.19–20). The poem consists substantially of directions, with gross sexual innuendo, for managing the ship. In doing so the poem reveals that this Edinburgh prostitute, as most if not all prostitutes, exists and functions at the wish of men and of their culture. In Edinburgh, as in many towns until the Reformation, brothels were legal even if disapproved.[21]

The second poem purports to defend 'crissell sandelandis', jailed for being unlawfully with a man (187). While seeming to argue for the accused Crissell by referring to the innocent Susanna, the poem soon reveals its satiric nature by labelling Crissell as one of 'dame venus virgenis' (l.6), an oxymoronic reference that distinctly undermines the preceding intimation of her innocence. Similarly, the narrator's rhetorical question to the accusers, asking if they believe that virgins are so quickly won, seems to imply Crissell's virginity, yet the narrator again undercuts such advocacy by immediately remarking that 'men may bourd' and that women are 'nocht the wor Quhen that is done' (ll.19–20). We are obviously meant to understand Crissell is not a virgin; from the narrator's viewpoint, subsequent sexual activity for her is of little relative consequence since Crissell has already lost her virginity.

To follow these poems about women Bannatyne termed 'slicht', he chooses a work that details, from a male perspective, the consequences for an unmarried woman of sexual activity (189). The tone of the narrator who overhears the speech of the abandoned and pregnant maiden is light and mocking throughout, even as he records her woe, fear, and anguish. The maiden relies on euphemisms to describe her circumstances, lamenting that a mandrake had bitten her and caused her 'littill finger' and other bodily parts to swell; despite many and varied attempts to abort the pregnancy, she is unsuccessful. The narrator declines to take her dilemma with any seriousness and mockingly warns all 'Trew maidis' to keep their 'littill finger' from the 'mandraikis snair' (ll.79–80). He not only trivialises her plight but also assigns responsibility for sexual activity and its consequences exclusively to women.

At the end of this cluster of poems about unmarried but sexual women after the initial poem advising men on sexual conquest, the three poems about prostitutes, and the poem of the abandoned and pregnant maiden Bannatyne places Alexander Scott's 'Ane ballat maid to the derisioun And scorne of wantoun wemen' (190). This last poem's denigration is not confined to women who are considered 'wanton', however, but applies to all women; the narrator charges that even the wisest of women 'May sone / Sedusit be and schent' (ll.17–18). The narrator gives to women abundant and specific instructions about interactions with men, warning women, for instance, that 'It settis not madynis als / To latt men lowis thair laice' (ll. 41–42). When the reader recalls Scott's poem that began this cluster and its detailed directions to men on seduction techniques (185), many of the commands to women in this poem that ends the cluster seem ironic indeed. In many ways this poem seems a summary of the preceding poems as it refers to male seduction, to female weakness, to lasciviousness, to pregnancy, and to illegitimate birth. Certainly Bannatyne recognised connections among these poems and the ideas they elucidate, and obviously he saw how Scott's 'ballat' codified those ideas and provided to this cluster a forceful culmination. Whether Bannatyne was also aware of the cultural hypocrisy thereby exposed is another matter. In his choice and arrangement of these poems, however, Bannatyne had overt moral and socio-political messages for the readers. Examining the nature of representative images in these sixteenth-century Scottish manuscripts thus illuminates the narrow roles for women in this literature as icon or stereotype. Moreover, these poems in aggregate manifest the importance of those prescribed images of women and their direct relationship to the maintenance of the prevailing social system. In so doing, this poetry attests the ideological function of literature in sixteenth-century society and culture.

NOTES

1. In quotations from the Bannatyne Manuscript and the Maitland Folio Manuscript I modernize thorn and yogh, and silently provide conventional expansions. Poems in both manuscripts are for convenience designated here by Arabic numerals rather than the Roman numerals used for designation in Ritchie's and Craigie's editions.

2. See Sarah Dunnigan, 'Scottish Women Writers c.1560–c.1650' in Douglas

Gifford and Dorothy Macmillan, eds. *History of Scottish Women's Writing* (Edinburgh: 1997), 15–43; and Dunnigan's 'Reclaiming the Language of Love and Desire in the Scottish Renaissance: Mary, Queen of Scots and the Late Sixteenth Century Female-voiced Love Lyric', presented at the Conference on Medieval and Renaissance Scottish Language and Literature (Oxford, August 1996), and my own initial research into women's 'voices' in Scots manuscripts, 'The Female Voice in Selected Middle Scots Poetry' both forthcoming in Sally Mapstone and Juliette Wood eds. *Later Sixteenth-Century Scots Literature.*

3. On the ways in which female and male thinking and values differ, see Carol Gilligan's germinal book, *In a Different Voice* (Cambridge, MA, 1982).

4. E. Newlyn, 'Of Vertew Nobillest and Serpent Wrinkis: The Taxonomy of the Female in the Bannatyne Manuscript' *Scotia*, 14 (1990), 1–12.

5. Joan Cadden, *Meanings of Sex Difference in the Middle Ages: Medicine, Science, Culture* (Cambridge, 1993), 167–227. See also Linda Lomperis and Sarah Stanbury eds. *Feminist Approaches to the Body in Medieval Literature* (Philadelphia, 1993).

6. *The Bannatyne Manuscript Writtin in Tyme of Pest*, 1568, ed. W. Tod Ritchie, (4 vols, London, 1928–34); and *The Maitland Folio Manuscript*, ed. W. A. Craigie, (2 vols, Edinburgh and London, 1927).

7. See, for example, the Middle English poem no 33 as edited by Maxwell S. Luria and Richard Hoffman, *Middle English Lyrics* (New York, 1974), 31–33. Also an iconic love song by Dante, 'Al poco giorno e al gran cerchio d'ombra,' Willard R. Trask, ed. and trans. *Medieval Lyrics of Europe* (New York, 1969) and a poem by the trouvere Colin Muset, no 29, Frederick Goldin, ed. and trans. *Lyrics of the Troubadours and Trouveres* (Garden City, NY, 1973).

8. *Bannatyne Manuscript*, iii, 276–78.

9. See Katherine Ackley ed. *Misogyny in Literature* (New York and London, 1992). Sheila Fisher and Janet Halley, *Seeking the Woman in Late Medieval and Renaissance Writings: Essays in Feminist Contextual Criticism* (Knoxville, 1989). Christiane Klapisch-Zuber ed. *A History of Women in the West: Silences of the Middle Ages* (2 vols, Cambridge, MA, 1992). Rosemary Horrox ed, *Fifteenth-Century Attitudes: Perceptions of Society in Late Medieval England* (Cambridge, 1994), especially P. J. P. Goldberg's chapter, 'Women,' 112–31. Susan Aronstein, 'Cresseid Reading Cresseid: Redemption and Translation in Henryson's "Testament,"', *Scottish Literary Journal*, 21 (1994), 5–22. Also useful is Mary Erler and Maryanne Kowaleski eds. *Women and Power in the Middle Ages* (Athens, GA, 1988).

10. *Bannatyne Manuscript*, iii, 252–54.

11. For example, Paul's prescription of women's silence in the presence of male authority (I Corinthians 14:34).

12. *Bannatyne Manuscript*, iii, 87–100. See also 'The Cupar Banns' announcing Lindsay's 'Satyre of the Thrie Estaits' discussed in E. Newlyn 'Traditions of Myth and Fabliau in the Cupar Banns' in G. Caie et al eds. *The European Sun* (East Linton, forthcoming).

13. *Maitland Folio*, i, 61–2.

14. E. Newlyn, 'The Function of the Female Monster in Middle Scots Poetry:

Misogyny, Patriarchy, and the Satiric Myth' in Ackley ed. *Misogyny in Literature*, 33–66.

15. A good source for tracing such ideas is Alcuin Blamires ed., *Woman Defamed and Woman Defended: An Anthology of Medieval Texts* (Oxford, 1992). Also, Martha Lee Osborne, *Woman in Western Thought* (New York, 1979); George H. Tavard, *Woman in Christian Tradition* (Notre Dame and London, 1973); E. Newlyn, 'The Political Dimensions of Desire and Sexuality in the Poems of the Bannatyne Manuscript' in S. McKenna ed. *Selected Essays on Scottish Language and Literature* (Lewiston, 1992), 75–96.

16. 'Luve, Lichery and Evill Wemen. The Satiric Tradition in the Bannatyne Manuscript' *Studies in Scottish Literature*, 26 (1991), 283–93.

17. *Bannatyne Manuscript*, ii, 325–342.

18. E. Newlyn, ' "The Wryttar to the Reidaris": Editing Practices and Politics in the Bannatyne Manuscript,' forthcoming in *Studies in Scottish Literature*, 31. This essay is part of a larger scholarly project on women in Middle Scots literary manuscripts.

19. Denton Fox, 'Contents of the Manuscript,' *The Bannatyne Manuscript, National Library of Scotland, Advocates MS.1.1.6*, Facsimile edition (London, 1980), xxix.

20. Poem no 188 weighs the merits of female tapsters.

21. *Extracts from the Records of the Royal Burgh of Edinburgh* (Scottish Burgh Records Society, 1869–92), ii, 40.

CHAPTER SIX

Women of the Gàidhealtachd and their Songs to 1750

Anne C. Frater

THE STORY OF Gaelic-speaking Highland women before 1750 is one of subservience and subjugation but also of rebellion. While to a large extent they were treated as mere property by their husbands, brothers and fathers, in other ways Gaelic society treated them favourably. Women of high status, paradoxically, probably had less freedom than women lower down the social scale. The more important the stature of a woman's father, the more likely she was to be married off on the basis of political expediency, whereas lower-caste women were more able to follow their hearts. However, this did not mean that there was any less heartbreak. A high-caste woman might be married against her will to a man she did not love, but the class system also prevented lower-caste women from marrying above themselves.

But marriage was not the be-all and end-all for these women. Many songs of the time boast of having a lover of high degree, even having children by him, but no shame or blame is involved. In Gaelic society of this period, men of noble birth generally acknowledged their illegitimate children to the extent of bringing them up in their households (whether or not their wives objected). Such children were recognised as belonging to the leadership of the clan, although they were not considered as heirs to their father. It was a source of pride rather than shame for a woman of low birth to have a child by a man of high degree, for she thereby ensured that her child would move up the social scale even if she herself could not.

A song that illustrates this mixture of love for the child, acceptance that she could never marry the father, and love for the father himself is 'An Cùl Bachalach'.[1] Beathag Mhór's song to Màrtainn a Bhealaich concerns their illegitimate child. She had evidently been the mistress of Martin Martin and had borne him a son; but she must have been well below him on social scale, and thus unable to marry him. Martin was probably the eldest son of Donald Martin of Beallach, who married a daughter of Lachlan Maclean of Vallay in North Uist.[2] Beathag seems to bear him no grudge for not marrying her, and her words reveal that, although the thought of him taking another as his wife grieves her, she still loves him; she even gives him advice on his choice of wife:

Ma Théid thu dh'Uibhist an eòrna
Thoir té bhòideach dhachaidh as.

Thoir dhachaidh té shocair chiallach
Riaraicheas na caipteanan.[3]

(If you go to Uist of the barley
Take a beautiful bride home.

Take home a gentle, sensible bride
Who will be approved of by the clan leaders.)

Some verses have been recorded in which Beathag shows a less charitable attitude to some contenders for Martin's hand:

Ma bheir thu bean a Sìol Leòid
Gun iarr i mòran fhasanan.

Ma bheir thu ban a Sìol Tharmoid
Marbhaidh i le macnas thu.[4]

(If you take a wife from the MacLeods
She'll want a lot of fashions.

If you take a wife from the MacLeods of Lewis
She'll kill you with wantonness.)

Despite her love for Martin, Beathag's main concern is the future welfare of her child, who will be brought up by his father and his new wife. This is why Beathag takes such an interest in Martin's choice:

Thoir dhachaidh té mhodhail chiùin
Dh'ionnsaicheas mo mhac-sa dhut.[5]

(Take home a modest, quiet bride
Who will teach my son for you,)

Her protectiveness of her child is illustrated by the misfortune she wishes on any woman who would mistreat him, but she also blesses the woman who would be loving towards him:

Is ma bhuaileas i le feirg e
Guma meirg thug dhachaidh i.

Is ma bhuaileas i le fuath e
Guma luath 'na chlachan i.

Ach ma bhuaileas i le gràdh e
Guma blàth fo d'achlais i.[6]

(And if she hits him in anger
A curse on the one who brought her home.

> And if she hits him in hatred
> May she soon be in the grave.
>
> But if she hits him out of love
> May she be warm in your arms.)

One can only imagine the heartache suffered by Beathag Mhór at the thought of giving up her child to the care of another, even though it might be in his own interests. This song illustrates the acceptance of illegitimacy. The child was acknowledged and brought up by his father, and the mother does not mention any hardship or shame which she has suffered because of having borne a child outside wedlock.

While it was neither unusual nor frowned upon for a man of noble birth to have a liaison with and children by a woman of lower status, the same could not be said of a noble woman who had an illegitimate child by a man of a lower class. According to the traditional story, a daughter of Dòmhnall Gorm MacDonald of Sleat fell in love with her father's cowherd and bore him a child. The child was taken from its mother and sent to foster-parents in Uist; Dòmhnall Gorm's daughter was sent to the household of Maclean of Coll, where she acted as a maidservant, while her unfortunate lover was literally ripped apart – tied between two horses which were then driven off in opposite directions. MacDonald's daughter composed the song '*Biodh an deoch-s' air làimh mo rùin*',[7] on being reunited with her brother after years of separation, when he visited Maclean of Coll.

> Young Clanranald was greatly charmed with the tablemaid, chiefly because she resembled his erring sister. When he was ready to leave Coll she sang the song to him. He was glad to find her, and took her with him to Uist.[8]

The rebellion of women of this period consisted not in a physical struggle, but in breaking the taboos of the time, most notably in their song-making. Women were permitted to compose lullabies, work-songs, laments and love-songs, but political and praise-poetry was the domain of the learned bardic order, a hereditary male occupation. This did not stop women such as Màiri nighean Alasdair Ruaidh,[9] Mairearad nighean Lachlainn[10] and Sìleas na Ceapaich[11] from composing panegyric and political poetry, leading in Màiri's case to her temporary exile from the household of her patron, Sir Norman MacLeod of Berneray.

Women had no political sway, and their fortunes depended wholly on decisions taken by men. All they could do was comment on the political situation, and lament events which adversely affected their clan. One such poetess was Mairearad nighean Lachlainn, whose poems give an account of the downfall of the Macleans of Duart in Mull. She firmly lays the

blame at the door of the Campbells, who profited from the disastrous
loyalty of the Macleans to the Stuart kings:

> Na Leathanaich bu phrìseal iad,
> Bu mhoralach nan inntinn iad;
> 'N diugh crom-cheannach 's ann chìtear iad,
> 'S e teann lagh a thug strìochdadh asd';
> Is mairg a bha cho dileas riutha
> 'Riamh do righ no 'phrionnsa.

> Gu 'm b' fheàrr 'bhith cealgach, innleachdach,
> Mar 'bha ur nàimhdean mìorunach;
> 'S e 'dh'fhàgadh làidir, lìonmhor sibh.
> 'S e 'dhèanadh gnothach cinnteach dhuibh,
> A bhith cho faicleach, crìonnta
> Is gu 'm b' fhiach leibh a bhith 'tionndadh.[12]

> (The Macleans were greatly valued,
> Their minds were dignified;
> Now they are seen with bowed heads,
> It was a hard law which caused them to submit;
> Never were any as faithful as them
> To King or to prince.

> It would be better to be deceitful and cunning
> As your malicious enemies were;
> That would leave you strong and numerous.
> It would make things certain for you
> If you were so wary and cautious
> That treachery was worth your while.)

The poetess Sìleas na Ceapaich, another partisan Jacobite, gives her views
on the 1715 Rising,[13] and does not hesitate to attribute blame for its
failure in her songs on the Battle of Sheriffmuir. In her eyes, only Clan
Donald acquitted themselves well, while the leaders are accused of
betraying the rising to preserve their own titles and lands:

> Rinn sibh cleas a' choin sholair
> Thug a cholbha 'n a chraos leis:
> Nuair a chunnaic e fhaileas
> Thug e starradh g' a fhaotainn;
> 'Nuair a chaill e na bh' aige
> Dh' fhàg sin acrach re shaogh'l e.[14]

> (You have done what the foraging dog did,
> Who carried his limb of meat in his mouth:
> When he saw its reflection

He made to catch it:
When he lost all he had
It left him hungry for the rest of his life.)

Another taboo was broken by Fionnghal Chaimbeul, a seventeenth-century bardess. Marriages amongst the Gaelic nobility were generally political rather than romantic in motivation. Clan alliances were formed by intermarriage, but some bonds were stronger than others. A woman's ties with her own clan were considered broken when she married into another, and especially once she had children, but Fionnghal went against this. She was the wife of Iain Garbh Maclean of Coll who, along with their son Hector Roy, fought for Montrose and the Royalist cause in 1645. She was also the sister of Campbell of Auchinbreck, commander of the Covenant forces, who lost his life in battle against Montrose's army at the battle of Inverlochy. Fionnghal seems to have been treated badly by the Macleans, and opens her song by lamenting the fact that she ever went to Coll, describing how her husband's clan behaved towards her:

Rinn iad mo leab' aig an dorus
Comaidh ri fearaibh 's ri conaibh;

'S thug iad am bràisd as mo bhroilleach,
'S m' usgraichean 's mo chneapan corrach . . .[15]

(They made my bed at the door
Made me eat with the men and the dogs.

They took the brooch from my breast
My jewels, and my rounded buttons.)

Her bitterness against the Macleans knows no bounds, as she curses her own son, Hector Roy, thus:

Eachainn Ruadh de'n fhine dhona,
'S coma leam ged théid thu dholaidh,
'S ged a bhiodh do shliocdh gun toradh.[16]

(Hector Roy of the bad clan
Little I care if you should be harmed
And if your line should be without fruit.)

Fionnghal feels totally alone in Coll, where there is nobody to share her grief for her brother, and she expresses her wish to be in Inveraray, where there would be tearing of hair and beating of hands over the death of Auchinbreck.

The strongest expression of her emotions, and her loyalties, is reserved for the final stanza. This is full of venom against the Macleans and Clan Donald, whom she holds responsible for the death of her brother:

traditional accounts, indeed, attribute Auchinbreck's death to Alasdair
Mac Colla, Montrose's Captain General and a MacDonald:

> Nan robh mis' an Inbhir-Lòchaidh . . .
> Dheanainn fuil ann, dheanainn stròiceadh,
> Air na Leathanaich 's Clann Dòmhnall;
> Bhiodh na h-Eireannaich gun deò annt',
> Is na Duibhnich bheirinn beò as.[17]
>
> (If I was in Inverlochy . . .
> I would shed blood, I would tear asunder
> The Macleans and Clan Donald;
> The Irish would be lifeless,
> And I would take the Campbells out alive.)

It is said that 'soon after Inverlochy [Fionnghal] went mad', and David
Stevenson comments 'whether or not this is true, the poem starkly
portrays a woman in the first wild paroxysms of grief, torn between
the conflicting claims of her loyalty of Campbells and Macleans'.[18] From
the actual text of the song, however, it seems that Fionnghal's grief stems
not so much from conflicting loyalties as from the fact that her loyalty lay
with one side, while she was the wife and mother of members of the
opposing side, and living in the lands of a clan that was fighting against
her own. One can only imagine the agony of her position and, if she did
lose her mind, it is understandable.

One woman whose rebellion consisted in action as well as words was
the daughter of Campbell of Glenlyon. Unusually for the songs of this
period, there is a historical record of the circumstances in which her song
'*Cumha Ghriogair Mhic Ghriogair Ghlinn Sreath*',[19] also known as
'*Griogal Cridhe*', was composed. Glenlyon's daughter had run away
and married Gregor MacGregor of Glenstrae against her family's wishes,
who wished to marry her to the Baron of Dall, and later watched her
husband being put to death by her own father and uncle. Gregor Roy's
crime seems to have been that he preferred his own name to that of his
feudal superior, Colin Campbell of Glenorchy to whom the earl of Argyll
sold the twenty merkland of Glenstray along with the ward and marriage
of Gregor in 1556.

> Possibly Sir Colin might have befriended him if he had been willing
> to give up his own Clan, but Gregor evidently preferred to cast in
> his lot with his persecuted brethren. His name is found in several of
> the complaints against the MacGregors, and . . . it must be
> supposed that there were some feuds, the history of which has not
> been transmitted, or other causes to excite the malignity of
> Glenurquhay . . .[20]

Perhaps the 'other cause' which led to Gregor's death was his love for Glenlyon's daughter who:

> Having met with young Gregor MacGregor of Glenstrae she gave up to him her heart's warmest affections and which he fully returned. In spite of all opposition, she left her father's house, and married him. Duncan was bitterly vexed, so were the then heads of the eastern Campbells, Sir Colin of Glenurchay and his son 'Black Duncan'. In consequence Gregor and his wife were followed with the most unrelenting enmity . . . On the night preceding the 7 of April 1570, they had rested under a rock on a hillside above Loch Tay. Next morning . . . they were surrounded by a band of their foes, and carried off to Balloch. Gregor was at once condemned to death, and beheaded at Kenmore in presence of Sir Colin; his wife, daughter of the Ruthven, who looked out of an upper window; Black Duncan; Atholl the Lord Justice Clerk, and Duncan Campbell of Glenlyon. Most pitiful of all, the unutterably wretched wife was forced to watch her Husband's execution. Immediately thereafter, with her babe in her arms, she was driven forth by her kindred helpless and houseless . . . In her great anguish she composed the song . . . and sung it as a lullaby to her babe.[21]

This account contains some basic oversights, if we accept the records in the Black Book of Taymouth. According to these Gregor Roy had two sons by the daughter of Duncan Campbell of Glenlyon, indicating that they were fugitives for quite some time before Gregor's capture, even if John, the second son, was born posthumously. Also the song gives the date of Gregor's capture as *Là Lùnasd*, Lammas morning, not the day previous to Gregor's execution. On the latter point, however, Derick Thomson suggests that the original version of the song may have referred to *Là Thùrnais* or Palm Sunday, which in 1570 fell on 19th March. Thomson points out that it is highly unlikely that Gregor would have been held captive from August 1569 until April the following year, whereas 'the interval between [19th March] and 7th April would have allowed the 'great justiciar' time to invite the 'Erle of Atholl, the justice clerk, and sundrie uther nobillmen' to Taymouth Castle to witness so effective a demonstration of Campbell authority in the former MacGregor territories.[22]

The song itself appears in two separate and distinct forms: a short version and a long one, with a different chorus for each. The short version summarizes the story given in the long one, for which up to eighteen verses are given in some sources. This longer song is in ballad form, telling the story of Gregor's capture, his widow's love for him, her grief over his death, and her hatred of those who have caused such anguish:

Mallachd aig maithibh is aig càirdean
Rinn mo chràdh air an dòigh,
Thàinig gun fhios air mo ghràdh-sa
Is a thug fo smachd e le foill.[23]

(A curse on gentles and friends
Who have rent me thus with pain,
Who caught my darling unawares
And made him captive by guile.)[24]

Naturally, the characteristic objectivity of the strict ballad form is not found here, as the song is charged with emotion. Although composed as a lullaby to Nighean Dhonnchaidh's child, the son of Gregor, it is actually a poignant lament for her husband.

There exists another song ascribed to Nighean Dhonnchaidh,[25] concerned with the same event, and addressed to Duncan Campbell of Glenorchy, or Donnchadh Dubh a' Churraic. The author of this song was evidently a Campbell who was married to a member of an opposing clan, and whose father brought about the death of her husband:

Gun logh an Rìgh sin do m' athair,
Gur caol a sgair e m' fheòil diom;
Thug e bh' uamsa m' fheara-tighe,
Gu 'm bu sgafanta roimh thòir e.[26]

(May God forgive my father,
He has torn my flesh from me;
He took my husband from me
Who was brave before his pursuers.)

As well as intermarriage, the practice of fostering was a way in which clans forged alliances, with the children of nobles of one clan being brought up in the household of a member of another clan. Songs by a *muime* (foster-mother) to a *dalta* (foster-child) are common, and the pride shown in her *dalta* could not be any more maternal.

A song that gives a telling insight into the relationship between *muime* and *dalta* is that composed by Màiri Nic Phàil to Eachann Òg Maclean of Tiree,[27] who was drowned between Tiree and Barra. The song uses some of the formulaic imagery of bardic elegy, such as '*Chaill mu ubhlan mo chrann*', but also contains strikingly imaginative similes of the bardess' own:

Gun do sgaoil e mo shic,
'S tha mo chridhe 'na lic,
'S e mo ghnàths bhi air mhisg gun òl.[28]

(It has ruptured my insides,
My heart is a stone,
I seem drunken although I drink nothing.)

What is most interesting about this poem, however, is that it is composed as a lament to her foster-son, when her own son drowned in the same incident. Although the song runs to nine stanzas, her son is mentioned only in the very last one.

> Gun robh cuilein mo rùin,
> Fear na camagan dlùth,
> 'S e a' seòladh ri d' ghlùin,
> Gus 'n do dhalladh a shùil
> Ann am mire nan sùgh gun deò.[29]

(The love of my heart,
He of the thick curly hair,
Was sailing at your side,
Until his eyes were blinded
And he was lifeless in the rolling waves.)

The loss of the young Maclean would understandably have been seen by the clan as more important than the loss of his foster-mother's son, but it is strange that the bardess herself seems to think in the same way; the primary subject of her lament is Eachann Òg. However, this should not be taken as evidence that the loss of her own son was the lesser grief, merely that the *dalta* was of noble birth, and therefore convention demanded that his death be given priority.

A similar convention is seen in Catrìona nighean Eòghainn mhic Lachlainn's lament 'Tha mi falbh an cois tuinne',[30] where, because the subject of the song is a woman, she is referred to in terms of her male forebears. The song is addressed to Catrìona Maclean, daughter of Maclean of Brolas, and wife of Lachlan, son and heir of the laird of Coll. It seems that this Catrìona was also a foster-child of, or very closely acquainted with, the poetess, as she is referred to as '*mo leanabh*'.[31] The poem begins with the familiar image of the poetess looking out to sea:

> Tha mi 'falbh an cois tuinne
> 'S tha mo shùil air na grunnaibh
> 'Dh'fheuch am faicear leam culaidh fo sheòl.[32]

(I walk by the shoreline
With my eye on the deep
To see if I can see a boat under sail.)

The poetess is awaiting news of Catrìona, and proceeds to describe her, using stock images and phrases, before revealing that she already knows

that Catrìona is dead. Catrìona is identified in terms of her male ancestry
on her father's side; her maternal grandfather, Allan of Ardgour, being
'the most improvident of his race',[33] who almost ruined his estate through
his extravagance, would not be considered a praiseworthy subject, and is
ignored:

> Nighean Dhòmhnaill mhic Lachlainn . . .
> 'S [iar?] ogha Dhomhnaill mhic Eachainn nan sròl.[34]
>
> (Daughter of Donald son of Lachlann . . .
> And [great?] granddaughter of Donald, son of Hector
>   of the [banners].)

This is the cue for the focus of praise to move from Catrìona to her father,
Donald, third Maclean of Brolas, who 'received two severe wounds on
the head in the battle of Sheriffmuir'.[35] These injuries, and the circumstances in which they were obtained, are referred to by the poetess in a
way which implies the bravery he has previously lauded:

> Ged bha comharr' ad shiubhal,
> Rinn thu gniomh bu mho pudhar,
> 'S dh' fhàg thu luchd nan ad dubha fo leon.[36]
>
> (Although it left its mark in your gait
> You performed a deed of power,
> And you left the black-hatted band wounded.)

The poetess then brings the situation of the clan to our attention, with no
chief, and a child as his heir, and with, seemingly, no-one else to lead the
clan:

> Dhuinne dh' èirich an diombuaidh,
> Gu'n do dh' fhalbh ar ceann-cinnidh,
> Gun do thaoitear bhith 't ionad 'nad lorg.
>
> Tha do mhuinntir fo imcheist,
> 'S do mhac fhathast òg leanabail,
> Bho dhubh sheachdain na Caingis 'so 'dh'fhalbh.[37]
>
> (A great misfortune has befallen us,
> Our Chief has left us,
> And there is no Tutor to take your place.
>
> Your people are anxious,
> Your son is still young and childish,
> Since this black Whitsuntide week that has passed.)

Donald of Brolas died in 1725, so the song can reasonably be dated to this
period. The poem itself is evenly balanced, the first of five stanzas directed

at Catrìona, the middle stanza placing her in relation to her father, and the remaining five stanzas addressed to Donald himself. In common with several other songs of the period, the poem is addressed to one person, but ends up with the focus of attention on another. Perhaps this results from pride in the initial subject extending to pride in their forebears and relations, or it could be a kind of filling-in device: when the subject of the poem has not achieved much glory in his or her own right, this is supplied through reference to illustrious relations and ancestors.

This leads to a surprising – to modern readers – feature of Gaelic women's songs up to 1750, namely the paucity of songs composed by women about other women. Out of over 200 songs by women that I managed to collect,[38] only fifteen were composed to or about other women. These are mainly laments, although there are also satires, taking the form of versified slanging-matches between bardesses from rival clans. Perhaps there were more songs to women which have not survived, but even then, the balance is still tipped in favour of poetry addressed to men, if we assume that the proportion of each type of song lost was similar. Then again, if women were discouraged from composing the type of poetry which was seen as the preserve of the bards, the panegyric poetry, and also from praising anyone other than their chief, it may also have been frowned upon for a woman to praise the chief's wife as a person in her own right, and not merely as her husband's chattel. Thirdly, the reason may be that women themselves did not think highly enough of their own gender to praise them in the same manner as they would a man. There is evidence that at least one poetess has little pity for a girl who has been raped, instead praising the man who attacked her:

> An cuala sibhs' a' mhoighdeann cheutach
> Air an tug Niall Bàn an éiginn
> Air taobh beinneadh ri latha gréineadh?
> 'S truagh, a righ, nach b' e mi fhéin i.
> Cha sraicinn broilleach do léineadh.
> Nan sracadh, gum fuaighinn fhéin i . . .[39]

> (Did you hear about the beautiful maiden
> Who was raped by fair-haired Neil
> On the mountainside on a sunny day?
> Pity that it was not me.
> I would not tear the front of your shirt.
> Or if I did, I would sew it up . . .)

This implies that the poetess thinks that a nobleman remains attractive and praiseworthy, even if his actions are ignoble. She thinks the raped girl should have been pleased to have gained the attention of such a powerful man, and not resisted his advances.

Men were the key to power and position, and the only way in which a woman could improve her social standing was to marry a man higher up on the social scale than herself or, if she could not marry him, to bear him a child which would then enjoy the protection and some of the privileges of his father's status. Given these circumstances, repellent though they seem to a modern woman, we cannot condemn too severely the attitude displayed by the song's composer. Her mention of the raped girl is used as a prelude to her declaration that she herself would not have resisted, but, although declaring herself willing to become his mistress, she seems to hold no hope of actually marrying Niall Bàn. This indicates that his attention and affection are all that she can hope for, presumably because of her lower social status.

This underlines the position of women in the society of the time: reliant on men for their status, protection and power, and having little control over the direction of their own lives. Husbands were chosen for them by their fathers, and if the woman expressed her own views on the matter she was punished; for the most part the education of a woman was neglected in favour of that of her brothers: they were property, not people, with ownership passing from father to husband. Poetry was a means of escaping the narrow world into which they had been born, and, in some cases, with certain types of poetry, to stray a little into the world of men.

For the most part, it would seem that Highland women espoused the very system which kept them subjugated. But then, these were times of great political instability, and the ultra-conservative clan and caste system were the only set of rules that remained fairly constant. And what was a woman to do if she did not embrace the system? A woman could not inherit the chiefship of a clan; very few owned land in their own right (and even then only until they married) and a woman would not have been able to live as a *creachadair* (cattle raider), the only other available option. So they became wives and lovers, mothers and *muimes*; they either ran a household or worked in one and, in the most part, if they were unhappy with their lot, their only means of expressing their discontent was in their songs.

NOTES

1. *Gairm Magazine*, no. 9, 47.
2. A. and A. MacDonald, *Clan Donald* (3 vols, Inverness, 1896–1904), iii, 561.
3. *Gairm Magazine*, no.9, 47.
4. Ibid.

5. Ibid.
6. Ibid.
7. A. Maclean Sinclair, 'A Collection of Gaelic Poems', *Transactions of the Gaelic Society of Inverness*, 26 (1904–7), 236–38.
8. Ibid, 238.
9. *The Gaelic Songs of Mary MacLeod* ed. W. J. Watson (Edinburgh, 1965).
10. A. Maclean Sinclair, *Na Bàird Leathanach* (2 vols, Charlottetown, 1898–1900).
11. *Bàrdachd Shilis na Ceapaich* ed. C. Ó. Baoill (Edinburgh, 1972). See also D. U. Stùibhart in this volume.
12. *Na Bàird Leathanach*, i, 187.
13. *Bàrdach Shìlis*, 16–48.
14. Ibid, 46.
15. Sinclair, 'Gaelic Poems', 238.
16. Ibid.
17. Ibid.
18. David Stevenson, *Alasdair MacColla and the Highland Problem in the Seventeenth Century* (Edinburgh, 1980), 160.
19. Catherine Kerrigan ed. *An Anthology of Scottish Women Poets* (Edinburgh, 1991), 56–58.
20. A. G. M. MacGregor, *History of the Clan Gregor* (Edinburgh, 1989), i, 53.
21. Ibid, 158–9.
22. Derick Thomson, 'A Disputed reading in "Cumha Ghriogoir Mhic Ghriogoir"', *Scottish Gaelic Studies*, 10 (1963), 68–70.
23. Kerrigan, *Women Poets*, 56.
24. D. S. Thomson, *An Introduction to Gaelic Poetry* (London, 1974), 108.
25. A. and A. MacDonald, *The MacDonald Collection of Gaelic Poetry* (Inverness, 1911), 179.
26. Ibid.
27. A. Maclean Sinclair, *The Gaelic Bards from 1715 to 1765* (Charlottetown, 1892), 150–2.
28. Ibid.
29. Ibid.
30. *Na Bàird Leathanach*, i, 60–1.
31. Ibid.
32. Ibid.
33. A Sennachie, *Account of the Clan Maclean* (London, 1838), 269.
34. *Na Bàird Leathanach*, i, 60–1.
35. *Account of the Clan Maclean*, 228.
36. *Na Bàird Leathanach*, i, 60–1.
37. Ibid.
38. Anne C. Frater, 'Scottish Gaelic Women's Poetry up to 1750' (University of Glasgow, unpublished Ph.D thesis, 1994).
39. K. C. Craig, *Òrain luaidh Màiri nighean Alasdair* (Glasgow, 1949), 9–10.

PART THREE

'Women in mischief are wyser than men'

'Dragonis baith and dowis ay in double forme': Women at the Court of James V, 1513–1542

_____ *Andrea Thomas*

A faire huire is a suete poyson.
Women in mischief ar wyser than men.
Women is moir pietefull than men, moir invyous than a
serpent, moir malycious than a tyraunt,
moir deceytfull than the devill.
Woman's counsale is waike and a chyldis unperfyte.
Woe be to that citie quhair a woman beirith rule.
It is better to be in companye with a serpent than with
a wikit woman.

IN DECEMBER 1542 Master George Cook, scribe of the Privy Seal, scribbled these slogans onto the fly-leaf of the last volume of *The Register of the Privy Seal* for James V's reign.[1] James V had just died and the new monarch was a girl in the arms of a young, vigorous and foreign dowager. Cook's preoccupation with the nature of women therefore had a certain urgency about it, yet the conclusions he reached were not original. The same feminine vices were listed by the court poet, William Dunbar, in his *Ballate against evil Women* as sensuality, envy, deceit, inconstancy and an inability to bear authority.[2] Dunbar was too humane and tolerant an observer of human foibles to sustain this vilification. Many of his poems suggest that he liked the company of women. The title quotation is from *The Tua Mariit Wemen and the Wedo*. Here he presents his subjects as bawdy, vain, scheming and deceitful, but implies that this is no worse than their menfolk deserve because they are possessive, jealous, lecherous, bumbling, gullible and impotent.[3] Dunbar was well placed to observe the ladies of the court of James IV and he indulged in the little games of 'courtly love' there. In *To a Ladye*, he melodramatically declares that he will die if she is so heartless as to reject his offers of love, whilst elsewhere he maintains that chastity is the paramount feminine virtue.[4] He is sharp with ladies who distribute their sexual favours at court to further their material interests.[5] When he praises women he sets them upon exalted pedestals from which any mortal woman would inevitably fall. For Dunbar, Queen Margaret Tudor was an icon of national and chivalric significance. She was beautiful, good, bounteous, of imperial birth and dignity, young, vigorous and likely to have healthy children.[6] With such expectations, disappointment was almost inevitable.

At the court of James IV, especially after his marriage in 1503, ladies held a prominent place. However, if the poetry of Sir David Lindsay of the Mount is a reliable indicator, the role of women at the court of James V was much less significant. An index of historical persons mentioned in Lindsay's works lists 110 people, of whom only ten are women and four of them are queens and one a saint.[7] Lindsay rarely generalised about the nature of women in the manner of Dunbar, but in his *Contemptioun of Syde Taillis* he makes a conventional, if rather tongue-in-cheek, attack on the excesses of female fashions and feminine vanity.[8] Elsewhere he is more serious for in *The Testament of the Papyngo* he discusses Queen Margaret's position during James V's minority, acknowledging her authority, but stressing how transient political power can be. In *The Monarche* he denies that women are fit to bear rule, but this poem dates from the chaotic minority of Mary, Queen of Scots. Lindsay's only poem specifically dedicated to a woman is *The Deploratioun of the Deith of Quene Magdalene*, in which he mourns the passing of one so young, noble, beautiful and sadly childless. However, he seems to regret most of all the cancellation of grand pageants that were to have been staged for her reception, which he had helped to organise.[9] Other poets of the court such as William Stewart, George Steill and Sir George Clapperton also repeat the prejudices and wry comments of Dunbar and Lindsay about female subjects. It is therefore difficult to excavate satisfactory information about the lives of individual women from literary sources.[10]

If male poets give a conventional and stereotypical view of women at court without indicating who most of the women were, other sources can be equally unhelpful. For example, the financial accounts where the woman of Falkland employed to wash sheets in 1540 and some of the nurses engaged for the king's children remain anonymous.[11] Yet some women are named and designated members of the royal household. An index of James V's household between 1528 and 1542 contains over a thousand names, yet only thirty of them are female.[12] The king's household was dominated by men who even did tasks regarded as 'women's work' in the kitchens, brewhouse and wardrobe. Of the thirty household women, there were seventeen children's nurses, five laundresses, three seamstresses, one brewer and four general servants. Most of them seem to have been of fairly obscure social origins, perhaps from the burgess families of royal burghs and several of them served continuously for many years. Some even transferred from the service of Margaret Tudor to that of her son. Only three of them were demonstrably of some social standing, and may therefore be considered to have had some influence at court. Firstly the king's senior laundress, Mavis Atkinson, who appeared in the records continuously from 1516 to 1542 and married John Tennant of Listounschiels. He was an influential and favoured chamber servant, simultaneously in charge of the king's purse and his wardrobe.[13] Secondly, there was Janet Douglas, the king's seamstress between 1522 and 1540 and wife of the poet and senior herald Lindsay.[14] Thirdly, there was Katherine Bellenden, who held a position in the wardrobe between 1537 and 1542.[15] She was the sister of John Bellenden, translator of Boece, and wife of Oliver Sinclair of Pitcairn. As one of the Sinclairs of Roslin, he was related to the Sinclair Earls of Caithness and was another favoured chamber servant of James V, as cupbearer and captain of Tantallon Castle. English reports of 1542 credit her with housing one of the king's mistresses at Tantallon.[16] These three women came from respectable families and filled what would be described today as middle-management positions, yet none of them feature in narrative sources for the reign. If they exercised any influence at court beyond their household functions it would probably have been through their prominent husbands.

In Mary of Guise's household, between 1538 and 1542, one might expect to find a much higher proportion of women, but there was only a modest increase. Eighteen out of 106 recorded members of her household were women and of these, six were the wives or daughters of men in her service.[17] They served as ladies in waiting, maids of honour and women of the bedchamber, with one laundress, one jester and a dwarf. All the servants of the queen's kitchens, pantry, cellar, stable and wardrobe (and even some in her chamber) were men. All of the women and three-quarters of the men were French, although some later married into Scottish families such as Marie Pierris, who married George, fourth Lord Seton, and Jehanne Gresmor, who married Robert Beaton of Creich.[18]

In a court that regularly numbered around 500 people in the late-1530s, only ten per cent are known to have been women.[19] However, there may well have been more women whose presence went unrecorded in the accounts. For instance, many of the men in the king's service were married and, if they held positions in the kitchens, stables, wardrobe or any of the other departments whose service was required continuously, it would be reasonable to infer that their wives and children lived with them nearby. There are occasional glimpses of these arrangements in the accounts when wives are recorded receiving payments on behalf of absent or ill husbands. The wife of James Aikenhead, master of the cuphouse, received several such sums in 1529 as did the wife of David Bonar, a groom in the stable, in 1540 and there are other scattered examples.[20] It would be reasonable to speculate that wives of nobles, lairds and knights who came to court to conduct business or circulate socially would have sometimes accompanied their husbands. Occasions when the presence of noble ladies was specifically demanded at court are few, but at the coronation of Mary of Guise in February 1540, it was regarded as appropriate to the dignity of the Queen to be attended by as many ladies of good birth as possible.[21]

One of the most frustrating gaps in the record is the lack of reference to the king's many mistresses. Their presence at court has to be deduced from the recorded provision made for their children. It is speculation to suggest that they would have been housed with their mothers, at least when they were very young. However, both Maurice Lee and Peter Anderson agree that James and Robert Stewart retained strong links with their mothers and maternal kin throughout their lives.[22] James V's amorous career began at fourteen or fifteen years old when he was deliberately encouraged into promiscuity by the Angus regime in order to distract him from exercising political power.[23] James's list of conquests included Elizabeth Shaw, the daughter of Alexander Shaw of Sauchie, Master of the King's Wine Cellar. She bore him a son, James, in 1529 when the king himself was only seventeen.[24] We know nothing more of her except that she received a payment of £20 and the nurse's fee in 1532 and died sometime before 31 August 1536. The boy was made commendator of the abbeys of Kelso and Melrose and granted some of the forfeited Douglas lands.[25] There was also Margaret Erskine, the daughter of John, fourth Lord Erskine, captain of Stirling Castle. She was already married to Sir Robert Douglas of Lochleven before James became interested in her. She bore the king another son named James in 1531 and seems to have been his favourite mistress.[26] In 1536, whilst he was theoretically engaged to Marie de Bourbon, daughter of the Duke of Vendôme, James attempted to divorce Margaret Erskine from her husband so that he could marry her. The petition was refused and she was then granted 500 merks a year from the Edinburgh customs, perhaps as compensation.[27] Their son was granted the lands of Tantallon and made commendator of the Priory of St Andrews.[28] These sons were clearly accorded some dignity and status, given lands, preferment and a good education. One might speculate that their mothers would have shared their glory.[29]

Other mistresses included Christina Barclay, perhaps from the family of the captains of Falkland. She produced another James probably in 1532, who seems to have died young.[30] Then there was Euphemia Elphinstone, daughter of the first Lord Elphinstone, who produced a son, Robert, in 1533, later appointed commendator of the Abbey of Holyrood.[31] Elizabeth Carmichael, daughter of Sir John Carmichael, captain of Crawford, and wife of Sir John Somerville, gave birth to a son, John, in 1531 who became commendator of Coldingham Priory.[32] Eleanor Stewart, daughter of John, third earl of Lennox, produced yet another son, Adam, who was given a pension from the Charterhouse of Perth.[33] Finally, there was Elizabeth Beaton, the daughter of Sir John Beaton of Creich and a cousin of Cardinal David Beaton, James's keeper of the Privy Seal and one of his Ambassadors to France. She produced the king's only illegitimate daughter, Lady Jane or Jean Stewart, who as a child was placed in the household of Mary of Guise and then in that of her legitimate half-brother, the short-lived Prince James. As an adult she married the fifth earl of Argyll, a match that was possibly arranged within her father's lifetime.[34] There may have been a second Robert, who became commendator of the Priory of Whithorn, but his mother is not recorded.[35]

Apart from this catalogue of names, kinship connections and births virtually nothing is known about James V's mistresses. They were almost all the daughters of nobles or lairds in the king's service and so, presumably, were present at least on the periphery of the court before they became mothers of royal bastards. The children were suitably provided for but very little is recorded about the financial support of the mothers. Some of them subsequently made respectable marriages for Elizabeth Beaton married Lord Innermeith, Eleanor Stewart married the sixth earl of Errol and Euphemia Elphinstone married John Bruce of Cultmalindie. If they subsequently had any significant role within the court circle, sources do not mention it.[36] There is certainly no suggestion that James ever imitated the French practice of having an official mistress with luxurious apartments in the royal palaces, a rich endowment of lands and titles and considerable influence in politics and diplomacy.[37]

The only remaining category of women at court are the queens. Only a few remarks about their role at court are appropriate as the lives of Margaret Tudor, Madeleine of France and Mary of Guise are well documented.[38] The king's mother, Margaret Tudor, was a force to be reckoned with until her death in October 1541. His first wife, Madeleine of France, was married in Paris in January 1537 and survived only a few weeks in residence at Holyrood before she died of consumption. His second wife, Mary of Guise (or Mary of Lorraine as she is styled in contemporary sources), arrived near St Andrews in June 1538 and produced two princes who died in infancy before she bore Mary, Queen of Scots, in December 1542 days before the king died. All three were foreign princesses brought to Scotland as young women as the human manifestations of alliances between Scotland and the lands of their birth.[39] Margaret was only thirteen when she married the thirty-year old James IV in August 1503 after the so-called Treaty of Perpetual Peace, and still only twenty-three when she was widowed by the Battle of Flodden. Madeleine was sixteen when she married the twenty-four year old James V and had not reached her seventeenth birthday when she died.

Mary of Guise was more mature, for she was already a twenty-two year old widow, with a young son left behind in France, when she married the twenty-six year old James V.

The letters, diplomatic despatches and narrative sources of the period make it clear that there were certain expectations of the role a queen would play in her new realm. First and foremost she was responsible for the production of a male heir and barren queens or queens who only had daughters might be put away, the most famous example being Katherine of Aragon, Henry VIII's first wife. Of course, daughters were not totally unwelcome since they could be bartered on the international marriage market. The daughters of James I of Scotland were used particularly effectively here, yet sons were essential to carry on the dynasty.[40] Although James V's reputed comment on his deathbed, 'it come witht ane lase, it will pase witht ane lase' may well be apocryphal, it sums up very well the contemporary view that an heiress, through her marriage into another family, signalled the end of a dynasty.[41] It is significant that Mary of Guise was not given a coronation until she had been in Scotland for twenty months and was visibly pregnant.

As well as bearing children, a queen was expected to supervise the disciplined order of her household and to provide for the education and training not just of her own children, but those of noble or landed families entrusted to her care as pages, maids of honour or wards. The French poet, Pierre Ronsard, came to Scotland as a page to Queen Madeleine and later wrote a glowing account of James V as a vigorous, gracious and regal monarch.[42] Mary of Guise took her household responsibilities seriously since many of her accounts are checked and signed in her own hand and she had the reputation of taking a keen interest in the marriages of her ladies, two of whom are noted above. She is also credited with treating her husband's illegitimate offspring with some consideration and even affection.[43] If this was so, it underlines the fact that however robust, capable and overwhelmingly masculine these children may have been, they were no threat to the rights of her daughter.

The public role of a queen consort was largely decorative. She was expected to preside as a gracious figurehead at banquets, tournaments, pageants and ceremonies. Contemporary narratives often describe in detail how queens were dressed and how they appeared to be gratified by the attentions they received, but they do not usually show them doing anything more strenuous than nodding and smiling.[44] Speeches were sometimes made to them and about them, but never by them. Elaborate preparations made for the official reception of Queen Madeleine in 1537 were never carried out and the only Scottish state ceremony in which she took part was her own lavish funeral at the Abbey of Holyrood. According to George Buchanan this was the first time that mourning dress was worn in Scotland.[45] Mary of Guise made ceremonial entries into the burghs of St Andrews, Edinburgh, Dundee, Perth and Aberdeen, attended several tournaments and was given a coronation for which new regalia was produced by the royal goldsmiths.[46] The household accounts also make it clear that the king and queen would preside together at court for the major feasts of *Yule* and *Pasche* (Christmas and Easter), even if their itineraries might separate at other times of the year.[47]

Queens were also expected to specialise in acts of piety, charity and mercy. For example, Margaret Tudor, when a refugee at her brother's court in 1517, joined with her sister, Mary, the Queen Dowager of France, and her sister-in-law, Queen Katherine of Aragon, in a carefully stage-managed plea for clemency for the London apprentice boys held responsible for the riots of 'Evil May Day'. With their hair loose upon their shoulders, the three queens knelt weeping before Henry VIII until he was moved to pardon the miscreants.[48] Margaret was also a regular patron of Scottish shrines as was Mary of Guise who visited St Adrian's on the Isle of May and the shrine of the Virgin of Loretto at Musselburgh. In 1540–1542, when she was approaching the birth of one of her three children by James V, Mary made arrangements for offerings to be made at several Scottish and French shrines in the event of her death.[49]

Queens were also expected to be leaders of fashion and patrons of the arts. As the courts of both England and France were wealthier and more sophisticated than that of Scotland, they played some part in introducing cultural novelties. English portraits and painters were sent to the Scottish court when the Princess Margaret was first betrothed to James IV and English musicians may well have come north in her train, bringing with them pieces of English music that found their way into the *Carver Choirbook*.[50] It is also possible to detect English influence in the architecture of the palaces of Linlithgow and Holyrood as developed by James IV and James V.[51] Even more pervasive was the French influence on the architecture, art, etiquette, clothing and jewellery of the Scottish court after James V's marriage to Madeleine.[52] James had gone in person to the court of Francis I to secure the hand of his daughter and stayed there for nine months as an honoured guest of the French king and at his expense. He returned to Scotland in a fleet of ships laden with French wines, tapestries, fabrics, jewels, *objets d'arts* and artillery pieces, some of which were his but many were his wife's possessions. After Madeleine's death her jewels and other movable goods were bequeathed by Francis I to Mary of Guise on her marriage to James.[53] Mary's parents were later commissioned to find the best French masons, goldminers, armourers and falconers and send them to Scotland. Mary took an interest in all these transactions.[54]

Despite all the sixteenth-century controversy about female rulers, queens consort did have a clearly defined, if rather tricky, political role to play.[55] The splendour of a queen's attire, the size and social status of her entourage and the manner in which she was escorted and housed within her new realm were all regarded as a reflection not only of the dignity of her husband but also of the honour in which her father or brother was held. In political and diplomatic exchange, a queen was not supposed to have an agenda of her own but act as a channel of communication between the king she had married and the king she had left behind. These expectations did not take into account the fact that a queen might have a mind of her own. Whatever Francis I and James V expected from Mary of Guise, she seems to have regarded her marriage as an opportunity to further the cause of true religion in a land that was wavering.[56]

When the terms of the peace treaty or alliance that accompanied the marriage were upheld and there was goodwill on both sides, a queen's duty might be fairly straightforward. When diplomacy failed and warfare became a threat or a reality, her position was a very difficult one. Margaret Tudor spent thirty-seven of her fifty-two years in Scotland. For twenty-seven of them Anglo-Scottish relations could be described at best as tense and at worst as hostile.[57] It is quite clear that Margaret was neither a paragon of virtue nor a skilled politician. She had weaknesses in her character and made many errors of judgement that are familiar to historians.[58] Yet some of her grievances and complaints may have been too lightly dismissed as hysterical or self-indulgent, without any serious consideration being given to them. During the adult rule of her son, when the anarchy of his minority had been quelled, Margaret's complaints to her brother were largely concerned with her inability to appear in public as a personification of the English realm. When James's two French queens arrived she was especially worried about being embarrassed in front of them.[59] These complaints are usually considered to be indicative of her greed, vanity and insatiable desire for new finery, but considering the political symbolism of such matters, there was probably more to it than that.[60] Henry VIII, impatient though he often was with his sister's demands, sent her a gift of £200 (sterling) and interceded with James V on her behalf on the occasion of Madeleine's arrival. Margaret's career as Queen Dowager was not a success. Even if she had been one of the most skilful of Scottish queens, she would still have faced many difficulties.[61] Mary of Guise, on the other hand, was a talented politician, though the example of her years as dowager is not an encouraging one. With French money, troops and diplomacy behind her, she struggled to maintain the interests of her daughter, her faith and her two realms through eighteen years of widowhood (the last six of which she was Regent of Scotland). Even before her death in June 1560, many Scots were rejecting the French alliance and Roman church. Seven years on they would reject her daughter as well.[62]

In surveying the role and status of women at the court of James V it is often necessary to read between the lines to draw inferences and speculations from sources produced by contemporaries who clearly did not consider the subject to be of any great interest. It would appear that the position of women at the court reflected many of the experiences of women in the wider society of the sixteenth century. In this they were expected to operate within the limited spheres of family, household and traditional occupations such as nursing and sewing. Court poetry suggests that the models they were exhorted to emulate were idealised icons of saints and queens. The untidy complications of real life do sometimes emerge from the sources in references to illegitimate unions and the political struggles of the dowager queens. These snippets of information occasionally illuminate a dim corner of the history of sixteenth-century Scotland.

NOTES

1. *Registrum Secreti Sigilli Regum Scotorum* [*RSS*], eds. M. Livingstone et al (Edinburgh, 1908–) ii, 773.
2. *The Poems of William Dunbar*, ed. J. Small (3 vols, Scottish Text Society [STS], 1893), ii, 266–8. See also Priscilla Bawcutt, *Dunbar the Makar* (Oxford, 1992).
3. *Poems of William Dunbar*, ii, 30–47.
4. Ibid, ii, 223, 272–3.
5. Ibid, ii, 168–9.
6. Ibid, ii, 183–9, 251–3, 274–5, 279.
7. *The Works of Sir David Lindsay of the Mount, 1490–1555*, ed. D. Hamer (4 vols, STS, 1931–6), iv, 298–302.
8. Ibid, i, 117–22.
9. Ibid, i, 55–90 (especially lines 542–8, p. 72), 197–386 (especially lines 1051–76, p. 230 and lines 3235–64, p. 295), 105–12 (lines 92–175, p. 109–11, deal with the Scottish plans).
10. *The Bannatyne Manuscript*, ed. W. Tod Ritchie (4 vols, STS, 1923–5); *The Maitland Folio Manuscript*, ed. W. A. Craigie (2 vols, STS, 1917–27); *The Maitland Quarto Manuscript*, ed. W. A. Craigie (STS, 1920); J. MacQueen, ed. *Ballatis of Luve* (Edinburgh, 1970); A. A. MacDonald, 'William Stewart and the Court Poetry of the Reign of James V' in J. H. Williams, ed. *Stewart Style, 1513–1542: Essays on the Court of James V* (East Linton, 1996), 192–4.
11. A. L. Murray, 'Accounts of the King's Pursemaster, 1539–1540,' Scottish History Society [SHS], *Miscellany*, x (1965), 44; *Accounts of the Lord High Treasurer of Scotland* [*TA*], eds. T. Dickson & J. Balfour Paul (Edinburgh, 1877–1916), vi, 40, 417, 446.
12. A. Thomas, 'Renaissance Culture at the Court of James V, 1528–1542' (University of Edinburgh, PhD thesis, 1997), appendix A, 299–375.

13. *The Exchequer Rolls of Scotland* [ER], eds. J. Stuart et al (Edinburgh, 1878–1908), xiv, 287–8; *TA*, v, 196, viii, 101 *etc*; Murray, 'Pursemaster's Accounts'.

14. *TA*, v, 196, vii, 315 *etc*. See C. Edington, *Court and Culture in Renaissance Scotland: Sir David Lindsay of the Mount* (Edinburgh, 1994), 26–41.

15. *TA*, vi, 298, vii, 87 *etc*. Cf. Theo van Heijnsbergen, 'The Interaction Between Literature and History in Queen Mary's Edinburgh: The Bannatyne Manuscript and its Prosopographical Context' in A. A. MacDonald, M. Lynch and I. B. Cowan, eds. *The Renaissance in Scotland: Studies in Literature, Religion, History and Culture Offered to John Durkan* (Leiden, 1994), 191–8.

16. *TA*, vii, 125. *ER*, xvii, 164 and elsewhere; *The Hamilton Papers* [Hamilton Papers], ed. J. Bain (Edinburgh, 1890–92) i, 329, 338; R. Lindesay of Pitscottie, *The Historie and Cronicles of Scotland* (STS, 1899–1911) i, 403–5; cf. P. D. Anderson, *Robert Stewart, Earl of Orkney, Lord of Shetland, 1533–1593* (Edinburgh, 1982), 26–41.

17. Scottish Record Office [SRO], Despence de la Maison Royale, E.33/1, fos 8r.-15v. *TA*, vii & viii and *ER*, vxii; Thomas, 'Renaissance Culture', app. A.

18. *Foreign Correspondence with Marie de Lorraine, from the Balcarres Papers* (SHS, 1923–5), i, 245; *TA*, vii, 166, 328.

19. Thomas, 'Renaissance Culture', app. A.

20. *TA*, v, 372, 378, 383; Murray, 'Pursemaster's Accounts', 46.

21. *TA*, vii, 282, 302; Thomas, 'Renaissance Culture', 70, 261–5.

22. M. Lee, *James Stewart, Earl of Moray* (New York, 1953), 18; Anderson, *Robert Stewart*, 1–2.

23. Lindsay, *Works*, i, 46 (*The Complaynt*, lines 237–254); G. Buchanan, *The History of Scotland*, translated by J. Aikman (Glasgow & Edinburgh, 1827–9), ii, 324; Pitscottie, *Historie*, i, 383, 408–9.

24. *Historical Manuscripts Commission* [HMC], sixth report (London, 1893), app. 670; *RSS*, ii, 336.

25. *Registrum Magni Sigilli Regnum Scotorum* [RMS], eds. J. M. Thomson et al (Edinburgh, 1882–1914), iii, 1425, 1620; *TA*, vi, 40; *The Letters of James V*, eds R. K. Hannay & D. Hay (Edinburgh, 1954), 279, 287, 425; Thomas, 'Renaissance Culture', 72.

26. HMC, sixth report, app. 670; *The Scots Peerage* [SP], ed. J. Balfour Paul (Edinburgh, 1904–14), vi, 369; Lee, *James Stewart*, 17.

27. *RSS*, ii, 2138; *The Letters of James V* [James V Letters], eds. R. K. Hannay & D. Hay (Edinburgh, 1954), 320.

28. *RMS*, iii, 1620; *James V Letters*, 343.

29. *TA*, vi, 289, 353, 430; I. D. McFarlane, *Buchanan* (London, 1981), 48–9.

30. *TA*, vi, 180; Anderson, *Robert Stewart*, 156.

31. *RSS*, ii, 3127; *James V Letters*, 357; Anderson, *Robert Stewart*, 1–6, 154.

32. *Acts of the Lords of Council in Public Affairs 1501–54*, ed. R. K. Hannay (Edinburgh, 1932), 502; *James V Letters*, 426–7.

33. *RSS*, v, 915; Anderson, *Robert Stewart*, 156–8.

34. *TA*, vii, 478; *SP*, i, 25, 342, iv, 155, ix, 21.

35. *SP*, i, 25.

36. *RSS*, ii, 2206, 4016, 4525; Pitscottie, *Historie*, i, 381; W. Fraser, *The Elphinstone Family Book* (Edinburgh, 1897), i, 83.

37. R. J. Knecht, 'The Court of Francis I', *European Studies Review*, 8 (1978), 9–10; Knecht, *Renaissance Warrior and Patron: The Reign of Francis I* (Cambridge, 1994), 117, 290, 396, 407, 421, 498, 551, 558 *etc.*

38. P. H. Buchanan, *Margaret Tudor, Queen of Scots* (London, 1985); R. K. Marshall, *Mary of Guise* (London, 1977); A. Strickland, *Lives of the Queens of Scotland and English Princesses,* (8 vols, Edinburgh, 1850–59), i, 272–334.

39. E. Bapst, *Les Mariages de Jacques V* (Paris, 1889); N. MacDougall, *James IV* (Edinburgh, 1988), 112–55; Thomas, 'Renaissance Culture', 247–61.

40. J. C. Parsons, ed. *Medieval Queenship* (Stroud, 1994), 63–78; M. Brown, *James I* (Edinburgh, 1994), 110, 154, 162–3, 203.; R. Marshall, *Virgins and Viragos* (London, 1983), 19. See also P. Bawcutt & B. Henisch in this volume.

41. *The Works of John Knox*, ed. D. Laing (Edinburgh, 1846–64), i, 91; Pitscottie, *Historie*, i, 407.

42. M. Simonin, *Pierre de Ronsard* (Mesnil-sur-l'Estrée, 1990), 52–77.

43. SRO, Despence de la Maison Royale, E.33/1, fos 3v.-8r., E.34/8/1, E.34/8/3; Marshall, *Mary of Guise*, 73; Anderson, *Robert Stewart*, 8.

44. Teulet, *Papiers*, i, 292–303; D. Stevenson, *Scotland's Last Royal Wedding* (Edinburgh, 1997), 63.

45. *TA*, vi, 334, 349–52, 313–4, 330–2, 354–5; Buchanan, *History*, ii, 315; Thomas, 'Renaissance Culture', 280–2.

46. *TA*, vii, 254, 285–6; Pitscottie, *Historie*, i, 378–81; Thomas, 'Renaissance Culture', 256–9, 261–5.

47. SRO, Royal Household Books, E.31/1-8, E.32/2-8, E.33/1-2; Thomas, 'Renaissance Culture', 163–4, 173–7 & app. C, 386–423.

48. M. A. E. Green, *Lives of the Princesses of England from the Norman Conquest* (6 vols, London, 1849–55), iv, 254; Strickland, *Lives*, i, 146.

49. SRO, Royal Household Book, E.31/8, fo 99v; *Balcarres Papers*, i, 78–9; J. Lesley, *Historie of Scotland* (2 vols, STS, 1888–95), ii, 253.

50. *TA*, ii, 341, 405; J. D. Ross, *Musick Fyne: Robert Carver and the Art of Music in Sixteenth Century Scotland* (Edinburgh, 1993), 6; Thomas, 'Renaissance Culture', 153–9.

51. Richard Fawcett, *Scottish Architecture from the Accession of the Stewarts to the Reformation, 1371–1560* (Edinburgh, 1994), 308, 322; Thomas, 'Renaissance Culture', 92–109.

52. J. Lesley, *The History of Scotland 1436–1561* (Edinburgh, Bannatyne Club, 1830), 154.

53. C. d'Espence, *Oraison Funebre es obseques de . . . Marie . . . Royne douairiere d'Escoce* (Paris, 1561), 39.

54. *TA*, vii, 48, 182, 184, 193–4; *Balcarres Papers*, i, 16–33, 71–3.

55. See C. Jordan, 'Woman's Rule in Sixteenth-Century British Political Thought,' *Renaissance Quarterly*, 40 (1987), 421–51.

56. D'Espence, *Oraison Funebre*, 29, 39, 66–7.

57. G. Donaldson, *Scotland: James V – James VII* (Edinburgh, 1990), 17–62.

58. Cf. Buchanan, *Margaret Tudor*; Green, *Lives*, iv, 49–505; Strickland, *Lives*, i, 1–267.
59. M. A. E. Wood, *Letters of the Royal and Illustrious Ladies of Great Britain* (3 vols, London, 1846), ii, 323–333, iii, 18–20; *Hamilton Papers*, i, 38, 42–3, 48–51.
60. Buchanan, *Margaret Tudor*, 248, 254, 261–2; Strickland, *Lives*, i, 253, 257–8, 262–3.
61. Wood, *Letters*, ii, 330–333; Buchanan, *Margaret Tudor*, 250–3; Green, *Lives*, iv, 494–7; Strickland, *Lives*, i, 258.
62. Marshall, *Mary of Guise*, 108–266.

CHAPTER EIGHT

Politicking Jacobean Women: Lady Ferniehirst, the Countess of Arran and the Countess of Huntly, c.1580–1603

_____ *Ruth Grant*

DISCUSSION OF EARLY modern aristocratic women in Scotland is commonly restricted to marriage alliances, the production of heirs (preferably male) and, occasionally, matters of religion. Although these roles are in themselves important and certainly had political repercussions, Jacobean aristocratic women also had the opportunity, if they so wished, to play a more active role within national or local politics. However, the paucity of information on aristocratic women in standard secondary texts could lead to the impression that if they did indeed have such a role, it was certainly very circumscribed. Nor is it unusual for aristocratic women to be discussed merely as extensions of their spouses. Naturally, whilst furthering their husbands' interests, they were also looking to their own welfare as well as that of their children. They also paid close attention to the interests of their own kin networks, for Scotland's co-agnatic society meant that a woman's family influence was just as important as that of her husband's. Indeed, this played a key role in determining many marriage alliances. Aristocratic women were not eclipsed by their husbands' kin, for they could and did act in their own right. Status and position within the court could easily derive from these women and may have been the primary means through which family interests were protected. The subjects of this chapter exemplify all or some of these traits: Jean (or Janet) Scott, lady Ferniehirst, Elizabeth Stewart, countess of Arran and Henrietta Stewart, countess and first marchioness of Huntly.[1]

Primary material indicates that although aristocratic women rarely came to the forefront of politics they could nevertheless exercise considerable influence. Those active in politics usually worked behind the scenes, perhaps utilising the opportunities presented at court or overseeing the affairs of the locality during the absences of their husbands. Lady Ferniehirst and the Countesses of Arran and Huntly were all politically active, influencing the course of national politics. Certainly, both Lady Ferniehirst and the Countess of Huntly approached politics in a fairly traditional way by taking advantage of their position to enhance or create networks, as well as working in the background. Perhaps it was because they did not challenge the natural order of politics that they were

so successful in achieving their objectives, whereas the Countess of Arran
attempted to navigate uncharted territory and encountered considerable
opposition. Her political dominance in national government even threatened the male hierarchy and although she probably achieved her political
zenith in 1584–5, her fall was swift and complete.

Perhaps one of the most traditional roles adopted by aristocratic
women was supervising the affairs of the estates in the absence of their
husbands. Both the Countess of Huntly and Lady Ferniehirst were well
practised in this role. For instance, Sir Thomas Ker of Ferniehirst's open
espousal of Catholicism had resulted in periodic banishments from the
realm. In April 1581, he received licence to return to Scotland after
banishment for his role in the murder of Mary, Queen of Scots' second
husband, Lord Darnley. His recall and pardon were procured by Esmé
Stewart, duke of Lennox, whose subsequent fall from grace put Ferniehirst into exile again until the autumn of 1583.[2] Whilst he was abroad
Ferniehirst's estates and personal interests were overseen by his wife, Jean
Scott. In May 1583, she wrote to Thomas Blair, desiring him to sign and
ratify an act of pacification at her lawyers' request. She signed her letter,
'your assured frend at pauar', a term infrequently used by women, but
Lady Ferniehirst was then factor for her husband and had full power of
attorney during his absence. The endorsement on the letter indicates that
the act of pacification referred to Ferniehirst, rather than Jean Scott.[3]
After her husband's return she still took action regarding his affairs, for in
October 1584 Sir Cuthbert Collingwood of Eslington in Northumberland
wrote to remind her of an overdue debt for £30 sterling. This had been
lent to her husband and she had promised to repay it at Michaelmas.[4]
This seems to indicate that she had a recognised role concerning her
husband's financial affairs.

On 1 September 1583, Lady Ferniehirst wrote to her husband from
Falkland Palace, having been at court for a month petitioning King James
VI to allow the laird to return home. Her persistence with the aid of the
Earl of Huntly, finally paid off as she obtained the king's letters granting
Ferniehirst leave to return. She instructed him not to come home with
Ludovic Stewart, second duke of Lennox, but to arrive in the north,
where he was to stay with Huntly until his affairs were sorted out. She
also sternly admonished him that he was 'mekill bund to that gentil man
for his gud offyces and contenuall payne and travel he taks for you at all
tymes, quhairoff I think ye will neid be . . . myndfull'.[5] Her familiarity
with court politics and the contacts that she made certainly facilitated her
husband's later integration into the Arran government.

Lady Ferniehirst's sojourn at court was far from atypical. Records are
replete with references to aristocratic women attending court in order to
elicit favours for others and to tend to their own affairs. These women

appear to have been adept at developing or using court networks and manipulating the system. This facilitated their access to those in different levels of government and thus enabled them to advance their causes. For example, the Countess of Huntly, daughter of the first duke of Lennox, enjoyed the protection of James VI and interceded on behalf of Lord Maxwell in June 1588. By May 1589 she was at court making suit for her husband following the discovery of his secret correspondence with Spain and his treasonable raising of troops against the king at Brig O'Dee.[6] Following the discovery of the infamous Spanish Blanks in 1592, that involved her husband and others, the countess journeyed to Aberdeen in order to obtain the king's grant for their houses and rents.[7] She continued to plead for her husband throughout the 1590s, which will be discussed below.[8]

Outwith court intrigues Jean Scott had an interesting role in covert Marian politics. She was a regular correspondent with the exiled Mary, Queen of Scots and in the early 1580s appears to have acted as an intermediary between King James VI and his mother. James's correspondence with this deposed Catholic queen filled the English with trepidation, but spurred on both Scottish and European Counter-Reformers. It fuelled their hopes for his eventual conversion to Catholicism and subsequent promotion of the Counter-Reformation in Britain. Just as importantly, Lady Ferniehirst was also a means for other Scottish nobles to contact Mary. Her exchange of correspondence, particularly with the younger nobility, contributed greatly to keeping the Marian interest alive in Scotland. The young earl of Huntly is but one example of this. In a lengthy letter of 22 October 1583, Lady Ferniehirst forwarded letters from Lord Seton and introduced Huntly to Mary, informing her that he was 'very desirous to hear from your majesty . . . and to command him with anything he is able to do for the advancement of your majesty's service'. Following on from this, in February 1584, she gave refuge to four or five English Catholics, who intended to shelter in the north with Huntly, 'to whom . . . they were commended by' Queen Mary. The role of Lord Seton has often been recognised as vital in maintaining Scottish contact with Queen Mary and for receiving mission priests and Catholic refugees.[9] The role of Lady Ferniehirst, however, in covert Marian politics during the early 1580s has been overlooked, yet it was equally important and revealing.

A less discreet approach to politics was adopted by Elizabeth Stewart, countess of Arran, formerly countess of March and lady Lovat, and eldest daughter of the Earl of Atholl. Whilst still Countess of March, she became pregnant with Arran's child and very publicly had her marriage to her elderly second husband annulled on grounds of his impotency or, according to Moysie, 'because his instrument was not guid'. She then married the politically aspiring James Stewart, earl of Arran on 6 July 1581 which latterly earned her the epithet 'Lady Jezebel'. Their first child was born on 8 January 1582 and the couple were compelled to do 'ecclesiastical penance for the irregularity, much against her will'.[10] The earl of Arran's political ascendancy followed the collapse of the anglophile Ruthven Regime in June 1583, causing, according to one chronicler, many noblemen to leave either the country or the court. This was 'to the gret contentment of the Erle of Arran and his wyf, to gyd all ther allane', while another stated that 'nothing was done in courte but by him and his ladey'.[11] Although written some years later, these quotes encapsulate the relationship between the countess and her husband working together as a political team. Although this was not a unique arrangement if one draws a parallel with the Drummonds during the reign of David II, their partnership and the Countess's prominent and decidedly non-traditional role in Scottish national politics between 1583 and 1585 earned her opprobrium from across the political spectrum. However, it may well have been the special circumstances at court in the 1580s that accentuated Elizabeth Stewart's role. Until Arran's government, there had been neither a queen consort, queen dowager, nor wife of a regent at court. The dexterity with which the countess filled this vacuum made her all the more conspicuous and perhaps prey to greater criticism.[12] Additionally, in what could be perceived as an insult to her husband, she was suspected by the English politician, Walsingham, of being the brains behind the Arran administration.[13] Indeed, since Arran was elevated to the peerage only three months before his marriage to Elizabeth Stewart, she may have been vital to Arran securing his place at court.[14]

Elizabeth Stewart's greatest enemy may well have been her own forwardness, for in November 1583, when a brawl broke out between the earl of Bothwell and Lord Hume, the countess encouraged the king 'to strike off' Bothwell's head! It is questionable if such an impetuous comment would have been taken lightly when placed within the context of her husband's partial responsibility for the executions of the earl of Morton, for complicity in the murder of Lord Darnley (1581), and of the earl of Gowrie, for involvement in the unsuccessful coup attempt in 1584. Concerning Gowrie, it was reported that she had consulted 'Highland oracles' who informed her that Gowrie would fall; she then merely 'helpit fordwart that prophesie the best sche culd'. If she did further Gowrie's demise, it would not have been out of character, as the lands of Gowrie and his wife (Dorothy Stewart) were subsequently acquired by her husband and herself.[15]

This was the first association of the countess with supernatural powers, which were subsequently pursued by her critics. In April 1584 a man from Atholl affirmed that 'he heard a witch say that the Ladie Arran had used witchecraft against him, and if he provided not for contrare venome, it would come to his distruction'. The proclamation of the Lords at Stirling on 22 April 1584 referred to her as 'depending on the response of witches and enemie to all human society'. Again, in 1585, she was described as a 'lasciuous viccked woman, and one blundered of witchcrafte'.[16] The link between descriptions of Elizabeth Stewart as a witch and her unconventional political role does not seem merely coincidental. Sources such as Calderwood were writing in a period when witchcraft was an issue. Her unpopularity can be partially attributed to her avaricious nature as she reputedly plundered Mary's jewels and clothing.[17] More invidious, in the eyes of her contemporaries, was her great influence once Arran became chancellor in 1584. Nor is it coincidental that her name was consistently linked with her husband's concerning both policy and finance throughout his chancellorship from May 1584 to November 1585. During this time Arran's political enemies tried jointly to indict him and his wife. One 1584 excerpt reads:

> The effaires and state of the realme is by *them* misgoverned and abused; the proofe wherof plainlie appears by that libertie and commandement which that pestilent persoun, *and his divelish wife*, have usurped in Secreit Counsell and Sessioun, wherin by *their* minacings and boastings, *they* preceeselie commanded suche as are of the lower and meaner ranke, and by *their* vitious and outrageous language overhailed suche of the nobilitie, and others of greater authoritie, that would not consent to *their* affections.[18]

In August 1584 the English ambassador wrote that nothing could be done in the Privy Council 'without the privitye of my Lady'.[19]

By February 1585 it was rumoured that the countess of Arran was made 'Lady Comtroller',[20] and was supposedly not averse to raising funds for the treasury (or herself) when administering justice. According to Calderwood, in the justice courts the poor were 'sold and ransomed at the hundreth punds the score', without regard to guilt or innocence. Lady Arran, sitting in judgement, 'caused sindry to be hanged that wanted their compositions, saying What had they beene doing all their dayes, that had not so much as five punds to buy them from the gallows?' Additionally, the pursuit of justice had to be purchased, 'the impudent Arran ladie hath found out for shamelesse scafferie, in taking angels, crownes, and . . . thrittie shilling peeces, to be soliciter for calling of bills'. She was also accused of appointing Catholic judges, supposedly to the detriment of Protestants.[21]

There seem to be no obvious parallels with the consistent descriptions of the countess's role in government. No other minority government in early modern Scotland mentions involvement of a regent's or chancellor's

wife in national affairs to a similar degree. Although she does not appear
in records listing her formally as comptroller, neither can she be traced as
presiding over any justice courts. This does not necessarily negate the fact
that she did exert real influence and control in these capacities. Her
gender certainly precluded her from official recognition in the records,
though her presence or control may have been taken as given. Such
pervasive malignment in primary texts could not have been baseless. This
can only lead to the conclusion that the countess did indeed play a
prominent political role. This aberration was bitterly resisted, provoking
accusations of witchcraft and descriptions of her as 'a monster of
nature'.[22] Just as John Knox referred to the rule of female monarchs
as 'the monstrous regiment of women', so was it considered equally
unnatural for an aristocratic woman to dominate what was considered an
almost exclusively male sphere of influence.

The third 'politicking woman' is Henrietta Stewart, countess of Huntly.
She did not aspire to pulling the strings of government, yet her political
influence operated through her close relationships with both King James
VI and Queen Anna. This was revealing and perhaps much more effective
than the countess of Arran's approach. Henrietta's kinship to the king
furthered her interests as he referred to her as 'his doughter, and beloved
of his blud'.[23] The countess began to attend Queen Anna in December
1590 and their ensuing friendship was another significant factor in her
success in influencing royal decisions and in further insulating herself and
her husband from many of the kirk's demands.[24] Ministers complained
about her Catholicism in November 1596, but the king reminded them
that 'the kirk had the wyte [blame], that dealt not with her'.[25]

Raised in France, Henrietta arrived in Scotland to marry George
Gordon, sixth earl of Huntly in 1588. This was a marriage strongly
encouraged by both Queen Mary in 1584 and King James himself, who
paid 5,000 merks for their marital celebrations.[26] The king granted
Huntly the commendatorship of Dunfermline to be used as her tocher.
These lands were later surrendered to Queen Anna, upon reversion to the
countess when the queen died.[27] Her residence in Dunfermline was
pivotal in providing easy access to the court when it was in Edinburgh
or Falkland and it was used extensively by the couple until 1590. Like
Lady Ferniehirst, she paid careful attention to her locality by receiving the
king's gift to appoint a sheriff of Aberdeen in 1597 or through settling a
dispute between John Ross and Grant of Freuchy in 1610.[28] Her main
strengths, however, lay at court.

The countess was described as 'a vertuous wyff and prudent lady; who
providentlie governed her husband's affairs, and carefullie solicited his
business at home dureing his banishment from Scotland' after 1594.[29]
She furthered their affairs through her close attendance upon the queen.

As early as 1590, the English ambassador speculated that 'it is thought that under the shadowe of her abode about the Quene that her husband shall gitt longer tyme to abide here and in courte'.[30] It is significant that during any period of crisis or when the favour of the king or queen was needed, the countess was invariably at court. In conjunction with courtiers who promoted their interests, such as Sir Patrick Murray, Lord Hume, the master of Glamis and Lord Spynie, she was usually successful in achieving her objectives. Huntly's autonomy in the North East, especially during his feud with James Stewart, earl of Moray, and the protection of his political interests depended largely on the nexus of power he had carefully built up within the king's bedchamber. This was mirrored by his countess's power base within the queen's bedchamber for in 1590 she even persuaded the king to suspend for fifteen days Huntly's bond of £20,000 for keeping the peace with Moray, who did not receive a like suspension and complained of partiality.[31] Likewise, from 1592 when the Spanish Blanks were found until Huntly defeated Argyll at the Battle of Glenlivet in 1594, the countess was conspicuously present in court.[32] Intermittent residence in court provided the perfect opportunity for friends and servants of her husband, who conveniently attended upon her, to pursue their petitions on the earl's behalf. For example, Huntly's personal servitor, Alexander Duff, and the Laird of Pitlurg accompanied her to court in 1592 in order to petition the king and Council to intercede with the kirk regarding Huntly's repentance for murdering Moray. Perhaps more importantly, she also provided a line of communication between the king and her husband during 1592–94. It was frequently suggested that James or Anna deliberately summoned her to court in order to find out what Huntly's position was. Thus, while James publicly refused to read Huntly's letters, mostly for the benefit of the kirk and Elizabeth I, he was still intimately acquainted with the position of this errant earl.[33]

The vital connection, however, seems to have been between the countess and Anna of Denmark, who exerted considerable influence on national politics in her own right. Ministers of the kirk and Anglophiles incessantly petitioned for her removal from the queen's court, fearing 'no good fruit in religion coming by her company to the Queen'. Their fears may well have been justified for one Jesuit credited the countess of Huntly with introducing the queen to Catholicism.[34] Despite these numerous petitions, the queen refused to remove her and showed increasing signs of favour towards the countess. In April 1594 it was remarked that when the countess left court, 'her rewards in the Queen's chamber were liberal and far exceeding the common order and proportion used here'.[35] She attended the queen at the birth of Princess Elizabeth in 1596 and was named her godmother. In response to the howls of protest from the kirk, James replied that she 'was a good discreit ladie, worthie of his affection'.[36] In 1599 the Earl of Huntly was elevated to a marquisate and one year later they both played a prominent role in the baptism of Prince Charles. It was reported that the Marchioness, instead of the nurse, held the baby for the duration of the sermon.[37] This may have been due to her position as the closest female relative to the young prince, but her relationship with his royal parents cannot be entirely discounted.

Early modern aristocratic women not only could but did play pivotal roles in Scottish politics. They were by no means, with the exception of Lady Arran, atypical of élite women of their era. High-ranking women could wield political power through a variety of means, ranging from maintaining a high profile at court to manoeuvring in the murky arena of covert politicking. Although the countess of Huntly and Lady Ferniehirst exercised considerable political influence, the former through the court and the latter through the cultivation of connections with the exiled Queen Mary, they have gone largely unnoticed by political historians. Perhaps this is because of the nature of their roles and the discreet means through which they effected their objectives, yet the quasi-official and highly contentious position of the Countess of Arran has similarly passed without notice. Aristocratic women constitute a vital part of the early modern political record and though the evidence is not as abundant as for their male counterparts, it nonetheless exists. It may well be that historians are simply not accustomed to looking for female influence; this provides exciting opportunities for future research.

NOTES

1. See also the portrait of Dame Jean and the illustration of Henrietta Stewart in this volume.
2. D. Calderwood, *The History of the Kirk of Scotland* (8 vols, Wodrow Society, 1842–9), iii, 510, 576.
3. Scottish Record Office [SRO], Lothian Muniments GD40/2/ix/65. I am grateful to Dr Maureen Meikle for allowing me to see an advance copy of 'Victims, Viragos and Vamps: Women of the Sixteenth-Century Anglo-Scottish Frontier', in P. Dalton and J. Appleby, eds, *Government, Religion and Society in Northern England, c.1000 to 1700* (Gloucester, 1997), 172–184.
4. SRO, GD40/2/ix/71.
5. SRO, GD40/2/ix/68.
6. *Calendar of Letters and Papers relating to the affairs of the Borders of England and Scotland* [CBP], ed. J. Bain (London, 1894–6), i, 51; *Calendar of State Papers relating to Scotland* [CSP Scot], eds. J. Bain et al (Edinburgh,

1898–69), x, 85, 332, 335. See R. Grant, 'The Brig O' Dee Affair, the sixth earl of Huntly and the Politics of the Counter-Reformation', in J. Goodare & M. Lynch, eds. *James VI: Court and Kingship* (Tuckwell Press, forthcoming).

7. *The Historie and Life of King James the Sext*, ed. T. Thomson (Bannatyne Club, 1825), 268; Sir Robert Gordon of Gordonstoun, *A Genealogical History of the Earldom of Sutherland, From its Origins to the Year 1630; With a Continuation to the Year 1651* (Edinburgh, 1813), 221; *CSP Scot*, xi, 72; Calderwood, *History*, v, 238. See T. G. Law, 'The Spanish Blanks and the Catholic Earls, 1592–4', in P. Hume Brown ed. *Collected Essays and Reviews of Thomas Graves Law, LL.D* (Edinburgh, 1904), 244–76.

8. Calderwood, *History*, v, 441–3; *The Autobiography and Diary of Mr James Melville*, ed. R. Pitcairn (Wodrow Society, 1843), 247–8.

9. *CSP Scot*, v, 638; vii, 24–5; for Seton, cf. British Library [BL], Add. MS. 38,823, fo. 11r.

10. D. Moysie, *Memoirs of the Affairs of Scotland, 1577–1603*, ed. J. Dennistoun (Maitland Club, 1830), 34. Calderwood, *History*, iv, 484–8. *The Scots Peerage*, ed. J Balfour Paul, (Edinburgh 1904–14), i, 396–7. Her first husband, Lord Fraser of Lovat, died in January 1580.

11. Sir J. Melville of Halhill, *Memoirs of his Own Life*, ed. T. Thomson (Bannatyne Club, 1827), 301; *The Historical Works of Sir James Balfour*, (4 vols, Edinburgh, 1824–5), i, 383.

12. I am grateful to Prof. Michael Lynch for commenting on this.

13. *CBP*, i, 165.

14. Captain James Stewart was declared tutor to the mentally ill Earl of Arran, *The Register of the Privy Council of Scotland*, [RPC], eds. J. Burton et al (Edinburgh, 1877–), iii, 356 and assumed his title by charter on 22 April 1581, *The Acts of the Parliaments of Scotland*, eds. T. Thomson & C. Innes (12 vols, Edinburgh, 1814–75), iii, 251.

15. *Registrum Secreti Sigilli Regum Scotorum* [RSS], eds M. Livingstone et al (Edinburgh, 1908–), viii, nos. 2089, 2150, 2400, 2399; Calderwood, *History*, iii, 759; Melville, *Memoirs*, 324–5.

16. Calderwood, *History*, iv, 28–9, 35; Balfour, *Works*, i, 383.

17. *Letters and Papers relating to Patrick Master of Gray*, ed. T. Thomson (Bannatyne Club, 1835), 5.

18. Calderwood, *History*, iv, 29. Emphasis my own.

19. *Master of Gray*, 1, 3, 5.

20. *Original Letters of Mr John Colville*, ed. D. Laing (Bannatyne Club, 1858), 83–4. There is no formal record of the Countess of Arran assuming the office of comptroller.

21. Calderwood, *History*, iv, 411, 439.

22. Ibid, iv, 410.

23. *Master of Gray*, 168; *CSP Scot*, x, 109; *History of the Church of Scotland . . . by the Rev. John Spottiswoode*, eds. M. Russell & M. Napier (3 vols, Spottiswoode Society, 1844–5), iii, 7, 464.

24. BL Cotton, Caligula, DII.94; SRO, CH2/89/1, fo 30r; *CSP Scot*, x, 429; *Acts and Proceedings of the General Assembly of the Kirk of Scotland*, ed. T. Thomson (3 vols, Bannatyne Club 1839–45), ii and iii, 1024, 1025; J. Row,

History of the Kirk of Scotland 1558–1637, ed. D. Laing (Wodrow Society, 1842), 192.

25. *CSP Scot*, xi, 594; Calderwood, *History*, v, 452; R. Grant, 'George Gordon, sixth earl of Huntly: a study in Counter-Reformation politique, c. 1576–1617', University of Edinburgh, PhD thesis, in progress.

26. SRO, GD24/5/57/15; *CSP Scot*, vii, 341; ix, 587; *RPC*, iv, 103; Gordon, *History of Sutherland, 208*; Calderwood, *History*, iv, 686–7; Row, *History*, 137.

27. SRO, GD 44/66/3; *Registrum Magni Sigilli Regnum Scotorum* [*RMS*], eds. J. M. Thomson et al (Edinburgh, 1882–1914), no. 126; *CSP Scot*, x, 86, 109, 298–9, 334, 552; *Master of Gray*, 168; Calderwood, *History*, iv, 613.

28. *Records of the Sheriff Court of Aberdeenshire*, (New Spalding Club, 1904–7), i, 377, 387, 475; W. Fraser, *The Chiefs of Grant*, (Edinburgh, 1883), ii, 39–40.

29. BL, Harleian 1423, fo 141r. *Genealogical History of Sutherland*, 208. R. Grant, 'Scotland and the Wars of the Counter-Reformation', in E. Cameron & F. Watson, eds. *Scotland and War*, (Association of Scottish Historical Studies, 1995).

30. *CSP Scot*, x, 429. Grant, 'George Gordon'.

31. *CSP Scot*, x, 437, 547, 650, 752, 764, 780. K. M. Brown, *Bloodfeud in Scotland, 1573–1625* (Edinburgh, 1986), ch. 6.

32. *CSP Scot*, xi, 89, 93, 97, 171, 176, 181, 301, 362–3, 370, 382; Calderwood, *History*, v, 250, 336.

33. *CSP Scot*, x, 782; xi, 23, 77, 83. Grant, 'George Gordon'.

34. *CSP Scot*, x, 591; Row, *History*, 205–6; M. Dilworth, 'Three Documents Relating to St John Ogilvie', *The Innes Review*, 34 (1983), 61.

35. *CSP Scot*, xi, 91, 181, 321.

36. *CBP*, ii, 226; Calderwood, *History*, v, 452, 454–6; Spottiswoode, *History*, iii, 12, 13, 31; William Scot, *An Apologetical Narration of the State and Government of the Kirk of Scotland since the Reformation*, eds. D. Laing and J. Anderson (Wodrow Society, 1846), 70.

37. Folger Shakespeare Library (Washington, D.C.), N.a. 102, fo. 8. I am grateful to Dr Maureen Meikle for this reference to an account of Charles' baptism.

CHAPTER NINE

'Holde her at the Oeconomicke rule of the House':[1] Anna of Denmark and Scottish Court Finances, 1589–1603

_____ *Maureen M. Meikle*

ANNA OF DENMARK married King James VI in 1589.[2] She was the second daughter of Frederick II of Denmark and his consort Sophia of Mecklenburg. Anna was only fifteen years old when she landed at Leith in May 1590, yet she quickly learned the ways of her adopted country, its language and its court. The Scottish Court had been without a resident queen since the abdication of James' mother, Mary, Queen of Scots in 1567. Changes were therefore inevitable. To begin with another household had to be established for the new queen with its own financial administration. This was not unusual as most European monarchies had separate households for their kings and queens.[3]

Anna's household was funded from her jointure, which consisted of Falkland and Linlithgow Palaces with a third of their demesne. After her marriage the lands of the earldom of Ross and the Abbey of Dunfermline (north of the Forth) were added. This made a large estate by Scottish standards, though it was not excessively affluent in comparison to Western European states. Scotland was not a rich country and was frankly incomparable to the riches of Anna's native Denmark. Denmark included Norway in those days and had a lucrative income from shipping tolls levied from vessels passing through the Sound. Many lavish items in Anna's trousseau would not be unpacked until a suitable palace had been found for them in Scotland. Although rapid repairs were made to Holyrood prior to her arrival, it would be at the rebuilt abbey of Dunfermline that Anna finally established her own household.

Anna's Danish advisors appointed the first managers of her household, who were later replaced by Scottish courtiers. This was part of the naturalisation process that most queen consorts of foreign birth were expected to go through in Scotland and France. It was more acceptable for female retainers to stay on, than men who might threaten the political order.[4] Therefore only a handful of Danish servants remained after a year, and only one stayed with Anna throughout the rest of her life. This was her devoted maid Anna Roos.[5]

Anna's first encounter with Scottish Court finances was the negotiations surrounding her tocher (*anglicé* dowry) and subsequent jointure. Admittedly these negotiations were carried out by her Danish advisors, but they would have kept the youthful queen consort informed of their discussions and diplomatic efforts. Queen Sophia was adamant that a good dower had to be agreed in exchange for her daughter's dowry of 75,000 rixdollars or 100,000 gold florins, which was approximately £150,000 Scots. James had hoped for a larger dowry, but the Danes drove a hard bargain. The agreed jointure was thought to be worth twice her tocher and was probably the best the impoverished Scottish exchequer could offer.[6] The Danish ambassadors had suggested that she receive an annual income of £4,000 Scots for her daily expenses. The final total was £4541 Scots in money, plus substantial amounts of wheat, barley, oats, capons, hens and geese. In 1590 this may have been adequate, but inflation and the depreciation of the Scots pound would eat away at this amount.[7]

James lost no time in distributing the tocher amongst the royal burghs in the form of a loan, with interest set at ten per cent. Edinburgh headed the list with £40,000 Scots, whilst smaller burghs such as St Andrews and Haddington received £2,000 Scots. However, what had begun as deposit accounts turned into current accounts within a few years. This was due to heavy spending by both James and Anna. Nevertheless, most of this money went on quelling the earl of Bothwell's rebellion (1593) and paying for the baptism of the royal couple's first child, Prince Henry.[8] In July 1594 Anna had borrowed back £4000 Scots from St Andrews and Anstruther. This was to support 'the apparelling of hir laydis maydynis of honnour, gentilwemen and serving wemen' at Henry's baptism celebrations. Her everyday household finances were insufficient to support extra expense such as this. As much of her tocher had been spent, future extraordinary expenditure would have to come from borrowing and this would be detrimental to Scottish Court finances.[9]

Anna's ordinary household spending was high as she had so many people to feed, clothe and pay wages to. In 1591 an account of the queen's household lists many people including her master of household, master stabler, secretary, carver, preacher, tailor, furrier and goldsmith. They all had their own servants within the household, again to be provided for by the queen. Then there were many lesser ranking servants of Anna such as 'ane moir', 'Hans, maister cuke', 'a notair of the expenssis of the quenis house' and several pages and lackeys.[10]

At the royal dining tables there was a strict segregation of the king's and queen's households. They sat at separate tables with foodstuffs furnished from their own supplies. Nothing was wasted as surplus foodstuffs were passed on to other tables in a descending social order. The top tables had wine, meats, bread and ale, whilst those at the bottom only received bread and ale.[11] The meats included were typical of an élite household with beef, mutton, veal, capon, chicken, lamb, fish, dove, tongue, geese and wild meat in season. The only exceptions to all this meat were forty apples and 100 eggs. We know that Anna was particularly fond of beer, rather than the inferior Scots ale, and James ordered beer especially from London for her in 1595. As it was made from hops, English beer travelled well, but it was another example of James and Anna's expensive tastes.[12]

Extravagance such as this would become the basic cause of the royal couple's financial troubles. Anna managed to remain within her basic budget until 1596, when her household expenses doubled. They doubled again by 1601 and by 1603 they were approximately £23,210 Scots. Even allowing for rapid inflation this was a huge increase that owes more to extravagance than common sense. Her children were accounted for separately in the treasurer's accounts and therefore did not contribute to these increasing costs.[13] Anna found temporary relief through her new goldsmith and moneylender George Heriot. Heriot acted in an unofficial capacity from May 1593 until he was made Anna's court-appointed goldsmith in 1597. His career really took off in 1593 with this new patronage. It was a relationship of mutual benefit for the nobility and lairds placed orders with Heriot as a result of his work for Anna.[14] For her part Anna adored jewels, yet she also appreciated that money could be borrowed against them. An intriguing note, obviously scribbled down quickly records Anna asking 'Gordg heriatt I ernestlie dissyr youe present to send me tua hundrethe pundes vithe all expidition becaus I man hest me away presentlie'. The note is undated, but probably was written in 1594 when Anna was still perfecting her use of the Scots language in written form.[15] He presumably obliged his most important patron as this note has survived in the Heriot papers. This pattern of commissioning jewels and borrowing money against them continued for many years.

Anna's love of jewellery is well known and accounts for many accusations of frivolity levelled against her. Anna had been accustomed to wearing expensive baubles since her childhood in Denmark. She had brought a jeweller from Denmark called Jacob, but he made off with some of her treasures in May 1594. For this crime he and his accomplice, one of Anna's French footmen called Guilliam, were arrested in North Shields and sent back to Scotland for execution.[16] This was fortuitous for George Heriot, who now slipped into the role of chief goldsmith to the queen. Their accounts continued until 1616 though, interestingly, Heriot had none of the sophistication of his later years in 1593 and duly itemised Anna's accounts in the Scots tongue. This meant, for example, that exquisite earrings were described as 'twa hingeris for lugis set with sevin dossane rubyes'.[17] Whilst it is true that she spent a large amount of money on jewels, it should be remembered that she was the queen consort and was entitled to wear the finest jewels that George Heriot could make for her. Anna also gave away jewels as gifts, so she cannot be accused of spending vast amounts on herself. At first, she had been able to meet most of Heriot's bills. For instance in 1594 she instructed the chamberlain of Dunfermline to pay Heriot 832 crowns out of the Abbey's rents for jewellery and goldsmith work. This work included elaborate commissions for fans inlaid with oriental agate, bracelets of gold and pearl and a horse set with diamonds and rubies. The jewels became even more elaborate and expensive as time wore on and included embroidered clothes with interwoven jewels such as 'ane stomacher inbroiderit with gold and silver' at twenty-three crowns.[18] Very few of these royal jewels have survived, which is a pity as Anna's jewels were worth at least £400,000 sterling when she died in 1619.[19]

James was as good a patron of Heriot as his wife, so her level of expenditure was not a singular vice. He sanctioned Heriot having his own apartment within Holyrood House to transact business.[20] This was just as well for the inevitable financial crises that would beset the royal couple in the later 1590s and early 1600s. Heriot, as well as helping Anna out of temporary financial predicaments, took jewels in pawn from James. Sometimes this meant pawning Anna's jewellery to Heriot on the king's behalf. Anna, true to the dictates of the era, appeared the dutiful wife in this sensitive matter. Nonetheless her compliance was probably due more to the fact that James, to settle a major row between them, had given Anna 'the greatest part of his jewels' back in 1593. Pawning large numbers of jewels was to remain a source of royal friction and embarrassment, for in 1599 James ordered the treasurer to 'prefer his payment to all others for the relief of our said dearest bedfellow's jewels engaged, and our honour and promise cause'.[21] When James dared not hawk Anna's jewels again he secured loans against property such as the Chapel Royal of Stirling Castle. Heriot returned the deeds to the chapel in January 1603, but by then many other crown lands in Scotland had been mortgaged as well.[22]

Considering the financial mess that James was in by the late 1590s, it was somewhat ironic that he had appointed a council of the queen in 1593 to sort out her business affairs.[23] These councillors, Blantyre, Pluscardine, Mr Thomas Hamilton, Mr John Lindsay and Mr James Elphinstone would develop into a group known as the Octavians. They were so successful at sorting out her affairs that she recommended them to the spendthrift James. Anna's economies would not be confined to the balancing of her rent books. During 1595–96 she twice ordered dresses to be remade to avoid the expense of purchasing new ones. On 18 September wardrobe accounts record that four and a half ells of white satin were purchased 'to reforme your majesties quhyt saittern gown' and on 26 January three and a half ells of 'twa pyle velvet to be new bodeie and slevis to ane velvet goun' were ordered.[24] At New Year 1596, when the royal family traditionally gave and received gifts, Anna had shamelessly paraded 1000 pounds in pieces before James. They were the result of profitable management of her estates by her councillors. She dutifully gave 600 pieces to James, but then taunted him to appoint her advisors to sort out his affairs since they were so competent in financial matters. James duly appointed them on 9 January 1596, but his finances were in a more desperate state. The Octavians tried to overhaul the king's 'whole living' with some success at first, but they encountered strong opposition from greedy sycophants at court.[25]

The undeniable financial success of Anna's councillors may well have prompted a back-handed compliment from James to Anna in his *Basilikon Doron*. This was a book of instruction for young Prince Henry, first published in 1599, more for James's own enjoyment than for the reading delights of a four-year-old. He carefully instructed Henry about a future wife, noting that he should 'suffer her neuer to meddle with the Politicke gouernment of the Commonweale, but holde her at the Oeconomicke rule of the house'. Anna's good economic rule of her household had clearly been noted as it is highly probable that James was reflecting upon his own marriage when writing this section of *Basilikon Doron*.[26]

Unfortunately, the initial good work of the Octavians was undone by 1598. Neither Anna nor James were taking the advice of their councillors by then and they unwisely cast off the financial stringencies imposed by the Octavians. This was not a prudent move as the visit of Anna's brother Ulric, duke of Holstein, cost £4000 sterling which the Scottish crown could scarcely afford. When the English ambassador wrote that 'againe money is scant' in December 1598, he was not exaggerating.[27] Anna's dislike of the Octavians' previous advice was foolish, but should not be dismissed as female frailty. By 1598 the likely succession of James and Anna to the English throne was probably colouring their financial judgement. It was as though they were overspending in hope that their debts would be settled by an unburdened Scottish exchequer, after their removal to England. This did happen, but the amassed debts took many years to settle.

Some additional household bills came from Anna's interests in theatre and architecture. These pursuits would become far more elaborate in England, yet they added significantly to her household accounts during the last years of her Scottish queenship. In 1599 she may have paid some of the expenses of English 'comedians' and in 1601 Anna paid £200 as half payment to English actors, (with James paying the other half).[28] James helped her out in 1600 with a new year present of over £4000 Scots, but this did not really improve Anna's overall debts. When news finally arrived in 1603 that Queen Elizabeth had died there was a flurry of activity in Anna's household. New clothes and riding equipment were ordered for the queen and her retinue for their journey south. This quadrupled the usual expenses on these items, but there were savings on salaries after the court moved south.[29]

Anna left Scotland some weeks after her husband on 2 June 1603, accompanied by Prince Henry and Princess Elizabeth. The elaborate journey would take approximately a month at a cost of £2000 sterling to the English exchequer.[30] She received many of Elizabeth I's ordinary jewels before leaving Scotland. In sending these jewels north James was showing his affection for Anna after a distressing miscarriage. However, he also knew that these baubles would hurry her journey south to inspect the remaining English crown jewels!

NOTES

1. James VI and I, *Political Writings* (Basilikon Doron), ed. J. P. Sommerville (Cambridge, 1994), 42.
2. D. Stevenson, *Scotland's Last Royal Wedding* (Edinburgh, 1997). See also the portrait in this volume.
3. Cf. chapters by J. Finlay and A. Thomas in this volume.
4. I am grateful to Dr Alison Rosie for her helpful discussion on the naturalisation of queen consorts' retainers.
5. G. Nichols, *The Progresses, Processions and Magnificent Festivities of King James the First, His Royal Consort, Family and Court . . .* (London, 1828), iii, 531, 549 & 541.
6. *Calendar of State Papers relating to Scotland* [*CSP Scot*], eds. J. Bain et al (Edinburgh, 1898–69), x, 103; *Registrum Magni Sigilli Regnum Scotorum* [*RMS*], eds. J. M. Thomson et al (Edinburgh, 1882–1914), v, 1731–33; A. Montgomerie, 'King James VI's Tocher Gude and a Local Authorities Loan of 1590', *Scottish Historical Review* [*SHR*], 37 (1958), 13.
7. T. Riis, *Should Auld Acquaintance Be Forgot . . . Scottish-Danish Relations c. 1450–1700* (Odense, 1988) i, 270, 272; A. J. S. Gibson & T. C. Smout, *Prices, food and wages in Scotland, 1500–1780* (Cambridge, 1995) 5–7.
8. Cf. Montgomerie, 'Tocher Gude', 11–16.
9. *The Register of the Privy Council of Scotland* [*RPC*], eds. J. Burton et al (Edinburgh, 1877–), v, 151–2.
10. *Papers Relative to the Marriage of King James the Sixth of Scotland, with the Princess Anna of Denmark* (Bannatyne Club, Edinburgh, 1828), 27–9.
11. A. Gibson and T. C. Smout, 'Food and Hierarchy in Scotland, 1550–1650', in L. Leneman, ed. *Perspectives in Scottish Social History* (Aberdeen, 1988), 33–9.
12. *CSP Scot*, xi, 550. See also E. Ewan in this volume.
13. Cf. Riis, *Auld Acquaintance*, i, 274–7.
14. B. P. Lenman, 'Jacobean Goldsmith-Jewellers as Credit-Creators: the cases of James Mossman, James Cockie and George Heriot,' *SHR*, 74 (1995) 166, erroneously states that Heriot's career took off in 1597.

15. Scottish Record Office, [SRO], George Heriot's Trust, GD421/1/3/4.
16. *CSP Scot,* xi, 339, 342–4, 356–7. Other thefts occurred in 1607 and 1619, cf. *Criminal Trials in Scotland from* 1488 to 1624, ed. R. Pitcairn (3 vols, Edinburgh, 1833), ii, 544–57; Nichols, *Progresses,* iii, 548–9.
17. SRO, GD421/1/3/5.
18. SRO, GD421/1/3/6,7 & 22.
19. Nichols, *Progresses,* iii, 532.
20. W. Steven, *Memoir of George Heriot,* 3rd edn (Edinburgh 1872), 7.
21. SRO, GD421/1/3/2; *CSP Scot,* xi, 237; J. O. Halliwell, *Letters of the Kings of England* (London 1846), 96–97.
22. SRO, GD421/1/3/3.
23. *CSP Scot,* xi, 120, 343, 472, 537.
24. SRO, E35/14 fos 13v & 14v.
25. *CSP Scot,* xii, 90, 93, 112–13, 117; A. L. Murray, 'Sir John Skene and the Exchequer, 1594–1612', *Stair Society Miscellany I,* 26 (1971), 125–31.
26. Cf. *Basilikon Doron,* 42; J. Wormald, 'Basilikon Doron and The Trew Law of Free Monarchies', in L. L. Peck, ed. *The Mental World of the Jacobean Court* (Cambridge, 1991), 48–9. For the reference to politics cf. M. M. Meikle, 'A meddlesome princess: Anna of Denmark and Scottish Court politics, 1589–1603', in M. Lynch & J. Goodare, eds. *The Reign of James VI* (Tuckwell Press, forthcoming).
27. *CSP Scot,* xiii, 172, 189, 206, 215, 217, 261, 362–3.
28. Cf. Riis, *Auld Acquaintance,* i, 274–5.
29. Ibid.
30. *The Dictionary of National Biography,* (London, 1963–4), i, 435.

CHAPTER TEN

In Search of the Antecedents of Women's Political Activism in Early Eighteenth-Century Scotland: the Daughters of Anne, Duchess of Hamilton

Karl von den Steinen

IN EARLY 1716, Margaret, countess of Panmure, began what would become a seven-year political campaign to avert the consequences of her husband, James, fourth earl of Panmure's, active role in the failed Jacobite Rebellion of 1715. Margaret was one of many eighteenth-century Scotswomen who became politically active. The lives of those who did so suggest that the most important antecedent of such activity was the perceived political victimisation of their husbands. Such victimisation might come from other politicians or political groups and, if it could be traced to English roots, the political trauma became yet greater.

Margaret was the youngest of three sisters. The eldest, Katherine, first duchess of Atholl, became politically active at a particular point in her life and continued so until her death, but the middle sister, Susan, never became politically engaged. Their shared heritage included an excellent role model for women's political activism: their mother, Anne, duchess of Hamilton. Though she sometimes declined political engagement, Duchess Anne actively supported the political pre-eminence of Presbyterianism and intervened to favour members of her family.[1] All of her sons became politically active. That her daughters should also incline toward political engagement might be expected, yet two became active whilst one did not.

Nothing of their lives suggests significant differences in their backgrounds before marriage.[2] The evidence of their own correspondence shows all three to be clear of thought and action and firm of conviction. In the absence of striking differences in background, the key to Katherine's and Margaret's political activities, and to Susan's inactivity, lies in their experiences after they married.

The case of Katherine, the eldest, provides the clearest correlation between specific events and the onset of political engagement. Between her marriage to John Murray on 24 May 1683, and his appointment as a secretary of state for Scotland early in 1696, little of politics appeared in Katherine's correspondence.[3] Katherine's perception of her husband as the victim of political intrigue and her serious interest in politics began soon after his appointment.[4] As early as February 1696 she first recognised political double dealing with regard to her husband:

it would appear things had been done on purpose before you should have the opportunity to speak to his Majesty. I assure you some people here are not idle to improve things to their own designs and those who you would little think has spoke pretty openly.[5]

Her awareness of political intrigue expanded quickly, as Duchess Anne asked Katherine to burn her letters and assured that she did the same, a resolution fortunately broken.[6] Katherine soon received George Mac-Kenzie, viscount Tarbat, and 'found his errand was to pump me to know how soon you was to be back . . . but his Lordship went away as little wiser as when he came'. She urged her husband 'to keep your resolutions as quiet as you can . . .'[7]

Katherine's political concerns intensified in 1697 with the efforts of her husband, by then earl of Tullibardine, to gain the appointment of Sir William Hamilton of Whitelaw as president of the Court of Session. This appointment quickly became a trial of strength between Tullibardine and his rivals, Queensberry and Argyll.[8] With Tullibardine in London, Katherine became his principal source of political intelligence from Edinburgh. She warned that 'Q[ueensberry] and his party are mighty high insulting upon it', and encouraged him that, 'although you say if partys are contriving to put you out of court it will be no great mortification to you . . . I confess the more they were striving against me would not make me the easier part with it'. Later in the year, Katherine found the English parliament still ill humoured, and accurately predicted that 'for our African company you may expect no favour from thence'.[9] Her awareness of English interests as a source of trouble thus sharpened.

The events that most significantly politicised Katherine occurred in Edinburgh in August 1698. Tullibardine, with his brothers James and Edward, accosted the Laird of Balnagoun about his mis-statements on the sensitive subject of Simon Fraser of Beaufort, then on trial for his recent abduction, forced marriage and rape of Tullibardine's sister.[10] Tullibardine and his brothers invited Balnagoun into their nearby lodgings and allegedly beat him.[11] Although no evidence suggests that Tullibardine's enemies had deliberately provoked him, the incident provided a perfect opportunity to harass him. They were placed under house arrest and then released promising to keep the peace until the matter could be heard in November.[12]

Tullibardine's protests went unheard and they prompted Katherine, though pregnant, to her most vehement political correspondence to date. She urged her brothers to intercede and cautioned them against believing government versions of the story. Katherine urged her brother, James, by now Duke of Hamilton, to 'be not slow in showing yourself very active in this affair . . .'[13] This provoked from him the unusual initiative of writing to leading politicians to hinder false accounts. The conduct which Katherine's letters inspired in him even won him rare praise from their mother.[14] To her brother, Charles, earl of Selkirk, with direct access to the King, Katherine wrote, 'I expect dear brother you will not at this time be idle but lay out yourself to vindicate my Lord . . .' He accordingly reported the affair to the King, who responded that Tullibardine 'had no reason to expect favours from him but that he would examine the matter and that would do justice of everybody'.[15] Tullibardine's acquittal followed.[16]

Katherine recognised that the Balnagoun affair represented a new level of secular activity that distracted her from spiritual matters.[17] None of this lessened her anger at Tullibardine's enemies, particularly his former ally Marchmont. She reported that he 'has dealt most ungratefully with my Lord', and that 'Lord Argyll has now the sole management' of Marchmont, who 'says he will venture his neck and fortune to humble my Lord Tullibardine'. She remarked that 'E[arl] Argyll threatens nothing less than ruin to us all, but big words is to frighten children and fools'.[18]

Until 1702, with Tullibardine out of office, Katherine's political engagement subsided, although the strength of her opinions appeared occasionally. In February 1700, for example, she wrote of the failure of the Darien project:

> The hard treatment we meet with from the English is most unaccomptable . . . I am in such a passion at them that its best for me to say nothing for only I hope we shall yet live to see the day that they shall be made to repent their unworthy unneighbourly doings.[19]

The 1702 elections brought Katherine renewed political involvement and new experience of political betrayals. With Tullibardine in London, she worked for the election of his brother, Lord James Murray, for the burgh of Falkland. She discovered an opposition built around one Alexander Robeson, previously a staunch Tullibardine supporter. She quickly rallied Murray's supporters and told Tullibardine:

> You are downright betrayed. Nobody has been entrusted with it but those two knaves that ten hangings is too little for especially that Robeson every day brings out more and more of it, and it will be found he's betraying the town as well as you . . .[20]

She cautioned Tullibardine 'to set your heart off your brother's election . . .' yet consoled him that 'the discovery of this man is of more importance than you can understand at a distance, and it has discovered some others as well as him'.[21]

The 'Queensberry Plot' of 1703 again activated Katherine through the targeting of her husband. Queensberry had authorised the outlawed Simon Fraser to discover a Jacobite plot with the intention of implicating Katherine's husband, now lord privy seal and earl of Atholl. Forewarned, Atholl confronted Queensberry before Queen Anne and forestalled the attempt.[22] Katherine supported him throughout, gathering and forwarding intelligence about Fraser's activities in the Highlands, and warning Atholl of treachery in Scotland. She cautioned him to 'answer for no man breathing but yourself' and urged him to 'be wary to whom you speak or write . . .' Once again, political intrigue aimed at Atholl had engaged Katherine.[23]

The final occasion of Katherine's political activism involved the proposed Act of Union. As early as 23 April 1702, two days before giving birth to her twelfth child (of thirteen), Katherine wrote to Tullibardine that 'I cannot believe . . . that any English are serious for an union with Scotland on any honourable terms for us'.[24] Atholl's dismissal as privy seal in 1704 for his support of the Act of Security, which asserted Scotland's independent right to decide the succession, only served to increase Katherine's suspicions about English designs.[25] She even penned a verse against the Union, but Katherine died on the night of 9 January 1707 and therefore did not live to see the Union.[26]

The middle Hamilton daughter, Susan, experienced nothing comparable to the provocations that faced Katherine. Her first marriage, in November 1684, to Lord John Cochrane, later earl of Dundonald, invited nothing of political engagement. Although eligible to attend the 1689 session of the Convention Parliament, he did not do so. Dundonald's death in May 1690 left her a twenty-three year old widow with three children.[27]

Susan's widowhood left her in command of her children's education and health, and her own remarriage. When contemplating remarriage, she insisted on visiting her mother with her brother, Selkirk, because 'the more unity there is now in the family the better, for it has enemies enough to take advantage of the least appearance of discord . . .'[28] Susan finally accepted the proposal of Charles Hay, Lord Yester, late in 1697. Although some of her brothers preferred another suitor, her mother assured Yester's father that 'my daughter is at her own disposal . . .' She married Yester in December, but the marriage brought little political vulnerability.[29] Although his father had flirted with Tullibardine's opposition, Yester did nothing to provoke attack from the Government. In 1698, during the Balnagoun affair, Yester came briefly into disfavour, but Seafield

has writ plainly that the opposing of the King's designs in
Parliament was the reason, but this does not hold as to my Lord
Yester, for which there can be no reason given but his marrying
your Grace's sister, for he has done nothing in council or out of it
to deserve it . . .[30]

No evidence suggests that this provoked Susan into political engagement
comparable to Katherine's.

Susan's marriage to Yester shows only minimal political interest.
Neither the Act of Union nor even the '15 itself provoked significant
comment in her correspondence. A single appeal for her intervention on
behalf of her Jacobite brother-in-law, William, second baron Nairne,
evoked no action.[31] Susan's political passivity should not, however, be
seen as part of a general passivity. After Dundonald's death, she had
taken a firm hand in choosing her second husband in a manner similar to
other élite widows. Susan also resisted her brother Orkney's idea that her
young son, John, fourth marquis of Tweeddale, should marry Madame
von Kielmannsegge's daughter.[32] To prevent the marriage, she rushed to
London and successfully dissuaded him, and later cautioning 'that our sex
are sometimes very dangerous and ensnaring for we are not easily
known'.[33] The remaining years of Susan's life were not of a political
nature and she died, aged seventy, in February 1737.[34]

The political activity of Margaret, countess of Panmure, like Katherine's, involved provocation, and yielded the most extensive involvement
of the three sisters. Margaret's husband was a staunch Episcopalian
Jacobite educated in France. In 1686 he was the only Scottish privy
councillor to resist James VII and II about rescinding penal laws against
Roman Catholics. James dismissed him and this was the first instance of
his political victimisation, just after Margaret married him on 5 February
1687.[35]

The arrival of the Prince of Orange brought Panmure political difficulties from another direction. In January 1689 he journeyed to London
'to do all he could for the King's interest . . .' but William quickly placed
him under house arrest.[36] William soon released him to attend the
convention of estates in Scotland, where he unsuccessfully opposed
William's nominee for president of the convention. After an abortive
attempt to aid an armed rising against William, Panmure retired and
applied himself to his studies and estates in Angus. He placed himself in
the permanent role of political victim because 'he would never be
persuaded to take the oaths or comply in any manner or way with the
usurpers . . .'[37] His Jacobitism thus assured him even greater disadvantage than his Episcopalianism.

Margaret's own political involvement only began to emerge in 1697, when Panmure declined Tullibardine's offer of an appointment. She advised Katherine that she had told Panmure that 'I'm afraid he will not have such offers again . . .' and described him as 'a little too strict on the head . . .'[38] Margaret also first wrote of her resentment toward English obstruction of the Darien project:

> I think all Scots folks should stand up for it and certainly if they did the English would not be so well able to obstruct it, but it seems some thinks a bird in the hand is worth two flying. There are many that have not yet payed . . . but for the most part it is people that is in the government that has not yet payed . . .[39]

Panmure's commitment to the sinking Darien project continued through 1700, but little more of Margaret's views emerged save for regrets at its demise.[40]

Upon Queen Anne's accession, Margaret hoped that Hamilton, Tullibardine, and Tweeddale might be favoured, but 'I have some fears that fair words will be all they'll get . . .'[41] From then until the outbreak of the 1715 Rising little further evidence appears of Margaret's political involvement.[42] Even the attempted Franco-Jacobite invasion of 1708 offered no provocation to Margaret. The government remarkably omitted Panmure when it arrested suspected Jacobites, although he had received letters from James III and Louis XIV, and had met the Jacobite agent, Nathaniel Hook.[43]

The turning point for Margaret's political involvement, which would exceed even Katherine's, came with Panmure's participation in the '15. When Panmure was summoned to appear 'before the criminal court' as a suspected Jacobite, he joined the rising and proclaimed King James III at Brechin. He then raised a regiment of foot at his own expense, joined Mar, fought at Sheriffmuir, suffered severe wounds and capture, but escaped. Panmure was recuperating at Dundee when James III arrived in Scotland.[44]

Although Margaret later claimed that 'I can take God to witnesse to that I never gave my consent to his going out but did what I could to have prevented it but could not prevail with him', she did entertain James III.[45] When she later disputed charges of her own Jacobitism, she did slip that 'God knows I liked the cause'.[46] As the rising collapsed, Panmure accepted James III's advice and fled to France.[47] Mitigation of the consequences of Panmure's actions then fell to Margaret, who remained in Scotland.

Margaret recognised that the solutions to Panmure's problems would be political. To prevent his attainder, she wrote 'to all that I thought my letters would have any influence with . . .' including Hugh Campbell, earl of Loudoun, to whom she urged that Panmure 'has never broke any engagements to the Government having never taken any oaths since the Revolution'.[48] She noted that attainders sometimes secured jointures to the wives of the attainted, but her efforts for Panmure failed as he was among those attainted.[49]

With her husband's attainder, Margaret faced a triple challenge. She pursued the overlapping political goals of obtaining parliamentary legislation for the grant of her jointure, delaying the sale of Panmure's estates, and obtaining a remission for him. The jointure and the delay of the estate sale became entangled, as award of the jointure required settling outstanding accounts. Once settled, these would have the counterproductive effect of hastening the sale.

The most pressing problem lay with Margaret's jointure. If granted, it would secure her livelihood and allow her to contribute to Panmure's support.[50] She proposed to the earl of Stanhope, then secretary of state, that her name be included in an act of parliament that would grant jointures to the wives of leading Jacobites. He agreed to present her petition to the King, but this miscarried when Stanhope met Selkirk, Margaret's 'little too officious' brother, at court. He proposed to present the petition to the King, with Stanhope to support it afterwards.[51] Stanhope demurred, but Selkirk persuaded him to do it. The bill, however, 'was ordered to be ingrossed and your name not mentioned with that of the duchess of Ormonde, Lady Mar, and Bolingbroke'.[52] When Margaret learned of her brother's intervention, she became incensed, noting that Stanhope 'told me he did not doubt of obtaining my jointure for me' and attributing 'the misfortune of this to its having been taken from him'. Selkirk's attempts to defend his conduct only earned him the rebuke that 'I am told it is now evident that I and others have been remarkable ill used on account of being related to the family of Hamilton'.[53]

Margaret understood this failure to obtain her jointure as a further instance of English abuse of the Scots. She remarked that 'the husbands of those ladys that have met with so much favour are I think full as criminal as mine is and unless my being a North Britain is the cause I can find no other . . .'[54] Assurances of success in the next session of Parliament brought only the tart response that 'I suppose that is but an offput. It's now happy for a Scotsman to get an English wife. If so you had a better chance for a livelihood'.[55]

With the new session of parliament in 1717, Margaret renewed her campaign for her jointure. Upon the advice of her friends, she made the distasteful trip to London, wrote to her brother Orkney and to Cadogan, and met Stanhope to assure his continued support.[56] The first glimmer of hope came in June when she petitioned the House of Commons 'who has received it and has given orders for a bill to be brought in to enable the

King to grant the desire of my petition . . .' Her bill passed by 28 June and received royal assent on 15 July.[57]

Margaret's success with parliament gave her the opportunity to deal with a bureaucratic maze to try to obtain actual payment. She first met delays with the barons of the Scottish exchequer because its two English members were in London while the three Scots were in Edinburgh. They reported in January 1718, but the treasury did not deal with her jointure until April, and then only to refer it to the solicitor and attorney general to determine whether it should be for life, or during pleasure.[58] She soon appeared before Attorney General Nicholas Lechmere to advance her case. Another favourable report from the Scottish barons of the exchequer came in June. Yet another referral to the attorney general excluded from the settlement an additional £10,000 bond that Panmure had granted for Margaret's earlier success in clearing his debt.[59] She then faced another obstacle, as the commissioners for the forfeited estates declined to pay her until she accounted for the crops and rents of 1715.[60] Her struggle with the commissioners continued for weeks as they pressed her for accounts and bonds. By October 1720 the commissioners even demanded accounts for 1714, as Panmure had not settled them before his flight. She finally extracted a precept for payment of one year's jointure in November 1720, although it proved difficult to obtain because South Sea Company investments had drained Scotland of available funds.[61] Margaret herself was among the many Scots who lost through South Seas investments, of which she reported, 'it's said that almost as many are ruined by it as was by the Rebellion . . .'[62] She first received partial payment in January 1721. More followed in March 1721, July 1722 and August 1722, but the matter was still open just before Panmure died in April 1723.[63]

Margaret's efforts to protect Panmure's estates attest to her determination. From the outset, she realised the value of retaining physical possession of the estates because 'I believe my being here at this time has prevented some inconveniences that might have otherways happened . . .'[64] She obtained tacks of Panmure House and Brechin Castle from the lords of session, the commissioners for forfeited estates and the eventual purchaser of the estates, the York Building Society.[65] She failed, however, in her ultimate purpose of averting the sale of the estates. The commissioners, frustrated by the delaying tactics, finally sold the estates before the determination of all claims. The York Building Society purchased them on 9 October 1719 for £60,500: by far the largest of the attainted Jacobites' estates.[66]

Panmure's remission proved to be the most difficult task of all. The woman who succeeded with parliament about her jointure and who struggled so tenaciously to obtain its payment could not persuade her husband to meet the preconditions necessary for his remission. Margaret believed that if Panmure would guarantee his future conduct he might be remitted and allowed to returned to Scotland. She repeatedly begged him to promise his future good conduct so that she could pursue the matter.[67] In the end, Panmure praised her profusely as

> a virtuous discreet woman of good understanding, good nature, and a great humour, with whom he had lived very comfortably, there always having been great unanimity, concord, and love betwixt them . . .[68]

Although she begged him to give the guarantee, even pointing out that they were too old for him to do much anyway, 'unanimity, concord, and love' went just so far: he finally refused.[69] Her outspoken response to that refusal is the only one of her 147 surviving letters to him that does not bear the salutation, 'my dearest heart.' She wrote:

> I am both very much grieved and astonished to find that you are so nicely scrupulous as to resolve that you will not so much as give security for your peaceable behaviour in time coming in case your attainder is taken off . . . If you refuse this, don't complain of the government being severe for in reason they cannot be blamed . . .[70]

Margaret certainly deserved her anger toward Panmure's refusal. To this point she had been as diligent in the campaign to secure a parliamentary remission for him as she had been in the matter of her jointure. She had extended her unpleasant stays in London solely to pursue his remission.[71] She wrote to many leading politicians to persuade them to reverse the attainder.[72] Her disappointment at this refusal to guarantee his future conduct became even greater in 1719 during her visit to Panmure in Paris. She discovered that his relations with James III and his court had been embittered for some time, a theme upon which Panmure himself dwelt, but of which he had only hinted to Margaret.[73] Even after Panmure's refusal to co-operate, however, she doggedly pursued the remission until his death. Thereafter Margaret lived quietly until her death, aged fifty-five, in December 1731.[74]

Margaret's seven years of intense political effort, though limited in success, exceeded that of her sisters. Like Katherine, she had witnessed what she perceived as her husband's political victimisation and, although she only became politically active in 1715, she remained so until his death. Favours granted to the English wives of Scottish Jacobites periodically reinforced her sense of victimisation. This perception of victimisation, particularly of the husband, and particularly if English inspired, stands as the most evident distinction between Katherine and Margaret, who became politically engaged, and Susan, who did not.

NOTES

1. Blair Castle, Duke of Atholl MSS [Blair MS], 29.I.(8).60.
2. R. K. Marshall, *The Days of Duchess Anne* (London, 1973), 146–7.
3. Blair MS 29.I.(3).96; 29.I.(7).17 & 31; National Library of Scotland [NLS], Correspondence of Anne, Duchess of Hamilton, MS1031, fo 195; Scottish Record Office [SRO], Hamilton Muniments, GD406/1/7354.
4. Blair MS 29.I.(8).60.
5. Ibid.
6. Blair MS 29.I.(8).95.
7. Ibid, 29.I.(8).110.
8. P. W. J. Riley, *King William and the Scottish Politicians* (Edinburgh, 1979), 119–23.
9. Blair MS 29.I.(9).4 & 505.
10. Ibid, 29.I.(10).213 and 44.VI.(465).274.
11. Ibid, Bundle 1720.
12. SRO, GD406/2/4252; GD406/1/6642.
13. SRO, GD406/1/6721.
14. Blair MS 29.I,.(109);29.I.(10).205; SRO, GD406/1/6792 & 6793.
15. Blair MS Bundle 1720; SRO, GD406/1/6760, 6766 & 6722.
16. SRO, GD406/1/6442, 6672 & 8093.
17. Blair MS Bundle 1625.
18. Ibid, 29.I.(10).208; SRO, GD406/1/6675.
19. SRO, Dalguise Muniments, GD38/2/2.
20. Blair MS 45.(2).186, 193, 195 & 203.
21. Ibid, 45.(2).207.
22. Ibid, 45.(3).164.
23. Ibid, 45.(3).169, 172, 173, 176 & 179.
24. Ibid, 45.(2).114.
25. SRO, GD406/1/7971.
26. Blair MS 45.(6).133.
27. SRO, GD406/1/8384 & 9226; Riley, *King William, 166.*
28. NLS MS 1031, fos 199–200.
29. Blair MS 28.I.(9).452; NLS, Yester Papers, MS 14414, fo 103; SRO, GD406/1/6291, 6336, 6411, 6429, 6428, 6430 & 7568.
30. SRO, GD406/1/6672.
31. NLS, Yester Papers, 14419, fo 202.
32. Blair MS 45.(14).5; NLS, Yester Papers, MS 14420, fos 11, 15, 16–17; SRO, Dalhousie Muniments, GD45/14/220/54.
33. Blair MS 46.(I).5; NLS, Yester Papers, MS 14420, fos 16–18, 20, 234–6.
34. Blair MS 45.A.JAC.C.I.(6).28, 46.(I).5; NLS MS 14420, fos 234–6.
35. NLS, MS17804 Panmure Autobiography, hereafter cited as Panmure AB, fos 2 & 3; SRO, GD406/1/6164.
36. NLS, Panmure AB, fo 4.
37. Ibid, fo 5.
38. Blair MS 44.VI.(172).258.
39. Ibid, 29.I.(9).452.

40. SRO, GD406/1/7908.
41. Blair MS 45.(2).263.
42. Ibid, 45.(4).169; SRO, GD45/14/245/8, GD406/1/5341.
43. NLS, Panmure AB, fos 6–7; J. S. Gibson, *Playing the Scottish Card: The Franco-Jacobite Invasion of 1708* (Edinburgh, 1988), 97; H. Maule, *Registrum de Panmure* (Edinburgh, 1874), ii, 346.
44. NLS, Panmure AB, fos 8, 9–17, 18.
45. Royal Archives [RA], Windsor, Stuart Papers, 6/5; SRO, GD45/14/276.
46. Huntington Library [HL], LO 12232; SRO, GD45/14/276.
47. NLS, Panmure AB, fos 19–21.
48. HL, LO12232; SRO, GD45/14/251, GD124/15/1159.
49. SRO, GD45/13/260 & 14/276; G. E. Cokayne, *The Complete Peerage* (London, 1929), i, app. E, 476.
50. SRO, GD45/14/220/7.
51. SRO, GD45/14/276, 14/220/8 & 41/278.
52. SRO, GD45/14/278.
53. SRO, GD45/14/261/2, 264 & 278.
54. SRO, GD45/14/276 & 278.
55. SRO, GD45/14/220/12, 30 & 60.
56. SRO, Clerk of Penicuik Collection, GD18/5246/5/42, GD45/14/220/27 & 31, 14/276.
57. NLS, Panmure AB, fo 280; SRO, GD45/14/220/34, 35 &˒37.
58. SRO, GD45/14/220/41, 50 &56.
59. NLS, Panmure AB, fo 8; SRO, GD45/14/220/64/4, 14/220/68/1, 17/944, 220/57, 276, GD124/15/1182/2.
60. SRO, GD45/14/220/83.
61. SRO, GD45/14/220/112, 114 & 116.
62. SRO, GD45/14/220/110 & 112.
63. SRO, GD45/14/220/117, 118, 121, 140, 142 & 146.
64. SRO, GD45/14/220/3 & 9, 14/276.
65. NLS, Panmure AB, fos 280, 282; SRO, GD45/14/220/131.
66. RA, Stuart Papers, SP47/149; SRO, GD45/12/292, 14/220/98.
67. SRO, GD45/14/220/23, 25 & 31.
68. NLS, Panmure AB, fo 280.
69. NLS, Panmure AB, fo 280; SRO, GD45/14/220/31, 32, & 38/1 & 2, 62.
70. SRO, GD45/14/220/73, 74 & 75.
71. SRO, GD45/14/220/43, 58, & 68.
72. SRO, GD45/14/220/46 & 58, 14/276.
73. NLS, Panmure AB, fos 24–41, 280–285; SRO, GD45/14/220/42,53 & 82, 14/291 & 297.
74. SRO, GD45/14/220/88, 89, 91, 93, 116, 123, 124, 125, 127, 128, 129, 139, 144, 145, 147.

PART FOUR

'brew upon their own adventure'

'For Whatever Ales Ye': Women as Consumers and Producers in Late Medieval Scottish Towns[1]

_____ *Elizabeth Ewan*

UNTIL RECENTLY, most work on the economy of medieval Scottish towns has tended to focus on overseas trade, rather than the local economy. However, some recent studies, with their detailed examinations of goods and prices, have provided the basis for new assessments of the local economy.[2] This chapter uses late medieval town court records to look at the role of women in this economy, focusing specifically on brewing.[3] It will argue that to a large extent women's role on the production side of the economy – manufacturing and retailing – grew out of their role as consumers, purchasers of goods for the household.

Brewing can reveal much about women's roles in the medieval urban economy.[4] Unlike most crafts, it could be carried on intermittently. Ale was perishable and time-consuming to produce. The most efficient way to ensure an adequate supply was for households to produce it in rotation, purchasing more raw material than needed for domestic use and selling the surplus, then buying ale between brewings.[5] The provision of ale thus involved women in consumption, production and retailing.

Because regulations for brewing and selling ale are very prominent in town legislation, there is more surviving evidence about brewing than most urban crafts. In the thirteenth-century gild laws of Berwick, almost twenty-five per cent of the laws on trading or marketing were concerned with brewing. Most laws assumed the brewers were female; they refer to brewsters (female brewers) or to women who brew.[6] Examining the brewing industry is one way to get a glimpse into the lives of medieval townswomen.

Because ale was such an important part of the Scottish diet, towns gave priority to ensuring an adequate supply for their citizens. Most urban families relied on purchasing the necessities of life, rather than trying to supply them all themselves. Buying such goods was thus an integral part of women's domestic role.[7]

Around 1500, the poet William Dunbar complained about the noise and raucousness of Edinburgh market-women. Court cases illustrate market disputes between sellers and buyers and between customers; many of those involved were women. They could be discriminating buyers. A Dunfermline woman irritated a fishseller by picking over his fish and then refusing to buy.[8] Such cases show marketing was an important part of women's household duties. The laws officially prohibited married women from buying anything with their husband's money, but an exception was made for necessary purchases, goods for the household.[9] Marketing was a common activity for medieval women and gave them useful skills should they wish or be forced to enter the world of retailing.[10]

As consumers, women benefited from local regulations designed to ensure a steady supply of necessary foodstuffs to townspeople at reasonable prices. Town councils regularly declared the assize of bread and ale, the prices at which they were to be sold. The Aberdeen town records record the assize every four or five weeks.[11] Penalties for offenders were high. The offender could have her brewing vessels taken and the bottom struck out, and be forbidden from brewing for a year and a day.[12] In England, fines for brewing were imposed so regularly that historians have argued that they were in reality a tax on the trade. However, as Nicholas Mayhew has pointed out in his study of Aberdeen brewing, in Scotland the penalty of being stopped from brewing, and even having one's cauldron destroyed, as well as the fact that fines could be suspended during good behaviour, suggests that these were real fines and not taxes.[13]

Consumers were protected as far as possible from faulty products. Town-appointed ale tasters supervised quality and price.[14] Another concern was false weights and measures. Everyone was to use local measures, which were checked and marked. In Dundee in 1521 two women were convicted of using false peck measures. The council warned that anyone else doing the same would be banished from the town. Jonet Howlat was banished for the crime in 1523.[15]

One concern of town governments was that all consumers had an equal chance to buy; the motivation was partly self-interest for they were themselves consumers, and partly a wish to preserve social harmony. Rules were intended to protect the local market's integrity in the interests of both consumers and vendors. On market days, all commodities were to be brought to the market and certain goods such as wheat, bread, barley, malt and ale were to be sold at specified prices. Goods were to be displayed openly so that all had an equal chance to buy, with those purchasing household supplies being given the chance to buy before processors or those who bought to resell later. No-one was to purchase goods before they came to the market.[16] As far as possible, towns attempted to cut out the middleman or woman between the producer and the consumer in the local economy, although ironically that very role was the basis of the fortune of many overseas traders.

The urban regulations prescribed an ideal, one not always met, judging both by the number of times the laws were promulgated and the numbers of people prosecuted for breaking them. Many consumers bought illegally. Vendors brought goods to the town secretly or produced them in town and sold them privately from house to house, either at a cheaper rate to undercut competitors who paid market tolls, or more expensively at times of shortage.[17] Townsfolk forestalled the market, buying up goods outside the town and then reselling them. Such vendors might only sell to favoured customers, instead of to all. In Dundee in 1523 Jonkyn Inch's wife was accused of only selling ale to those she chose, while in 1521 Janet Howlk was accused of buying barley in great quantity before it came to market and keeping it in her house to sell, along with eggs, butter, poultry and cheese.[18] This practice was severely punished by town councils who attempted to ensure that all goods from outside the burgh came to the market cross where, in theory at least, all had an equal chance to buy. Janet was warned that if she was caught again she would be banished from the town. Brewsters sold ale privately to neighbours, without quality checks and in unofficial measures. Prosecutions show that women were heavily involved in this underground commerce, as buyers and sellers.

How did women pay for their purchases? Credit was an essential part of marketing. Debt cases suggest that deferred payment, sometimes with goods pledged as security, was often used for small purchases. Barter might also be used.[19] Credit could be given by buyer or seller. In 1470 an Aberdeen man charged Alexander Turbe and his wife with not delivering the twenty-one bolls of wheat that he had bought from them.[20] Pledges were often common household goods which women had readily available.

Although many countries officially barred married women from making contracts, court records show this did not prevent them in practice. Studies have suggested that women were involved in ten to fifteen per cent of credit transactions appearing in the courts.[21] The cases represent only the tip of credit transactions, successful ones generally leaving no trace. Many small debts did not come to court, either because the sum was not worth the expenses to pursue, or because they were verbally contracted, and difficult to prove. As women tended to be predominantly involved in such small loans, their participation in credit is even less well-represented in court records than men's.[22]

A large number of women's credit transactions involve contracts for goods for household consumption. A Scottish law stated that brewsters and bakers had to be willing to sell on credit, although if a customer defaulted they could refuse to extend credit to that person again. There are several instances of credit being extended for the purchase or sale of malt – in Dundee in the 1520s about twenty-five per cent of women's recorded credit transactions involved malt.[23] Most of the debts were for irregular amounts rather than rounded sums, implying that they were payments for exact costs, not loans.[24]

These transactions show the close relationship between consumption for household use and production for sale. Most of the recorded purchases were large enough for there to have been a surplus for sale outside the household. Such purchases could be used in two ways. Items such as malt or flour could be processed for household use and any excess sold. Finished products could be bought in greater quantity than the household required and sold again in smaller quantities to those who could not afford to buy wholesale in the market. Women followed both practices with ale.

Women could purchase drink supplies for their families in one of three forms, barley to be malted and ground, malt to be brewed, or ale. Most recorded purchases by women are for malt or ale, and it seems likely that most women alternated between buying malt and ale, although some also had the facilities and time to process barley. Some town properties had brewhouses and kilns to produce malt. A kiln in Edinburgh had a steipstane used in the malting process and a well to provide the necessary water.[25] Perth excavations have revealed drying kilns that could be used in the malting process to end the germination of the barley, while carbonised grains of barley, accidentally burned in the drying process, have been found on several urban sites.[26] Separate ordinances for maltmakers and brewsters suggest the two activities were separate by the fifteenth century. Malting was time-consuming and required space and drying kilns; it was perhaps carried out more effectively on a professional basis. The sixteenth-century Perth maltmakers were organised as a separate craft, although not formally incorporated. Maltmaking fit the patterns of women's work less well than brewing, and it appears that, although there were women maltsters, the industry was dominated by men.[27]

Brewing was a skill expected of all adult medieval women. Brewing equipment was part of the possessions of most urban households. Inheritance laws ordered burgesses to pass on to their heirs a lade and mashing vat, a wort vat, cauldrons and kettles. Records of inheritance goods often included brewing implements. In Dunfermline in 1506 the goods included several large vessels for holding ale, a masking vat, and a measure.[28]

Brewing was ideally suited to women's work patterns which tended to be temporary, short-term and fitted around other household responsibilities. Unlike men who generally followed one craft for life, women had to be adaptable, changing occupations with their marital status, the occupation of father or husband, and differing family responsibilities through the life-cycle.[29] Medieval legislation recognised this by officially allowing women to follow several occupations while attempting, without great success, to restrict men to one. Scottish gild ordinances restricted the pursuits of their members, but wives were allowed to carry on secondary occupations – many craftsmen's wives appear as brewsters. One law ordered craft families making ale to use a different lade to brew in than they used for their crafts – as this was addressed to dyers, shoemakers, and butchers, one can understand the authorities' concern.[30]

Studies elsewhere have shown that up to half of a community's families could be involved in producing ale for sale at some point in their life course. Although we lack population figures for Scottish towns which would enable us to quantify this, the lists of brewsters that appear for Edinburgh and Aberdeen suggests that brewing was very common among urban families. In Aberdeen eighty-eight women were amerced in 1472, over 150 in 1509; in Edinburgh 110 brewsters were amerced in 1499.[31]

Studies of English brewers suggest most brewed only intermittently; the Scottish evidence seems to fit this pattern. Early laws distinguished among those who brewed three times a year or less, half a year and all year.[32] Many brewsters engaged in other remunerative activities as well. Some baked bannocks of barley or oats which competed with the baxters' wheat loaves – in Aberdeen women appeared before the courts for this almost as often as for brewing. The occupations which women undertook varied between towns. In Peebles, the authorities assumed most bakers were women, while in Aberdeen and Edinburgh baking was largely practised by men.[33] Some women undertook a variety of activities to raise income, not all of them legal. In 1468 Ellen Bessat of Aberdeen was charged with being not only a brewster and a cake baker, but also a seller of second-hand shoes and a receiver of stolen goods.[34]

Most women brewed their own ale and then sold it, but there were also other arrangements. In Dundee in 1521 John Robertson and his wife agreed to brew ale for Will Lawson for a year, he providing the malt, and giving them a boll of malt in payment. Will may have been a maltster – later he pursued a woman for a debt of twenty-two shillings that she owed him for malt.[35]

Which women brewed? Married women usually dominate the lists – seventy-eight out of eighty-eight were wives in Aberdeen in 1472, eighteen out of twenty-nine in Dundee during the early 1520s.[36] The exception is Dunfermline where in 1490–1521 thirty-five women of single or unclear status appear as opposed to eight married women. Men may have been answering for their wives as David Fawsid did in 1491. In 1493 eleven brewsters were amerced, seven men and four women; the women were all single, suggesting that wives were answering under their husband's name.[37] Because brewing was a household activity which involved several members of the household, it was most easily carried out if a woman had the support of a household.

Although most women sold ale intermittently and mainly to supplement the household income, brewing could be profitable enough to be a full-time profession. In 1530 the Edinburgh council commented in disgust that it seemed as though every servant woman who could save five or six merks (about £2) set up on her own as a brewster or huckster selling ale. Even if she could not afford her own brewing equipment, she could hire it, a practice the council tried to prohibit. The authorities preferred brewing to be done by wives who combined it with their other duties; the idea of independent women was anathema to the officials. If women brewed, they should do so within a household. Servants could 'brew upon their own adventure', giving part of the ale to the mistress, but later the council ordered all suspicious women living alone to leave the town and restricted brewing and selling ale to freemen, their wives and widows, unless the brewster had a special licence. In 1546 the council insisted brewsters be married women or widows.[38]

Despite the authorities' preferences, women from all parts of burgh society brewed for sale.[39] The authorities in fact allowed for this by permitting women who did not fit into the stipulated categories to apply for licences. Another way to allow such women to participate was to sell them stallanger licenses which permitted them to set up a stall and sell in the market without being burgesses.[40] Some women could not even afford the stallanger fee. Edinburgh town council had to stress that its prohibitions against people trading unless they were burgesses or stallangers referred to all traders including brewsters. Brewsters had to be 'honest and substancious persons' and licensed to brew,[41] otherwise they could be banished.

Periodic attempts were made by town governments to restrict brewing to the upper reaches of urban society. In Edinburgh in the early sixteenth century it was restricted to burgess families. Aberdeen adopted a two-price policy restricting the brewing of the most expensive ale to gild brethren in 1442.[42] As with similar restrictive ordinances elsewhere, however, these seem to have been short-term responses to particular situations, and were likely ignored by many. In Edinburgh in 1530, 314 brewsters swore to keep the statutes on the price of ale. Over one-tenth of the women broke the statutes again the following year. The council also banned the selling of ale from Leith,[43] implying that many of the women were retailers rather than brewers. Perhaps one of the reasons that brewing suited women was that it was difficult to supervise, making it easy to evade regulations, especially if it was not clear whether the brewing was for domestic use or sale.

Through their experience as consumers, women learned marketing skills – the best places to sell, seasonal fluctuations in supply and demand, who were trustworthy suppliers. Knowledge of local families' needs, useful

1. The Prioress Anna of the nunnery at Iona as depicted on her tombstone. From H.D. Graham, *Antiquities of Iona* (1850).

2. Eleanor, fourth daughter of James I. Original in the Kunsthistorisches Museum, Vienna.

3. Margery Bowes or Margaret Stewart, wife of John Knox. Scottish National Portrait Gallery.

4. Dame Jean or Jonet Scott, Lady Ferniehirst, shown as a widow in 1593. In the collection of the Duke of Buccleuch and Queensberry KT.

5. Anna of Denmark, consort of James VI and I. Scottish National
Portrait Gallery.

6. The family of Sir William Dick of Braid. In a private Scottish collection.

7. Washerwomen of Dundee, as depicted by John Slezer in 1678.
From his *Theatrum Scotiae*. University of Guelph Library, Special
Collections.

8A. Esther Inglis, calligrapher, printer and embroiderer of book-bindings. From *Proceedings of the Society of Antiquaries of Scotland*, December 1865.

8B. Title pages of Bibles printed by Agnes Campbell in 1707. From Dr. John Lee, *Memorial for the Bible Societies in Scotland* (1824).

for selling door-to-door, came from friendship networks, developed in common tasks such as fetching water or helping with childcare and marketing, and conversations with neighbours.[44] Such skills were integral to women's urban life. Ale suited this type of distribution – because it soured quickly, there was little incentive to buy it in large quantities at the market. It was a commodity in demand among visitors to the burgh who might consume it on the street or in an alehouse, rather than carry it home.[45] It was also in demand at public building projects. In Dunfermline three women were paid for providing ale for workers on the town ports.[46]

Retailers included brewsters selling their own product. Burgh laws stipulated that, when they had ale ready, they must erect an ale-stake to indicate they had ale for sale and summon the ale-taster to check its quality and declare the price.[47] However, because ale was sold throughout the town, not only in the market, prices were hard to enforce. More women were charged with breaking the assise of ale than any other crime.

Tapsters bought ale and sold it in small measures, in the street or door to door. Some were hired by brewsters.[48] Retailing of foodstuffs was a common activity for women. In Dunfermline in 1490 four women were amerced as 'dry tapsters', sellers of small measures of ale.[49] Hucksters were disliked by authorities who saw them profiting from a commodity without adding any value to it. Most towns passed statutes to ensure that hucksters could only buy goods after the burgesses had first chance to buy at the market, or that they were licensed by the town.[50] They were tolerated for performing a necessary function by providing necessities for the poor who could not afford to buy in large quantities at the market or from brewsters who usually sold their ale in gallon measures. Huckstering also provided an income for those who otherwise had to rely on charity.[51] They helped dispose of poor quality produce which might have been wasted. Huckstering was closely related to women's role as consumers.

Some women ran alehouses. As well as serving customers in the alehouse, the owners provided drink to townspeople who brought their own measures and carried it home.[52] This latter activity avoided some of the hazards caused by drunken customers. A Dunfermline woman ejected such a customer from her house and locked the door on him. However, he had already paid for his drink and sued her for his money.[53]

In England, brewing in the sixteenth century became increasingly dominated by men.[54] Unlike many crafts, the brewsters never formed a gild, although on occasion they were recognised as having a collective identity. In 1527 the Aberdeen council ordered the bakers, brewsters and fleshers to decorate the burgh for a royal visit, each one for their own craft.[55] For other crafts, recognition of a craft identity led to incorporation as a guild. This did not happen with ale-brewing, perhaps because the activity was dominated by women [56] (although a few women were

members of the London guild of brewers).[57] Women, barred from
political office, could not lead their own craft.

From 1508 Edinburgh leased out its common lands for large-scale
malting operations,[58] making possible a larger, more capital-intensive
brewing industry. The late medieval introduction to Scotland of beer that
lasted longer and did not need to be produced as frequently, made it less
suitable for those who only wished to participate occasionally on a small
scale. It required the purchase of expensive hops, imported from overseas,
putting it beyond the financial means of small-time brewers and breaking
the link between consumption and production. As with many crafts, the
move towards professional organisation helped lead to the increasing
exclusion of women, at least at the more profitable levels of the occupation.[59] It has been argued that the professionalisation of the Edinburgh
beer-brewing industry, marked by the establishment of the Society of
Brewers in 1596, 'probably did more than any single other act to
undermine the economic status of women, whether as wives or widows.'[60] However, as Mayhew argues, there is no evidence that women's
involvement in ale-brewing declined as a result.[61]

Although ale-brewing was crucial to the town's well-being, it did not
confer high status on those involved. Partly this was due to a traditional
dislike of food purveyors; because of their dependence on them, customers suspected them of dishonest practices and price-gouging.[62] Officials
suspected their honesty. Ale-tasters were to taste ale outside the brewster's home, not after they had 'filled their bellies' drinking inside the
house.[63] Since ale could impair the judgement, it was easy to suspect the
worst of the seller. But the status of brewing probably suffered most from
the fact that most brewsters only engaged in the occupation part-time and
informally in a time of growing organisation and professionalisation of
urban industry. Brewing was a secondary occupation which grew out of
women's primary role as providers of food and drink for their families. In
the urban world, this meant that their role as producers was closely linked
to their role as consumers.

NOTES

1. I would like to thank the Social Sciences and Humanities Research Council
   of Canada for financial support for this research. My thanks also to Pat
   Dennison, Judith Bennett, Helen Dingwall, and especially Nicholas Mayhew
   for their valuable discussion about various points of medieval brewing.
2. E. Gemmill and N. Mayhew, *Changing Values in Medieval Scotland. A
   study of prices, money, and weights and measures* (Cambridge, 1995); A. J.
   S. Gibson and T. C. Smout, *Prices, Food and Wages in Scotland 1550–1780*
   (Cambridge, 1995). See also E. Sanderson, *Women and Work in Eighteenth-*

century *Edinburgh* (Basingstoke, 1996) and Helen Dingwall, Gordon Des-Brisay and Alastair Mann's papers in this volume.

3. *Early Records of the Burgh of Aberdeen, 1317, 1398–1407* ed. W. C. Dickinson (Scottish History Society, 1957) [*Aber.Recs.*]; *Extracts from the Council Register of the Burgh of Aberdeen* (Spalding Club, 1844–8) [*Aber. Extracts*]; Aberdeen City Archives, Council Registers [ACR]; Dundee Archives, Book of the Church [DBC]; *The Burgh Records of Dunfermline* ed. E. Beveridge (Edinburgh, 1917) [*Dunf.Recs.*]; *Extracts from the Records of the Burgh of Edinburgh* (Scottish Burgh Records Society, 1869–92) [*Edin. Recs.*]; *Charters and Documents Relating to the Burgh of Peebles* (Scottish Burgh Records Society, 1872) [*Peebles Chrs.*]; *Extracts from the Records of the Royal Burgh of Stirling* ed. R. Renwick (Glasgow, 1887–9) [*Stirling Recs.*]; Central Region Archives, B66/15/1, Stirling Council Minutes [SCM].

4. N. Mayhew 'The Status of Women and the Brewing of Ale in Medieval Aberdeen', *Review of Scottish Culture*, 10 (1996–7). For England see Judith Bennett, *Ale, Beer, and Brewsters in England. Women's Work in a Changing World, 1300–1600* (Oxford, 1996) and 'The Village Ale-Wife: Women and Brewing in Fourteenth-century England' in B. Hanawalt, ed. *Women and Work in Preindustrial Europe* (Bloomington, 1986); H. Graham, '"A woman's work": Labour and Gender in the Late Medieval Countryside' in P. J. P. Goldberg ed. *Woman is a Worthy Wight. Women in English Society c.1200–1500* (Stroud, 1992); M. Kowaleski, 'Women's Work in a Market Town: Exeter in the Late Fourteenth Century' in Hanawalt ed. *Women and Work*; Jane Laughton, 'The Alewives of Later Medieval Chester' in R. Archer ed. *Crown, Government and People in the Fifteenth Century* (New York, 1995).

5. Bennett, *Ale, Beer and Brewsters*, 17–18.

6. *Statuta Gilde* in *Ancient Laws and Customs of the Burghs of Scotland 1124–1424* (Scottish Burgh Records Society, 1868). Also *Leges Burgorum*, in ibid c.63 'what woman will brew', c.67 'all brewsters who sell ale'.

7. *Edin.Recs.*, i, 143. A. Gibson and T. C. Smout, 'Scottish Food and Scottish History, 1500–1800' in R. Houston and I. Whyte, eds. *Scottish Society 1500–1800* (Cambridge, 1988), 60.

8. *William Dunbar: Selected Poems*, ed. P. Bawcutt (Harlow, 1996), no. 42; *Dunf.Recs.*, 134; *Aber.Recs.*, 43.

9. *Leges Burgorum*, c.118.

10. M. Wiesner Wood, 'Paltry Peddlers or Essential Merchants? Women in the Distributive Trades in Early Modern Nuremberg' *The Sixteenth Century Journal*, 12 (1981), 7; Laughton, 'Chester Alewives', 199–200.

11. *Aber.Recs.*, 39, 41, 46, 53–4. See also *Dunf.Recs.*, 19, 46, 101; *Edin.Recs.*, i, 12, 62, 75; *Peebles Chrs.*, 128, 147, 166; SCM, fos 2v, 7v, 13r.

12. *Edin.Recs.*, i, 12; *Dunf.Recs.*, 102; *Stirling Recs.*, 12.

13. Mayhew, 'Status of Women', 18. For England, see, for example, Bennett, *Ale, Beer and Brewsters*, 4, 100, 161–3.

14. *Articuli Inquirendi* in *Ancient Burgh Laws*, c.21; *Peebles Chrs.*, 111; *Juramenta Officiariorum* in *Ancient Burgh Laws*.

15. DBC, fos 48v,156v. *Dunf.Recs.*, 154. Also see *Edin.Recs.*, i, 118, 133, 232. See also the illustration of washer women near Dundee in this volume.

16. *Ancient Laws* passim; E. Ewan, *Townlife in Fourteenth-Century Scotland* (Edinburgh, 1990), 65–7. For England, see C. Dyer, *Standards of Living in the Later Middle Ages* (Cambridge, 1989), 198–9.
17. *Edin.Recs.*, i, 53; *Dunf.Recs.*, 129; DBC, fos 143v, 150v.
18. DBC, fos 124v,45v.
19. DBC, fo 57v. *Edin Recs.*,i,13; J. Kermode, 'Money and Credit in the Fifteenth Century: Some Lessons from Yorkshire' *Business History Review*, 65 (1991), 480; Bennett, *Ale, Beer and Brewsters*, 53–4.
20. ACR, vi, fo 100.
21. W. C. Jordan, *Women and Credit in Pre-Industrial and Developing Countries* (Philadelphia, 1993) 17–20; DBC, fo 17v; *Dunf.Recs.*, 124; SCM, fo 19r.
22. Jordan, *Women and Credit*, 18; Kermode, 'Money and Credit', 486, n.35.
23. *Fragmenta Collecta* c.1 in *Ancient Burgh Laws*; DBC, passim.
24. Kermode, 'Money and Credit', 485.
25. *Protocol Book of James Young 1485–1515*, eds. H. M. Paton and G. Donaldson (Edinburgh, 1941) nos 150, 445, 1505, 1741. See also *Dunf. Recs.*, 156; *Stirling Recs.*, 40; 'Protocol Book of John Darow' (forthcoming), nos 306, 443; *Leges Burgorum*, c.50. My thanks to Alan Borthwick for allowing me to consult the typescript of the Darow Protocol Book.
26. Ewan, *Townlife*, 31–2.
27. *Iter Camerarii* in *Ancient Burgh Laws*, c.26; I. Donnachie, *A History of the Brewing Industry in Scotland* (Edinburgh, 1979), 50; M. Verschuur, 'Merchants and Craftsmen in Sixteenth-century Perth' in M. Lynch ed. *The Early Modern Town in Scotland* (Wolfeboro, 1987), 38; DBC, fos 72v,83v; ACR, i, fo 406; *Dunf. Recs.*,29; N. Mayhew, 'The Brewsters of Aberdeen in 1509' *Northern Studies*, 32 (1997), 78.
28. *Leges Burgorum*,c.56 ; ACR,v/1, fo 2; *Dunf.Recs.*, 163. See also *Dunf.Recs.*, 209; *Peebles Chrs.*,119.
29. E. Ewan, 'Mons Meg and Merchant Meg: Women in Edinburgh in the Later Middle Ages'in T. Brotherstone and D. Ditchburn eds. *Freedom and Authority: Scotland c.1050–c.1650* (East Linton, forthcoming); Kowaleski, 'Exeter', 155–8; K. Honeyman and J. Goodman, 'Women's work, gender conflict, and labour markets in Europe 1500–1900' *Economic History Review*, 2s, 44 (1991), 610.
30. ACR,vi, fos 167–8; *Leges Burgorum*, c.94. Honeyman and Goodman, 'Women's work', 612.
31. ACR,vi, fo 27; R. Houston, 'Women in the economy and society of Scotland, 1500–1800' in *Scottish Society*, 122; *Edin. Recs.*, i, 75. For England, see Kowaleski, 'Exeter', 148; Bennett, *Ale, Beer and Brewsters*, 18–19,41.
32. *Leges Burgorum*, c.36; *Fragmenta Collecta*, c.41.
33. *Peebles Chrs.*, 147, 150; *Aber.Extracts*, 9; *Edin.Recs.*, i, 14.
34. ACR, vi, fo 36.
35. DBC, fos 51v, 56v.
36. ACR, vi, fo 27; DBC, passim; Mayhew, 'Brewsters of Aberdeen', 71–7. For England, see Bennett, *Ale, Beer and Brewsters*, 182–6.
37. *Dunf.Recs.*, 29, 41. Mayhew, 'Status of Women', 17, n.7; Graham, 'A woman's work', 136–44; Bennett, *Ale, Beer and Brewsters*, 163–70.

38. *Edin.Recs.*, ii, 27, 24–5, 40, 124. Cf. a Chester servant, Laughton, 'Chester Ale-wives', 198,204. For the move towards professional married brewsters in England after 1350, see Bennett, *Ale, Beer and Brewsters*, 43–59.
39. ACR, vi, fos 27, 82, 105, 117.
40. *Edin.Recs.*, ii,8; *Dunf.Recs.*, 66; ACR, i, fo 410; *Edin.Recs.*, i, 36, 40; *Peebles Chrs.*, 214.
41. *Edin.Recs.*, i, 40–1, 65, ii, 8.
42. M. Lynch, 'Continuity and change in urban society, 1500–1700' in *Scottish Society*, 108–9; *Aber.Extracts*, 42.
43. *Edin.Recs.*, i, 17, ii, 19, 20, 24–6, 44, 45–6, 51. These lists, which appear in full in the Edinburgh City Archives, will be more fully analysed elsewhere.
44. Wiesner Wood, 'Paltry Peddlers', 7, 10.
45. P. Clark, *The English Alehouse. A Social History 1200–1830* (Harlow, 1983), 22.
46. *Dunf.Recs.*, 98. See also *Peebles Chrs.*, 215.
47. *Iter Camerarii*, cc 6, 10; ACR, vii, fo 1066.
48. Central Region Archives, B66/15/1, fo 26r. In England, they were called 'tipplers', Bennett, *Ale, Beer and Brewsters*, 45–6.
49. *Dunf.Recs.*, 23.
50. ACR,v/2, fo 757; *Aber.Extracts*, 16; *Peebles Chrs.*, 166; *Edin.Recs.*, ii, 16.
51. S. Wright, ' "Churmaids, Huswyfes and Hucksters": The Employment of Women in Tudor and Stuart Salisbury' in L. Charles and L. Duffin eds. *Women and Work in Pre-Industrial England* (Croom Helm, 1985), 110.
52. *Edin.Recs.*, ii, 112; *Dunf.Recs.*, 61. Bennett, *Ale, Beer and Brewsters*, 45–6.
53. *Dunf.Recs.*, 132.
54. J. Bennett 'Women and Men in the Brewers' Gild of London, ca. 1420' in E. DeWindt ed. *The Salt of Common Life* (Kalamazoo, 1995), 181–2; J. Bennett, 'Misogyny, Popular Culture and Women's Work', *History Workshop Journal*, 31 (1991), 168–9, 174–82.
55. *Aber.Extracts*, 115. See also *Edin.Recs.*, i, 67.
56. *Edin.Recs.*, i and ii. M. Kowaleski and J. Bennett, 'Crafts, Gilds, and Women in the Middle Ages' in J. Bennett et al eds. *Sisters and Workers in the Middle Ages* (Chicago, 1989), 20–5.
57. Bennett, *Ale, Beer and Brewers*, 60–76.
58. *Charters and Other Documents Relating to the City of Edinburgh* (Scottish Burgh Records Society, 1871), no. 62; *Edin. Recs.*, i, 187–9, ii, 56, 60, 82.
59. M. Howell, 'Women, the Family Economy, and the Structures of Market Production in Cities of Northern Europe during the Late Middle Ages' in Hanawalt, *Women and Work*, 215–6. For the effect of beer on English brewsters, see Bennett, *Ale, Beer and Brewsters*, 77–97.
60. Lynch, 'Continuity and Change',109.
61. Mayhew, 'Status of Women ',17; H. Dingwall, *Late Seventeenth Century Edinburgh; a demographic study* (Aldershot, 1994), 202, although also see Mayhew, 'Brewsters of Aberdeen', 78. The situation c.1550–1650 requires more study.
62. For England, see Bennett, 'Misogyny, Popular Culture'. The popular image of Scottish brewsters will be explored elsewhere.
63. *Iter Camerarii*, c.6.

CHAPTER TWELVE

Embroidery to Enterprise: the Role of Women in the Book Trade of Early Modern Scotland

Alastair J. Mann

THE USUAL PERCEPTION of women in the society of early modern Scotland encompasses the roles of wife and mother, ignoring responsibilities in wider economic and social development. To these 'traditional', dual familial roles we might add that of responsible widowhood. Thus the fate of the domestic and commercial estate of the husband must be managed to secure the future for offspring, to sustain the widow on her own account, and even to offer the prospect of a second marriage which might benefit surviving assets and relatives. For all commercial trades in the early modern period, from apothecaries to tenant farmers, we find this culture of inheritance – booksellers, bookbinders and printers were no different. In these commercial areas there is much evidence of independent decision making by wives and widows. It is ironic, therefore, that in order to test the hypothesis of the significance of women in the book trade the historian is forced to turn to family records, and in particular to the details of marriages, wills and testaments. A combination of male oriented contemporary record keeping, and similarly tainted modern historiography, makes it virtually impossible to shake off the effects of the ascendancy of male gender.

Scotland's early modern book trade was relatively deregulated and along Dutch rather than English lines. There was no Scottish equivalent of the Stationers' Company of London to restrict entry to the trade, and regulation under the government was devolved to the magistrates of the printing burghs – Edinburgh, Aberdeen and Glasgow. Burgh book trade regulation in Scotland, therefore, had a sophistication without parallel in England. In burgh manufacturing and retailing of books there were, of course, many participants – typesetters, editors, correctors, agents, patrons, publishers as well as bookseller and printer – and so confirmation of responsibility is extremely difficult. The lines of demarcation between master and apprentice are also hard to clarify. Agnes Campbell, the relict of Andrew Anderson, in trade from 1676 to 1716, had numerous apprentices and journeymen, and perhaps five presses at her peak.[1] There were no Stationers' regulations placing a limit of two to three presses per printer. It is impossible to ascertain the extent to which Campbell was directly responsible for the entire output of her presses and the quality of printing executed. Nevertheless, decisions taken to expedite publication and sale would fall to the owner of the press or bookshop, whether male or female. The degree of ownership by women in book businesses of this period should then provide some guidance as to the significance of women in the book trade.

As well as their capital women brought their labour, as skilled individuals or as emergency support for their book merchant spouses, eldest sons, and fathers. For Scotland there is scant direct evidence of the involvement of women in the press room, but given the regulation of burgesses and apprentices in a masculine environment it is likely that 'family' female labour existed on an informal basis, with little or no remuneration and record keeping.[2] There were, naturally, some highly physical tasks in the print shop for which hardy women were capable,[3] although the likes of setting type, mixing inks, and correcting proofs were certainly not beyond the physical abilities of all. No physical qualifications need have applied to the trade of bookseller, and this acted as a greater encouragement for women booksellers in assisting the family, learning the trade and, in some cases, running their own business.

In sixteenth- and seventeenth-century Scotland there was a small band of skilled book women. *The Accounts of the Lord High Treasurer* indicate that James V had a taste for fine bookbindings. The king's most astonishing commission was in 1538 to complete the binding and a cloth bag for his personal bible. This task involved the use of 'purpure welvet . . . sewing gold . . . purpure silk [and] crammesy (crimson) sating', and similar treatments were given to the 'mating bukes' of the king and queen in 1539. The key craftswoman for this work was the embroiderer Helen Ross who worked from 1538 to 1543. Sadly her bindings, and most tragically her magnificent bible, have not survived.[4] A tradition of exotic book binding continued into the reign of James VI, and the fine calligrapher Esther Inglis (1571–1624) may even have embroidered her own manuscript bindings, though she was never a commercial bookbinder.[5] Great skill could be submerged within the commercial book houses of the period. It was to the credit of Janet Kene, the widow of Andro Hart, that she and not the king's printer was chosen by the magistrates of Edinburgh to produce the special edition of poems Εισοδια *Musarum Edinensium in Carole* presented to Charles I to commemorate his coronation visit in 1633.[6] Women with the requisite management and technical abilities had some opportunities within the book trade.

The tracing of the activities of female book makers and sellers is, nevertheless, problematical. Recent Dutch and English studies of bibliographical history, such as those concerning the great female, bible printing dynasties of late seventeenth-century Amsterdam, and the key presses of female Puritanism in England from the 1630s to 1650s, point the way to the rigorous analysis required for Scotland.[7] From 1600 to

1750 perhaps up to thirty Scottish women were steeped in the professional book trade of their nation (see appendix). Women printers traded in the names of fathers, husbands and sons, although some booksellers did so under their own names. Before 1600, excluding the already mentioned Helen Ross, only Katherine Norwell, the widow of Thomas Bassandyne, who in the 1580s went on to join in businesses and matrimony with the printer Robert Smyth, could be included, although details of the Norwell-Smyth business activities are murky.[8] The provisional post-1600 check-list is dominated by widows, with the exceptions of Margaret Reid, daughter of the Edinburgh printer John Reid, senior (1680–1712), the daughters of the bookseller James Harrower (1638–51), and Janet Hunter (Mrs Brown), a co-printer with a number of partnerships of Glasgow printers in the 1730s who, along with the booksellers Martha Stevenson, Anne Edmonstoun and Jean Smith, traded before widowhood.[9]

Excluded from the list are a number of vague references for which no corroborative details are available to indicate the longevity or scale of trading. Although some bibliographers have adopted a 'list all' approach,[10] because not all book trade widows were certainly in trade omissions have been made. Included, however, are those widows or relatives who kept printing and bookselling businesses turning over for a short but quantifiable period prior to dismemberment by auction, sale as a going concern within the trade, before sons came of age, or until a suitable, swift and fortuitous second marriage was joined. Delays between a husband's death and the registration of testaments provide evidence of continuity when assets were intact.

In the category of 'seeking a second marriage' was Beatrix Campbell, widow of the bookseller and printer Archibald Hislop (1670–78) and sister to Agnes Campbell, who maintained her husband's bookselling business for at least twelve months following his death up to and after her marriage in 1679 to the 'wryter', turned stationer, Robert Currie. The Hislop press was, according to James Watson, sold off to John Cairns, while the Hislop children and the family bookselling business went on to suffer hereditary injustice and protracted litigation. Issobel Harring (Herron), widow of the printer Robert Bryson (1637–45) acted in a similar manner to Beatrix Campbell before her second and more prudent marriage to the printer Gideon Lithgow – she printed as the 'Heirs of Robert Bryson' in 1646.[11]

The recourse to litigation to protect rights and licences also acts as a useful guide to the trading maturity of these women, especially for those who could afford lawyers. The 1632 appeal of Janet Kene to the lords of exchequer against a twenty-year licence as Scotland's royal printer granted to the Englishman Robert Young, indicates a single-mindedness of purpose and an appreciation of legal process.[12] The litigious behaviour of Agnes Campbell and her husband is more frequently referred to by bibliographical historians.[13] Her lawyers were certainly very tenacious, pleading from bailie court to House of Lords to protect her patents and restrict the trade of others. Indeed, she mixed intimately in the legal circles of Edinburgh, and actually rented property to lawyers, including James Erskine, Lord Grange, a lord of session, which adds some novel colour to her relationship to the Edinburgh élite.[14]

This degree of independent action is also highlighted in the bold activities of Margaret Reid, daughter of the printer John Reid, senior. On the death of her father in August 1712, Margaret Reid took over the use of some of her father's type, acquired the printing office of Andrew Symson, who, Watson informs us, died about this time, and set up on her own. This appears to be the only example in the period of a Scottish woman setting up a printing press without the 'partnership' of a male, dead or alive, and may account for the anonymity of her printings. This seemingly unique book woman ended her known printing activity in dispute with the poet and bookseller Allan Ramsay. Her printing of one of his poems without prior permission led him to mock her in his 'Elegy on Lucky Read'.[15] Nevertheless, Margaret Reid, like Janet Kene and Agnes Campbell exhibited the qualities of a professional book merchant. Indeed, women participants, full-time and part-time, major or minor, while representing only perhaps ten per cent of all Scottish book traders in the early modern period, were a prominent, surprisingly numerous, yet only occasionally independent minority.[16] Such a proportion suggests women book traders were more common in Scotland than in England.

The marriage contract itself was, however, the point of conception for potential commercial activity. Marriages were frequently within the trade. In this respect the book trade was no different from others in the social mixture of peers and fellow craftsmen. Elizabeth Brown, daughter of the major Edinburgh printer, bookseller, bailie and council treasurer Thomas Brown (c.1658–1702), married the Edinburgh book-seller John Vallange (1691–1712). Thomas Brown's first wife was Marian Calderwood, probably a relative of the stationer John Calder-wood (1676–82), and Brown himself entered into various bonds and deeds with his son-in-law and Agnes Campbell in the 1680s and 1690s. In addition, Campbell's eldest daughter Issobel married the Edinburgh bookseller William Cunningham in 1676 and, in an act mirrored many times in the book trade, enabled her husband to be made a burgess of Edinburgh in 1677 'by right of his spouse Issobel, daughter to umquhyle Andrew Anderson'.[17] Everywhere networks of family connections were complex and interwoven, and as a result many a bride, before marriage, will have been instilled with some experience of the mechanics of book merchandising. The dowry of a 'burgess ticket' (the licence to trade as a burgess) must, in addition, have sweetened the marriage contract.

Some wives, such as James Watson's widow Jean Smith with her second husband Thomas Heriot, and Anne Edmonstoun with George Stewart (1713–45), 'formally' worked with their spouses,[18] but such family co-operation was usually reserved for mothers and sons, especially after the death of the father left the son too young to run the business. Katherine Boyd sustained the bookbinding business of her dead husband John Gibson with her son David at least from 1600 to 1606.[19] In a more curious example of family responsibility Margaret Cuthbert, the widow of the Aberdeen printer John Forbes, the younger (1675–1704), continued the business from 1704 to 1710 by which, at her death, her daughter Margaret and son-in-law James Nicol were ready to take control.[20] The importance of maintaining the continuity of family ownership was seen as an essential objective, and even the recourse to second marriages did not lessen the ideal of continuing in trade for the benefit of the original family. The second marriages of Katherine Norwell, Beatrix Campbell, and Issobel Harring were all examples of attempts to continue trading through the commercial *mariage de convenence*.

Wedlock brought opportunity but the chief basis for the importance of women in the early modern book trade was inheritance, and this applied to estates of whatever size. The wealth of book traders could vary enormously ranging from the considerable wealth of merchants like Andro Hart, and Andrew Wilson, to the small bookbinders and chapmen living in the shadow of poverty. The contrasting legacies of the partners in Scotland's first bible printing, Thomas Bassandyne and Alexander Arbuthnot, provide a useful illustration. Bassandyne's widow Katherine Norwell inherited an estate of over £2000 Scots in 1577, while Arbuthnot's widow Agnes Pennycuik received an estate of only £100 in 1585. But limited prospects were even more common for provincial book traders, such as the meagre £50 estate left in 1673 to Janet Stevenson, widow of the Irvine bookseller Matthew Paton.[21] From humble legacies the prospects for women continuing to trade must have been relatively slim, and the most likely outcome was the transportation of remaining stock to Edinburgh for sale by auction.

The decision by widows to dispose of an estate through auction, or sale to other book merchants, was often necessitous. For pressing financial reasons Margaret Rowan, the wife of the printer John Ross (1574–80), was forced to sell her husband's materials and type to the publisher Henry Charteris, and similarly the brothers and sisters of Margaret Wallace, who pre-deceased her husband Robert Charteris (1600–1610), were compelled to realise the assets of the Charteris press and sell them to Andro Hart in 1610.[22] Another alternative, however, was the sale of only part of the business, and typically this would involve selling the printing presses, type and press rooms while continuing the bookselling activity. Thus, in 1724, Jean Smith the widow of James Watson sold the presses and rights of her husband to John Mosman and William Brown, including Watson's part of the gift of king's printer, and then independently ran the family bookshop until in 1725 she went into marriage and partnership with Thomas Heriot.[23] Yet such assets could, of course, quickly lose their value if the beneficiaries neglected maintenance. The Edinburgh printer, bookseller and paper-mill owner John Moncur (1707–29) bequeathed to his wife Agnes Lathem book stock, three presses, a paper-mill and various annuities in 1729 but, by the time his will was proved in 1736, much of the unbound stock in the warehouse and shop had been 'eaten and destroyed by rats and other ways'. It was not, however, always necessary for widows to be actively in trade to profit from inherited assets. The arrangements contracted by Marie Johnson, widow to the Edinburgh bookseller John Porteous (1699–1700), have to be admired. Although *c.*1700 her husband's stock was sold to George Warrander and John Vallange, she contracted a share in their profits and took rental from them for the shop premises.[24]

Part of the inherited rights of widows and children were those related to copy patents and appointed offices. Heirs succeeded to the term of book licences, while over appointments the authorities were sympathetic to the claims of heirs over licensed offices, although official confirmation was required. It was particularly common for widowed mothers to seek to secure the rights in the name of young sons. The widow of George Anderson, for Andrew Anderson, in November 1647, and his widow Agnes Campbell, for James Anderson in 1676, obtained confirmation from local magistrates of the inherited right of their sons to be burgh printers.[25] Equally, when George Mosman (1669–1707), printer to the General Assembly, died in the winter of 1707–8, his widow Margaret Gibb was able to convince the church that she should and could continue as church printer. Agnes Campbell's renewed efforts to claim the right were dismissed in the face of heritable notions and a pious widow.[26] But in all these cases the key requirement was proof to the burgh, crown or clerical authorities that the widow controlled the material and skills necessary to carry out the office. Proof of competence was an effective weapon against potential attack based on gender, even though the threat was usually inferred rather than blatant as seen in the impatience of the government over the petitions of Janet Kene (1630s) and Agnes Campbell (1680s).

Women contributed to fields political and religious as well as commercial. Across Scottish society political and religious controversies were certainly fuelled by print of ink as well as word of mouth, although the general involvement of women in the dissemination of nonconformist literature is not immediately obvious. Again the key to understanding is the family. A continuous line of book merchants can be traced from the clerical subscription crisis of 1584–5 to the covenanting revolution of 1638–39 (see figure 1). The key individuals in this line were Andro Hart and his third wife Janet Kene, although the first book merchants to be involved in nonconformity from the 1580s were the brothers Edward and James Cathkin. Both were banished in the summer of 1584 for refusing to subscribe to James VI's Episcopalian policies, and both, along with Andro Hart, were among those arrested in the Edinburgh Presbyterian riots of December 1596. This was followed in June 1619 by the well-known investigation into the printing, importation and selling of David Calderwood's *Perth Assembly*. Hart and Lawson's houses and booths were searched and James Cathkin, happening to be in London, was interrogated by the king himself.[27] Little action was taken against these merchants although undoubtedly they had distributed Calderwood's works and much else of a Presbyterian flavour.

After James Cathkin died in 1631 his wife Janet Mayne, sister-in-law to Richard Lawson, continued bookselling until her death in 1639. Janet Kene, 'Widow Hart', printed with the aid of her sons until passing on the press to James Bryson in 1639, and on her death her bookshop appears to have passed to John Threipland who, to emphasise this remarkable network, had trained and worked for James Cathkin. Moreover, Janet's sister Margaret Kene married the printer John Wreittoun who had been operating a press from at least 1624.[28] There was clearly then an extensive range of book trade and nonconformist connections that led up to the revolution of 1638/9. When the Covenanting government required to explain its policies and actions to the parliament in England, and the wider world, it turned to the presses of Bryson and Wreittoun, along with numerous tracts imported from the presses of Amsterdam and Leiden from 1638 to 1640.[29] It was a flood of propaganda to date unparalleled in Scottish history. Meanwhile, this distinct book trading community was held together by the five families, Hart, Cathkin, Bryson, Kene and Mayne. The two sets of sisters, Mayne and Kene, connected the bookselling and printing branches of Edinburgh book commerce, and bridged the gap between the old Melvillian nonconformity and that of the National Covenant. These families were not revolutionary 'fifth columnists', yet the coincidence of political and social connections goes beyond links arising from normal trade intermarriage.

No credible account of female book merchants of this period can ignore the unique features relating to Agnes Campbell, Lady Roseburn, who in 1676 succeeded her husband Andrew Anderson as king's printer in Scotland. The redoubtable lady inherited not only the king's gift but

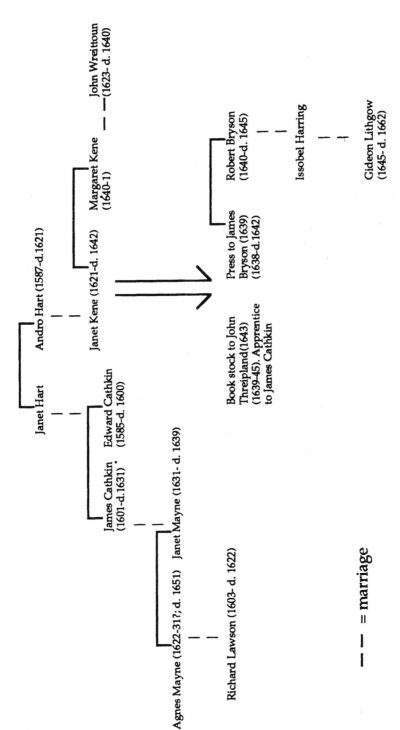

Figure 1: Book trade dynasties and nonconformity (with trade activity dates)

the remaining thirty-six years of its forty-one year licence, as well as unprecedented supervisory and monopoly powers over the Scottish press.[30] As a result 250 years of historiographical vilification have followed in her wake.

On the basis of scale her achievements were astonishing. She was by some distance the most wealthy Scottish book maker in the early modern period, with an estate valued at over £78000 Scots at her death in July 1716. This represented a miraculous turn around considering the financial circumstances of her husband who was in debt to the tune of £7451 in 1676.[31] That she was the largest printer in Edinburgh is not in doubt – in 1678 she had at least sixteen apprentices and journeymen.[32] Her printing and paper supply business had become the hub of a large trading zone beyond Edinburgh, and sweeping out to all the burghs of Scotland, into Ireland and the north of England. She clearly acquired stock, and had business dealings, with many of the major book makers of London. Just as remarkable is the extent to which she lent money to book traders, in Ireland as well as Scotland.[33]

Until the revisionism of John Fairley in the 1920s, bibliographical historians, with a mixture of antiquarianism and a modern dislike of monopoly, have condemned the Anderson press for poor quality printing, and a stifling and regressive grip on the book trade of the period. But the most damning criticism levelled at Agnes Campbell by Principal John Lee concerns her counterfeit bible printing of 1707. After years of complaint and protest about the damage to her trade done by English bibles entering Scotland, she printed an edition of her own with the imprint 'London, printed by Charles Bill'.[34] If the Scots wanted London bibles let them be printed in Edinburgh. This charge, more than any other, outrages John Fairley. He points to the cracked printing block of the page design which 'gives the game away' too blatantly; the fact that such an edition has not survived; that an elderly Mrs Anderson could not have policed all the output of her press, and that there was, in any case, no market available in England for such bibles. And yet, Agnes Campbell maintained her faculties into old age, even starting a paper-mill in 1709 and, after a twenty year campaign, at last became printer to the church in 1712. The production of false editions was also common, as with the numerous pirated and profitable almanac editions that circulated throughout Scotland after the Restoration.[35] Finally, the commercial attractions of printing such an edition in the year 1707 are fairly obvious.

In Holland the production of bibles with false imprints was a major industry, and many Dutch printings of English bibles arrived in Scotland through Glasgow.[36] Why should Agnes Campbell not engage to some degree with this illicit trade? In 1684 the king's printers in England even admitted to the House of Lords that they had carried out similar acts of falsification.[37] Agnes Campbell prosecuted through the courts whenever necessary, restricted the actions of competitors, and curtailed the freedom of her apprentices. She used her press to petition on her own behalf, and to manufacture illicit and false editions to hurt the competition and increase the profits of her house. Yet, in all of this she behaved in a manner not uncommon to contemporaries, and in a way that was copied, and sometimes surpassed, by her greatest opponent James Watson. Her only crime was commercial pragmatism.

The high profile of Campbell is, however, atypical and establishing the role of women in the early modern book trade requires considerable detective work. The need to look for the man before you find the woman is especially unfortunate. Nonetheless, it cannot be denied that it is through the family that historiography locates these women and through their family ties that they entered the business of books. The small selection of women considered in this paper by no means represent the entire number of women traders in the period, and more names will be uncovered over time. In many respects the identified group of Scottish book women reflect the variety of the Scottish book trade as a whole. These were after all the wives and daughters of wealthy stationers, moderately comfortable printers and booksellers, small and large book-binders, apprenticed printers and street traders and chapmen. Meanwhile, that journey from the crimson silks of the bindings of Helen Ross to the counterfeit bibles of Agnes Campbell seems a strange passage, but a suitable metaphor for the movement from the culture of craft to the exigencies of commerce. As female literacy expanded with that of men, women played a crucial role in the dynamics of the Scottish book trade. It is a role that should be recognised more widely.

Appendix: A Provisional Check-list of the Major Women Book Traders, 1600-1750

Name	Activity	Trade	Spouse	SomeKey References
Katherine Boyd	1600–6(?22)	bookbinder	John Gibson	*Bann. Misc.* ii 222–3; cc8/8/51(Feb. 1623)
'widow Waldegrave'	1604	printer (Edinburgh/London)	Robert Waldegrave	McKerrow, *Dictionary of Printers, 1557–1640, 277–9*
Janet Kene	1621–42	printer (to 1639/ bookseller	Andro Hart	*Bann. Misc.* ii 249–9 (Hart testament), ibid, 257–9 (Kene)
Agnes Mayne	1622–31?	bookseller	Richard Lawson	*Bann. Misc.* iii, 199–205; cc8/8/65(Mayne, Oct. 1651)
Janet Mayne	1631–39	bookseller	James Cathkin	*Bann. Misc.* ii 249–52 (Cathkin testament), ibid, 253–4 for Mayne
Margaret Kene Agnes Readick	1640–41? 1642–46	printer/bookseller bookseller	John Wreitoun James Bryson	*Bann. Misc.* ii 255–257. No books survive with her imprint. Not mentioned in Bryson testament *Bann. Misc.* ii 259–62; see Plomer,
				Dictionary of the Booksellers and Printers 1641 to 1667, 37; Aldis, 110 and *Edin. Marriages,* 99 (21 Dec., 1630)
Issobel Harring	1645–6	printer/bookseller	Robert Bryson	*Bann. Misc.* ii 263–269; Plomer, *Dictionary of the Booksellers and Printers 1642 to 1667, 37*; Aldis, no. 1241. Married Lithgow 1646; *Bann. Misc.* ii 279–281
Issobel Aitcheson	1648–53	printer(Glasgow/ Edinburgh	George Anderson	International Geneology Index (IGI) 0.423.632, MacLehose, *Glasgow University Press,* 20–31, G. Chalmers, 'An Historical Account', 239–43
Janet Patterson	1650–1	bookseller	James Harrower	cc8/67 (May 1654) and cc8/8/67 Aug.1654)
Marian & Jeanet Harrower	1651–54	bookselers	- - - - - - - - - - -	cc8/67 (May 1654) and cc8/8/67 Aug.1654)
Elizabeth Mortimer	1654?	bookseller	Andrew Wilson	*Bann. Misc.* ii 277–279
Agnes Campbell	1676–1716	printer/ paper merchant	Andrew Anderson	*Bann. Misc.* ii. 284–9; cc8/8/86(July, 1711) cc8/8/112.1:(Oct. 1748) for Anderson *Bann. Misc.* ii. 282–284 and cc8/8/75 (Aug.1676)
Beatrix Campbell	1678–82?	bookseller	Archibald Hislop	cc8/8/76 (July, 1679) and cc8/8/80; (June, 1697) CS 157/66/2; *Edin. Marriages,* 169 (22. Sep. 1679)
Christian Auld	1682–3	bookseller	John Calderwood	*Bann. Misc.* ii 289–292

Name	Dates	Occupation	Associate	Source
Bessie Sheills	1684–9	bookseller(Glasgow)	John Andrew	cc9/7/44 (Jan.1684) and cc9/7/48 (Dec.1689)
Marion Bell	1692–1710	bookseller	John Johnstone	cc8/79 (Johnstone: Jan.1693) and cc8/8/84 (Bell; Sep.1710)
Mrs Beiglie	1696	bookseller	– – – – – – – – – –	Plomer, *Booksellers and Printers, 1668–1725*, 28
Marie Johnston	1740–4(?)	bookseller	John Porteous	cc8/82 (Sep. 1704)
Margaret Cuthbert	1704–10	printer(Aberdeen)	John Forbes, ygr	Edmond, *Aberdeen Printers*, iv, lvi-vii and Aberdeen Council Records (MSS), 58, 3 and 215–6
Margaret Gibb	1708–11	printer	George Mosman	SRO. ch1/1/18 Records of the General Assembly, 1702–8, 521. No testament for Mosman. For inventory see SRO.RD.2.92.no. 1772, 870–872 (Nov.1707)
Martha Stevenson	1690–1732	bookseller	Alexander Ogston	cc8/8/85 (her son James Ogston, Aug. 1714), and cc8/8/100 (Stevenson, Jan. 1735); Grant, J. (ed.), *Seafield Correspondence from 1685 to 1708*, (SHS, 1912), 90, 95–6, 150.
Margaret Reid	1712–20	printer	– – – – – – – – – –	Plomer, *Dictionary of the Printers and Booksellers 1668 to 1725*, 251; for her father, cc8/8/86 (May, 1716)
Agnes Knox	1716	newsvendor (Glasgow)	Thomas Sheills	*Glasgow Recs*, 4, 603–4.(supplier of diurnals)
Jean Smith	1722–31	bookseller	James Watson, ygr	cc8/8/86 (Watson: Dec. 1722) and cc8/8/104 for testament of Anne Smith sister to Jean (Dec. 1740)
Janet Hunter	1722–35	printer(Glasgow)	James Brown	MacLehose, *Glasgow University Press*, 124; c cc9/7/55 (Hunter, Nov. 1736)
Agnes Lathem	1729–35	printer, bookseller, paper maker	John Moncur	cc8/8/97 (Moncur testament, June, 1735).
Anne Edmonstoun	1734–44	bookseller	George Stewart	R.H. Carnie and R.P. Doig. 'Scottish Printers and Booksellers 1668–1775; a second supplement', *Studies in Bibliography*, xii. (1961–2), 115 and *Edin. Marriages*, 170 ('Anna')(1712)
Mary Cameron	1742	bookbinder/bookseller (Glasgow)	Alexander Miller	cc9/7/57(Sep.1742)
Susan Trail	1764	printer (Aberdeen)	James Chalmers	Aberdeen Council Records (MSS), 63, 20

Notes: The activity dates must be seen as best guesses based on bibliographical and testamentary evidence. Dates will alter as our knowledge improves

NOTES

1. John Fairley, *Agnes Campbell, Lady Roseburn: Relict of Andrew Anderson: A Contribution to the History of Printing in Scotland* (Aberdeen, 1925); James Watson, *The History of the Art of Printing* (1713), preface 10–24; George Chalmers, 'An Historical Account of Printing in Scotland' (*c.* 1825) National Library of Scotland [NLS],Adv. MSS. 17.1.16. fos 270r-276v.

2. R. A. Houston 'Women in the Economy and Society of Scotland, 1500–1800' in R. A. Houston and I. D. Whyte eds. *Scottish Society 1500–1800* (Cambridge, 1989), mentions the 'manual labour' of bookselling and printing but does not discuss examples of female book traders.

3. Joseph Moxon, *Mechanick Exercises on the Whole Art of Printing* (1683–4), eds. Herbert Davis and Harry Carter (Oxford, 1962), 294–5, 318.

4. *Accounts of the Lord High Treasurer of Scotland* eds T. Dickson and J.B. Paul (13 vols, Edinburgh, 1877–1916), vii, 113; ibid, 142, 161. William Smith Mitchell, *A History of Scottish Bookbinding 1432 to 1650* (Aberdeen, 1955), 18–20.

5. A.H. Scott-Elliot and Elspeth Yeo, 'Calligraphic Manuscripts of Esther Inglis (1571–1624): A Catalogue', *The Papers of the Bibliographical Society of America*, 84 (1990), 11–86 and NLS, MS 8874 which she may have helped bind. See also her portrait in this volume and her self-portrait in NLS, 8874, fo 4v.

6. H. G. Aldis, *A list of books printed in Scotland before 1700 including those printed furth of the realm of Scotland before 1700* (Edinburgh, 1904, reprinted 1970), no. 802.

7. P.G. Hoftijzer, *Engelse boekverkopers bij de beurs: De geschiedenis van de Amsterdamse boekhandels Bruyning en Swart* (Amsterdam, 1987) and Maureen Bell, 'Hannah Allen and the Development of a Puritan Publishing Business 1645–51', *Publishing History*, 26 (1989).

8. For testaments of Bassandyne, Norwell and Smyth see *The Bannatyne Miscellany* [*Bann. Misc.*] (3 vols, Bannatyne Club, 1827–55), ii 191–203; 218–221; 233–5 and summary; Robert Dickson and John P. Edmond, *Annals of Scottish Printing, 1507–1610* (Cambridge, 1890, reprint Amsterdam, 1975), 272–306, 475–484.

9. Reid: Henry R. Plomer ed. *A Dictionary of the Printers and Booksellers Who Were at Work in England, Scotland and Ireland from 1668 to 1725* (Oxford, 1922), 251, for her father Scottish Record Office [SRO], Commissary Court Records [CC] CC8/8/86 (11 May, 1716), and my thanks to John Morris of the National Library for some additional details; Janet Hunter: James MacLehose, *The Glasgow University Press 1638–1931* (Glasgow, 1931), 124 and CC9/7/55 (15 Nov. 1736); Stevenson: CC8/8/85 (her son) and CC8/8/100 herself (20 January, 1735) and see also Rosalind K. Marshall, *Virgins and Viragos: A History of Women in Scotland from 1080–1980* (1983), 155–6; Edmonstoun: R. H. Carnie & R. P. Doig, 'Scottish Printers and Booksellers 1668–1775: a second supplement', *Studies in Bibliography*, 12 (1961–2), 115 and *Edin. Marriages*, 170 ('Anna') (7 Dec., 1712); Smith: SRO, CC8/8/86 (Watson testament, 19 Dec., 1722) and CC8/8/104 for testament of Anne Smith sister to Jean (12 Dec., 1740).

10. For example Maureen Bell, 'Women in the English Book Trade, 1557–1700' *Leipziger Jahrbuch Buchgeschichte*, 16 (1996), 13–45.

11. John Grant, 'Archibald Hislop, Stationer, Edinburgh, 1668–1678', *Papers of Edinburgh Bibliographical Society*, 12 (1925), 35–51; SRO, CC8/8/76 (10, July 1679) and CC8/8/80 (8 June, 1697). Watson, *History of Printing*, 14. Sir John Lauder of Fountainhall, *The Decisions of the Lords of Council and Session from June 6th 1678 to July 30th 1712* (2 vols, Edinburgh, 1759–1761), i. 487 and SRO, Court of Session records [CS] 157/66/2. Issobel Harring: *Bann. Misc.* ii. 263 (testament Robert Bryson), ibid, 276 (testament Lithgow).

12. Robert and James Bryson, 'Information anent His Majestie's Printers in Scotland', *The Spottiswoode Miscellany* (2 vols, Spottiswoode Society, 1844–5) i, 299–300, William Cowan, 'Andro Hart and His Press', *Papers of the Edinburgh Bibliographical Society*, 1 (1896), no.12. 6, *Extracts from the Records of the Burgh of Edinburgh [Edin Recs.]*, 1626–41 ed. M. Wood (Edinburgh, 1936)109; *The Acts of the Parliaments of Scotland [APS]* eds. T. Thomson and C. Innes (12 vols., Edinburgh, 1814–75), v, 52.

13. Dr John Lee, *Memorial for the Bible Societies in Scotland* (Edinburgh, 1824), 160–169; G. Chalmers, 'Historical Account', fos 190r, 270r-276v; James Chalmers, MSS 'Materials' for 'An Historical Account of printing in Scotland from 1507 to 1707', (2 vols, c.1845); NLS, Adv.MSS 16.2.21 and 22. W. J. Couper, 'James Watson, King's Printer', *Scottish Historical Review*, [SHR] (1910), 253–8; Couper, 'The Pretender's Printer', *SHR*, 15 (1917), 107–10

14. For trade disputes see *Register of the Privy Council [RPC]* eds. J. H. Burton et al (14 vols, Edinburgh, 1877–) iii, v. 141–2, (March, 1677) *RPC*, iii, vi. 418–9 (March, 1680). For disputes with apprentices *Fountainhall's Decisions*, i. 104; *RPC*, iii, vii. 3–4; ibid , 31–32; *RPC*, iii, viii. 250–51; Sir John Lauder of Fountainhall, *Historical Notices of Scottish Affairs, 1661–1688*, (2 vols, Edinburgh, 1848), ii. 464–5. For lawyer contacts of Campbell see her full testament: SRO, CC8/8/86, fo 336r.

15. Plomer, *Booksellers and Printers 1668–1725*, 250–1, 258–9. Margaret was daughter to the elder John Reid and not widow of the younger as indicated by Plomer. SRO, CC8/8/86(11 May, 1716). Watson, *History of Printing*, 18.

16. Houston, 'Women in the Economy and Society of Scotland', 123.

17. SRO, CC8/8/82 and CC8/8/88 (Thomas Brown, 29 Nov., 1703 and 30 May, 1722), beneficiaries John Vallange and his son John; CC8/8/85 (John Vallange, 9 Apr., 1713); Marriage Brown to Marian Calderwood, *Edin. Marriages*, 93 (9 Oct., 1667); SRO, Register of Deeds [RD] 3/77. 297 (Recorded 23 July, 1692 but dated 1 June, 1683); Fairley, *Agnes Campbell*, 19.

18. R. B. McKerrow ed. *A Dictionary of Printers and Booksellers in England, Scotland and Ireland, 1557–1640* (Oxford, 1910), 272–3; SRO, CC8/8/88 (Watson, 19 Dec., 1722); no testament exists for Jean Smith but her sister Anne Smith's will was proved 12 Dec., 1740. SRO, CC8/8/104. Marriage Jean Smith to Heriot, *Edin. Marriages*, 504 (6 July, 1725); Carnie and Doig, 'Printers and Booksellers, 1668–1775', 115 and *Edin. Marriages*, 170 (7 Dec., 1712).

19. SRO, CC8/8/51.
20. Aberdeen City Archives, Aberdeen Council Records (MSS), lviii. 3 and 215–6. J. P. Edmond, *The Aberdeen Printers, 1620 to 1736* (4 vols, Aberdeen, 1884), iv. preface p. lvii
21. Andro Hart's estate (d. 1621): £19, 528 and Andrew Wilson's (d.1654): £15,424 *Bann. Misc.* ii. pp. 241–9 and 277–9; *Bann. Misc.* ii. 191–204, 207–8; SRO, CC9/7/41 (Paton, 23 April, 1674)
22. Dickson and Edmonds, *Scottish Printing, 1507–1610*, 349; McKerrow, *Printers and Booksellers 1557–1640*, 67.
23. John Lee, *Additional Memorial*, (Edinburgh, 1826), 105, 153; Plomer, *Booksellers and Printers, 1668–1725*, 54, 212.
24. SRO, CC8/8/97 (23 June, 1735). A. G. Thomson, *The Paper Industry in Scotland, 1590–1861* (Edinburgh, 1974), 129,153; SRO, CC8/8/82 (Porteous, 11 Sept., 1704).
25. *Extracts from the Records of the Burgh of Glasgow, 1630–62*, (Scottish Burgh Records Society, 1881) 126–7 (27 Nov., 1647); Edinburgh City Archives, Moses Bundles, 67, 3043 (22 June, 1676).
26. SRO, CH1/1/18, Records of the General Assembly, 1702–8, 521 (27 Apr., 1708).
27. *History of the Church of Scotland by Mr David Calderwood* (8 vols, Wodrow Society, 1842–9) iv, 78–9 and *Calendar of State Papers relating to Scotland* eds. J. Bain et al (13 vols, 1898–1969), vii, no.171; Calderwood, *History*, v, 510–2, 520–1; vii, 348–9; ibid., 382–3 and *Bann. Misc.* i, 199–215 for Cathkin's account of his own interrogation; Calderwood, *History*, vii, 433–4 and 439–442.
28. McKerrow, *Printers and Booksellers 1557–1640*, 63–4; Kene testament: *Bann. Misc.* ii, 258 (Threipland a debtor); Plomer, *Booksellers and Printers 1641–47*, 180; Mayne testament: *Bann. Misc.* ii, 253–4 (Threipland described as 'servant'); Wreittoun testament: *Bann Misc.* ii, 255–7 (25 June, 1641).
29. For example from these presses came *The Protestation of the Noblemen and Wariston's A short relation of the state of the Kirk of Scotland* (Wreittoun, 1638); *The Protestation of the General Assembly* (1638–1639), *the Remonstrance of the Nobility* (1639) and *Information from the Scottish nation to all . . . English* (1640), (James Bryson), and *Intentions of the Army of Scotland* (1640) (Robert Bryson)
30. She adopted the title Lady Roseburn from 1704 having acquired property to the north west of Edinburgh. *APS*, viii. 206–7. c.147. and Lee, *Memorials* appendix no. xxvii, 56–61. Marshall, *Virgins and Viragos*, 156–7.
31. For testament extracts see *Bann. Misc.* ii, 284–9 and for the entirety and of her grandchildren SRO, CC8/8/86 (10 July, 1676) and 112.1. (28 Oct., 1748); for Andrew Anderson, *Bann. Misc.* ii, 282–284 and SRO, CC8/8/75 (18 Aug., 1676). Fairley, *Agnes Campbell*, 4–6; ibid.,14–19. Agnes had at least eight children, most dying young, and the only son to reach adulthood, James, died in 1693.
32. *RPC*, iii, v. 441–2.
33. SRO, CC8/8/86, 333r–336v.
34. See the illustration of the title pages in this volume.

35. Lee, *Memorials* 160–3; Fairley, *Agnes Campbell*, 23–26.
36. For Dutch bibles inported through Glasgow in the 1670s see Gemeentearchief Amsterdam [GAA], Notarial Archive, GAA NA. 4779. 101–2 (8 and 15 Mar., 1679). J. W. Stoye, *English Travellers Abroad, 1604–1667* (1952), 256–7. P.G. Hoftijzer, *Engelse boekverkopers bij de beurs: De geschiedenis van de Amsterdamse boekhandels Bruyning en Swart* (Amsterdam, 1987), 110.
37. *Historical Manuscripts Commission*, vol.17. House of Lords i. 1678–85. no. 498. 274. Affidavit dated 5 July 1684.

CHAPTER THIRTEEN

The Power Behind the Merchant? Women and the Economy in Late-Seventeenth Century Edinburgh[1]

Helen Dingwall

UNTIL FAIRLY RECENTLY it has been accepted by many social and economic historians that by 1700 women were becoming much less able to contribute independently to the economy, and that they had been reduced to a supporting role in household or workshop. In her pioneering study of early modern English women, Alice Clark took the view that 'Restoration women were but shadows of the vigorous personalities of their grandmothers';[2] this, however, may be more true of the surviving records than of the women themselves, and recent work has concluded that at least in some areas of the economy women continued to have the opportunity to contribute independently and actively.[3] While individual women may have enjoyed less economic prominence as industrialisation brought in significant social and economic change, particularly in the growing towns, it may be argued that collectively women maintained their economic importance, though its focus and manifestation may have been changing. As the pre-industrial period progressed in Scotland, women were still crucial to the economy, but, increasingly, in rather different ways. If some previously prominent Edinburgh women were rendered less economically important, this may have been to a considerable extent the result of general socio-economic realignment, in which new skills and organisations were acquired by men, and in which the occupational balance was changing, rather than simply the apparent economic subjugation of women in a male-dominated society.

Those who seek to assess the independent economic contribution of Scottish women have to make do with less than plentiful source materials. Quantitative sources are particularly lacking in comprehensive household information, usually revealing occupational details about the head of the household only. Single female householders were often widows and designated thus, so that any gainful pursuit is not divulged. However, for Edinburgh a number of imperfect sources survive, including Poll Tax records and port books,[4] which provide an opportunity to assess some late-seventeenth century women. Edinburgh was at the forefront of· professionalisation and tertiary services, and it will be argued that in Scotland's capital, while a fair number of women could and did maintain a high economic profile, an important barrier to continued progress was that women could not enter the professions. Tertiary services were not well established, nor indeed essential, in rural or less urbanised areas, and Edinburgh was unique among Scottish towns; however a unique situation demands individual attention. More conventional views on the changing status of women in this period may hold good for the rest of Scotland, and even for Edinburgh in part, but there were additional factors. This chapter will, therefore, attempt to highlight the role and functions of late seventeenth-century Edinburgh women against a background of changing social and economic structures. In particular, the role of women in the merchant and retailing trades will be examined, together with their functions in other, less visible, areas of the economy. While the economic contributions of unskilled women remained consistently important, no matter the structure of society or stage of industrialisation, higher-status women were more susceptible to the vagaries of trade and changes in social structures – as indeed were their husbands.

Industrialisation has been regarded as a major factor in the apparent reduction in the independent economic importance of women, although this view has also been challenged, particularly by historians writing from a feminist perspective, who regard gender conflict rather than industria-lisation *per se* as the source of growing discrimination or eclipse of women from leading economic roles.[5] It has been argued that in medieval times women could participate on equal terms with men in most occupa-tions, but that the advent of organisations such as merchant and craft guilds, to which women could not belong, served to prevent them from acquiring new skills, thus effectively relegating them to the realms of unskilled work.[6] The gradual separation of work from the home also played a part. It has also been argued, though, that in the industrialisation process in Scotland, 'a major facilitating factor was the ready availability of female, and child, labour'.[7] It may be that women and children were important because they were the groups more readily available to transfer their labour to industrial processes, but whatever the case, they were constantly necessary. It is, therefore, essential to try to reassess Edinburgh women at the beginning of the crucial transition of the capital from merchants' town to Enlightenment city. Edinburgh, with its complex socio-economic profile, would not industrialise in the same way as Glasgow, and this may have allowed some women to maintain their economic position longer.

The sex-ratio of late seventeenth-century Edinburgh was skewed sig-nificantly, the ratio for the burgh as a whole being seventy-six males to 100 females. In the highly urbanised and central Old Kirk parish, the ratio was 71:100, but in the much more rurally-configured peripheral parishes the ratio was considerably closer to parity, the norm for more rural societies, at 89:100.[8] The unusual ratio in the inner parishes may be explained by the presence of large numbers of female domestic servants, who lived and worked in the households of merchants, craftsmen and professionals, together with a fair number of widows heading large households and employing female servants. These female servants, numbering well over 3000, out of a population of some 40,000, clearly influenced the economy, however indirectly, by their household work (including the lucrative and important work of the highly-paid wet nurses), their assistance in manufacturing processes, and also by their 'sideline' pursuits of ale, butter and cheese selling, which they did either on behalf of their employer or on their own account.[9] This was not an age of single-occupation work at any level of society. Individuals worked in their 'designated' occupation, but supplemented their incomes by undertaking all sorts of additional economic activities, from ale selling to moneylending. Domestic servants were involved in these pursuits despite the seemingly all-inclusive nature of their primary employment. While these women were perhaps not individually crucial to the economy of Scotland's capital, collectively they certainly were, and indeed higher-status women depended on them.

The occupational profile of Edinburgh was uniquely complex, with over 180 different occupations appearing on Poll Tax returns, ranging from arithmetician to executioner, quaich maker, royal trumpeter and fencing master. Professional occupations, particularly in the central parishes, accounted for as much as thirteen per cent of all stated occupations.[10] Although some women appeared in this category as schoolteachers, they could not enter the church or the rapidly-expanding legal and medical professions from which Edinburgh's wealth was increasingly derived.

The foundation of the Merchant Company of Edinburgh in 1681 heralded a new type of institution. Unlike the old Merchant Guild, it was not just a protectionist body defending the privileges of its members; it also indulged in corporate trading on its own behalf. Membership was deemed necessary before a merchant could trade overseas, though this proved difficult to enforce. In its early years a few women joined, although female admissions declined during the following half century. Importantly, though, the membership of women allowed their husbands to enter the Company; this has elements of continuity with the old burgess regulations, which allowed cheaper purchase of freedom if the applicant were married to the daughter of a burgess. That a woman could provide her husband with a passport to a new type of trading organisation illustrates the continuing value of women to their husbands as well as to the economy in their own right. In 1702, for example, Robert Lightbody was accepted into the Company when his second wife, Mary Campbell, had 'consigned her dues'.[11] This practice did not long survive the seventeenth century, but it indicates that at least a few Restoration Edinburgh women could still offer a boost to their husbands' merchant careers and emulate their allegedly more forceful grandmothers.

In her recent detailed study of women in the clothing and retail trades in eighteenth-century Edinburgh, Sanderson has shown that the Merchant Company kept a close watch on female workers, who were obliged to obtain a licence from the Company before they could sell their wares. This was a rather different state of affairs from the very early days of the Company, when women were full trading members in their own right.[12] The pursuit of non-licenced traders of both sexes has rather more to do with the maintenance of exclusivity than the persecution of women.

Examination of the intermittently-extant Edinburgh and Leith port books for the later seventeenth century reveals a small but consistent number of women, designated as 'merchants', signing for cargoes on their own behalf, and not on behalf of their husband or other male merchant, despite the efforts of the new Merchant Company to restrict foreign trade to its membership. Indeed, there are also some instances of men signing for goods destined for females.[13]

Between 1660 and 1700 some eighty women appear in the port records as importers or exporters of various commodities. This is a small group in comparison to the several hundred male merchants operating in the period, but these women were there and were trading independently. In general the amounts of goods credited to females were smaller than the often considerable quantities traded by men. Anna Ker, wife of Adam Darling, a practising and prosperous surgeon, was active in the 1660s, appearing on several occasions as importer and exporter of a variety of textile goods. In May 1667 she imported '160 ells flannel and other stuffe', at a duty of £8; a few months previously she had been responsible for the export 'be land for England of 1 pack and a half coarse cloth'.[14]

While many of these merchant women had husbands who were trading actively on their own account or following one of the professions, a number were widows, though this did not prevent them from participating in 'official' business. An entry in the import registers in January 1685 in the name of Lilias Douglas, widow of merchant Robert Douglas, stated that she had been authorised 'by warrant from the Lords of the Privy Council date 16 Sept last to import from England 250 ells of red cloath at 6d or 9d the ell for cloaths to the earl of Airlies troup'.[15] Several entries around this time referred to the import of material for army uniforms, reflecting the uncertainties of the short but turbulent reign of James VII, with its potential for armed conflict,[16] rendering it necessary to kit out troops in anticipation of unrest.

A number of women were involved in sending quantities of stockings to England and then re-importing them after they had been dyed. As part of a varied package of imports in August 1667, Anna Ker was credited with '40 pr Scots stockings dyed and returned';[17] while in September 1682, Isobel Stirling sent off '55 doz worsted stockings' to London.[18] She was one of the more active of the women during the 1670s and 1680s, her interests appearing to lie solely in textiles, including calico, silk, linen and lace, in addition to the stockings. Interestingly, all of the women were able to sign their names in the port registers, whereas a small number of male merchants were obliged to mark rather than sign.

Female traders may have been relatively few but they confirm that it was still possible for them to participate in business. The 'power behind the merchant' may have been behind him in terms of quantities of goods and numbers of women involved, but it was there and it was important. Many male merchants dealt in a wide variety of goods, and if some of their wives were able to organise the textile side of the operations, then they could concentrate on dealing in iron, wood and other heavier items. Women do not appear to have been involved in the wine trade.

The available port books before 1690 suggest that women were concerned almost exclusively with the movement of textiles (apart from the occasional foray into other goods, such as the forty-five pounds of tobacco imported by Janet Seaton in 1662,[19] or the large quantities of sugar, pepper, carrot seeds, currants, raisins and mace credited to Isobel Jollie in 1667).[20] However, from the early 1690s another aspect of women's activities appears. This may not have been a new development; it is possible that incomplete records masked the practice previously. Whatever the case, the port books begin to show a number of women branching out into the importing of a much wider range of goods, many of which were destined to stock the shelves of retail shops, owned or rented by women. Possibly towards the end of the century the retail shop, as opposed to sales from the front of a manufacturing workshop, became more common. These separate shops seem to have appeared rather later in Edinburgh than in England, where it has been suggested that by the early seventeenth century the larger towns were served by 'shops catering principally for the retail trade'.[21]

A local taxation roll for 1699[22] contained details of 115 commercial premises in Edinburgh, including seventy-two shops, twenty-two of which were owned or rented by women. Some women owned whole tenements, having perhaps benefited from carefully-drawn up, complex marriage contracts that ensured good and lasting financial provision. Scots law allowed women to retain greater control over heritable or immovable property after marriage than in England,[23] and this may have helped at least some Edinburgh women to remain economically active.

Among the female shop owners was Mrs Graham, member of the Merchant Company, who also featured in port books as an overseas merchant. Mary Campbell, who facilitated her husband's entry into the Merchant Company, was not on the 1699 list of shopkeepers, but the 20,000 pins she imported in 1690, together with quantities of crepe, soap and needles, seem rather too many for her own use.[24] Another active female trader, Isobel Campbell (Mrs Melville), did not appear on the taxation roll as a shopkeeper, but it seems reasonable to conclude that the many and varied goods she imported were intended to be shop stock for some of the listed shopkeepers rather than household items. She appears in the port ledgers on several occasions; one entry, dated September 1690, credited to her a mixed cargo containing: cradles, vinegar, saltpetre, iron snuffers, dishes, brass weights, ounce balances, nutmeg, mace, cloves, pepper, raisins, currants, rice, soap, dry confections, wet confections, writing paper, glasses, hat brushes, floor rubbers, hair besoms (brushes), and earthenware bowls.[25] This list has the appearance of stock for a general store, and supports the view put forward concerning English women's work, that 'women were very active in retailing'.[26] The shops kept by Edinburgh women were not temporary stalls or the rather more durable luckenbooths, but rather permanent properties which were assessed for rental value as a basis for contributions to local taxation, which was based upon property valuations rather than personal financial assets.

The limited information available confirms that some women could function at a reasonably high economic level, either in parallel with their husbands, or as widows attempting to support themselves. The retail shop offered an opportunity for women to set up this type of business and the provisions of marriage contracts probably helped some women continue in the retail trade after being widowed. Thus, in the trading and retailing aspects of late seventeenth-century Edinburgh, women could indeed provide welcome assistance, if not power, to their husbands, and in their own right. This was a period before banking had been firmly established, when business was built on precarious financial foundations, including complex property transactions, many of which involved women. Women functioned as moneylenders, lending to men and again providing indirect economic support. Elizabeth Antone, who appears on the 1699 shopkeeper's list, lent 300 merks (£200 Scots) to Andrew Brown, a well-known Edinburgh clockmaker.[27]

No assessment of late-seventeenth century Edinburgh women would be complete without reference to perhaps the most powerful woman of all, Agnes Campbell (Mrs Anderson), who succeeded her husband as royal printer and printer to the Tounis College (University) and ran a large and flourishing business for many years. Although Clark took the view that no women 'ever engaged in the manual process of printing',[28] Campbell was by no means a non-executive director. She imported paper for the works, undertook negotiations with the Town Council to find room in the University to set up a printing press, and dealt in person with Sir John Clerk of Penicuik for the lease of ground on his estate on which to erect a paper mill. The latter transaction is detailed in a document dated 23 April 1709, granting Agnes Campbell

> the tack (lease) of the Penicuik Mill lands with wells to carry the samen from the fountainhead thereof to her paper mill which she is to build upon the saids lands . . . with liberty to the said Agnes to erect and build a paper miln (mill) with as many office houses she shall think necessary upon any part of the forsaids lands she shall judge most convenient and that for the space of nineteen years.[29]

The cost to Campbell was to be £60 Scots entry money and an annual rental of £86, together with 'two rimms (reams) of fynest white paper and two rimms of coarser white paper made at the said miln'. An amusing additional clause was that a local minister, Mr McGeorge, was to receive 'as much paper as may write his sermons' free of charge.[30]

Agnes Campbell was a power in her own right, as well as having assisted her husband in building up the business. Her testament, recorded at her death at the age of 80 in 1717, notes that her business inventory included some 50,000 books deposited in various Edinburgh warehouses, including 29,000 Bibles, together with copies of acts of parliament, the valuation of the stock being over £11,000 Scots, and her total assets over £78,000 Scots.[31] Her position as University and royal publisher was prestigious; she was not the only printer in Edinburgh, and it may be concluded that she had proved herself more than capable of running what was clearly a substantial business concern, and also that she had enough political acumen (or helpful contacts) to survive the turbulent state of Scottish politics in the period. She may have been one of a few, but she was a woman who survived in a changing society in which it was increasingly difficult for women to head enterprises such as this.

Edinburgh had long been, and continued to be, a major focus of foreign trade, but the occupational distribution of the capital was changing. Merchant fortunes were declining by the end of the century, and the new pivot of the economy and of the realigned socio-economic profile was the professions. Professionalisation is a complex process and historiographically controversial,[32] but there is little doubt that the rapid expansion of professional occupations, particularly law and medicine, during the second half of the seventeenth century, meant that women could not participate in the aspect of the economy that was growing most steadily. This is not just a matter of gender differentials; these occupations were also closed to unqualified men.

The one area of the professions in which some women could become involved was education. The records show that a number of, mostly single, women designated themselves 'schoolteacher'. This was, though, on the lowest rung of the professional ladder. Indeed, it is debatable whether they should be accorded the designation of professionals. Masters in the prestigious grammar schools such as the historic High School of Edinburgh were highly qualified, with university degrees, and prepared their students for the University. Female teachers had to settle for rather less. Most of the women appearing on the Poll Tax returns as schoolteachers paid tax at the lowest level and were clearly close to the poverty line. They most probably taught very basic literacy, a little music and economically-useful skills such as sewing. Christian Porteous, a widow, managed to sustain herself by teaching 'a few children',[33] and Elizabeth Campbell, in similarly straitened circumstances, who 'doth only keep a skool', claimed to have no financial assets whatsoever.[34]

The increasing prominence of the professions in the socio-economic profile of Edinburgh was a significant factor in reducing the potential economic strength and influence of some women. Female merchants were one thing; female doctors and lawyers quite another. It is not sufficient, though, to view this process in terms of gender conflict; unskilled and unqualified men faced the same decline in their economic potential. Professionalisation meant that medical and legal men imposed standards and entrance examinations in order to bring about exclusivity to their professional bodies. Women were thus prevented from participating in these new, economically-fruitful areas, not merely because they were women, but because they could not acquire the necessary qualifications – a problem shared by many men.

All was not lost, though. In addition to their moneylending activities, women were involved in a less active, but nonetheless important, role – the ownership of properties, which were rented out for residential accommodation. Many individuals owned substantial properties – often complete tenement buildings – but chose to rent their own dwelling houses from another owner. The reasons for this are unclear, but records show that a substantial number of women in most Edinburgh parishes owned properties. These may have been acquired as the result of marriage contracts, or as payment of debts by transfer of assets ('physical' rather than cash payments were still common in the period before banking began to become more formalised – the advent of cash-based banks was yet another indirect means of excluding women from some aspects of economic activity). Whatever the case, this was yet another area in which women could and did operate. Of the 2738 hearths listed for the central Old Kirk parish in the Hearth Tax returns of 1691, 460 (fifteen per cent) were owned by thirty-two women (twenty-one per cent of the owners).[35] Mrs Wood owned a total of thirty-three hearths, divided into fairly substantial properties; one of these comprising eight hearths, was let to Sir William Binning. In the nearby Tron parish, the female owners, who accounted for seventeen per cent of the hearths, included Widow Heriot, one of whose tenants was the Marquis of Douglas, who rented a property with seven hearths, while Mrs Cessford owned no fewer than seventy hearths, her own spacious dwelling comprising twelve hearths.[36] Even in the poorer suburbs, which were much more 'rural' in socio-economic configuration, women still featured as property owners. In the large and sprawling West Kirk parish, which almost completely encircled the inner town, women comprised thirteen per cent of the house owners, and owned twelve per cent of the hearths.[37]

This is, perhaps, a rather indirect aspect of the economy, but confirms that women could be substantial property owners. The rentals on their properties provided them with an income, part of which could be let out at interest, or used in retailing or trading. The urban setting provided opportunities for women in many areas of the economy in its widest sense, and property ownership was one means by which they could remain independent. It may be that this type of activity was more feasible for Scottish women because their husbands could not dispose of their property without their permission; whatever the case, though, the pre-banking world continued to offer opportunities.

The question of the continuing role of women in the economy of late-seventeenth century Edinburgh is complex and must be viewed on several levels. Unskilled women had always been, and would continue to be, economically vital in terms of their numbers and physical labour. Women who had been able to deal independently and run retail businesses faced the same difficulties as did their husbands in a period of economic downturn, not helped by the 'ill-years' of the 1690s, nor by the French and Dutch wars, nor by the ill-fated Darien Scheme, which resulted in the loss of a quarter of Scotland's liquid assets. The power behind the merchant was weakened, but so was the power of the merchants themselves. Edinburgh entered the eighteenth century with a rather different occupational configuration from that with which she had begun the seventeenth. The position of women was similarly altered, but in many respects they were just as important and necessary to the economy as they always had been.

NOTES

1. I am most grateful to Dr Anne Laurence of the Open University for her helpful comments and suggestions on an earlier draft of the chapter.
2. A. Clark, *Working Life of Women in the Seventeenth Century* (London, 1919), 41.

3. For Scotland, see H. M. Dingwall, *Late Seventeenth Century Edinburgh: A Demographic Study* (Aldershot, 1994), 201–11; R. A. Houston, 'Women in the economy and society of Scotland, 1500–1800' in R. A. Houston and I. D. Whyte eds. *Scottish Society 1500–1800* (Cambridge, 1989), 118–47; E. C. Sanderson, *Women and Work in Eighteenth-century Edinburgh* (Basingstoke, 1996). For England see P. Earle, 'The female labour market in London in the late seventeenth and early eighteenth centuries' *Economic History Review*, 2nd ser. 43/3 (1989), 328–53; B. Hill, *Women, Work and Sexual Politics in Eighteenth-Century England* (London, 1989); A. Laurence, *Women in England 1500–1700* (London, 1994); I. Pinchbeck, *Women Workers in the Industrial Revolution 1750–1850* (London, 1930); P. Sharpe, *Adapting to Capitalism. Working Women in the English Economy, 1700–1850* (Basingstoke, 1996).

4. Scottish Record Office [SRO], E70/4/1–11, 1694 Poll Tax; E72, port books.

5. K. Honeyman and J. Goodman, 'Women's work, gender conflict, and labour markets in Europe, 1500–1900' *Economic History Review*, 44/4 (1991), 608–628.

6. Ibid, 610–1.

7. C. A. Whatley, 'Women and the economic transformation of Scotland c.1740–1830' *Scottish Economic and Social History*, 14 (1994), 19.

8. Dingwall, *Edinburgh*, 28–9.

9. Ibid, 44–9, 144–5, 206–7, 292.

10. Ibid, 142, Table 5.1.

11. Merchant Company of Edinburgh, MS Roll of Members, 1702.

12. Sanderson, *Women and Work*, 7–40.

13. SRO, E72/15/5, 21 Feb. 1667.

14. SRO, E72/8/3, 16 May 1667; E72/8/3/, 1 Nov. 1666.

15. SRO, E72/8/15, 22 Jan. 1685.

16. K. M. Brown, *Kingdom or Province? Scotland and the Regal Union, 1603–1715* (Basingstoke, 1992), 160–9.

17. SRO, E72/8/3, 1 Aug. 1667.

18. SRO, E72/8/11, 18 Sept. 1682; E72/8/14, 8 Sept. 1684.

19. SRO, E72/8/1, 19 Nov. 1662.

20. SRO, E72/15/5, 25 March 1667.

21. U. Priestly and A. Fenner, *Shops and Shopkeepers in Norwich 1660–1730* (Norwich, 1985), 2.

22. Edinburgh City Archive, Stent Roll, 1699.

23. Houston, 'Women in the economy and society of Scotland', 128–34.

24. SRO, E72/15/45, 4 March 1690.

25. SRO, E72/15/45, 30 Sept. 1690.

26. Laurence, *Women in England*, 130.

27. SRO, RH15/7/3, business papers.

28. Clark, *Working Life of Women*, 65, although H.S. Bennet, *English Books and Readers 1603–1640* (London, 1970) refers to female printers. On this point see also Alastair Mann's paper in this volume.

29. SRO, GD18/889/2, Clerk of Penicuik Papers.

30. SRO, GD18/5278, 4 Sept. 1711.

31. *Bannatyne Miscellany*, ii (Bannatyne Club, 1836), 285–9.

32. M. Burrage and R. Torstendahl, eds. *Professions in Theory and History. Rethinking the Study of the Professions* (London, 1990).
33. SRO, E70/4/7, Poll Tax, Tron Parish.
34. SRO, E70/4/6, Poll Tax, Tolbooth Parish.
35. SRO, E69/16/2, Hearth Tax.
36. SRO, E69/16/2.
37. SRO, E69/16/3.

PART FIVE

She 'upbraidit hir, and bad hir kis her ers'

A Scotch Woman

CHAPTER FOURTEEN

Women and Legal Representation in Early Sixteenth-Century Scotland[1]

_____ *John Finlay*

IN HIS *Practicks*, written around 1579, Sir James Balfour of Pittendreich listed those who were permitted to act as the procurators, or representatives, of others in the courts of law.[2] Amongst those debarred from doing this were the mute, the deaf, the mentally ill, the illiterate and those who, not falling into any previous category, simply happened to be women.[3] To Balfour's legal mind women did not rate highly when it came to the rational resolution of judicial matters: not only were they unable to act for others, but they were allowed neither to give evidence nor to sit on juries.[4] Balfour was outlining the law of post-Reformation Scotland and it would seem reasonable to conclude from this that the role of women in the courts was minimal. But the uncritical use of the *Practicks* for the elucidation of pre-Reformation Scots law and legal practice is fraught with danger. Balfour also excluded churchmen as procurators, but medieval churchmen were very active in this role. In this paper, evidence drawn mainly from the court record will be used to assess the extent to which the rules outlined by Balfour reflect the social reality of the role of women in legal practice in Scotland in the early sixteenth century. In particular, it will be argued that the part played by women at all levels of the court structure in later medieval Scotland was significant and multi-faceted.

In procedural terms before any person could be represented by another in the courts of medieval Scotland the latter had to be properly constituted as a procurator in court and given sufficient authority to act. This normally involved a litigant personally appearing before the court and authorising a named person or persons to represent him or her either generally, in all actions that might arise, or specially, that is, in a particular action. Whatever the particular powers specified in the procurator's constitution, normally he had the power to win or lose the case on his client's behalf and the client invariably undertook to ratify ('to hald ferme and stable') whatever the procurator did within the scope of his constitution. On 14 July 1518, before the lords of council:

> Comperit Elene douglas lady Levingstoun and constitute
> procuratouris M[aster] Robert galbraith M[aster] thomas hamilton
> in the actioun movit be hir aganis James Douglas for away takin of
> ane horss *et promisit de Rato*.[5]

Helen, appearing in court personally, promised to ratify whatever her procurators did in pursuing her summons against James. Leaving aside for the moment the question of whether women could represent others, it is clear that women could, and often did, represent themselves in actions before the court, and that, as a consequence of this, they could authorise professional men of law to act on their behalf. Thus on 7 December 1530, Janet Strachan compeared and constituted procurators to represent her in an action raised against her by Lady Moncrieff.[6]

Even the stereotypical damsel in distress[7] would go to law rather than wait to be rescued by some late medieval display of chivalry. In 1540 Margaret Kinloch's advocate, Thomas Marjoribankis, presented her case against William Edmonstone of Duntreath alleging that he:

> with his complices maisterfully & by force haldis hir in subiectioun
> & firmance & bidis to gar hir mary quhair thai pleiss contrar hir
> will to that effect that thai may gett hir landis & heritage to thaim
> & to dishereiss hir thirof to greit apperand scaith.[8]

Edmonstone was threatened by the lords of session with denunciation as a rebel unless he put Margaret 'to fredome & liberatioune' within twenty-four hours. At the same time he was ordered to produce her so that the lords could ascertain whether she was being held against her will. Margaret is named as the party bringing the action; this perhaps implies that Marjoribankis had been constituted by her under a general procuratory at some earlier date and that he was acting on that authority. The context makes it unlikely that Margaret had been able to give any fresh authority to Marjoribankis to appear on her behalf.

Although cases of this kind may give the impression that women were rather ineffectual in the legal world, the bulk of evidence is to the contrary. Women are often found in the courts defending their rights and the rights of their children or husbands. In 1532 Elizabeth Scrimgeour, wife of Sir Thomas Erskine of Brechin, the king's secretary, appeared by her procurator to defend her husband's interests while he was on embassy in France.[9] As was customary, for the duration of such periods abroad, Erskine was exempt from having actions raised against him in the courts. Nonetheless Sir John Carnmaneth had taken this opportunity to purchase royal letters by which he intended, it was alleged, to poind and distrain certain lands belonging to Erskine for non-payment of an annualrent which he claimed was due to him. With Erskine abroad, it was up to his wife to act and this she did by instructing Henry Lauder, an experienced advocate, to persuade the lords to suspend Carmaneth's letters. This was successfully achieved.

Margaret Kinloch and Elizabeth Scrimgeour were wealthy women. Although some of the women mentioned in the court record are much

more obscure figures whose backgrounds are unknown, a high proportion of those who appear were socially significant. At the apex, of course,
was the queen. There is evidence that queens had their own procurators as
early as the mid-fifteenth century. In 1443 John Dishington of Ardross,
one of the lords of council, was described as procurator for Queen Joan,
the widow of James I.[10] During the minority of James III, in 1461, Mr.
Gilbert Heryng, *advocato domine regine* is recorded in the Exchequer
Roll.[11] The *domina regina* referred to was Mary of Gueldres and Gilbert
had received a payment for coming from Edinburgh to Falkland probably
to proffer advice in relation to prospective litigation. Such references, few
as they are, coincide with periods of royal minority. The next royal
minority during which the queen mother was still alive was that of James
V. Margaret Tudor regularly used procurators before the central courts.
It was during her late husband's reign that the office of king's advocate
had developed and it is not surprising to find that by the 1520s the queen
should as of right have had her own advocate.

As James IV's widow, Margaret had been entrusted with the regency of
the kingdom and tutory of the heir to the throne on condition that she did
not re-marry.[12] When, in 1514, she married the Earl of Angus, the lords
reacted quickly and robustly, declaring that she, having 'contractit
marraige and past *ad secundas nuptias*', had thereby lost the office of
tutory. They ordered all lieges, temporal and spiritual, in the king's name
not to obey the queen nor to accept any reward from her that properly
belonged to her son the king. Anyone who did so 'salbe reput as
conspiratouris agane the commoun weile and gud public of the realme'.[13]
Margaret's representative before the lords, who met with no success in
arguing her case, was her new husband's kinsman the poet Gavin
Douglas, at the time postulate of Arbroath and later Bishop of Dunkeld.[14]
This unsatisfactory outcome may have persuaded Margaret to seek more
professional legal assistance in future; but in difficult circumstances,
including a period of exile from September 1515, her interests were
represented in the meantime by a variety of procurators including some
Englishmen.[15] By the time it is possible to identify a regular man of law
representing Margaret she had returned from exile and her relationship
with her husband had broken down. The advocate she employed, Robert
Galbraith, was a former professor of law in Paris who remained in the
front rank of Scottish practitioners as both procurator and judge until his
death in 1544. He first represented Margaret from her return to Scotland
in June 1517, and retained his position even after he became a lord of
session in November 1537. The fact that he is specifically referred to as
'advocate' when representing the queen, and not the more usual 'procurator', may indicate that his role was seen as equivalent in status to that
of the king's advocate. In the reign of James IV the use of the word

'advocate' was virtually synonymous with the newly-created office of king's advocate and it is a matter of conjecture whether Margaret was consciously imitating this office. There is no evidence that Galbraith, who was also treasurer of the Chapel Royal at Stirling, was paid a yearly retainer by Margaret although it is likely that he was; he certainly seems to have enjoyed the other rewards that went along with representing the widow and mother of a king.[16]

It is worth looking at part of a letter from Margaret to her advocate dated 23 April 1531 not least because it is a very rare example of early sixteenth-century correspondence between client and man of law:

> Advocat It is our will and we pray zow rycht effectiouslie and als charge that incontinent eftir the sicht herof ze ansir to the summondis raisit aganis our derrest soun and ws at the instance of our lovit ad[am] stewart of schawstoun . . . as ze will have severale thank of ws therfor and do ws singular emplessyr and ansyr to ws thirapoun subscrivit with our hand togeddir with the subscriptioun of oure derrest spous in signe of his consent to the promiss.[17]

The concluding part of this missive, in its wording, is similar to a letter which James IV wrote to his own advocate a few months prior to Flodden although, of course, that earlier letter bore no reference to – nor did it require – spousal consent.[18]

A wide variety of women appeared in civil cases on their own behalf and also hired procurators to represent them. For example, Janet Homyll, widow of the Edinburgh burgess Lancelot Fery, brought an action against her late husband's brother, David, in 1514. She claimed that David had arrested certain goods in France that belonged to Lancelot's children, in contravention of acts of parliament which specified that such mercantile actions had to be raised in Scotland. In the action Janet is designated as being 'personaly present'. This does not necessarily mean that she acted personally: it was quite normal, when the clerks noted the presence of the parties, for them not to include the name of their representative – such an inclusion would in those circumstances be otiose. In this instance it is likely that Janet was represented; two days prior to this appearance the court record bears a note in which actions between Janet and David are referred to arbitration. Janet had selected as her arbitrators Mr. Adam Otterburn and James Logan.[19] Otterburn had acted on occasion as king's advocate during James IV's reign and would do so again under James V; Logan was sheriff depute of Lothian: either could have acted on Janet's behalf in her later action and, indeed, Otterburn had acted as her forespeaker at the end of January when he was described, in what must have been a lively exchange with David Fery, as 'ane gegar' or liar.[20]

It is beyond dispute that women were often physically present in court and it is perfectly feasible that they were representing themselves in legal disputes. Normally it is impossible to tell from the way the clerks kept the record whether or not a party who was personally present had professional assistance. However a man of law appearing in court for a client who was also present was almost invariably designated as 'forespeaker' rather than 'procurator' and the application of the former designation normally indicates that his client was within the court. When, for example, James Carmuir appeared as 'forespeaker' for Elizabeth Gray, Lady Dunlop, it is safe to assume that she stood beside him at the bar of the court as he argued her case.[21] In such a situation the client was in a better position to control and influence the line of reasoning put forward by her man of law in his argument before the judges. But this is not the only indication that women were present in court looking after their own interests. Although constitution by letter became increasingly common, the formal rule was that any person who wished to constitute a procurator had to do so personally in court before the judge.[22] This meant that women, unless married, generally appeared personally to constitute a procurator. Thus in October 1515, Elizabeth Hepburn constituted procurators to defend her in an action already raised against her by David Lindsay of Gareston.[23] Until this moment Elizabeth had no procurators and since no one else had the power to do so, it may be concluded that she did in fact personally appear in order to constitute them. By far the most significant category of women likely to appear in court for this purpose were widows since they were freed from the control of husbands and fathers.[24]

In contrast, females not old enough to marry were often represented by their father or another male relative. If that male relative happened to be a legal expert so much the better. In 1515 William Wawane, Official of Lothian, acted as procurator for his widowed niece Christine, Lady Dirleton, and also as tutor to her daughters Janet, Margaret and Marion Haliburton, before the lords of council.[25] More often than not, a man of law was instructed in a testamentary writing to represent the interests of female heirs and to act as tutor or curator in the event of their father's death. Robert Galbraith is found acting by this means in the capacity of tutor to Margaret and Elizabeth, the daughters of the late William Sinclair of Hirdmanston against their mother and William's widow, Beatrice.[26] It transpired that Beatrice and her accomplices had removed the children from school in the abbey of Haddington where they were being educated at Galbraith's expense.[27] Galbraith obtained a summons from the king's chancery requiring Beatrice to restore the girls to him as tutor in compliance with their father's wishes or to appear before the lords within three days to explain why she had not done so. The matter was quickly resolved when the lords ordered that the girls be restored in terms of Galbraith's petition and just over a week later Beatrice asked that it be recorded that she and her accomplices had complied with the lords' decreet.[28] In the absence of a male relative, a man of law could also act as the procurator of an orphan apparently without requiring to have the status of tutor or curator. Thus the six daughters of David Cunningham, a deceased Dundee burgess, who had been served as his heirs by an inquest were represented not by a relative but by Master John Lethame, one of the advocates of the College of Justice, in an action in which it was decided that the inquest had wilfully erred in their favour.[29] Nor was it only in their minority that females could be represented by their fathers. Christine Cockburn, the widow of David Stewart, was represented by her father in an action she brought as a result of being cast out of lands in Kelso that she held on a lease issued to her late husband by Andrew, Bishop of Caithness and Commendator of Kelso.[30]

The married state itself had particular consequences for any woman contemplating litigation. In one case it was argued that Helen Campbell, who was betrothed to Thomas Kennedy, could not pursue a summons because it ran in her name alone and bore no indication that Thomas knew of, or consented to, the action.[31] This argument was rejected, presumably because, as Helen's procurator put it 'thai war nocht spousit yit'. Until Thomas actually married Helen he had insufficient interest in the matter to render his consent legally necessary. Once the marriage had taken place, however, the husband was entitled to constitute a procurator on his wife's behalf or revoke any previous constitution which she might have made. For example, in October 1532, Henry McCulloch appeared in his wife's name and constituted one of the advocates of the College of Justice to represent her, perhaps in conjunction with Henry himself.[32] This may be contrasted with the example of Baldred Blakadder who in 1494 revoked all procuratories previously made by him and also those made or to be made by his wife, Margaret.[33]

It was common for the husband himself to be named as one of his wife's procurators. When Lady Herries named five procurators to represent her, including James Wishart and Robert Galbraith, she put her husband, the Master of Hailes, at the top of the list even though Wishart was at the time the king's advocate and thereby the leading man of law in the realm.[34] In the fifteenth century it was often the case that the husband alone acted as his wife's procurator, but increasingly it became the practice that the husband in conjunction with one or more experienced men of law would be constituted as procurators. Where a husband did act as his wife's procurator it was sometimes necessary to find caution that she would ratify whatever he did in her name. The husband himself occasionally acted as cautioner, as when Gilbert Wauchop of Niddrie Marischal appeared to offer caution that 'his wif suld hald ferme and stable quhat he did' on her behalf 'undir the pane of double'.[35] Another procurator could also act in this capacity; early in 1533 Master John Lethame, one of three procurators of the Perth burgess Thomas Houston and his wife Katherine Scott, acted as cautioner that Katherine would ratify any undertaking made by them on behalf of her husband and her.[36]

The rule expressed by Balfour in his *Practicks* notwithstanding, there is evidence that women did act as procurators in the courts. In an action brought against Agnes Eldar, daughter and heiress of the late John Eldar, and her tutors, Agnes is said to have appeared by Margaret Wallace, Sir John Inglis and Master James Carmuir her 'tutoris & procuratouris'.[37] Margaret was Agnes' mother and it might be better to analyse her appearance in court on Agnes' behalf more in terms of her role as tutrix than as a procurator strictly speaking even though that term is also used. Much the same might be said of similar later examples such as Alexander Newton who compeared by Margaret Kerr his 'modir (mother) tutrix & governour' and John Murray who appeared by Agnes Cockburn his 'modir & tutrice'.[38] It should be noted that a woman appearing as a pupil's tutrix need not be that pupil's mother. For example, Marion Douglas was tutrix testamentary of William Douglas of Moffat (presumably her nephew) and represented him in an action brought against William and his widowed mother Margaret Herries.[39] The word 'tutrix' was not used when George, Agnes, Elizabeth and Margaret, the children of the late Lord Glamis and his wife Janet Douglas, were noted 'comperand be jonet douglas thir moder procuratoure & factour'. They were pursuing a summons that was raised at their instance against John Lyoun and his accomplices for 'spuilzie', or dispossession without warrant or consent, of sixteen oxen which belonged to them and had been in their mother's keeping.[40] In an interesting dispute concerning the ownership of a black gown lined with velvet which had been left in his will by George Hepburn, the late dean of Dunkeld, Margaret Cornwell appeared as procurator for her son Master Adam Cockburn and argued that the gown had been gifted by the dean to the bishop of Dunkeld.[41] There is no question of Margaret acting as tutor in this case.[42]

Women clearly acted in court as procurators for their children (whether pupils or not) but did they act for their husbands? Of interest here is a constitution of procurators by David Heriot of Trabroun in January, 1531. Heriot constituted 'M[aster] John Lethame Sir Alexander Scott M[aster] robert calbraith M[aster] thomas merioribankis *and marioun cokburn his spous*' his procurators in his action against William Hepburn 'eme' to the Earl Bothwell and in all his other actions.[43] Nor is this unique. A fragment from the burgh court of Edinburgh, belonging to the reign of James IV, contains a constitution of procurators by John Cant which includes the provost Alexander Lauder, Master James Henryson (who was at the time the king's advocate) and Agnes Carkettle who was

Cant's wife.[44] This was a general constitution, empowering procurators to appear in all actions concerning Cant in both spiritual and temporal courts.

When Margaret Moncreiff, widow of Robert Mercer, brought an action against Robert's son and heir also named Robert, to act as her warrantor and to defend lands assigned by him as her terce after her first husband's death, she not only appeared for herself but also as procurator for her present husband Henry Luvell.[45] Likewise Margaret Somerville, wife of the Edinburgh burgess Robert Adamson, appeared in person on behalf of her husband and herself to pursue an action of spuilzie against Sir John Sinclair of Driden and his son.[46] In one case it was alleged by the king's advocate that John Cant had broken an arrestment made by royal authority of a ship in the port of Leith.[47] The arrestment was made because the ship was carrying Norwegian timber and by statute no merchant was to purchase any foreign timber brought into the realm until the king had the opportunity of doing so. Cant appeared by his wife to defend the case against him. The argument put forward on his behalf was that he was 'vesyit (visited) with the hand of god in greit seiknes' three weeks before and until some four or five days after the skipper of the ship had delivered the timber to his wife; during this time he never handled the timber nor was he aware of the arrestment. The penalty for breaking the king's arrestment was severe – escheat of movable goods and imprisonment for a year and a day – and it is indicative of Cant's faith in his wife that he should allow her to represent him in court.[48] These were women entrusted with the same authority to act in the name of their husbands as was customarily exercised by husbands in relation to their wives. This can be clearly seen from the activities of Elizabeth Blair the wife of Ninian Stewart, sheriff of Bute. Elizabeth, together with Master Duncan Lennox, vicar of Kingarth, appeared as Ninian's procurator in an action concerning rent owed by the latter to the comptroller for his lordship of Bute. Master William Gibson, dean of Lestalrig, gave caution that Ninian would pay the comptroller £40 by Michaelmas while Elizabeth and Duncan undertook to stand as surety for his relief in the event that Ninian failed to pay.[49]

Such examples raise a serious question mark against Balfour's broad statement that women could in no circumstances act as procurators. They clearly could do so.[50] It is evident that they could also be given a general mandate. Perhaps the acid test is the situation identified near the beginning of this chapter in the example of Elizabeth Scrimgeour who instructed a man of law to intervene in her husband's affairs when he was abroad on the king's business. One example, although later in date, indicates that a wife herself could act as procurator in such circumstances. In April 1565 Isobel Balfour, Lady Carraldston (Careston) is recorded acting 'in name and behalf of Johnne Seytoune hir spouse as his lauchtfull procuratour in his absence furtht of this realme'.[51]

To conclude, the court records reveal a large number of cases involving women in a number of roles. Sometimes they represented themselves, sometimes they were represented by their father, husband, or son,[52] or, equally likely, by a professional man of law. Some of the most interesting references are to incidental details in cases which concern women only obliquely. For example, in 1540 Walter Scott of Branxholme alleged that John Scott and his accomplices had appeared at his house and chased his wife with a long Jedburgh staff and would have killed her had they been better horsemen.[53] In 1528 a domestic dispute was recorded involving Elizabeth Cunningham, the wife of John Lord Hay of Yester, and her husband. Elizabeth alleged that she had been compelled in fear of her life to lock herself in her chamber and she was corroborated by her son who alleged that he dared not stay in the house.[54] But this is not to suggest that women were always passive when it came to acts of wrongdoing. In 1517, for example, the wife of the advocate Adam Otterburn was accused of having offered 'ain doublit and ane pair of hois' to a certain John Elphinstone as a bribe in return for his making a deposition.[55] More severe than an allegation of subornation of perjury was the case of Marion Craig who in 1556 was sent to the 'thieves hole' in the Tolbooth for six months for uttering slanderous words to the senators of the College of Justice.[56]

The evidence that exists can sometimes be fragmentary but it clearly shows that the courts in the late fifteenth and early sixteenth centuries were not solely the preserve of men. From the queen dowager and her granddaughter Queen Mary, to the widows of the king's gunner and his master mason;[57] from significant landowners such as the Countess of Bothwell[58] to those at the other end of the spectrum represented by the advocate for the poor, the opportunity existed to bring the complaints and the concerns of a wide range of women into the courts. The evidence suggests that they used it.

NOTES

1. I am grateful to Mr W. D. H. Sellar for his comments on earlier drafts of this paper.
2. For Balfour's *Practicks*, see Winifred Coutts in this volume. On Practicks in general see *An Introductory Survey of the Sources and Literature of Scots Law* (Stair Society, 1936), 25.
3. J. Balfour, *Practicks* ed. P. G. B. McNeill (2 vols, Stair Society, 1962–3), ii, 298–9.

4. Balfour, *Practicks*, ii, 378.
5. Scottish Record Office [SRO], CS5/31 fo 105v.
6. SRO, CS5/41 fo 142r.
7. For a captive woman described as a 'damsel' see SRO, CS6/14 fos 14r, 33v.
8. SRO, CS6/13 fo 107v. For a similar case see M. F. Tweedie, *The History of the Tweedie or Tweedy Family* (London, 1902), 26–30; J. W. Buchan and H. Paton, *History of Peebleshire* (Glasgow, 1927), iii, 403–4, 425 ff; SRO, CS5/35 fos 44r-v, 77r-v; CS5/41 fos 4v,155r, CS5/42 fos 2v, 4v, 6r, 7r, 8v, 24r, 30r, 64v, 93r-94r, 150r-v, 153r, 192r; SRO, Justiciary Court [JC]27/2/2; JC27/3.
9. SRO, CS6/1 fo 75v.
10. *Historic Manuscripts Commission*, 10th Report, appx. I, 63, no. 9.
11. *The Exchequer Rolls of Scotland* eds. J. Stuart et al (Edinburgh, 1878–1908), vii, 59.
12. See G. Donaldson, *James V to James VII* (Edinburgh, 1976), 31–3; C. Edington, *Court and Culture in Renaissance Scotland* (East Linton, 1995) chapter 1; W. K. Emond 'The Minority of James V' (unpublished PhD thesis, University of St Andrews, 1988); J. Cameron, 'Crown Magnate Relations in the Personal Rule of James V' (unpublished PhD thesis, University of St Andrews, 1994).
13. SRO, CS5/26 fo 168r.
14. P. Bawcutt, *Gavin Douglas* (Edinburgh, 1976).
15. SRO, CS5/26 fo 82v; CS5/27 fo 70r; CS5/28 fos 33v, 41r.
16. *Protocol Book of John Foular 1528–1534* ed. John Durkan (Scottish Record Society, 1985), no.221; SRO, RH 6/1057; *Registrum Magni Sigilli Regum Scottorum* eds. J. M. Thomson et al (Edinburgh, 1882–1914), iii, no.869.
17. SRO, CS5/43 fo 168r, entry dated 26 February 1531/2.
18. *Historical Manuscripts Commission*, Fourth Report, appx, 503.
19. SRO, CS5/26 fo 70v.
20. SRO, CS5/26 fo 60r.
21. SRO, CS5/41 fo 2v, also fo 55r. For another example see CS5/27 fo 210r.
22. National Library of Scotland, Adv. MS. 25.5.7, Foulis MS, *Regiam Majestatem*, lib 3, cap. xi. Written *c.*1475.
23. SRO, CS5/27 fo 86v.
24. R. A. Houston, 'Women in the Economy and Society of Scotland, 1500–1800' in R. A. Houston and I. D. Whyte eds. *Scottish Society 1500–1800* (Cambridge, 1989).
25. SRO, CS5/27 fo 84r.
26. SRO, CS5/43 fo 66r. For Galbraith and William Sinclair, see CS6/1 fo 97r, *Calendar of Writs preserved at Yester House 1166–1503* eds. C. C. H. Harvey and J. Macleod (Scottish Record Society, 1930), nos 424,500; *Registrum Secreti Sigilli Regum Scotorum* eds M. Livingstone et al (Edinburgh, 1908–), ii, no.820; SRO, B30/1/2, Protocol Book of Alexander Symsoun.
27. SRO, CS5/43 fo 67v.
28. SRO, CS5/43 fo 82v.
29. SRO, CS6/1 fo 82r.
30. SRO, CS5/26 fo 27r.
31. SRO, CS5/34 fo 110v. For betrothal and handfasting see Rosalind K.

Marshall, *Virgins and Viragos: A History of Women in Scotland from 1080–1980* (London, 1983), 27–8.

32. SRO, CS6/1 fo 9v.
33. *The Acts of the Lords of Council in Civil Causes* eds. T. Thomson et al (Edinburgh, 1839, 1918–95), ii, 349.
34. SRO, CS5/27 fo 144v.
35. SRO, CS5/27 fo 197r. For similar entries see CS5/28 fos 121v,80r and CS6/2 fo 31v (although here the woman is not designated as a spouse).
36. SRO, CS6/2 fo 107r.
37. SRO, CS5/26 fo 82v. 22 February 1513/14.
38. SRO, CS5/28 fo 48v. 5 November 1516; CS5/33 fo 88v. 12 December 1522.
39. SRO, CS5/31 fo 82v. 9 July 1518.
40. SRO, CS5/40 fo 102r. 9 October, 1529.
41. SRO, CS5/38 fos 49r-v.
42. Cf SRO, CS5/31 fos 117v,134v,143r.
43. SRO, CS5/41 fo 155v. 14 January 1530/1. Emphasis added.
44. SRO, B22/23/1.
45. SRO, CS5/39 fo 169v. 13 March 1528/9.
46. SRO, CS5/36 fo 98v. 19 October 1526.
47. SRO, CS5/37 fos 185r, 188r.
48. Cf. similar representation in SRO, CS5/37 fo 220v.
49. SRO, CS5/40 fos 92v-93r. 11 August 1529.
50. Other examples include SRO, CS5/28 fo 121v; CS5/29 fo 197r; CS5/31 fos 12r, 115v, 148r; CS5/32 fo 2r; CS5/41 fo 58v.
51. B52/1/16 fo 17r, Benet's Protocol Book. At Tranent. I am indebted to Dr Alan R. MacDonald, University of St Andrews, for this reference.
52. For example, SRO, CS5/28 fo 66r.
53. SRO, CS6/14 fo 86r. See also CS5/31 fo 150r.
54. SRO, CS5/38 fos 171v-172v.
55. SRO, CS5/28 fo 175v. For Otterburn's family, see J. A. Inglis, *Sir Adam Otterburn of Reidhall* (Glasgow, 1935), 116–7.
56. SRO, CS6/29 fo 14v.
57. SRO, CS6/2 fo 23v; CS6/1 fo 87v.
58. SRO, CS6/3 fo 78v.

CHAPTER FIFTEEN

Wife and Widow:
The Evidence of Testaments and
Marriage Contracts c. 1600

_____ *Winifred Coutts*

THE LEGAL POSITION of married women in late-sixteenth and early-seventeenth century Scotland was inferior to that of men, although the mutual obligations and moral responsibilities of marriage were virtually the same for both sexes. Non-fulfilment, adherence and divorce law bore equally on both.[1] A woman on marriage kept her maiden name, but this may simply imply that marriage was a link between two kin-groups.[2] A wife had fewer legal rights than her husband, an unmarried woman over twenty-one, or a widow. All women were inferior in law in that, apart from as a mother or nurse proving someone's age, they could not be witnesses in civil cases heard in the supreme court.[3] Although women could be executors, none was appointed in a testament to act as an overseer to supervise the fulfilment of the testator's wishes. Many wives and widows, however, were not as legally constrained as theory might suggest; this can be shown by an examination of surviving testaments, marriage contracts, and the court cases in which such documents featured.

Information about the legal position of women around 1600 can be gleaned from several extant legal sources. Principal among these is Balfour's *Practicks* (1579–83), a digest of contemporary laws based on Balfour's own judicial experience, old laws, decisions from a register now lost, and statutes.[4] *Ius Feudale* by Thomas Craig, a practising advocate, discusses conjunct infeftment, liferent, terce and courtesy, all of which affected wives and widows.[5] Hope's *Practicks*, the personal notebook of a busy legal practitioner, covers the entire range of contemporary practice between 1608 and 1633.[6] The most important sources for this study, however, are the manuscript sources in the Scottish Record Office. The seventeenth-century *Registers of Testaments* for Edinburgh and Dumfries[7] and the *Registers of Acts and Decreets of the Lords of Council and Session* for 1600[8] have been studied in detail along with the unindexed processes, *Warrants and Decreets*.[9] What can these sources tell us about wives and widows and the law?

On marriage a woman ceased to have an independent legal *persona*; she could not act without her husband's consent or contract personal obligations, although as head of the household she could pledge her husband's credit. He had to approve her pursuit or defence of any civil action.[10] Some cases before the Lords of Council and Session were raised by or against single women or widows but those involving wives bear the words 'A, relict,' (or daughter) 'of B and C her spouse for his interest'.[11]

On marriage all the wife's moveables, including rents from her heritable property, passed to her husband. Her paraphernalia (jewels and clothes) were her own to gift, but not heirlooms or household furniture.[12] A widow or single woman could make a testament, but a wife needed the approval of her husband as *dominus omnium bonorum*.[13] As Balfour puts it,

> ane woman that is fre and not under subiection to ane husband may mak ane testament of hir guids and geir . . . bot ane woman beand cled with ane husband and thairby in his powar and subiection, may dispone and give na thing in hir latter will without his consent . . . nevertheless the husband dois ane honest and godlie thing gif he permittis and grantis to his wife licence and powar to mak testament of that part of the gudis and geir quhilk sould have pertenit to hir, gif scho had happinit to live efter him.[14]

A wife who could make a testament seems to have been completely free to test as she wished. Although Balfour implies that a wife, like a husband, was legally compelled to give a third of the moveable estate to the spouse if there were children or a half if there were none, later jurists such as Stair and Hume clearly state that *legitim*, or bairn's part, affected the father only.[15] Actual testaments show how often mothers provided for their children. Euphemia Broomrig, whose husband and children were alive, left a will in three parts.[16] In each case the husband's prior consent is implied, although never specifically mentioned. Such consent may have been given because the wife had brought goods from a previous marriage; her current husband may have felt such goods were hers by right.

Husbands frequently tried to protect their wives through testaments. Time and again male overseers were appointed 'to see that nane do wrang to my wife and bairns'.[17] Some who could afford to do so reinforced this responsibility with a gift. Thus £10 was left to the Laird of Cowhill 'desiring him for Godis cause to be good to my wife' and a farmer left the Laird of Lag as 'protector, maintainer and defender of my wife and bairns . . . to suffer no man to do thame wrang, fortie punds or ane of my horses', whichever he pleased best.[18]

Husbands often appointed wives as executors. 'Jon Kirkpatrik nominat and constitute Isobell Kirkpatrik his dochter and Agnes Mcgowne his spous his onlie exe[cuto]rs and intro[mitte]rs wt his guids geir and dettis'.[19] A widowed mother could be appointed 'tutrix testamentary' by her husband, or 'tutrix dative' by the king or court, to a son until he was fourteen and to a daughter until she was twelve, although she forfeited the office if she remarried; after these ages the pupil became a minor and could choose the mother as curatrix until the minor reached twenty-one. This choice had to be ratified by the Court of Session. If the girl married before the age of twenty-one (she could marry at twelve years) she came under the power of her husband instead of under her curator.[20]

Although a widow was entitled to a third of her husband's moveable goods,[21] and his children, apart from his heir, to a further third, the remaining third, or 'deid's pairt' was the husband's to dispose of as he wished. Legacies from the 'deid's part' were made in money and kind. The Commissary of Dumfries left his wife '1,200 merkis in the coffer', while a farmer left five merks to each sister.[22] Most bequests provided the wife with something specific beyond her legal rights. One was given a house, a yard and a peat house to be a barn; their son was to furnish the house and labour the ground.[23] Friction between the family and widow was anticipated in a spouse being given £40 yearly 'if sche can nocht agrie in familie with hir son'.[24]

Some thought a contract more binding than a testament. Sir John Edmiston made a contract that his son Andrew should pay Christian Ker, his widow, and if she died, their daughter Isobel, the sum of 2000 merks. Andrew was to 'receive thame in houshald with himself and to interteine thame during the space that Cristiane sould happin to remane wedow allanerlie'. The sum was not paid to her, Andrew claiming that it was meant to be used to purchase lands or annualrents for Christian in liferent and Isobel heritably. He was content to do so. It was the other stipulation which caused problems, because

> said Cristiane hes removit hirself furth of the saidis Androis hous and is relaps in fornicatioun and hes borne twa bairns . . . and swa hes defylit hirself in respect quhairof the said Andro can not be haldin to interteine ane fornacatrix in his hous, and he hes ever sen the deceis of his said umquhile father intertenit the said Issobell hir dochter in houshald with himself, lyk as he intends to intereine hir in tyme cuming.

He protested that if he was compelled to give the whole 2000 merks 'sche will not fail schortlie to consume the samen, being ane woman, as is knawin to the lords, quha dois not behaive hirself honestlie'. The Lords ordered him to pay the 2000 merks to Christian and her to find caution that the said sum would be made forthcoming to Isobel after her decease.[25]

In the law of succession, based on the principle of male primogeniture, although a male always excluded females of equal degree, a woman could succeed in default of a male. In such an eventuality, the heritage was divided equally among the daughters. The preference for a male was over-ridden by the rule that descendants were represented by their descendants. A grand-daughter by a dead eldest son excluded a younger son.[26]

Such a wife's heritable estate differed from her moveable goods. Her husband administered it but never owned it. With his consent she could dispose of it *inter vivos* and on her death it passed to her heir.[27] Until he died, even if he remarried, the husband enjoyed the courtesy, the legal right, to the liferent of his wife's patrimony, provided she had borne a living child who would have been his heir, even if the child died.[28]

That there were advantages for women in marriage is indisputable. Marriage contracts refer to the husband 'takand the burdene upoun him'[29] for his future spouse. He was responsible for her misdemeanours and debts and he had to provide clothes and sustenance.[30] He could make a voluntary provision for her widowhood by assigning to her debts owed to him. In being compelled by law to give her a third of his moveable goods after the debts had been paid if there were children, half if there were none, a Scottish husband differed from his English counterpart. An English husband could make a will that left nothing to his wife or children if he chose. The widow's only recourse was to challenge the fairness of the will in a Court of Equity. It was only when an English husband died intestate that a widow was descerned by the ecclesiastical courts to be entitled to one third of his moveables, with the remaining two thirds divided equally among his children.[31] A Scottish widow was also entitled to terce, the liferent of a third of his heritable estate as it stood at the time of the marriage. Although this land did not belong to her, since she could not sell it, its purpose was to give her a source of food or income in widowhood or 'gif it happin hir husband to deceis befoir hir scho may the mair easilie be maryit with ane uther man'.[32]

Increasingly by 1600, terce was replaced by assignations by the husband or husband's family of lands in conjunct fee. In such an arrangement, husband and wife received investiture in a feu at the same time. On the death of one partner, the survivor enjoyed the liferent and the feu passed to the heir after the survivor's death.[33] Craig pointed out that those who could, bargained with their daughter's future spouse or his parents for the setting apart of some cultivable land as a unit in lieu of terce. They provided a tocher but stipulated that they required for their daughter something more than the rights which the law accorded to a widow. They insisted on half or even more of the husband's lands being set aside for their daughter's lifetime, should her husband predecease her. Thus conjunct fee arrangements provided greater security for life for their daughter.[34] Although meant to be instead of terce, this was a provision, not a legal requirement. Unless specifically renounced, the widow could still claim terce. All the widow's rights ceased, however, if the husband died within a year and a day, 'no bairns being gotten or born betwixt thame'. If the couple were divorced on the grounds of adultery, the guilty party forfeited his or her rights.[35]

As in England, although married women lost their *persona* on marriage, all their disabilities could be altered by provisions laid down in marriage contracts. The purpose of these contracts was to protect property from creditors, spouses or children by counteracting legal rights.[36] Most contracts were straightforward provisions for the marriage but some were far-sighted legal documents. They appear as evidence in court mainly because they had not been honoured or because a pursuer sought to impose what would have been his legal right if there had been no contract.

In a simple marriage contract in Dumfries in 1571, Thomas Newell optimistically promised 'to infeft Marioun Fergussone in hir virginitie in the lands of Dalbatholme and to provide her with thrie hundreth punds', still unpaid in 1600.[37] The contract in 1598 for the marriage between Mark Ker, son of Sir John Ker of Hirsel, and Jean Hamilton, second daughter of Alexander Hamilton of Innerwick, was a more complicated legal document.[38] Sir John promised to infeft Mark and Jean, and 'the langer levar (liver) of thame twa, in coniunct fie and the airis lauchfullie to be gotten betuix thame . . . in the lands and maynis of Spylaw and mylne thairof . . . and the landis of Littildeane and Maxtoun'. Financial details of the worth and yields of these and other lands followed and a further promise of 1000 merks was made. A house was to be built in three years; projected plans were outlined. Complicated renunciations of specific lands and reservations of liferents were set down. The contract tried to foresee every eventuality.

> Gif it sall happin thair be na airis maill (as God forbid) bot airis
> femell procreat betuix the saidis Mark and his future spouse . . . ;
> gif there be bot ane air femell the sowme of ten thowsand
> punds . . . ; gif there be twa airis femell the sowme of auchtene
> thowsand merkis to be equallie distributit betuix thame . . . ; gif
> there be ma airis femell nor twa, the sowme of tuentiefour
> thowsand merkis to be equallie devydit and distributit amangis all
> the saidis airs femell . . .

These sums were to be provided by any male heirs succeeding to the lands, in default of a direct male heir, for 'providing of thame to honorabill pairteis in marriage agreabill to thair estaitis and conditiounis'. Such sums were not to be paid until the daughter or daughters were past the age of sixteen years complete 'as gif thai war of pirfyt aige' (twenty-one years). In return they were to surrender all documents relating to the lands. Here the aim was to prevent the equal division of the lands among the daughters as heiresses as the law required,[39] by compensating them with money for tochers. Any daughter giving her body 'to ony persone unmareit . . . sall forfalt, tyne and amit the tocher'. Alexander Hamilton, for his part, obliged himself to pay to Sir John Ker and heirs, in two instalments, 11,000 merks in tocher.

Although usual, tochers were not an essential feature of a marriage. This is shown by a testament in which Janet Glover declared that 'for the love and respect I have to my husband Thomas Kirkpatrick who received no patrimony with me, I appoint him to be my executor and legator unto the whole guids and geir pertening to me'.[40]

Tochers were normally paid to a man by the father of his bride-to-be, but 500 merks Scots money was paid by Sir John Dalziel in name of tocher good with Barbara Cheslie together with the sum of 60 merks money foresaid 'in caice of failyie'. Here the master of a 'servitrix' may have been marrying off a reluctant illegitimate daughter or a discarded mistress.[41] Brothers too were sometimes helpful. In a responsible provision for his niece, James Beaton became

> bundin to pay to Cristiane Betoun my sister dochter . . . 6000
> merkis to the help and supplement of hir marriage quhen it sal
> happen and in sa far as I presentlie mynd, God willing, and am
> agaitward to France, for sundrie guid respectis moving me and that
> thairby it lykis better Cristiane to remane and be company with the
> said Luceis hir mother and Andro Wischart of Mylnden hir father
> in law nor in houshald with my familie . . . to pay and deliver to
> Cristiane Betoun fortie punds betuix the present and 10 November
> for hir sustentatioun this present yeir 1600 and yeirlie ay and
> quhile my returning in Scotland.[42]

Inability to afford the amounts so optimistically promised in marriage contracts was a fertile seed of grievance in marriage. Many such actions came before the Lords of Council and Session; for instance, 1000 merks were 'to be wairit upoun land [of Aberlady] to the utilitie of him and his spous and the airs to be gottin' but they were never paid.[43]

Most women who wrote testaments or litigated had been or were married. Single women were entitled to bring actions but relatively few who had never been married did so. This may have been because women did not feel confident about litigating without the support of a husband, father or brother.[44]

Remarriage was exceedingly common. There were sound economic reasons for remarriage, particularly if a widow had children. Although she lost the freedom to act in her own affairs, she hoped to gain for herself and her children the financial security provided by a husband. He gained control of her property unless a clause in a marriage contract restricted his power and he provided his children, if he had any, with a surrogate mother.

That remarriage was often hasty is suggested by the example of a widow who was left with large debts marrying the cautioner before the confirmation of the will less than a year later.[45] The evidence of testaments shows how one husband had two wives within two years.[46] The prevalence of brothers or sisters 'germane' may be indications of a man's remarriage; court actions by a woman, relict of one man and spouse of another, indicate a woman's remarriage.

Without a man to protect them, relicts and spinsters were open to oppression. There are many examples of widows not being paid 'fermes and dewties'.[47] Margaret Home, relict and tackswoman of the teind (tithe) sheaves of lands in the regality of Melrose had not been paid since 1594.[48]

Single women and widow tenants were frequently removed from someone's heritable property if the tack had expired. If she did not comply with the decree of removing, the landlord could obtain letters or a precept of ejection in order to authorise her ejection from the holding.[49] Sympathy for a widow's plight probably explains why the relict of Richard Fiddes was to have removed herself from the toun and lands of Gilmertoun by Whitsunday, 1598, but no action followed until Adam Tait entered to the property and was charged as succeeding in the vice and violent occupation thereof.[50] Mr David Ogle, minister at Barry, however, successfully ejected a widow from land designated to him 'in gleib'. Some women fought back. Two women tenant farmers protested against their ejection from lands in Lauder.[51]

Goods were often taken from a widow, perhaps justifiably by an inheritor or legatee. Thus 'twelf brod geis, ane gaunder and ane skeip of bees' were removed from Elizabeth Mure and 'horses, meirs with foils, bedding and fyre veschels' were forcibly removed from Helen Hal, relict in Banffshire.[52] Dame Jean Campbell, Duchess of Lennox, widow of the Master of Eglinton, brought an action for the

> spoliatioun of corns, the samen pertening to her . . . and in the
> wrangous outputting furth of the foirsaids landis, rowme and
> steding, the uplifting of the profeits sche micht have had, and in the
> wrangeous demolisching of the houses and biggings, away taking of
> the tymmer wark, stanes, joynit wark and uther materials.[53]

Actions were raised against women who, either through apathy or poverty, allowed property to become dilapidated. Isobel Hamilton, relict of John Whitelaw, had let two tenements of land in Haddington become 'ruinous and utterlie decayit'.[54] Her son was dead and she may have seen no reason why she should maintain property for a remote heir. Margaret Auchinleck 'being fallin in povertie and be hir debotchit lyfe and unhonest conversatioun, hes . . . sustenit the mylne houses and biggings of Ballumbie to come to rwyin, fall and decay'.[55]

Some women renounced their legal rights in return for some perceived benefit. Thus, Dame Jean Johnston, Lady Salton, renounced her 'third and terce of all and sundrie lands, lordschippis, barronies and possessiounis quhilks pertenit to hir said umquhile spous and to the leving of Saltoun'; for his part, George Lord Salton bound him, his heirs, executors and assignees

> to content and pay to the said Dame Jean Johnston yeirlie during hir lyftyme ten chalders cheritit victual, and in cais of not payment thirof, the sowme of ten merkis for ilk boll thairof, as the contract contening uther heids beirs.[56]

Dame Alice Ross, wife of Sir John Melville of Carnbie, renounced her liferent by giving consent to her husband to 'infeft William Moncreiff heritablie but [without] reversioun in all and haill the lands and maynes of Carnbie'. It had been agreed that she should be recompensed, but 'trew it is that the said William Moncreiff nevir as yit maid satisfactioun'.[57] In this way the anticipated benefit had not materialised but had provided a loophole for escaping from the contract.

A few women were determined to circumvent the law. Elizabeth Drummond used a contract to prevent certain family members inheriting her goods. For £300 she sold to Robert Drummond, her brother 'germane' 'the haill guids and geir, abuliament [clothes], insicht and plenishing in his possessioun in the place of Elphinstoun according to the particular inventar . . . reservand to hir use thairof during all the days of hir lyftyme'. He was to intromit with her goods if she died without heirs. She died childless and intestate. She had acquired further goods since the transaction and the intromitters with these goods refused to hand them over to the brother. The Court, however, found that her brother 'had guid ryt to the guids and geir pertening to umquhile Elizabeth Drummond'.[58] Margaret Winton sought, unsuccessfully, to defeat the course of law by passing on goods to her daughter on the view that these 'wald justlie befall and pertene to her as relict'. The son as executor dative claimed them because her dead husband's debts greatly exceeded his free gear and 'quhile the dettis be first payit, it cannot be . . . knawn quhat hir thrid part may extend to'.[59]

Margaret Dalgleish assigned her half of a liferent of a tenement in Edinburgh to her son after banns of marriage to her next husband had been called. She took the precaution of writing a backband, or a writing qualifying the assignation, to the effect that should her new husband die, her son must restore the liferent to her. One can understand her motive; the liferent must have come to her through her son's father and she may well have felt that by remarrying she was defrauding him. An advocate voiced her future husband's fury.

> In cais sic kynd of blokes (bargains) and dispositiounis be sustenit, the samen sall be ane grit defraude to all men quha maries wedows or heretrices or other frie wemen quha onlie contractis thameselffis in mereage without onie concernis or assistance of ony responsall persone quha binds for thame.

The Lords annulled the disposition as 'being given *contra bonos mores* without the consent of her husband quhomto sche was oblist and contractit in matrimony' and they 'restorit the said Margaret to hir awin ryt'.[60]

The married woman or widow of the late sixteenth and early seventeenth century, as she appears in legal textbooks, was downtrodden and in many ways 'widows, pupils and other poor and miserable persons'[61] needed protection. A healthy married woman could expect to have many children. She needed support and gender roles were clearly defined in the late sixteenth and seventeenth centuries. The fundamental difficulty for a wife lay in her requiring her husband's consent to all her actions. This meant that she was utterly dependent on her husband's sense of fairness. The principle governing the law was equity and reason but it was not necessarily the principle governing a marriage relationship.

Nevertheless the evidence of testaments and court records suggests that many wives were in fact well protected and had legal freedom in practice, whether it derived from the consent to write a testament given by a fair-minded and understanding husband or from conditions written into a marriage contract by a far-sighted father.

NOTES

1. J. Balfour, *Practicks* ed. P. G. B. McNeill (2 vols, Stair Society, 1962–3), 97, 99; *Acts of the Parliaments of Scotland* eds. T. Thomson and C. Innes (12 vols, Edinburgh, 1814–75), iii, 82 c.1.
2. David Walker, *A Legal History of Scotland. The Sixteenth Century* (Edinburgh, 1995), 641.
3. Balfour, *Practicks*, 378; J. Stair, *The Institutions of the Law of Scotland* 3rd edn (Edinburgh, 1770), 719. Some women appear as witnesses in burgh courts, *Protocol Book of Gavin Ross 1512–32* (Scottish Record Society, 1908), no. 89; *The Burgh Court Book of Selkirk 1503–45* (Scottish Record Society, 1969), 89, 113, 147. See also John Finlay's essay in this volume.
4. Balfour, *Practicks*, xxxii-lxiv.

5. Thomas Craig, *The Ius Feudale* trans. J. A. Clyde (2 vols, Edinburgh, 1934).
6. *Hope's Major Practicks 1608–1633* ed. J.A. Clyde (2 vols, Stair Society, 1937–8).
7. Scottish Record Office [SRO], CS5/8 and CS5/6.
8. SRO, CS7/185–193.
9. SRO, CS7/15/77–79.
10. G. C. Paton, 'Husband and Wife: Property Rights and Relationships' in *Introduction to the Study of Scottish Legal History* (Stair Society, 1954) 99,100; *Hope's Major Practicks*, ii, 17,10; Balfour, *Practicks*, 93.
11. For example, SRO, CS7/192 fo 223r; CS 7/189 fo 65v.
12. Paton, 100, 103; Balfour, *Practicks*, 93.
13. Balfour, 216; *The Decisions of the Court of Session, digested in the form of a dictionary* ed. W. M. Morison (Edinburgh, 1811), p. 5784 *Pennycook against Cockburn* (1582).
14. Balfour, *Practicks*, 216.
15. Balfour, *Practicks*, 217; Stair, *Institutions*, iii, iv, pp xxiv,458; *Baron David Hume's Lectures 1768–1822*, vol v ed. G. C. H. Paton (Stair Society, 1957), 190.
16. SRO, CC8/8/34. 25 February, 1600.
17. For example, SRO, CC8/8/41. January 1602.
18. SRO, CC8/8/35. 8 May 1600; CC8/8/45. 20 May 1608.
19. SRO, CC8/8/35. 8 November 1600.
20. SRO, CC5/6/1 fo 181r.
21. Balfour, *Practicks*, 217.
22. SRO, CC5/6/1 fo 39v; CC8/8 fo 39. 5 August 1600.
23. SRO, CC8/8 fo 45. April 1608.
24. SRO, CC5/6/4 fo 1r.
25. SRO, CS7/192 fo 133v. Ker v Edmestoun.
26. W. D. H. Sellar, 'The Common Law of Scotland and the Common Law of England' in R. R. Davies ed. *The British Isles 1100–1500: Comparisons, Contrasts and Connections* (Edinburgh, 1988), 89.
27. Paton, 100–104.
28. Sellar, 'Common Law', 90; Craig, *Ius Feudale*, 881–2.
29. SRO, CS7/186 fo 131v.
30. Hope, *Major Practicks*, 17, 13, 32; Paton, 20, 101; Balfour, *Practicks*, 95.
31. Amy Louise Erickson, *Women and Property in Early Modern England* (London, 1993), 28.
32. Balfour, *Practicks*, 93, 105, 107, 111.
33. Craig, *Ius Feudale*, ii, 854–7.
34. Craig, *Ius Feudale*, ii,, 859.
35. Balfour, *Practicks*, 95, 99, 111.
36. Paton, 20,114.
37. SRO, CS7/186 fo 131v. Newall v Fergussone.
38. SRO, CS15/78, 2. Hammiltoun v. Ker.
39. Balfour, *Practicks*, 223.
40. SRO, CC5/6/6 fo 439.
41. SRO, CC5/6 fo 666.
42. SRO, CS7/186 fo 252r. Campbell v. Betoun.

43. SRO, CS7/186 fo 407r. Hepburne v. Nicolsoun.
44. Cf. John Finlay's paper in this volume.
45. SRO, CC5/6/4 fo 42v; CC5/6 fo 70v.
46. SRO, CC5/6/1 fo 119v.
47. SRO, CS 7/190 fo 121r.
48. SRO, CS7/190 fo 316r. Home v. Carnetors.
49. SRO, CS7/190 fo 226r. Hay v.Chisholme; CS7/190 fo 155r, Menzies v. Forbes; P. Gouldesbrough, *Formulary of Old Scots Legal Documents* (Stair Society, 1985) 36,142.
50. SRO, CS7/186 fo.246. Lord Edmoston v Tait.
51. SRO, CS7/186 fo 264v; CS7/186 fo 344r. L. Lunplum v. Ogill; CS7/190 fo 145v. Lichtbodie v. Lichtbody.
52. SRO, CS7/190 fo 354v. Mure v. Barclay; CS7/187 fo 371r. Hall v. Watsoun.
53. SRO, CS7/187 fo 371r. L. Dutchis of Lennox v. L. Cathcart.
54. SRO, CS7/190 fo 311r. Quhitlaw v. Hammiltoun.
55. SRO, CS7/190 fo 254v. L. Secretar v. Auchinlek.
56. SRO, CS7/185 fo 285r. Ker v. L. Saltoun.
57. SRO, CS7/185 fo 234v. L. Carnbie v. Moncreiff.
58. SRO, CS7/186 fo 369v. Drummond v. Mur of Elphinstoun.
59. SRO, CS7/186 fo 221r. Meldrum v. Forret.
60. SRO, CS7/187 fo 344r. Hereot v. Crystie.
61. Balfour, *Practicks*, 658.

CHAPTER SIXTEEN

Women and the Church Courts in Reformation-Era Scotland

_____ *Michael F. Graham*

LATE IN NOVEMBER 1602, Christine Graham of Stirling complained to her parish kirk session that Ranald Campbell 'frequentis hir hous against hir will, straikis (strikes) and oppressis hir'. She had approached the burgh council which had forced Campbell to find a cautioner to guarantee his good behaviour in the future, but this measure had been ineffective. The town's bailies had been unwilling or unable to punish Campbell for his continuing harassment. The session decided sterner measures were required, and requested that the bailies confine Campbell until order could be taken with him.[1]

The records tell us little about the two parties. We know that Graham kept a house in Stirling, and the kirk session later determined she had necessary business there. She may have been a widow carrying on her husband's enterprise, although not so identified. Whatever her situation, she apparently approached the kirk session on her own, seeking protection that the burgh council could not offer her. This was not unusual. While local secular courts such as burgh councils might seem to enforce *public* order, they were in fact *private* concerns, primarily involved in defending the interests of the local oligarchy – those who in effect had a share in the corporation. The kirk session, even though its membership might overlap that of the burgh council,[2] represented a wider interest – that of the Christian community. This is not to say that the justice meted out by kirk sessions was always even-handed, either in terms of gender or social class.[3] But it does appear that women, particularly those without close ties to burgh authorities, found kirk sessions much more approachable and responsive to their needs for justice, support and protection. Indeed, women rarely sought the aid of burgh courts by themselves, tending instead to appear with husbands or by proxy through procurators.[4]

Whatever was done to 'take order' with Campbell did not keep him away from Graham. The kirk session eventually decided that she was partly to blame for this, and in May 1603 it requested the bailies to banish both because they had 'long slanderit this toun be suspitius behavier togither'. But Graham returned to the kirk session, pleading innocence. The session decided that Graham's house and business gave her a standing Campbell lacked. It ruled that she could stay provided she performed public repentance wearing linen clothing on three successive Sundays, that she found caution not to allow Campbell in her house again, and that she go to the bailies immediately if he entered against her will. The banishment order against Campbell stood, and this appears to have ended the matter.[5] Graham's reputation may have been sullied in the elders' eyes, but her rights as an independent householder had been upheld.

Much discussion of the Reformation's effect on women's lives has centred on the strengthening of the patriarchal family and on the limited outlets for female spirituality in a world which rejected the cloistered life.[6] But Reformed protestantism also brought with it a disciplinary apparatus that put private lives under unprecedented scrutiny as ministers and elders sought to enforce Christian codes of behaviour.[7] Merry Wiesner has suggested that institutional changes tied to the Reformation probably had a greater impact on women's lives than did changes in doctrine or theology.[8] Social discipline provides a case in point. Where Reformed protestantism took hold, clerically-dominated episcopal courts with large bailiwicks (both in terms of geography and claimed legal competency) were often replaced with parochially-based consistories controlled by, or at least primarily staffed by, laymen. Usually, these consistories restricted themselves to primarily disciplinary functions. Since they did not cover large circuits, they could devote greater attention to relatively obscure individuals whose low profiles or poverty had rendered them unlikely targets or plaintiffs in Catholic church courts. Further, the presence of lay elders helped to ensure that enforcement might better reflect community, rather than clerical, values. The perspective that those elders brought to the courts was still masculine, but it was a view informed by experience of marriage and parenthood. In Scotland, it was the kirk sessions and presbyteries which sought to mould the new order.[9] For many, the intrusions of kirk elders and ministers into their affairs (in many senses!) would have been the most dramatic and noticeable aspect of the Reformation.

Although both women and men felt the intrusions of social discipline and its conflicts with traditional society, it does not follow that they felt them in the same ways. How did the operations of these courts affect women, as members of families, parish communities, or the wider Christian community? Could the new courts be allies, offering women rights and opportunities to defend their interests? Might the increased intensity of oversight merely provide another weapon for the 'double standard' which winked at the sexual sins of men while regarding their female partners as guilty temptresses?[10] In practice, women may have found Reformed social discipline both empowering and repressive, or at least invasive. Janine Garrisson, in her study based on consistories and regional church assemblies in the French Midi in the late sixteenth century, opined that the Huguenot movement was a precursor of modernity because of the dignity it accorded to women.[11] Dignity is of course impossible to quantify. Christine Graham used the disciplinary system of the Kirk to protect herself from what modern western societies might define as harassment. The kirk session offered her power and protection that the burgh court did not. But it came with a price – the ritual of public repentance which held her up to community scorn. Likewise, when the widow Bessie Lin of the Ayrshire parish of Dundonald accused her servant George Wright of raping her in 1603, the kirk session ordered her to perform public repentance as a fornicator. His punishment was more severe, but she did not escape unstained.[12] We need to examine both sides of this equation of feminine empowerment and potential stigmatization which the Reformation introduced into the social mathematics of early modern Scotland.

The maintenance of a good reputation was critical to social standing in early modern Scotland, as in many other early modern societies. While male reputations rested primarily on honesty in business dealings, courage, and willingness to use violence to defend honour,[13] female reputations relied more on sexual probity and freedom from the taint of witchcraft. 'Witch', 'whore' and 'harlot' were the slanderous labels from which women most often sought to protect themselves.[14] When William Morris boasted in 1590 of having had sexual relations with Helen Menteith, a married woman, she (and her father) complained to the Stirling Presbytery. Since Morris' claim seemed to lack foundation, the presbytery ordered him to appear one Sunday in the parish kirk of Dollar, where Menteith resided,

> and thair to confes publictlie in p[rese]ns of ye haill congregatione yat he hes innocentlie sclandirit ye said hellein & yat ye words he spak of hir war fals, and [there]for to crave god, ye said hellein & ye kirk forgevenes. And to declair he knawis na thing to hir bot honestie.[15]

The parish kirk, with the whole community theoretically in attendance, provided a much more dramatic forum than the burgh mercat cross, the usual locus of punishment imposed by burgh courts. Morris' apology was delivered in the silence of the kirk, without the background noise and distraction of people going about their daily business. Margaret Richie in Stirling was forced to make a similar apology in 1587 after she accused Marjorie Robertson of taking away her cow's milk by witchcraft. Unable to provide any evidence, Richie was convicted of slandering Robertson, and the presbytery ordered the apology.[16]

. Menteith and Robertson both had the advantage of previously unsullied reputations, which might have suffered irreparable damage if the slander had gone unchallenged. Those already marked by ill repute had less protection. When Andrew Leving of Rothiemay Parish (Grampian) was accused by Agnes Lesley of having slandered her as an adulteress in 1607, he responded that he was not the first to do so. The kirk session elders were willing to accept this defence if Leving could cite other examples of such slanders which had not been challenged. Unable to do so, Leving was forced to make a public confession.[17] But when Nannis Melville became the leading accuser against William Ferny in an investigation of incestuous rape in Anstruther Wester (Fife) in 1594, he accused her of witchcraft, of which she had previously fallen under suspicion. Ferny got off the hook with a private confession before the kirk session (the victim, his daughter, had to do the same); Melville may have paid with her life.[18] Female honour was fragile, and once lost it was nearly irretrievable. Hence the regular resort by women seeking to protect their reputations to the courts of the Reformed Kirk.

William Ferny seems to have headed a dysfunctional family, while Helen Menteith sought to preserve her standing as a faithful wife. Such cases bring us inside the family, and it was in the area of marriage and domestic relations that women often sought to use the courts of the Reformed Kirk to defend their interests. Divorce suits were generally not heard in church courts,[19] but women used kirk sessions to press marriage claims and to seek protection from domestic abuse.

The pregnancy of an unmarried woman was the evidence which set most fornication or adultery cases in motion. The woman was brought before the elders and asked to name the father, so he could be charged and brought to the penitent stool as well. But women fornicators often alleged that their partners had promised marriage, and kirk sessions were willing to listen. John Lindsay was pursued by two women, both charging him with seduction under promise of marriage, before the St Andrews Kirk Session in 1563. One, Christine Howieson, was pregnant, and the kirk session ordered him to marry her.[20] There are also rare instances of women seeking to enforce marriage promises even when no sexual relations were alleged, as when Marjorie Pawy successfully pursued a claim of handfast marriage with William Kinnisman in November 1562. Since Kinnisman refused to deny under oath his 'spekyng and saying to hyr, be his hand he layd in hyrris, he suld marye hyr and never have ane other woman bot hyr', the kirk session ordered him to marry her.[21] But if a woman claimed seduction and the accused male provided evidence he was not her first sexual partner, he could avoid marrying her, although he would have to take his turn on the penitent stool.[22] This highlights once again the importance of female reputation.

John Scott, a merchant and deacon on the St Andrews Kirk Session, sought in 1579 to rid himself of his wife, Jonet Murray, by destroying her reputation. She used the forum of the kirk session to fight back. Scott had already admitted adultery with Grisell Motto (who testified that he regularly visited her while the burgh's residents were at common prayers!). He then tried to persuade Thomas Hunter to go to the commissary court in Edinburgh (which had the authority to grant divorces) and testify that he had committed adultery with Murray. Hunter refused, and Murray charged her husband with slander. The elders found him guilty, and ordered him to kneel before the congregation 'and pronunce thir wordis, handand his awin tung in his hand, Fals tung thow leid! and confes that he knawis na thing to the said Jonet bot gud and honestie'. Such a marriage could hardly have been happy, but Murray was determined to maintain her rights within it.[23]

This does not mean that kirk session elders were free of the gender prejudices of their era. They regarded male household heads as primary authority figures, and held them answerable, to a certain extent, for the behaviour of their wives, children and servants. The kirk session of Aberdeen in 1574 gave William Davidson 'many exhortationeis' that he 'suffer' his wife to perform public repentance for her adultery, but 'he answured stuburnely, that in no wayes wold he suffer hir to do any more then she had done'. No doubt he felt his honour, as well as hers, was threatened. Likewise the Canongate session in 1567 upbraided Cuthbert Ferguson, an elder, for allowing his wife to take Communion in Edinburgh when she was under censure in the Canongate for slander. Ferguson offered the unlikely excuse that he 'knew nocht that scho wes debarit'. His fellow elders ordered him to make a public profession of his ignorance, thus holding him up to possible scorn as the head of an unruly household.[24]

Another form of unruly household was one whose internal disputes became known to outsiders. Kirk sessions were not slow to intervene when quarrels between spouses turned violent, and such a policy could offer women significant protection. On the other hand, some women seemed violent themselves. When George Stene told the Canongate session in 1566 that he could not live with his wife (Jonet Murdo) on account of her cursing him 'and casting at him, with hir handis, stannis and dirt,' she replied 'I have gretter caus to complan upone him, for I dred bodelye harme of him'. The session held them both guilty, 'bot specialle the said Jonet' and ordered her to ask his forgiveness.[25] He may have threatened violence, but she practised it. When David Creighton and Isobel Smith, a married couple, admitted fighting to their kirk session in 1594, they had to find caution that it would not happen again. If their quarrels continued, they would both face public repentance, regardless of who was at fault.[26] Domestic peace benefited men as well as women, but the kirk's interest in censuring spousal discord clearly placed limits on husbands' powers of coercion.

Women also became involved in quarrels outside their families. Conflicts between neighbours ripped the social fabric; elders and ministers saw mending this as an important responsibility. In 1598, Katherine Brown of Anstruther Wester parish was called before the local kirk session for 'flyting' loudly on the Sabbath outside the kirk door, calling Kristin Scot 'drunk harlot'. Brown said she had been provoked, that Scot had 'upbraidit hir, & bad hir kis hir ers', a charge Scot denied. The session decided Brown was the more guilty of the two, since it was her words which had disturbed the Sunday service and she had behaved 'disdanfullie' before the elders.[27] Neither woman was very prominent in local society, so such conflict would have received little attention from a burgh court. But session elders were increasingly eager to censure sharp-tongued women. In 1591 the elders of St Andrews ordered Mirrabell Moody to sit on the 'goik stuill of this citee' for two hours on a Monday morning for having slandered Isobel Kay as a 'common huir'.[28]

Women could also be violent on occasion, and here elders tried to orchestrate communal disapproval in all its majesty. The murderess Marjorie Brison had already compensated her victim's kin and purchased royal letters of remission, thus settling the criminal aspects of her offence. But the Canongate Session demanded ritual satisfaction as well. In January 1566, she was ordered to make three successive appearances in church dressed in white, bareheaded and barelegged, holding a knife dipped in blood, and to ask the congregation's forgiveness. On the third occasion, an elder would receive her by the hand and take the knife from her.[29] Marion Adie had not killed anyone, but her violence placed the St Andrews Kirk Session in a difficult position in 1599. She was the daughter-in-law of a bailie and session elder. She had allegedly attacked her servant Margaret Parky, 'cutting hir heir by the plattis out of hir heid with ane knyiff, and . . . striking of hir, and burning of hir fleshe with ane hot irn tayngis, and specialie betuix hir leggis'. The act suggests sexual jealousy; Adie's husband had earlier been charged with adultery. Parky may have come up against the limits of early modern justice, even in the (relatively) progressive atmosphere of the kirk session. The elders consulted with the burgh council, and determined that nothing could be proved except the hair-cutting. Adie was privately rebuked for her 'pryid and misbehaviour', and the minister was to announce from the pulpit that nothing warranting public repentance had been discovered.[30] All men were not equal before the law, nor were all women, be it the law of burgh or kirk.

A major function of social discipline was the enforcement of order, whether religious, sexual or social. Discipline could marshall community disapproval when individuals strayed too far from the norm. When

women put on trousers (literally) and walked about as men, many felt
that the categories through which society was organised were in danger. .
While such cases are quite rare, some women were censured for dressing
as men. The Aberdeen Kirk Session fined Maggie Morrison 6s 8d for
'abusing of hir self in cla[th]ing of hir w[i]t[h] mennes cla[th]es' at a wake
in 1576. Later, it warned four women against their practice of donning
men's clothes and dancing. Jonet Cady in Edinburgh denied such a charge
in 1574.[31]

This was not the only form of ostensibly male behaviour on the part of
women that kirk elders felt the need to condemn. Christopher Smout
describes kirk elders as hypocritical in their refusal to censure usury,
despite official denunciations of the practice.[32] In the rare instances found
of kirk sessions discouraging usury, the accused usurers were female.[33]
Although the number of cases is insignificant, this is suggestive that elders
found sharp dealing repugnant primarily when women got into the act.

One profession in which women remained fairly secure was that of
midwifery. Reformed discipline left the practice of midwifery intact, but
saw midwives as potential sources of sensitive information. The birthing
process was a female preserve, so elders enlisted midwives as the eyes and
ears of parochial discipline there. In 1564 the Canongate Kirk Session
ordered that midwives report to it concerning all births 'that thairby the
Kirk may knaw gif it [the child] be gotting in harlatre, or quhair it is
baptissit, or in qhuhat maner'. The concern was both illegitimacy and
Catholicism. Midwives refusing to comply were threatened with a forty
shilling fine. Fathers needed to be identified both to face discipline, and to
be made to support their illegitimate offspring. The St Andrews Kirk
Session questioned midwife Marion Dawson closely in 1573 concerning
Christen Hagy's words when she was giving birth. She had apparently
mentioned James Mont as the father, and the session invoked a General
Assembly ruling that if a woman *in tempore partus* names someone as the
father of her child, and he admits to having had sexual relations with her
in the previous year, then he is to be regarded as such.[34] Information from
midwives was critical in making these determinations, and kirk sessions
sought to make sure they co-operated.

Sexuality affected a woman's reputation and might also have a significant impact on her relations with her husband (or husband-to-be), her
neighbours, and whether or not she gave birth, in or out of wedlock.
Female reputations largely stood or fell on the issue of sexual probity. The
majority (fifty-five per cent) of cases handled by Scottish kirk sessions
stemmed from charges of sexual misbehaviour, primarily fornication or
adultery. Was illicit sexuality regarded as a peculiarly female problem?
The evidence makes this seem unlikely, at least in the first fifty years of the
Scottish Reformation.

A database of disciplinary cases from kirk sessions and presbyteries [35] shows that of the 4,594 cases from kirk sessions, forty-one per cent of those charged with offences were women. If we focus on the 2,523 cases involving sexual behaviour, the proportion of female offenders increases to fifty-one per cent. Dividing these cases by gender, we find that forty-five per cent of all men summoned faced sexual accusations, while sixty-eight per cent of all women did. Thus women called before parish elders were considerably more likely to be charged with sexual sins than were men. The cases from presbyteries followed a similar pattern, although presbyteries were less concerned with sexual misbehaviour than were kirk sessions. Further, since presbytery cases often involved those who had managed to avoid punishment at the parish level, the presbytery caseload contains a higher proportion of male cases.

Are these differences significant? The fact that an individual woman hauled before her parish elders stood a two-thirds chance of being charged with sexual misbehaviour, while the chances of this happening to a male were less than even, may simply reflect the universe of possible offences. Certain misdeeds, such as political disloyalty, violent assault, or Sabbath breach, were regarded by kirk sessions and presbyteries as much more common in men than women. The kirk session of Edinburgh in 1574–5 charged ninety-two men, but only two women, with having supported the queen's party during recent civil war.[36] A factional take-over of the burgh council and kirk session of St Andrews in 1593 led to charges of political dissidence against twenty men, but no women.[37] Since women were not active in civic politics, they were incapable of political sins. Accusations against women for Sabbath breach or violent assault were more common, but men outnumbered women by large majorities. That women were much more likely than men to be charged with sexual offences is due to the narrower range of possible sins; males were seen as more versatile miscreants. The sins of women were generally restricted to sexuality, verbal quarrels, religious deviance and the occasional practice of magic.

Although some offences were regarded as largely gender-specific, the nature of most human sexual activity is such that ministers and elders would have had to display wilful bias if they sought to lay the blame on one particular gender. None of the cases involved charges of homosexual behaviour or masturbation, and accusations of bestiality were exceedingly rare. Virtually every sexual offence involved at least one male and at least one female. Did the ministers and elders view both parties as guilty and subject to similar sanctions? In general, yes. Kirk sessions charged 1226 men and 1282 women with sexual sins. At the presbytery level the situation was reversed, with 314 men and 258 women accused of sexual misdeeds. Some parishes displayed remarkable even-handedness; in

1582–1600 the St Andrews kirk session lodged sexual charges against 447 men and 447 women.

There were, however, some parishes where considerably more women than men were charged in sexual cases – the Canongate in the mid-1560s, and Edinburgh and Aberdeen in the mid-1570s. Significantly, these were urban parishes. In the tight and crowded confines of the early modern town, burgh councillors and session elders regarded a certain type of single woman as a danger to public morality. In the Canongate parish, a notorious red light district around the Cowgate occupied much of the kirk session's attention. In 1564, it drew up a list of sexual sinners 'within this reformit gait', for action by the civil magistrates. Twelve women were named, as were their partners, but the elders were clearly only after the women, some of whom were brought before the session on 2 December 1564.[38] A group trial of sexual sinners held before the kirk session, burgh bailies and the Justice Clerk of Scotland in 1565 considered the cases of sixteen women but no men, although one male did appear before the session the next day because he wished to marry one of the defendants.[39] Even when both partners were summoned, they might be treated differently. In October 1564 David Pearson and Isobel Mowtray in October 1564 admitted to having a child out of wedlock. She was ordered to leave the burgh within forty-eight hours 'under the pane of schorging', while he was given four hours in the branks [stocks], which he avoided by promising to pay forty shillings instead.[40] Some women targeted in these roundups seem to have worked as prostitutes, and the kirk session was eager to eject them from burgh society. In practice, this proved difficult. Whippings, head-shavings and banishments were ordered, but few seem to have been carried out.[41] By 1567, there were signs that the Canongate session was turning its attention to resolving conflicts within the parish community, and the sexual double standard was disappearing. A similar trend is evident in Aberdeen, where by 1577, men began to outnumber women among those charged with sexual misbehaviour.[42]

In smaller burghs such as St Andrews or rural parishes such as Anstruther Wester, Monifieth (Angus), Dundonald (Ayrshire) or Rothiemay, no such double standard seems to have existed, at least in terms of accusations by elders and attempts at punishment. Men outnumbered women among those accused of sexual impropriety. In most cases, both partners were named and summoned. Men found it easier to ignore summonses, delay proceedings, or shift blame on others. Since most of the women accused were pregnant and unmarried, it was difficult for them to flee or deny responsibility. But kirk sessions and presbyteries often went to great lengths to identify the fathers, get them to admit paternity, and force them to perform public repentance. A representative from Stirling's

Holy Rude Kirk Session petitioned the Stirling Presbytery to write to its counterpart in Glasgow in late 1581, seeking to track down a Glasgow-area laird who had committed adultery with Margaret Leiche in Stirling. The kirk session of Anstruther Wester in March 1591 tried to prevent any local skipper from hiring Alan Caddells until he performed public repentance for his relapse into adultery. This effort was unsuccessful; he sailed to the Orkneys before he had completed his punishment. But it is a testament to the elders' dogged determination that he appeared before them when he returned in 1592, again promising to perform his repentance. The case dragged into the following year, with no clear resolution, but the session displayed no inclination to let the matter drop.[43]

This is not to argue for an egalitarian, gender-neutral Reformation. Some Scotswomen felt its sting in ways that men could not. The Reformation shut off many avenues of female spirituality and in Scotland certainly contributed to the demonification of the witch and the prostitute. But by holding individuals – men as well as women – primarily responsible for their own behaviour, it militated against the maintenance of any double standard in the area of sexual ethics. In addition, by creating the kirk session, it established a forum for the complaints of the humble – male and female – in which they had the opportunity to identify their causes with those of the wider Christian community, regardless of the prominence of their adversaries.

NOTES

1. Stirling Council Archives [SCA], CH2/1026/1, 25 Nov. 1602.
2. See St Andrews University Muniments [StAUM], B65/8/1, fos 125v,130r; *Register of the Minister, Elders and Deacons of the Christian Congregation of St Andrews 1559–1600* [StAKS], ed. D. Hay Fleming (2 vols, Edinburgh, 1889–90), ii, 650. See also SCA, CH2/1026/1, 20 Nov. 1600; SCA, B66/20/ 2, fo 109.
3. See Michael F. Graham, 'Equality Before the Kirk? Church Courts and the Elite in Reformation-era Scotland,' *Archiv für Reformationsgeschichte*, 84 (1993), 289–310.
4. See StAUM, B65/8/1, St Andrews, 1588–92; SCA, B66/15/4, B66/16/1 and B66/20/2, Stirling, 1560–66 and 1598–1602; and *Court Book of the Regality of Broughton and the Burgh of the Canongate, 1569–73*, ed. Marguerite Wood, (Edinburgh, 1937) the Canongate, 1569–73. For rare exceptions, see SCA, B66/16/1, fo 143r (Annabel, countess of Mar); StAUM, B65/8/1 (Margaret Monipenny); *Court Book of Broughton and the Canongate*, 251–2 (Elizabeth Braidfoot and Marion Robeson); ibid, 262 (Alison Snype and Catherine McNabb).
5. SCA, CH2/1026/1, 19 May and 2 June 1603. See Michael F. Graham, 'The Civil Sword and the Scottish Kirk in the Late Sixteenth Century' in W. Fred

Graham ed. *Later Calvinism: International Perspectives*, (Kirksville, 1994), 237–48.

6. For example, Steven Ozment, *When Fathers Ruled: Family Life in Reformation Europe*, (Cambridge, Mass., 1983); Lyndal Roper, *The Holy Household: Women and Morals in Reformation Augsburg*, (Oxford, 1989); Merry Wiesner, *Women and Gender in Early Modern Europe*, (Cambridge, 1993), 186–203.

7. See Raymond Mentzer ed. *Sin and the Calvinists: Morals Control and the Consistory in the Reformed Tradition*, (Kirksville, 1994); R. Mentzer, '*Disciplina Nervus Ecclesiae*: The Calvinist Reform of Morals at Nîmes,' *Sixteenth Century Journal*, 18 (1987), 89–115; Ibid, 'Le consistoire et la pacification du monde rural,' *Bulletin de la société de l'histoire de protestantisme français*, 135 (1989), 373–390; Bernard Vogler and Janine Estèbe, 'La genèse d'une société protestante: Etude comparée de quelques registres consistoriaux languedociens et palatins vers 1600,' *Annales ESC* (1976), 362–387; Heinz Schilling, *Civic Calvinism in Northwestern Germany and the Netherlands*, (Kirksville, 1991); Robert Kingdon, 'The Control of Morals in Calvin's Geneva' in L. Buck and J. Zophy eds. *The Social History of the Reformation*, (Columbus, 1972), 3–16; Jeffrey Watt, 'Women and the Consistory in Calvin's Geneva,' *Sixteenth Century Journal*, 24 (1993), 429–39; R. Po-chia Hsia, *Social Discipline in the Reformation: Central Europe 1550–1750*, (London, 1989); Michael F. Graham, *The Uses of Reform: 'Godly Discipline' and Popular Behaviour in Scotland and Beyond, 1560–1610*, (Leiden, 1996). For Catholic and Lutheran areas, see B. Lenman, 'The Limits of Godly Discipline in the Early Modern Period' in K. von Greyerz ed. *Religion and Society in Early Modern Europe, 1500–1800*, (London, 1984), 124–45, at 127. Hsia, *Social Discipline in the Reformation*, 122–35.

8. Merry Wiesner, 'Studies of Women, the Family and Gender,' in William Maltby ed. *Reformation Europe: A Guide to Research II*, (St Louis, 1992), 159–89, at 164.

9. Gordon Donaldson, *Scottish Church History*, (Edinburgh, 1985), 40–52; Graham, *Uses of Reform*.

10. For the alleged double standard, see Lawrence Stone, *The Family, Sex and Marriage in England, 1500–1800*, (New York, 1979), 315–8.

11. Janine Garrisson-Estèbe, *Les Protestants du Midi, 1559–1598*, (Toulouse, 1980), 337.

12. *Dundonald Parish Records: the Session Book of Dundonald 1602–1731*, ed. Henry Paton, (Edinburgh, 1936), 30–3.

13. Keith M. Brown, *Bloodfeud in Scotland 1573–1625: Violence, Justice and Politics in an Early Modern Society*, (Edinburgh, 1986).

14. For other slanders see *The Buik of the Kirk of the Canagait, 1564–1567* [*BKC*], ed. A. B. Calderwood (Edinburgh, 1961), 60, 64.

15. SCA, CH2/722/2, 27 Oct., 24 Nov. 1590.

16. *Stirling Presbytery Records 1581–1587* [*SPR*], ed. James Kirk (Edinburgh, 1981), 244, 247, 249–50.

17. New Register House, Edinburgh [NRH], OPR 165/3, fos 24v-25r.

18. NRH, OPR 403/1, fos 85v-86r, 90r-v, 94r, 96r, 103r-v, 104v, 106r. See Graham, *Uses of Reform*, 235–8.

19. *Acts and Proceedings of the General Assemblies of the Kirk of Scotland*, ed. Thomas Thomson, (Edinburgh, 1839–45), i, 19, 31, 35; *The History of the Kirk of Scotland by Mr David Calderwood*, ed. Thomas Thomson, (Edinburgh, 1842–9), ii, 191–3; David Smith, 'The Spiritual Jurisdiction, 1560–64,' *Records of the Scottish Church History Society*, 25 (1993), 1–18.
20. *StAKS*, i, 184–5.
21. *StAKS*, i, 174. For the attack on handfast marriage, see Graham, *Uses of Reform*, 122–3.
22. *StAKS*, i, 178–9,304.
23. *StAKS*, i, 437–9,441–2.
24. *BKC*, 68; Scottish Record Office [SRO], CH2/448/1, p. 56.
25. *BKC*, 38.
26. NRH, OPR 403/1, fos 87r-v.
27. NRH, OPR 403/1, fos 117r-v.
28. *StAKS*, ii, 702.
29. *BKC*, 36.
30. *StAKS*, ii, 910,915.
31. SRO, CH2/448/1, fos 87,108; CH2/450/1, fo 15v.
32. T.C. Smout, *A History of the Scottish People, 1560–1830* (Glasgow, 1969), 150.
33. SRO, CH2/450/1, fos 23r,34r.
34. *BKC*, 10; *StAKS*, i, 382–3,391. See *BKC*, 28 (Molly Acheson).
35. Graham, *Uses of Reform.*
36. SRO, CH2/450/1, passim.
37. *StAKS*, ii, 770–6,778–9.
38. *BKC*, 11–12. However, several were Frenchmen and may not have been subject to the session's jurisdiction.
39. *BKC*, 34–5.
40. *BKC*, 8–9.
41. See *BKC*, 58,60,66. For the problem of enforcement generally, see Graham, 'Civil Sword,' passim.
42. See SRO, CH2/448/1, fos 106–134. For actions against female brothel-keepers or panderers, see ibid, 11, 28, 83.
43. *SPR*, 7; NRH, OPR 403/1, fos 62v, 68v, 69v, 71v, 74v-75v, 77r-v.

PART SIX

'of this marriage there are no sons,
but three daughters now existing'

A Highland woman

CHAPTER SEVENTEEN

A Woman's Place: Birth Order, Gender and Social Status in Highland Houses

Roxanne Reddington-Wilde

PEOPLE AND PLACE are intertwined. People relate to the land upon which they and others live. This chapter looks at land-owning families and others dwelling in Argyll in the Western Highlands during the late seventeenth and early eighteenth centuries.[1] The subject is the *House* – not the building in which people live, but the generations of a family who lay legal claim to a piece of ground. The system of land inheritance differs from that of other, moveable property and has an effect upon the organisation of families. Birth order is as important as gender in determining one's role within the family. Testaments (wills) and marriage contracts provide a large number of the examples utilised because they highlight the transfer of property and people amongst households. All family members are taken care of throughout their lifetime, but the manner in which they receive their upkeep and the social status accorded them varies depending upon their birth order and their gender. As individuals who cannot inherit land, women throw into relief the issues of land, kin and hierarchy. In the Campbell legal documents analysed, 276 women appear. Of these 176 appear alone in a legal document, without any other women. Women appear in fifty-seven marriage contracts, two testaments, nine bonds of provision that are akin to testaments and five liferent documents with similar intents. These seventy-three documents contrast with thirty-nine bonds in which women figure in an active role, sometimes lending money to male kinsmen. Thus, broadly speaking, women figure in 112 out of some 1,500 documents analysed.[2]

In the feudal ideology of landholding, the principle of which was accepted in the Highlands as well as the Lowlands, family land may only be inherited by the first born or oldest surviving male of the prior landholder. Even if this male is a small child, he has right to the land above that of any older male relatives of his father. No Campbell heiresses were found in the abstracts, though technically a female could inherit in the absence of a male heir.

A division of lineage lands would lead to a diminution of the family's strength. Gender is the first concern in determining eligibility for landholding. The individual must be male. This eliminates half the offspring. If more than one son is available, then the holding's ownership is passed whole to the eldest. Younger sons frequently farm a portion of the lineage land during their lifetimes, but at death the disposition of the ground passes back to the eldest male and his personal line.

In the non-feudal landholding system of Early Ireland, females were alienated from lineage lands in a similar way. This system of male inheritance of land is an ancient one throughout Northwest Europe, common to both Celtic and non-Celtic cultures. Land provides the basis of wealth and power. The continued existence of the family takes precedence over any of its individuals. Sons are socially valued in High-land society over daughters. This makes no comment on levels of affection in a family or implies that individuals prefer their boys to their girls. It simply means that, when it comes to the transferral of land and the continuance of the family name, a family hopes to have at least one son. That is the reason for the otherwise unnecessary comment in a bond mentioning that 'of this marriage there are no sons, but three daughters now existing . . .'[3] It then details the amounts of non-land or moveable property each daughter may inherit.

The above specifics apply only to the inheritance of land. 'Grund', as an estate or piece of farmland is still referred to in Scots, is a fixed, immovable commodity known in Scots law as 'heritable property' and contrasts with moveable resources such as livestock, furniture, clothing and of course the ultimate in moveable transactions – money.[4] In a rather complicated bond of 1712, John Campbell of Kenmore and his eldest lawful son, Archibald, promise to pay an annual rent or interest of forty-eight merks on 800 merks borrowed from John Campbell, a Dumbarton merchant. That interest is to be drawn off one of Kenmore's possessions, the farm of Barquile.[5] The example illustrates land resources from which this social class drew its power and the growing desire for additional money primarily controlled by merchants. They did not expect to pay off the debt quickly as the bond contains provisions for monetary interest to be drawn by several generations and several removes of the merchant's relatives. There is a clear preference here for legitimate or 'lawfully procreated' heirs, but their gender is immaterial. Priority is given to any male or female children of the merchant. Interestingly, birth order does not matter here. Specifically noted, however, is the person who is his immediate heir, his sister Helen Campbell in Inveraray. Because a merchant's wealth rests in money and other moveables, a woman may legally inherit it. A societal preference still exists, however, for closely related males if they are available. Moving down a generation, Helen's sons or 'heirs male' should inherit the annual rent. Only failing them do daughters come into the money. Should all else fail, any other male heirs, such as uncles or cousins, of the merchant brother and sister may receive the interest.

In this monetary bond, one sees a preference for legitimate, male heirs but an even greater desire to keep the money, moveable though it is, as close as possible to the original line of descent emanating from the merchant. This desire permits closely-related females to inherit money over more distant male relatives. As this merchant died without any male heirs, his sister Helen, widow of a John Campbell in the Horseguards, passed on the income 'in favour of Margaret Campbell, her only lawful daughter', in 1716.[6]

Often, a woman received her inheritance at the time of her marriage. This rite of passage marks not only her assumption of adult status, but her movement from her nuclear family – defined by the interests of her father and kin – to her husband's family. She brought wealth, in the form of tocher or dowry, into this new family to cement her status. She also laid claim to any moveables that might be coming to her from her own family, rather than wait until her parents were advanced in years and she herself a mother. When John Campbell, brother to Alexander Campbell of Sondochan, married Katherine Campbell, daughter of John Campbell of Balliclaven, her tocher was '£500 Scots, in satisfaction of all that she might claim by the decease of her said father, or Mary Campbell, his spouse'.[7] This *living* inheritance is not unusual in Europe as Early Medieval Saxon examples include *dowry*, direct and indirect, closely linked to the inheritance by females of parental property.[8]

In the early 1700's, the Kilberry branch of Campbells ran into financial difficulties with no direct male heir. Their legal deeds illustrate how a kindred had more than one option open to them in inheritance. In manipulating family resources and marriage ties to bolster 'the standing of the house of Kilberry', personal needs, particularly female ones, took second place to those of the family as a whole. The elder Dugald Campbell of Kilberry must have suspected he was dying in 1713, so he distributed his goods and property among his wife and four daughters.[9]

Goods are tangible objects such as clothing or other furnishings. Property can extend to animate beasts. Wealth on the hoof is as moveable as any piece of goods could be. Scottish society (as with Early Irish) had no trouble extending ownership of livestock to both sexes. The distribution of moveables is up to the individual owner. Dugald wishes his wife to receive half his wealth, while the four daughters are to split the rest, in effect receiving an eighth each.

Lacking a male heir, the Kilberry land was about to pass out of the hands of the immediate, all-female family. In order to keep effective control within the direct line of descent, the Kilberry women effect a union between the closer, female and more distant, male representatives of the family. Elizabeth Campbell, eldest daughter of Dugald Campbell of Kilberry, marries Captain Dugald Campbell, the new heir to Kilberry in

1717. With Kilberry interests safely consolidated, all the women transfer their assets to the new family head, who would deal with their debts. As she surrendered her liferent of 'Kilberry and Tiretian', Barbara Campbell, Dugald's widow was to receive an annuity of 600 merks. The dates indicate that Elizabeth marries at the same time as these legal proceedings. Marriage itself is not just the happy union of two people, it is a product of close negotiations to determine the assets of two families and arrange a transferral of these assets between generations.[10] Whatever their private plans for spending their inheritance, the Kilberry women recognise the claims of family standing to override any immediate, personal needs they may have. They will not be cast off destitute but are definitely expected to pass up an opportunity to exert their legal rights and to take a lesser share of income because of family problems.

A woman brings some of her family's property, in the form of her tocher, into the relationship with the new husband and his family. That new family, however, then physically supports her in that marriage and in any widowhood afterwards. This is the case with the aforementioned Elizabeth Campbell, 'boarded and maintained' by her mother 'till the time of her marriage in November last'.[11] While a man's income and well-being throughout life depend upon the resources of his birth family, upon reaching adulthood a woman depends upon the income of her new relations. Perhaps this is the reason why the Kilberry daughters and other Highland women are expected to sacrifice more of their inheritance and other monetary resources than men. Barbara Campbell, the elder Kilberry's widow, does not give up her share of 'inheritance' from her husband because her own birth relatives no longer support her. She needs this spousal income from her marital family to maintain herself and at least one of her daughters.

Campbell landholders and other arbiters of similar social standing who assembled a year after the original agreement to restructure the family finances understand that 'the circumstances of the family of Kilberry require this as much as any other families in the country'.[12] A shortage of ready cash, coupled with a desire to follow a fancier lifestyle than the Highlands previously pursued, left many families juggling their assets. Other women are on record as passing their monetary and other income rights to their family's males.

The eldest surviving male most closely associated with the main line of family descent wields the most official power within a lineage. Birth order and gender conspire to place him in this position. Birth order, while most dramatic in its separation of eldest from non-eldest child, subdivided the claims of younger siblings as well. The effect is most pronounced, as before, in inheritances where children are listed in order of birth.

Donald Campbell of Barichbeyan had eight children, six of who are listed in his will. His eldest son, George, acts as executor for the estate, dividing up some or all of the family's livestock and monetary moveables amongst his younger siblings; Mr Alexander, Ronald, Mary, Anna, and Janet (who is probably illegitimate). Birth order is recounted solely along gender lines, emphasising the separate roles each sex plays in a family. The testament first lists the inheritance due the males. The second son, Alexander, receives 4000 merks and all equine stock. The third son receives only half that money and any young bullocks useful for ploughing. These animals are of lesser value than horses cited. The eldest and next to eldest daughters are unmentioned. They are likely married and have either received their inheritances as tocher or are deemed not to need additional support. No money is forthcoming for the younger girls. They receive livestock only, the amount varying by birth order. Thus Mary has thirty, Anna twenty and Janet twelve.[13] 'Old-fashioned' marriage contracts found elsewhere provide a woman's tocher in cattle alone. Those with more 'modern' features include or substitute money. The girls here receive breeding cows, capable of producing both offspring and dairy products. From this stock, they can increase their personal resources more productively than from interest off a monetary bequest. The numbers of cows are within the range found in tochers and may represent the girls' dowries.

Margaret Campbell, Barichbeyan's widow, receives additional money above and beyond that legally called for by her marriage contract. Her inclusion reveals that her husband is not limiting himself to the barest legal minimum he must dole out to his family. He is also moved by a sense of personal responsibility and likely by affection as well. It is the more significant, therefore, that he gradates the inheritance, even within a gender, by birth-order. How to account functionally for the diminution of wealth as birth order increases is unclear. Unlike the category of 'women' as a whole, latter born children do not seem to be compensated in other manners for their loss of patrilineal inheritance. This is not a society philosophically based on egalitarian or democratic principals. Such discrimination based on birth order may have been justified as 'one's lot in life'.

In some ways, non-eldest sons occupy a similar social position in society to all women. These men do not automatically have access to that most powerful of social resources, land. Tradition and law mandate that a piece of land be handed over intact to one male member of the upcoming generation rather than divided into portions. Only moveable property passes on to a lineage's remaining, secondary children. Rather than view the issue of property inheritance as one that splits males and females into opposing camps, the divide becomes an uneven one separating the few, eldest males of a generation – to whom control of the land is granted –

against the rest (both male and female) who receive control of lesser, moveable resources. This imbalance reflects a greater, societal imbalance of power and status upon which the hierarchical Highland and Lowland Scottish societies are based. There is one major difference, however. Males of any birth order may play a public role, such as entering into legal deeds. Women are, for the most part, barred from active, public positions. The clearest illustration of this is the complete absence of women from any witness list, itself the least powerful role in a legal action.

Women predominately appear in marriage contracts and testaments. The passing on of property is an important part of both. In marriage, a woman also passes from her birth family to a new family. The inter-generational bond is stressed between a woman and her father in both these legal forms, while the marriage contract adds a new, primary relationship between husband and wife. This marital bond represents the start of a new, nuclear family.

A marriage contract involves several parties and generations, not just the bride and groom, for it legally marks the union of two separate families and not simply two individuals. The more socially prominent and land rich the families, the greater the attention to detail. The preferred form is for the father of the bride to give his consent or actually enter into the contract alongside or even on behalf of his daughter. The groom, particularly if he is the head of his kindred, is the only mandatory person on the other side, but his father may well appear too, signifying that family's acceptance.

A series of marriage and other contracts exists for a large family, the Campbells of Elister in Islay. Isobel Campbell's marriage contract to Alexander Stewart, saddler in Coleraine, Ireland, apparently because it documents a woman, sets out the basic family genealogy on her side. Similar genealogies do not appear in her brothers' contracts. Three brothers, a mother and a sister/daughter appear here, along with deliberate mention of a father and additional brother. The list brings in representatives of both active generations of the Elister family. Because her father is dead, eldest brother Colin as head of the family records his legal consent to the marriage. Somewhat unusually, their mother Elizabeth and two more brothers also place theirs on record. The contract concerns her entire family, which is passing over £35 pounds sterling (rather than pounds Scots) as well as watching a sister leave the family. Representatives of the groom's family are lacking. While not mandatory, their absence may be explained by the contract's setting in what was a nearby but still foreign country.[14]

When it comes time for eldest brother Colin to choose a bride and perpetuate the family line, he and his brothers look only a few miles north to old family friends. Margaret Campbell, as the eldest daughter of

Campbell of Sinderland, is an appropriate mate for the head of the house of Elister. The marriage cements long-term, local connections between two landowning families in the area. Colin's brothers and other Islay power brokers record their witness and satisfaction with the union.[15] Oddly, Margaret's father is not recorded as consenting to the contract, but his good will comes across in the next Elister marriage when Colin's younger brother, William, marries a younger daughter of Sinderland's, with the father's blessing. A final Elister brother, John, marries soon after to a sister of Ballinaby. Archibald Campbell of Sinderland is a witness to it.[16] Phrased this way, the interconnection between person and place, generation and kindred becomes explicit: land equals family. A wedding ties together not just individuals but territory. A web of marriage and future kinship ties is being cast across the western peninsula of Islay. From Sinderland to Elister to Ballinaby and smaller points in between, marriages and other legal actions link individuals, the families and places in which all live.

Wives and widows maintain considerable control over the affairs of land. A wife's consent in the rental or more permanent alienation of land is often needed. In fact, if the plot comes from her liferent lands, she may be the major power here even if a male is given pride of place in the writing of the document. The amount of land tied to a woman in marriage could be extensive. Lachlan MacLachlan of Fassifern in marrying Elizabeth Campbell, eldest lawful daughter of Mr Dugald Campbell of Kilmorie, agrees 'to bestow 30,000 merks in land for her liferent . . . and promising to infeft her . . . in certain of his lands in fulfillment thereof, viz. Clachaig, Glenlean, Garrochra, Bernie and others.'[17]

Within a marriage, a husband may place considerable trust in his wife's judgement. Alexander Campbell of Kirnan, writing from London, appoints his wife to act as his factor or 'agent' to manage his main lineage lands of Kirnanmore and Kirnanbeg. While she may run the home office, she does not go into the field herself. Several months later, probably in time for the autumn rents, Isobel appoints a man, Mr Alexander Campbell, minister at Inveraray, to act as her sub-factor to lift the rents.[18] The choice Kirnan made to invest his wife in a factorship was a personal one, based on his regard for her as an individual. It does not seem to derive from a standard set of social expectations as might the appointment of one's male heir to this land management. As always, individuals operate within a broad range of possible actions. They are simply more likely to follow the general norms of society than operate outside them. Kirnan's factory was permissible but somewhat unusual. His wife, in her sub-factory to a man, returns to the general expectations of society.

A woman gains yet more control after her husband dies and the provisions of the marriage contract come to fruition. Even though 'Janet

Campbell, widow of John Campbell of Strachur, and now spouse to Mr John Cunningham in Ardgartan' has remarried, she continues to tack or rent out the lifèrent lands which passed to her on her first husband's death. In this case, she reconfirms 'the nether half of the lands of Feorline' to two men already farming there.'

Women can receive an income from land. That income is frequently limited in its source and extent, but how much public power do these women receive along with that income? Kinship terms can carry a denotation of age and a related sense of status. A woman begins life as a daughter, living within the parameters of her own family. A daughter has no public role. She is represented legally by her father (or brother if the father is dead). When she marries, she becomes an adult and moves into a new status in a new family, her husband's. A wife may operate in public with the consent of her husband. When that spouse dies, however, a woman moves into her strongest, most public position. Jack Goody observes of early, Germanic society that 'land given as a marriage portion eventually came under the control of the widow if she survived [after her husband]'.[19] The position of Highland and Scottish widows are part of a Northwest European social set-up. Widows operate in their own right, at least in a limited way, in public. They enjoy considerable control over their liferent lands, although they may still be willing, as with Barbara Campbell of Kilberry, to give up much of this control to male relatives for the sake of the greater, family well-being.

The main reason women do not own land in this society stems from the primary system of descent reckoning. It is patrilineal. Membership in a family is determined through the male line. To keep the primary source of power – land – within the lineage, it can only be passed on to those members who remain in and transfer membership in the lineage. These are the men. While present society might view this set-up as chauvinistic and limiting, it provides for the up-keep of all family members and at the same time conserves the landed property. Adult men draw their income from family lands. A woman enjoys the support of her birth family before marriage, receives some of its moveable assets at marriage, and spends most of her life with her husband, jointly drawing upon his family's resources. Widowhood might see her as no longer integral to that family. To ameliorate that, legal custom specifically sets aside some of her husband's family lands for her to use in liferent at this time. As a widow, she can manage this land in her own right, rather than rely on the services of male relatives. Upon her death, the land reverts back to its primary owner, the patrilineage. Individuals pass away. Time and generations flow on, land and family intact.

NOTES

1. This chapter is based on Scottish Record Office, The Particular Register of Bonds . . . within Argyll, 1665–1794, SC 51/48 26 volumes. Henry Paton culled these into *The Clan Campbell: Abstracts of Entries Relating to Campbells in the Sheriff Court Books of Argyll at Inveraray* (Edinburgh, 1913), vols. i & iii. For greater discussion see R. Reddington-Wilde, 'The Power of Place: Spatial Analysis and Social Organisation of the Campbells in Early Modern Argyll, Scotland', Harvard University PhD thesis, 1995; now published (Ann Arbor, 1995).
2. Cf. Paton, *Clan Campbell*, i, 136.
3. Ibid, i, 202.
4. Cf. *Glossary: Scottish Legal Terms, Latin Maxims and European Community Legal Terms* (Edinburgh, 1988). See also D. U. Stiùbhart in this volume.
5. Paton, *Clan Campbell*, i, 130.
6. Ibid, i, 172–3
7. Ibid, i, 7.
8. J. Goody, *The development of the family and marriage in Europe* (Cambridge, 1983), 248.
9. Paton, *Clan Campbell*, i, 145.
10. Ibid, i, 170–1.
11. Ibid.
12. Ibid.
13. Ibid, i, 94–5. See also D. U. Stiùbhart in this volume.
14. Ibid, i, 175–5.
15. Ibid, i, 177.
16. Ibid, i, 182.
17. Ibid, i, 197. See also D. U. Stiùbhart in this volume.
18. Ibid, i, 149.
19. Ibid, i, 183–4.
20. Goody, *family and marriage*, 121.

CHAPTER EIGHTEEN

Wet Nurses and Unwed Mothers in Seventeenth-Century Aberdeen[1]

_____ *Gordon DesBrisay*

'IT WERE BEST', wrote Edinburgh physician James McMath in 1694, 'that all Mothers might nurse their own Children', but he went on to lament that few 'now a days do it, save the poorer'.[2] Most well-to-do women in Scotland and elsewhere in early modern Europe turned their newborns over to wet nurses, despite all medical advice to the contrary. Because lactation impedes conception, and perhaps too because of taboos against having sex during the nursing period, widespread wet-nursing shows up in the demographic record: in Aberdeen, women in the upper third of society bore significantly more children at shorter intervals than their poorer, breastfeeding (and possibly abstaining) neighbours.[3] But if rich women would not breastfeed for themselves, they could at least be urged to be careful as to whom they chose in their stead. The old adage 'as the nurse is, so the child will be', was taken literally, because everyone knew that a woman's milk conveyed character and temperament along with nutrients and contagions: 'in sucking her [the child] will draw in both the vices of her body and mind'.[4] These words echoed centuries of medical opinion in Europe, but Scottish readers could have been forgiven for thinking they were written especially for them, because the sucking in of vice was a matter of particular relevance in a country where respectable parents appear to have been much more likely than their English or western European counterparts to hire unwed mothers as wet nurses. Just as French and English parents were reporting difficulty finding suitable wet nurses, McMath blithely declared 'Nor are good Nurses hard to be got'.[5] He did not elaborate, but his Scottish readers all knew that prospective wet nurses were as close as the nearest church, where they could be found any Sunday, seated facing the congregation on stools of repentance. There is no reason to suspect that parents in Scotland cared any less for the moral and physical welfare of their newborns; nor were respectable Scots notably tolerant of sex outside of marriage, especially among the servants. Yet numbers of seemingly caring Scottish parents appear to have considered bastard-bearing, the literal embodiment of vice, no barrier to employment as a wet nurse to their child. Why was that?

In the providentialist universe of the seventeenth century, immorality of all sorts was thought to put entire communities in the way of God's wrath, but in Scotland as elsewhere the struggle to impose 'godly discipline' on unruly bodies and wayward souls tended to concentrate, even fixate, on sins of the flesh.[6] The country bristled with kirk sessions, one in every parish, each of them busy with many things but dedicated first and foremost to the detection, pursuit, and punishment of unwed mothers (and, slightly less often, fathers).[7] The chances that an unmarried pregnant woman would escape the attentions of the kirk were slim to nil in most parts of the lowlands.[8] Once caught, public shaming was assured and there was a heavy fine to pay.[9] Yet even so, comparatively high levels of illegitimacy persisted throughout the era of godly discipline (roughly 1560–1760) and beyond.[10]

Much has been written on Scottish illegitimacy, but that persistence remains to be fully explained. Of course, Scotland was a poor country and many young people could not afford to establish the separate household that marriage entailed, but we should not presume that every single woman entering into a sexual relationship, or even those who became pregnant, had marriage in mind. When hauled into court for bastardy, Scottish women, unlike their sisters in other countries, almost never claimed that the men had promised to marry them.[11] Church authorities did not push offending couples to marry, nor was irregular 'common law' marriage common in the seventeenth century, as suggested by the fact that nearly all the women who bore multiple illegitimate children did so by multiple men.[12]

If shotgun weddings and cohabitation were uncommon, there must have been other mechanisms in place to enable women to cope with unwed motherhood. Poor relief was seldom an option, because church and secular authorities rarely granted charity to young unwed mothers and their children. Women recently convicted of fornication almost never appeared on Aberdeen's poor relief rolls.[13] Some fathers promised to provide for their bastard children, and the kirk helped broker child support where private arrangements broke down, but given the low status of most fathers such payments were likely as meagre as they were unreliable.[14] In the nineteenth century, most unmarried mothers-to-be in the rural north-east moved back in with their parents until the child was weaned, leaving it with them when they returned to full-time employment as farm or domestic servants.[15] No doubt such arrangements were made in earlier centuries as well, though higher rates of mortality will have made grand-parents scarcer.[16]

The coping mechanism that concerns us here, wet-nursing, was more peculiar to the early modern period, since from the mid-eighteenth century rich women increasingly took to breastfeeding for themselves.[17] Historians have failed to note the earlier link between illegitimacy and wet-nursing, partly because it merited only occasional and generally oblique references in the kirk session records on which most studies of illegitimacy rest, and partly because it had not occurred to us that Scotland might diverge in this particular from English and European models, whereby (outside aristocratic circles) nearly all wet nurses are said to have been married women in villages taking in children from the nearby town.[18] Aberdeen's kirk session records, however, make the connection between unwed mothers and wet nurses explicit, and they show just how common live-in nurses were in the royal burgh.[19]

In the second half of the seventeenth century, Aberdeen was a compact, moderately prosperous place of about 7,500 people, with perhaps 2,000 more living in the immediate vicinity: a good-sized city by British standards. A busy North Sea port and a university town, it was the market and service centre for a mainly lowland hinterland of some 100,000 people.[20] The north-east was a poor region in a poor country, where the majority of the rural population were landless sub-tenants working the land and whatever else was going, being paid sometimes in cash, sometimes in kind. Rural poverty was Aberdeen's competitive advantage in the international woollens trade: urban merchants made fortunes by paying sub-subsistence wages to thousands of part-time, mainly rural, mainly female outworkers.[21] 'It is this' noted one north-east commentator, 'which bringeth money to the Commons, other ways of getting it, they have not'.[22]

There was another way of getting money, and that was to move to town. Like any city, Aberdeen attracted large numbers of migrants seeking work, most of them young single people from within a radius of about forty kilometres.[23] Because women's wages were so low, a majority of Aberdeen households, many of them modest indeed, employed one or more female domestics – about half of whom had moved into town from elsewhere.[24] Women aged fifteen to twenty-four arriving in Aberdeen to work as domestic servants outnumbered all male immigrants combined, contributing to a lop-sided sex ratio (seventy-one men to every 100 women in the 1690s) typical of early modern towns.[25] Many of these women likely intended only a short stay, perhaps a single six-month contract. Others were in it for the medium haul, trying to save money for a dowry or to support family back home.[26] Their position was always tenuous, because, after gender, the most fundamental distinction in urban society was between native-born and established residents, who were deemed *of* the town, and the mainly transient newcomers, who were merely *in* it.[27] This distinction was especially critical for migrant women, who might be dismissed by employers at any time but could make no claim on the city's poor relief rolls, reserved as they were for native and established residents of seven years or more.[28]

Living away from parental supervision in crowded quarters amongst mixed company, female domestics were at considerable risk of becoming pregnant: in the third quarter of the seventeenth century, this was the fate of just over twenty servants a year in Aberdeen.[29] The constant flow of people in and out of towns makes estimates of urban illegitimacy very difficult; contemporaries, alas, were not inclined to calculate illegitimacy ratios for us, but they knew a lot of sin when they saw it, and Aberdeen's city fathers responded with a particularly strenuous campaign for godly discipline.[30] For much of the seventeenth century, the Aberdeen kirk session drew yearly on the services of three ministers, five magistrates, and thirty-six elders and deacons, and after 1657 its efforts were re-inforced by a justice of the peace court that sent another thirty-six constables out into the streets to do what all those others were already doing – nosing around, keeping an eye out, bending an ear, whatever it took to root out the sins and misdemeanours of their servants and neighbours.[31] All office-holders were appointees, and there was a high annual turnover: between 1657 and 1687, about 450 different men stoked the engines of godly discipline in Aberdeen.[32] Even the humble deacons and constables had a taste of the power to bear witness or turn a blind eye, hear confessions and know secrets, punish and forgive: what-ever impact godly discipline had on the lower orders, it provided their (slightly) betters with a fruitful exercise in consensus building and male bonding.

Not that the agents of godly discipline didn't manage to keep busy. Over those thirty years, those 450 men saw to it that at least 629 women were convicted of fornication or adultery (107 of them more than once) on the basis of an unsanctioned pregnancy. Pregnancy featured in ninety-eight per cent of all prosecutions for fornication and adultery.[33] Upwards of ninety per cent of the women were servants, and most were guest-workers, as suggested by the fact that of ninety-four prosecutions for fornication and adultery 1659–1665, only one-third of the pregnancies yielded a baptism in the parish register.[34] Miscarriages, neonatal mor-tality and evading registration could account for some of the attrition, but court records for Aberdeen and across the country show that a great many of the women convicted of fornication in the cities fled, or more likely returned, to the country to give birth. Since most runaways were likely headed for their home parish, they were easily traced and made to return to undergo church penance and civil punishment in the parish where the sin was committed.[35]

In Aberdeen, the convoluted process of godly discipline helped to nudge unwed mothers-to-be towards wet-nursing in at least two ways: by making them appear before prospective employers in potentially advantageous circumstances, and by imposing financial burdens that made it hard to resist relatively well-paid work as a wet nurse. The story of a servant named Margaret Rolland offers a case in point.[36] In March, 1685 she was found to be pregnant out of wedlock and was summoned to appear in private before the Aberdeen kirk session. Here, the kirk's redemptive mission was the key, its insistence upon confession and its dependence upon the compliance and acquiescence of the accused.[37] The interview was the crucial point in the disciplinary proceedings, because only if she offered a detailed confession and a convincing show of contrition and remorse would she be allowed to proceed to the acts of public penance – three shamefaced Sunday appearances on the stool of repentance for a first offence – that would lead to her absolution and reintegration into the community of the faithful.

Margaret Rolland must have made a good impression, because the presiding minister, Dr George Garden, soon hired her to nurse his forthcoming child. She gave birth in May, about the same time as Garden's wife, and a month later was ensconced in the minister's house-hold. Garden immediately petitioned the elders to suspend their proceed-ings against Rolland until after his child was weaned – a courtesy routinely granted employers, but never unwed mothers nursing their own children. Unfortunately, the Gardens' child died the next spring.[38] Margaret Rolland had to face the congregation sooner than she might have expected, and having made her three appearances she was absolved of her sin in July, 1686, sixteen months after the initial accusation.

Church discipline depended on the cooperation of the accused, but secular punishment was straightforward and decidedly unilateral: female and male fornicators alike faced statutory fines of up to £10 Scots for a first offence, payable in full by the end of the week on pain of a public whipping and banishment if they failed to pay.[39] Because they nearly all earned less money than almost any man, the fine weighed especially heavily on women, and especially women in Aberdeen: in Edinburgh average wages were higher, in Glasgow average fines were lower, but Aberdonian employers and magistrates provided women with a double whammy of low wages and maximum fines.[40] £10 Scots was all the cash, less tips, that senior female domestics in Aberdeen earned in a year, and many women earned less. In 1695 the average wage for female domestics (not including wet nurses) was £8 14s, exclusive of room and board.[41] Some could call on family or draw upon dowry savings for their fine and some had items to pawn, while others borrowed, on terms that elude us, from relatives, friends, lovers, employers, fellow servants, or money-lending merchants.[42] Revenue from the fines was paid back out in the form of pensions for Aberdeen's 'deserving poor'.[43] Thus, pregnant servants (most often rural migrants) facing single motherhood, unemployment, loss of earnings, public shaming and mount-ing debt contributed to urban social services for which neither they nor their children were ever likely to qualify.

Poor women bearing illegitimate children were drawn by their fines deeper into the cash, credit and debt nexus. For domestic servants in Aberdeen faced with repaying the equivalent of a year's wages, the climb back was especially steep, even without the interruption in employment and the prospect of a new mouth to feed. But the city fathers who fixed the wages and imposed the fines also saw to it that the wage ceiling for wet nurses was £20 per year, double the top wage most single mothers could have earned before their pregnancy, with the prospect of handsome tips from the godparents if the child survived to be weaned.[44] Returning to our friend Margaret Rolland, it is worth noting that her brisk dealings with the justice of the peace court were completed before the critical interview with the kirk session. On 9 March 1685, she and her ne'er-do-well lover (who impregnated two other women over the next few months) were each fined £10 for fornication, and the accounts show that she, like ninety per cent of the women in her circumstances, somehow paid her fine within the week.[45] So when Margaret Rolland met with the minister and elders on 16 March, she had an added financial incentive to make a good impression. And she may well have known that the minister was in the market for a wet nurse.

Live-in wet nurses were a luxury reserved to the very rich in most parts of early modern Europe, but in Aberdeen they could be found in even quite modest households: in 1695, Christian Thomson was a wet nurse in the household of a stonemason in the bottom tax bracket.[46] Eighty couples listed in the poll book that year baptised children in the town: at least twelve of them reported a live-in wet nurse, and wage rates suggest there were as many as nine more.[47] Live-in wet nurses were overwhelmingly drawn from the ranks of unwed mothers: one-quarter of the women convicted of fornication or adultery in Aberdeen with Margaret Rolland in 1685 were hired as live-in nurses while still on the kirk's books, but there were surely many other unwed wet nurses who went unrecorded because they had completed their penance before being hired, or because they were convicted in another parish.[48] In 1695, city fathers tried to insist that 'non of the Inhabitants accept or intertaine any person to be nurses who are guiltie of uncleannes untill they produce ane testifcat bearing ther giveing satsifaction to the Church', just as in 1609 they had warned parents not to import rural ('landwart') wet nurses into the city until they had atoned for 'thair harlatrie and fornicationes'.[49]

Urban employers seem to have expected exclusive service from their live-in wet nurses.[50] What, then, became of the nurses' own children? High rates of infant mortality must have claimed many, and abandonment and infanticide may have claimed a few more (though such cases were rarely reported).[51] But what of those who survived? A sixteenth-century minister in Fife warned that some women turned to wet nursing 'not regarding quhat sal become of ther awin', and there is some evidence for this a century later in Aberdeen.[52] Around 1675, Andrew Dempster took his illegitimate child to court with him to complain that the child's mother owed him money. Janet Gordon was a live-in wet nurse employed by one of the magistrates: 'I am but a poor man', claimed Dempster, but 'she hath left the child with me and broken the arme thereof as apparentlie may be sein'.[53] There is no way of knowing how many wet nurses turned their children over to the care of the fathers, but infants needed to be breastfed and if there was no other nursing mother in the family, another, cheaper wet nurse would have to be hired. In Edinburgh, some live-in nurses appear to have turned half or more of their salary over to their own child's nurse, and it seems likely that similar arrangements pertained in Aberdeen and other cities.[54]

Aberdeen's wet nursing regime, then, was the product of four inter-locking factors: an illegitimacy rate so high as to ensure a steady supply of lactating single women available to live in; wages so low that even quite modest householders could afford a live-in nurse; fines so high that unwed mothers had to take the best paid work available; and parents who, in light of these material considerations, set aside any scruples they may have had about morally tainted milk. We might also speculate, ever so gingerly, as to whether the ritual of private confession before the ministers and elders, the key moment in the process of godly discipline, might have been understood by at least some prospective employers to have set in train a physical as well as spiritual and moral cleansing of the body, a filtering of sin so thorough as to render the milk of fallen women suitable for the tender infants of respectable parents.

Wet-nursing cannot have been a viable option for all of the newly delivered unwed mothers in early modern Scotland, but it did provide a way for some to rejoin the workforce, repay their fines, and make their own way in the world. Might the wet nursing option have encouraged some single women to become pregnant, or at least to take some sexual risks they might not otherwise have taken? Why not? Is this any less plausible than suggesting that the husbands and fathers who presided over godly discipline so arranged things as to ensure that some unwed mothers had little choice but to become wet nurses? Recovering the story of wet nursing helps us to see that godly discipline (like the modern campaign for family values) encountered, and to some extent generated, countervailing social and economic forces that helped entrench and perpetuate the very behaviours it set out to curb. There was a symbiotic aspect to the whole business, a feedback loop (if you will pardon the pun) that wound through the town and out into the country whence so many servants and wet nurses came, whereby the men sworn to punish illicit sex ended up hiring the women they prosecuted to suckle their own children.

NOTES

1. Funding for this chapter was provided by the President's SSHRC Fund of the University of Saskatchewan. I wish to thank Susan Blake, Chris Friedrichs, Pam Downe, Ron Harpelle, Kelly Saxburg, Kris Inwood, Jim Scott and the late Louise Scott for their help and encouragement, and to extend special thanks to Elizabeth Ewan for her expert advice and support.
2. J. McMath, *The Expert Mid-wife: A Treatise of the Diseases of Women with Child, and in Childbed* (Edinburgh, 1694), 387.
3. R. E. Tyson, 'The Population of Aberdeenshire, 1695–1755: A New Approach', *Northern Scotland*, 6 (1985), 122. Unless otherwise noted, all references to Aberdeen refer to the royal burgh of New Aberdeen, and do not include the adjacent burgh of Old Aberdeen. On the taboo, see M. E. Wiesner, *Women and Gender in Early Modern Europe* (Cambridge, 1993), 71; S. Shahar, *Childhood in the Middle Ages* (New York, 1992), 56, 69–70; A. McLaren, *Reproductive Rituals: The Perception of Fertility in England from the Sixteenth Century to the Nineteenth Century* (London, 1984), 67. Cf. David Harley, 'From Providence to Nature: The Moral Theology and Godly Practice of Maternal Breast-Feeding in Stuart England,' *Bulletin of the History of Medicine*, 69 (1995), 204.
4. F. Mauriçeau, *The Diseases of Women With Child*, trans. H. Chamberlen (London, 1683), 433; R. Marshall, *Virgins and Viragos: A History of Women in Scotland from 1080–1980* (Chicago, 1983), 118.
5. McMath, 388–89. V. Fildes, *Breasts, Bottles and Babies: A History of Infant Feeding* (Edinburgh, 1986), 156–57; C. C. Fairchilds, *Domestic Enemies: Servants and Their Masters in Old Regime France* (Baltimore, 1984), 196.
6. R. Mitchison and L. Leneman, *Sexuality and Social Control: Scotland 1660–1780* (Oxford, 1989). See also M. Graham, 'The Civil Sword and the Scottish Kirk, 1560–1600' in W. Fred Graham ed. *Later Calvinism: International Perspectives* Sixteenth Century Essays and Studies, XXII (Kirksville, 1994); and G. Parker, 'The "Kirk By Law Established" and the Origins of "The Taming of Scotland"' in L. Leneman ed. *Perspectives in Scottish Social History* (Aberdeen, 1988). See also Michael Graham's paper in this volume.
7. Mitchison and Leneman, *Sexuality and Social Control*, 21, 202–208; S. J. Davies, 'The Courts and the Scottish Legal System, 1600–1747: The Case of Stirlingshire', in V. A. C. Gatrell, B. Lenman, and G. Parker eds. *Crime and the Law: The Social History of Crime in Western Europe Since 1500* (London, 1980), 123–132.
8. L. M. Smith, 'Sackcloth for the Sinner or Punishment for the Crime? Church and State in Cromwellian Scotland', in J. Dwyer, R. Mason, and A. Murdoch eds. *New Perspectives on the Politics and Culture of Early Modern Scotland* (Edinburgh, 1982), 116–132.
9. G. DesBrisay, 'Authority and Discipline in Aberdeen: 1650–1700', (University of St Andrews, unpublished PhD thesis, 1989), 321–24, 403–416; and '"Menacing Their Persons and Exacting on Their Purses": The Aber-

deen Justice Court, 1657–1700', in D. Stevenson ed. _From Lairds to Louns: Country and Burgh Life in Aberdeen, 1600–1800_ (Aberdeen, 1986).

10. In addition to _Sexuality and Social Control_, see Leneman and Mitchison, 'Girls in Trouble: The Social and Geographical Setting of Illegitimacy in Early Modern Scotland', _Journal of Social History_, 21 (1988); 'Scottish Illegitimacy Ratios in the Early Modern Period', _Economic History Review_ 2nd ser. 40 (1987); and M. Flinn ed. _Scottish Population History, From the Seventeenth Century to the 1930's_ (Cambridge, 1977). For comparisons, see P. Laslett, 'Introduction: Comparing Illegitimacy Over Time and Between Cultures' in P. Laslett, K. Oosterveen and R. M. Smith eds, _Bastardy and Its Comparative History_ (London, 1980). For later centuries see A. Blaikie, _Illegitimacy, Sex and Society: Northeast Scotland, 1750–1900_ (Oxford, 1993); D. Gill, _Illegitimacy, Sexuality and the Status of Women_ (Oxford, 1977); and B. Thompson, 'Social Study of Illegitimate Maternities', _British Journal of Preventive and Social Medicine_, 10 (1956).

11. L. Leneman and R. Mitchison, 'Clandestine Marriage in the Scottish Cities, 1660–1780', _Journal of Social History_, 26 (1993), 846.

12. Mitchison and Leneman, _Sexuality and Social Control_, 151–52.

13. But see ibid. 58, 213–214.

14. For more positive assessments see ibid. 152–53, 200–207; and the unattributed comments of Wiesner, _Women and Gender_, 50.

15. A. Blaikie, 'A Kind of Loving: Illegitimacy, Grandparents and the Rural Economy of North East Scotland, 1750–1900', _Scottish Economic and Social History_, 14 (1994).

16. Ibid. 54–5.

17. V. Fildes, 'The English Wet-Nurse and Her Role in Infant Care 1538–1800', _Medical History_, 32 (1988), 163–164; _Breasts, Bottles, and Babies_, 164, 398–400; Marshall, _Virgins_, 119–20.

18. L. Campbell, 'Wet-Nurses in Early Modern England: Some Evidence from the Townsend Archive', _Medical History_, 33 (1989), 364–65; Fildes, _Wet Nursing: A History from Antiquity to the Present_ (Oxford, 1988), ch. 6; _Breasts, Bottles and Babies_, 158; G. D. Sussman, _Selling Mother's Milk: The Wet-Nursing Business in France, 1715–1914_ (Urbana, 1982), 2.

19. Scottish Record Office [SRO], CH2/44/6–24, Aberdeen St. Nicholas Kirk Session Minutes (1651–1700). See also Mary Lindemann, 'Love for Hire: The Regulation of the Wet-Nursing Business in Eighteenth-Century Hamburg', _Journal of Family History_ 6 (1981), esp. 385.

20. Tyson, 'The Population of Aberdeenshire'.

21. Tyson, 'The Rise and Fall of Rural Manufacturing in Aberdeenshire' in J. S. Smith and D. Stevenson eds. _Fermfolk & Fisherfolk: Rural Life in Northern Scotland in the Eighteenth and Nineteenth Centuries_ (Aberdeen, 1989); I. D. Whyte, 'Agriculture in Aberdeenshire in the Seventeenth and Eighteenth Centuries: Continuity and Change', _Review of Scottish Culture_, 3 (1987): 45–47; R. A. Dodgshon, _Land and Society in Early Scotland_ (Oxford, 1981), 265–271.

22. W. Macfarlane, _Geographical Collections Relating to Scotland_, eds. A. Mitchell and J.T. Clark, vol. 3 (Edinburgh, 1908), 225.

23. C. W. J. Withers, 'Highland Migration to Aberdeen, c. 1649–1891', _North-_

ern Scotland, 9 (1989); I. D. Whyte and K. A. Whyte, 'Patterns of Migration of Apprentices into Aberdeen and Inverness During the Eighteenth and Early Nineteenth Centuries', *Scottish Geographical Magazine*, 102 (1986); R. A. Houston, 'Geographical Mobility in Scotland, 1652–1811: The Evidence of Testimonials', *Journal of Historical Geography*, 11 (1985).

24. *List of Pollable Persons Within the Shire of Aberdeen, 1696*, ed. J. Stuart (2 vols, Aberdeen, 1844), i, 595–632; A. J. S. Gibson and T. C. Smout, *Prices, Food and Wages in Scotland, 1550–1780* (Cambridge, 1995), 289–97; I. D. Whyte and K. A. Whyte, 'The Geographical Mobility of Women in Early Modern Scotland', in Leneman, *Perspectives in Scottish Social History*, 97.

25. Whyte and Whyte, 'Geographical Mobility', 97; *List of Pollable Persons*. See also H. M. Dingwall, *Late Seventeenth-Century Edinburgh: A Demographic Study* (Aldershot, 1994), 13–21, 28; D. Souden, 'Migrants and the Population Structure of Later Seventeenth-Century Provincial Cities and Market Towns', in P. Clark ed. *The Transformation of English Provincial Towns 1600–1800* (London, 1984), 149–161; and J. de Vries, *European Urbanization: 1500–1800* (London, 1984), 178. See also Helen Dingwall's essay in this volume.

26. R.A. Houston, 'Women in the Economy and Society of Scotland, 1500–1800', in R. A. Houston and I. D. Whyte eds. *Scottish Society 1500–1800* (Cambridge, 1989).

27. DesBrisay, 'Authority and Discipline', 161–69; A. Sharlin, 'Natural Decrease in Early Modern Cities: A Reconsideration', *Past and Present*, 79 (1978), 126–138; M. Walker, *German Home Towns: Community, State and General Estate, 1648–1871* (Ithaca, 1971), 11–142.

28. Aberdeen City Archives [ACA], *Council Letters*, vii, no.243 (April 1699).

29. Leneman and Mitchison, 'Girls in Trouble', 483–97; C. Fairchilds, 'Female Sexual Attitudes and the Rise of Illegitimacy: A Case Study', in R. I. Rotberg and T. K. Rabb eds. *Marriage and Fertility: Studies in Interdisciplinary History* (Princeton, 1980), 163–204; ACA, *Justice Court Book* I(1), 1657–1687.

30. See DesBrisay, 'Authority and Discipline', 398–99.

31. DesBrisay, 'Menacing Their Persons', 76–78.

32. DesBrisay, 'Authority and Discipline', 277, 310–313, 377–86.

33. Ibid, 387–402. Davies, 'The Courts and the Scottish Legal System', 125.

34. ACA, *Justice Court Book* I(1) and New Register House, OPR 183/3.

35. Smith, 'Sackcloth for the Sinner', 123–30.

36. SRO, CH2/448/19.

37. H. Schilling, ' "History of Crime" or "History of Sin"? Some Reflections on the Social History of Early Modern Church Discipline', in E. I. Kouri and T. Scott eds. *Politics and Society in Reformation Europe* (Basingstoke, 1987).

38. ACA, *Treasury Accounts* ii (Mortcloths, 1685/6).

39. DesBrisay, 'Menacing Their Persons', 85–88.

40. Dingwall, *Late Seventeenth-Century Edinburgh*, 119–120; R. K. Marshall, 'Wet-Nursing in Scotland, 1500–1800', *Review of Scottish Culture*, 1 (1984), 48–49; SRO, CH2/173/1, Glasgow Barony Kirk Session Minutes.

41. DesBrisay, 'Authority and Discipline', 436. *List of Pollable Persons*.

42. L. Ewen, 'Debtors, Imprisonment and The Privilege of Girth,' in Leneman, *Perspectives in Scottish Social History.*

43. ACA, *Justice Court Accounts.*

44. See *The Account Book of Sir John Foulis of Ravelston, 1671–1707* ed. A.W. Cornelius Hallen (Edinburgh, 1894).

45. ACA *Justice Court Book* I(1); ACA *Justice Court Accounts.*

46. *List of Pollable Persons*, i, 596.

47. Tyson, 'Population of Aberdeenshire', 120; *List of Pollable Persons.*

48. SRO, CH2/448/19. See also Lindemann, 'Love for Hire', 379.

49. SRO, CH2/448/23 (4 Nov. 1695); *Selections From the Records of the Kirk Session, Presbytery, and Synod of Aberdeen* ed. John Stuart (Aberdeen, 1846), 69. See also Lindemann, 'Love for Hire,' 379.

50. Shahar, *Childhood in the Middle Ages*, 64–68, and L. L. Otis, 'Municipal Wet Nurses in Fifteenth-Century Montpellier', in Barbara Hanawalt ed. *Women and Work in Preindustrial Europe*, 86. But see also Dingwall, *Late Seventeenth-Century Edinburgh*, 27–8.

51. See Deborah A. Symonds, 'Reconstructing Rural Infanticide in Eighteenth-Century Scotland', *Journal of Women's History*, 10 (1998). I would like to thank Dr Symonds for providing an advance copy of her article.

52. New Register House, OPR 403/1, 35v, Anstruther Wester Kirk Session Register. I am grateful to Dr Michael Graham for this reference.

53. ACA *Justice Court Book* I(1) 97 (n.d., but bound with 1675).

54. *The Tron Parish Poll Tax Returns 1694* eds. R.M. Strathdee et al (Edinburgh, 1993), 2; *Edinburgh Poll Tax Returns for 1694* ed. M. Wood (Edinburgh, 1951), 10. See also Wiesner, *Women and Gender*, 72. See also Lindemann, 'Love for Hire', 386.

CHAPTER NINETEEN

Wed to the Manse: The Wives of Scottish Ministers, *c.1560 – c.1800*

_____ *Ian D. Whyte and Kathleen A. Whyte*

IN 1564 the reformer John Knox married Margaret Stewart, daughter of the Protestant Lord Ochiltree. It was one of the most famous, indeed notorious, marriages of a Scottish minister for Knox was fifty and his bride barely seventeen.[1] Contemporaries were perhaps struck more by the social disparity between bride and groom than the age difference. Here was a man from a humble background marrying the daughter of a member of the nobility whose family had links with royalty. It was an extreme example of social mobility in a society that was very status conscious. However, in terms of the marriages made by ministers in the late sixteenth century and after this was an unusual, though not unique, example. Ministers continued to marry into landed society but only rarely into the nobility. Their brides were seldom as young as Margaret Stewart though significant age disparities between bride and bridegroom were not uncommon.

Our knowledge of ministers' wives in early modern Scottish society is strictly circumscribed by the limitations of the source material. Previous reviews of women in early modern Scotland have, inevitably, adopted a 'top-down' approach, focusing on the wives and daughters of members of the landed élite whose character and activities are better recorded than those of women from humbler origins.[2] However, below the ranks of the landowners, ministers are one of the best chronicled social groups and we have correspondingly more information about their wives. Church of Scotland ministers formed an organised, tight-knit professional élite with a common ethos.[3] Makey has shown that in the mid-seventeenth century ministers whose social origins were known were mostly drawn from the ranks of landed proprietors, burgesses and from the families of other ministers in particular.[4] However, the social origins of about half the ministers studied by Makey were unknown. As he suggests, a significant proportion of these must have come from the ranks of small feuars, tenant farmers and tradesmen.[5]

Ministers were relatively well off financially and were often upwardly mobile. But what of their wives? Little attention has been paid to them by historians. Autobiographies and biographies of prominent Scottish ecclesiastics have concentrated on their political activities and their theology rather than their private lives.[6] A recent political biography of Archbishop

James Sharp refers to his marriage to Helen Moncrieff, daughter of the laird of Randerston, only incidentally.[7] What were the social origins of ministers' wives in early modern Scotland? How did ministers and their future brides first meet? What patterns of courtship ensued? What was the role of ministers' wives, not just within the family but within the community? What were their relationships with their husbands? This chapter attempts to outline some tentative answers to these questions.

Much information may be gleaned from manuscript material, including correspondence and some published diaries of ministers. However, a useful starting point for an introductory survey such as this is the Reverend Hew Scott's nineteenth-century biographical compilation, *Fasti Ecclesiae Scoticanae*.[8] Twenty-five presbyteries were selected for study within the synods of Lothian and Tweeddale, Fife, and Glasgow and Ayr. The area covered comprises most of the Lowlands south of the Tay, excluding Galloway.

Scott's work is problematical for whilst the lists of ministers in each parish are mainly complete, the amount of biographical detail for each incumbent varies from a couple of terse sentences to several pages. The information given about ministers' wives includes their name, social origin, date of marriage, date of and age at death, names of children, occupations of sons, and marriage partners of daughters. Previous and subsequent marriages of ministers' wives are sometimes noted. However, this full set of information is rarely recorded for any individual. Indeed in many cases wives are not even named, and the existence of a marriage may only be indicated indirectly through references to children. Moreover, although second and subsequent marriages are listed as such it cannot be assumed that all marriages have been recorded or that all marriages not listed as second or subsequent were necessarily first marriages.[9] Data on ministers' wives from the *Fasti* have a tendency to be more detailed for urban parishes than for rural and for the later seventeenth and eighteenth centuries more than earlier periods. Such information has to be treated with caution, but this source nevertheless provides some useful insights when the data are aggregated on a broad scale.

Within the twenty-five presbyteries 2,471 marriages made between 1560 and 1800 were analysed. The proportion of marriages for which the brides' social origins were given never rose above forty-six per cent for any quarter-century period and was as low as twenty-three per cent for the first quarter of the seventeenth century. The proportion of marriages that were only referred to indirectly dropped from twenty-nine per cent in the later sixteenth century to six per cent at the end of the eighteenth. However, even in the last quarter of the eighteenth century fifty-three per cent of wives were referred to by name only with no details of their social origins.

In many cases where the social origins of ministers' wives are not given they were probably relatively humble. It is unlikely that the daughters of many ministers or larger landowners would have escaped Scott's scrutiny. Very few brides whose origins were specified came from tenant backgrounds or below, although it is known that many ministers were drawn from this level of society.[10] In addition, cases of ministers being charged with antenuptial fornication with their domestic servants indicate that they married girls from modest social backgrounds.[11]

The known social origins of ministers' wives in the sample are shown in Table One. Despite the development of dynasties of ministers with father often succeeding son in the same parish, the proportion of ministers' wives who themselves came from the manse is not as high as might have been expected. In the late sixteenth century, before ministers were established in every parish, only twenty per cent of girls of known origins came from families of ministers. The proportion rose to thirty-two per cent in the first quarter of the seventeenth century and to over forty per cent in the second half of the eighteenth century. Of comparable or greater significance were marriages between ministers and girls from landed backgrounds. They made up sixty per cent of total known social origins in the late sixteenth century, falling to thirty-five to thirty-seven per cent for most of the eighteenth century. Within the landed group there were eighteen marriages involving daughters of peers, though these were often younger daughters and, in one instance, an illegitimate one. Thirty-nine marriages involved girls from the families of knights and baronets. The proportion of marriages involving families of peers and knights reached a maximum of thirteen per cent in the second quarter of the seventeenth century, but was usually much lower. The majority of the rest were lairds, (described as 'laird', 'of that ilk', or 'of') plus a few smaller landholders described as 'portioners'. As we have seen, this social group provided many of the kirk's ministers. Very few fathers of ministers' wives were described as 'tenant' or 'farmer' but a fluctuating proportion referred to as being 'in' rural or urban parishes, were presumably of relatively humble status. Within the professional classes some wives had fathers holding university posts, though these were mainly former ministers, while some came from legal backgrounds. Few daughters of schoolmasters were recorded. The towns provided eighteen per cent of ministers' brides in the late sixteenth century, perhaps reflecting the urban focus of the early Protestant church. Proportions fluctuated between seven per cent and thirteen per cent in the seventeenth and most of the eighteenth century. This rose to seventeen per cent at the end of the eighteenth century, possibly reflecting growing urbanisation. Fathers designated as provosts, baillies and merchants accounted for most of these with only a small proportion being craftsmen.

TABLE 1. The Social Origins of Ministers' Wives (percentages)

	1560–1599	1600–1624	1625–1649	1650–1674	1675–1699	1700–1724	1725–1749	1750–1774	1775–1800
Peerage	2		4	3	1	1	2		6
Knights	2	4	9	6	6	4	3	3	3
Lairds	54	37	31	38	28	32	28	26	25
Portioners	2	2			1		1		1
All landed	60	43	44	47	36	37	35	29	35
Tenants			1					3	1
Designation 'in'	2	15	7	21	16	10	9	6	4
Ministers	18	28	27	23	25	29	33	37	35
University	2	4	3		3	4	4	4	5
Law		2	3	1	2	7	4	5	
Medicine				1	3			1	
Schoolmasters			3		1		1		
Admin/Govt			2		1		2	3	2
Army					1		2	1	1
Provosts & Baillies	2	2	2	2	2	5	2	2	2
Merchants	14	6	4	4	10	7	5	8	13
Burgesses	2		3						
Craftsmen		1	1	1	1	1	4		2
All Urban	18	8	11	7	13	13	11	10	17

Age at first marriage can be worked out for ministers and their wives where date of marriage, date of death and age at death are given. Such data are more frequent for the later eighteenth century than earlier periods and more common for ministers than their spouses. Calculations of average age at first marriage are suspect due to the small size of the sample and the possibility that some of the marriages may not actually be first ones. Because of this medians, less susceptible than means to the influence of extreme values, have also been calculated. Data on age at marriage for ministers and their brides are presented in Table Two. For the late sixteenth and seventeenth centuries, the small sample of ten suggests that ministers' wives often married in their mid twenties, sometimes their late twenties. The mean of 24.4 years and the median of twenty-three compares with a figure of twenty-six to twenty-seven for a much larger sample of women taken from court depositions between 1660 and 1770.[12] It has been suggested that daughters of the landed élite in Scotland married early.[13] Although the average age at first marriage of ministers' wives in the earlier part of our period may have been a little below that of women in general, marriages involving brides under the age of twenty included only one out of ten in the late sixteenth and seventeenth centuries, and nine out of sixty-one in the eighteenth. For the eighteenth century both mean and median ages for brides, with larger samples, rose to twenty-six to twenty-seven. This was more in line with what we know of the average age of first marriage for Scotswomen in general. It must be remembered, however, that these calculations relate to brides originating from the middling ranks of society and above. Brides coming from more modest origins may not have married at quite the same age.

TABLE 2. Age at First Marriage of Ministers and Their Wives

WIVES

	MEAN	MEDIAN	SAMPLE SIZE
1560–1699	24.5	23	10
1700–1749	26.8	26	23
1750–1800	27.9	27	38

MINISTERS

	MEAN	MEDIAN	SAMPLE SIZE
1560–1649	31.0	32	18
1650–1699	31.7	32	34
1700–1749	34.5	33	81
1750–1799	34.5	33	175

For ministers, age at first marriage is clearer because a larger sample is available, though again data are scarce for the early part of the period. The average age of first marriage was 31.0 for the period 1560–1649 and 31.7 for the last quarter of the seventeenth century, rising to 34.5 a century later. The median figure was more stable at thirty-two for the seventeenth century and thirty-three for the eighteenth. Ministers thus married later than their brides. This can be explained by the long and rigorous training which candidates for the ministry had to undergo. After graduating with an MA from a Scottish university, postgraduate study of divinity led to an examination by a presbytery assessing his suitability for the ministry. Once a presbytery granted a licence to a candidate he might then serve as a temporary stand-in for various ministers within the presbytery. Alternatively such men might take up posts as chaplains or tutors to landed families, or work as schoolmasters. Even after being licensed it might take some time for a suitable parish to fall vacant. The whole process of training might take six or seven years or more following graduation.[14] As a result, ministers commonly entered their first parish in their late twenties or early thirties. Furthermore, there was no guarantee of a parish at the end of it. Given the system of patronage, candidates often needed suitable family connections in order to be presented to a vacant parish. An unknown proportion of hopeful young men must have ended up as 'stickit ministers', continuing as schoolmasters, sometimes too poor to marry, like Scott's caricature Dominie Sampson in *Guy Mannering*.

Ministers therefore generally delayed marriage until they had been entered into their first parishes. Where details can be calculated, sixteen per cent of ministers studied married in the same year that they entered their first parish, and seventy per cent of them within five years. Only three per cent married before they got a parish. In such circumstances it is likely that they had been engaged for some time but had postponed marriage until their future and financial security was confirmed. Many ministers delayed marriage for some years more until they had established themselves in their parish. Given this, it is not surprising that courtship was often prolonged. The diary of George Ridpath, minister of Stitchill in the mid-eighteenth century shows that he knew his future bride Wilhelmina Dawson, daughter of a merchant in Kelso, for many years before they married in 1764.[15] By this time conventions were changing and women had more independence and freedom of movement than in earlier times. Ridpath's diary between 1755 and 1761 shows him and Wilhelmina visiting each other's houses, walking and riding together (sometimes unchaperoned) on numerous occasions before he proposed to her.

How did potential brides come to meet their future husbands? Family links must have been a major source of contacts. Some girls married cousins who were ministers and in other cases a relationship is suggested by the similarity of surnames. Proximity in an early stage of a minister's career was also important. Grisel Kynnynmonth, a lady in waiting to the Countess of Buccleuch, married John Arthur who had been chaplain to the family.[16] That courtship was sometimes initiated by the girl is suggested by William Row's biography of his father-in-law in which he described how he had been courted by various girls before he proposed to Beatrix Hamilton.[17]

The mechanisms of courtship in the mid-eighteenth century are well described in the diary of John Mill, minister of a parish in Shetland. At forty, having had his parish for nearly ten years, he seems to have decided that it was time to get married. He courted various local girls without success. One preferred a local laird as life in the manse may have seemed too austere for 'she wanted to be a Lady and get Madam at any rate'. Another girl turned out to be already pregnant.[18] He set about finding a wife in Edinburgh when attending the General Assembly in 1754. Mill's account suggests that Edinburgh acted, at this time, as a major marriage market for Scotland's landed and professional classes. The social role of the General Assembly seems to have been as important to many ministers as its official business. He met his future wife, daughter of an Edinburgh baillie, while acting as best man for a fellow minister. Having discovered her real piety in conversation with her, he carefully sounded out other people who knew her regarding her character. Suitably impressed, he then persuaded the wife of a friend to make a proposal on his behalf.[19]

She died four years later, following the birth of their second child. In 1762 Mill was back in Edinburgh seeking another wife. The remoteness of his parish was a clear disadvantage whatever his personal qualities might have been. He courted the daughter of a knight and became engaged to her. They agreed to get married the following spring, but another minister living close to Edinburgh proposed to her. She broke her engagement to Mill and accepted the other man 'purely to be near her friends'.[20] Eventually he married Ann Young, daughter of a portioner near Edinburgh. He had met and considered her a possibility before he married his first wife. Her mother, however, had not wished her daughter to move to Shetland and was only persuaded with difficulty on this second occasion.

Objections to marriage were sometimes raised by the families of potential brides.[21] On the other hand even in the seventeenth century girls seem to have had considerable freedom of choice of partner, marrying on the basis of attraction as well as security. Margaret Bruce, daughter of James Bruce, minister of Kingsbarns, refused a proposal of marriage from the ambitious James Sharp, the future Archbishop of St Andrews, and married another minister instead.[22]

Given that so many ministers' wives came from landed backgrounds, they were often provided with substantial dowries. Sir Archibald Stewart of Blackhall gave his sister a dowry of 8000 merks.[23] John Mill's two marriages were both advantageous in financial, as well as personal terms, allowing him to build up a substantial estate.[24] Marrying purely for affection without thought for a dowry could cause difficulties. Robert Muire, minister of Drymen 1626–48 married an honest woman of low status who brought no money with her, to the distress of his family.[25] More detailed study of marriage contracts is needed to establish the range of dowries which ministers received. Their wives often inherited property and on occasion these were substantial estates. Ministers who married the daughters of merchants could also enjoy the benefits of being entered as burgesses, as well as the cash they received.

What qualities did ministers value in their wives? Contemporary epitaphs, incorporated into Scott's biographies and ministers' diaries, emphasise piety above all other qualities, followed by meekness and frugality.[26] Piety would doubtless have been required of ministers' wives in order to maintain their husbands' professional credibility, as well as suiting their personal inclinations. Meekness and frugality are likely to have been qualities valued more generally in early modern Scottish society, not merely within the ministry. Despite the relative affluence of many ministers a plain and unadorned lifestyle seems to have been the norm for their families. Although not all ministers' wives would have been well educated or even literate some certainly were. Christian Melville, daughter of a professor of Hebrew at St Andrews, was proficient in Hebrew and could translate it into English.[27]

There was scope within marriage for a wide range of relationships, including plenty evidence of real affection. For example, James Gordon, an Aberdeenshire minister in the late seventeenth and early eighteenth century, seems to have had a close and compassionate relationship with his wife.[28] Robert Blair was 'warmly attached' to his first wife, Beatrix Hamilton, and saved his second wife, Katherine Montgomerie, from drowning at the risk of his own life.[29] John Mill wrote of his 'great apprehension concerning his wife' during the birth of their first child and how, during the birth of their second 'I couldn't bear to hear her cries'.[30] John Moray, minister of South Leith 1603–9, moved to Dysart because of concern for his wife's delicate health.[31] Relationships could also turn sour as William Boyd, minister of Coylton 1739–51, is supposed to have died from grief due to his wife's infidelity.[32] Helen Stirling, wife of Andrew Allan, minister of Blackford, was convicted of adultery in 1611.[33] James Steele, minister of Heriot, 1678–83, is supposed to have resigned his charge due to the (unspecified) 'base conduct' of his wife, Mary Bain.[34] John Kello, minister of Spott, strangled his wife, Margaret Thomsoune and then tried to make it look as though she had hanged herself.[35]

The activities of ministers' wives are unlikely to have been confined to the manse. In managing their households they could call on the help of servants. Poll tax records of the 1690s show that ministers' households, though small compared with those of many lairds, commonly included two or three female servants plus a male servant, presumably to cultivate the glebe. Little information is available regarding their work within their parishes, yet bequests to the poor made by ministers' widows suggest an active involvement in helping the needy rather than mere general piety. The nature of relations between ministers' wives and other women in their parishes, and the degree to which their social circles spanned the divide between landed society and the tenantry remains a matter for speculation. Descriptions of ministers' wives as 'spouse and helper' suggest an active rather than a passive role.[36] There is evidence of ministers' wives acting independently, attending conventicles for example,[37] or petitioning ecclesiastical and secular authorities on behalf of their husbands and families. Elizabeth Knox, daughter of the reformer married John Welsche, minister of Ayr. He was imprisoned then exiled by James VI for opposing the king's religious reforms. When he wanted to temporarily return to Scotland, in order to join the colony in Nova Scotia, his wife petitioned James for permission. When he told her that her husband could return provided that he reconciled himself to episcopacy she retorted that she would rather have him beheaded than compromise his integrity.[38]

That activities of ministers' wives were by no means confined to the manse has been highlighted by Sanderson's recent study of women in eighteenth-century Edinburgh.[39] She cites examples of ministers' wives who continued after their marriages to work as dressmakers and milliners, or who rented rooms and kept shops.[40] Obviously in a city like Edinburgh the range of employment opportunities was much wider than in a rural parish or a small burgh. It has been suggested that the wives of professional men, including the clergy, in contemporary London did not normally work, yet it was clearly not unusual in Scotland.[41]

For a prospective bride marriage to a minister might have seemed to offer a life of some frugality and austerity, but also social respectability, security and a comfortable sufficiency, if not great riches. Life in the manse was not always easy or safe though. Society could be violent even without considering the 'rabbling' which many ministers and their wives endured with the revolution of 1688 that left many 'outed' ministers and their families living in Edinburgh in poverty.[42] In 1670 the wife of Alex Kinnear, minister of Neilston, was beaten when nine or ten men broke into the manse and plundered it.[43] In 1643 Jonet Cunynghame was sufficiently ill-advised to accompany her young husband, John Weir, minister of Dalserf, on a mission to help Protestants in Ireland, at the behest of the General Assembly. Sailing back to Scotland they were captured and imprisoned by Alasdair MacColla. Because she was pregnant she was set free, but her husband died from the rigours of his confinement. In 1645 she petitioned Parliament for the loss of 1,000 merks, a part of her dowry that her brother had given her in Ireland, and for further assistance. As her husband had only recently entered the ministry when captured he had little money of his own so she was granted 3,000 merks.[44]

The gap between the ages of ministers and their wives at marriage, where it can be ascertained, was commonly five to eight years, sometimes a dozen. Given this and the likelihood that ministers' wives, if they survived childbirth, would have lived longer, on average, than their husbands, many ministers' wives would have been left as widows. The details in Scott's biographies show that they often survived their husbands by many years. Some married again, but for others widowhood brought insecurity and poverty. From 1744 the Ministers' Widows Fund provided some security. Before then cases of ministers' widows reduced to poverty and seeking assistance from kirk sessions are not uncommon.[45] After the death of her husband, Patrick Rynd minister of Dron, Agnes Clerk, 'turned ane gangrell poore woman, selling some smallwares'.[46]

This chapter has only sketched the outlines of a neglected topic. While the origins and experience of ministers' wives have received no attention even the Scottish ministry as a profession has attracted little research.[47] However, limitations of source material are also evident. The reader will have noticed that most of the evidence presented has come from men writing about ministers' wives rather than from the women themselves. Scott's compilation proved less forthcoming about ministers' wives than had initially been hoped. Sources such as presbytery and synod records are likely to contain some useful information. Given that a substantial proportion of them came from landed backgrounds, more details of their experience may be gleaned from correspondence surviving in estate collections. In the seventeenth century Covenanters like James Nimmo recorded their religious experiences, but so did their wives.[48] It is likely that a good deal of relevant, if widely scattered, source material still remains unexplored.

NOTES

1. J. Ridley, *John Knox* (Oxford, 1968), 432. See also the portrait of Mrs Knox in this volume.
2. R. K. Marshall, *Virgins and Viragos* (London, 1983).
3. R. Mitchison, 'The social impact of the clergy of the reformed kirk of Scotland', *Scotia*, 6 (1982), 1–13.
4. W. Makey, *The Church of the Covenant* (Edinburgh, 1979), 95.
5. Ibid, 101–102.

6. *e.g. The Life of Mr. Robert Blair, Minister of St. Andrews*, ed. T. McCrie (Wodrow Society, 1848).

7. J. Buckroyd, *The Life of James Sharp, Archbishop of St. Andrews 1618–1678* (Edinburgh, 1987).

8. H. Scott, ed. *Fasti Ecclesiae Scoticanae*, 1st edn, (3 vols, London, 1866–71).

9. *e.g. The Diary of the Rev. John Mill, minister of the parishes of Dunrossness, Sandwick and Cunningsburgh in Shetland 1740–1803*, ed. G. Goudie, (Scottish History Society [SHS], 1889), xxiii. His first marriage is not listed in *Fasti* and his second is wrongly given as his first.

10. Makey, *Covenant,* 101–2.

11. Scott, *Fasti,* ii, pt 1, 60, 341.

12. R. A. Houston, *The Population of Britain and Ireland 1500–1750* (London, 1992), 37.

13. J. Ridley, *Knox, 142.* Cf. marriage age in the paper by Stiùbhart in this volume.

14. Makey, *Covenant,*102.

15. *The Diary of George Ridpath, Minister of Stitchel 1755–61*, ed. Sir J. Balfour Paul (SHS, 1922), *passim.*

16. Scott, *Fasti,* i, 165.

17. McCrie, *Blair,* 116.

18. Goudie, *Mill,* 27.

19. Ibid.

20. Ibid.

21. Scott, *Fasti,* ii, pt 2, 474, 615.

22. Ibid, 443.

23. Ibid, ii, pt 2, 464.

24. Goudie, *Mill,* xxv.

25. Ibid, 352.

26. Scott, *Fasti,* ii, pt 1, 98, 184, 307, 335; ii, pt 2, 208.

27. Ibid, ii, pt 1, 308.

28. R. A. Houston, 'Women in the economy and society of Scotland 1500–1800' in R. A. Houston and I. D. Whyte, eds. *Scottish Society 1500–1800* (Cambridge 1989), 142.

29. McCrie, *Blair,* xv, 138.

30. Balfour Paul, *Ridpath,* 23.

31. Scott, *Fasti,* i, 104.

32. Ibid, ii, part 1, 100.

33. Ibid, ii, part 2, 750.

34. Ibid, i, 273.

35. Ibid, i, 380.

36. McCrie, *Blair,* 117.

37. Scott, *Fasti,* ii, pt 1, 8, 197.

38. Ibid, ii, pt 1, 119.

39. E. C. Sanderson, *Women and Work in eighteenth-century Edinburgh* (London. 1996).

40. Ibid, 117–121, 203–13.

41. P. Earle, 'The female labour market in London in the late seventeenth and early eighteenth centuries', *Economic History Review,* 2nd ser, 42 (1989), 236–7.

42. H. M. Dingwall, *Late Seventeenth-century Edinburgh. A demographic study* (Aldershot, 1994), 133.
43. Scott, *Fasti*, ii, pt 1, 229.
44. Ibid, 277.
45. I. D. Whyte & K. A. Whyte, 'The geographical mobility of women in early modern Scotland' in L. Leneman, ed. *Perspectives in Scottish Social History* (Aberdeen, 1988), 99–100.
46. Scott, *Fasti,* ii, pt 2, 630.
47. Cf. R. Mitchison, 'social impact'; R. O'Day, *The English Clergy: the Emergence and Consolidation of a Profession 1558–1642* (Leicester, 1979) and J. H. Pruett, *The Parish Clergy Under the Later Stuarts* (London, 1978).
48. *The Narrative of Mr. James Nimmo 1654–1709*, ed. W. G. Scott-Moncrieff (SHS, 1889), xii.

CHAPTER TWENTY

Women and Gender in the Early Modern Western Gàidhealtachd

_____ *Domhnall Uilleam Stiùbhart*

TO DATE the history of women – to say nothing of social history – has been marginal in Gàidhealtachd[1] historiography; however, Gaelic literary criticism has been somewhat more favourable. This paper will give a brief impression of the variety of women's lives during the seventeenth and early eighteenth centuries, the constraints under which they lived, and how some were able to negotiate and even circumvent these according to individual circumstances. Where expedient I have used evidence from literature and oral tradition, though not to the extent of privileging them above or even as equal to more traditional sources. Finally, one hardly needs to point out that there is no generic 'Gàidhealtachd woman' for this or any other period of history.

Even more so than in Ireland, the culture of the early modern Scottish Gàidhealtachd was imbued with a strong patriarchal ideology. Classical or vernacular, male or female, secular Gaelic poetry was underpinned by the authoritative norms of the panegyric code, 'a coherent system of rhetoric of great resonance and evocative power'. This system was predicated upon notions of an assertive masculine independence based upon physical prowess and violence, heavily influenced by concepts of honour and shame, and above all intended to praise the hunter-warrior chief as defender of the clan.[2] It is highly likely that such an ideology was primarily indebted to the hybrid Norse-Gaelic culture of the Kingdom of the Isles. This was further strengthened as a result of the siege mentality engendered in the Gaels during the late medieval period, when the Lordship of the Isles strove to maintain an independent identity against successive Lowland encroachments.[3] The warrior hero became even more crucial to Gaelic society during *Linn nan Creach* (the Age of the Forays), that confused and violent era of bloodfeud resulting from the final collapse and balkanisation of the Lordship, with the apparent total disruption of the church throughout the western Gàidhealtachd, and the general economic crisis affecting Scotland as a whole by the mid-sixteenth century.[4]

By way of contrast, we might consider the remarkable absence of courtly love poetry – with one major exception[5] – from contemporary Scottish Gaelic classical literature, even from the seemingly representative collection of the Book of the Dean of Lismore, an early-sixteenth century compilation containing anti- and non-courtly literature aplenty. By contrast in Gaelic Ireland bilingual and multilingual poets from the Old English population served as a conduit for new love poetry deriving from continental and English models.[6] Such innovations found indigenous echoes in the ancient Irish poetic convention of the bride of the high king, and the cult of the Virgin. Grace Neville has stressed that *dánta grádha* (classical Irish love poems), are, in their objectification of the female subject, and indeed in their reflection of the assumptions of a male audience, necessarily permeated with patriarchal values.[7] Nevertheless, they do offer an outlet, however compromised or condescending, for the praise of women. Revealingly, it appears that courtly conventions enjoyed considerably less popularity in the literature of the Scottish Gàidhealtachd.

Patriarchy in the early seventeenth-century Scottish Gàidhealtachd was paradoxically stronger, firstly, because of the absence of theological underpinnings in the wake of the collapse of the church at a popular level following the Reformation[8] and secondly, in the absence of detailed and widely-known physiological justifications caused by the steady waning of continentally-derived medieval Gaelic medical traditions.[9] Such a culture had little need of constant policing of the boundaries of patriarchy; there is no evidence as yet of the 'acutely felt anxiety . . . about how women could best be governed and controlled' which some historians have discerned in early modern England.[10] Indeed, so well entrenched was the ideology that it can make little sense to speak of a prescriptive patriarchy in relation to the Gàidhealtachd of this period. Within the boundaries of the culture, it seemed natural and incontrovertible. In fact women at all levels of Gàidhealtachd society enjoyed considerably more freedom, or at any rate suffered somewhat less subordination, than we might be led to expect from prevailing cultural norms.

The overwhelming majority of the people of the early modern Gàidhealtachd lived at near-subsistence level, either as peasant farmers in *bailtean* (multiple-tenant farms), or as *sgalagan* (agricultural labourers or servants).[11] We should be somewhat wary of arguing for 'separate spheres' of men and women's labour. Ploughing and peat-cutting, for instance, counted as men's work, but women toiled beside them at the harrow and during harvest time. Again, the onerous labour of carrying peats, seaweed and manure was at the very least as much female labour as male. Certain tasks, however, were classed as women's work, unworthy of men: weeding crops, making and stooking sheaves, grinding corn, tending goats, sheep (including shearing), poultry, and milking cows, especially during the summer months at pasture in upland shielings. Above all, the wife was responsible for the domestic sphere, cooking food, dyeing, preparing and weaving cloth, washing and mending clothes, and, most importantly, caring for the children.[12] As Olwen Hufton has commented, the lower a family's position on the social scale, the more crucial the woman's role was to the household.[13] This must have been the case in the often famine-ravaged, epidemic-stricken western Gàidhealtachd.

From the early eighteenth century, young Gaels, including women, mainly but not exclusively from Argyllshire and the southern periphery of the Gàidhealtachd, found seasonal employment in reaping and shearing bands in the Lowlands. This development led to major changes in the yearly pattern of work in these areas.[14] For the great majority of women in the western Gàidhealtachd, however, life must have altered very little until the years following the Forty-Five rising, when the development of the flax industry offered a new source of income.[15] The subsequent rise of illegal whisky distilling, and the kelp industry, involved men and women alike. The growth of the herring fisheries on the west coast, as well as increased recruitment for the army, inevitably meant that the burden of agricultural work fell disproportionately upon women in the absence of their menfolk. The early modern period, then, was certainly no golden age for peasant women in the Gàidhealtachd. The drudgery, incessant toil and sheer strain of existing from year to year in a subsistence economy, not to mention recurring illnesses and above all the agonies of childbirth, come through clearly in later observers' accounts – haggard, worn out and prematurely aged by their exhausting labours.[16]

As one might expect, the importance of marriage alliances – and the concomitant exchange of property – to the upper classes and clan gentry can scarcely be overestimated, especially during an era of rivalry and occasional outright war between neighbouring clans. An important study of the genealogy of the gentry of the MacPhersons of Badenoch during the early modern period seems to suggest that, whereas men might be more likely to marry outside the clan, women tended to endogamy. By ensuring, therefore, that dowries were paid within the clan, this pattern would work towards preserving and expanding clan resources and power.[17] However, for a woman to live among her own kith and kin might be beneficial not only to clan finances, but also for the woman herself. In 1714, Greenock merchant Patrick Campbell desired that his daughter go home to Argyll 'and mary among her relations as other[s] do for I see many inconvenience's in women's going abroad'.[18] An extreme example of such 'inconvenience' might be the tragic fate of Elizabeth, daughter of Sir Coinneach Mackenzie of Coul, who emigrated to Ireland, disappeared, and in 1696 turned up, to the intense embarrassment of her family, wandering the streets of London quite out of her mind.[19]

As in Lowland Scotland, most daughters of the *fine* (clan élite), tended to marry young, apparently by the age of fifteen.[20] Some faint traditions survive, incidentally, that the chief once had the right to arrange such marriages. Among clan gentry, some forty or sixty cows were the usual *tochradh* (dowry), brought into the household, a number similar to contemporary Ireland.[21] However, there was a gradual shift to money dowries during the seventeenth century, especially at the level of clan nobility. This development, taken with the large jointures legally due to the widow, caused problems with family finances.[22]

What apparently distinguishes the western Gàidhealtachd from the rest of the country – and indeed from much of Europe – was the young marital age across society, possibly as low as eighteen for women. It may be noted, however, that the evidence is overwhelmingly literary and impressionistic in character, and may be vulnerable to later statistical research.[23] Many cases relate to small islands where delayed marriage might well have caused a great deal of unwanted competitiveness and strife among the young males.[24] The extreme case in this regard is tiny St Kilda, isolated for all but three months of the year, where girls married at twelve, or possibly even earlier.[25] The custom of the new couple stocking their household by thigging *faoighe* gifts from their neighbours suggests that, unlike in England, young people did not spend years saving money from service or apprenticeship in order to set up home together. John Ramsay of Ochtertyre commented that love-matches were more common than 'in commercial countries' and that many of them began whilst at the summer shielings, a supposition strengthened by a number of illegitimacy cases recorded in church session registers.[26]

Serial or trial marriage, the consequence of easy divorce permitted under Gaelic brehon laws combined with a somewhat cynical approach to the canonical marriage rules of the church, was not unknown, particularly among chiefs and clan gentry at the beginning of the early modern period.[27] The most notorious example is the five-times married Raghnall MacDonald of Benbecula (d.1636), described by the historian Niall MacMhuirich as '*duine maith do reir na haimsire ina ttarrla se*' (a good man according to his times).[28] Increased state and ecclesiastical control during the early seventeenth century, however, and the accompanying stress now laid upon legitimacy and primogeniture as the criteria of inheritance, meant that the custom rapidly became untenable for the clan élite. This is clearly demonstrated by the attempt of Domhnall MacDonald of Clan Ranald Domhnall Dubh na Cuthaige (d.1685), to divorce his wife Mòr, on the perfectly accurate grounds that she had borne a son to Norman MacLeod. In a grisly case replete with accusations of torture and imprisonment, which scandalised the entire country, Mòr was able to parry her husband by claiming that he was merely trying to 'palliat and cover his unjust deserting of her'.[29] Some evidence, however, suggests that the custom of irregular marriage may have continued among the rest of the Gàidhealtachd population even into the nineteenth century.[30]

Elite women at the beginning of the early modern period were potentially vulnerable both under Gaelic and Lowland law. Perhaps the most extreme case is the wretched Màiri (c.1542–c.1602), heiress to the MacLeods of Harris. Rejected and exiled by her own people in favour of her cousin Iain a'Chùil Bhàin, she spent her youth as a ward being shuttled around various predatory noble families before finally being married off to Dùghall Campbell of Auchinbreck.[31] One might also note the fate of disgraced noblewomen who bore illegitimate children, such as Anna MacDonald, daughter of Iain Mùideartach and sister of Domhnall Dubh na Cuthaige, or Seònaid, sister of Iain Garbh MacLeod of Raasay, both of whom composed songs to justify their case, and who appear to have been subsequently quietly married off to minor gentry.[32]

Other evidence, however, suggests that, once married, far from being mere chattels, many wives of gentry status and above enjoyed a considerable amount of independence and power. Under customary Gaelic law a divorced or widowed woman was entitled to reclaim the dowry she had brought to the marriage.[33] The extreme cases here are the redoubtable Lady Agnes Campbell and her daughter, Fionuala MacDonald, the 'Inghean Dubh' ('Dark-haired Maiden'). The control these women could exert over their military dowries, together with their superior standard of education, allowed them to play a crucial rôle as brokers in Ulster politics during the late sixteenth century.[34] The part wives played in the day-to-day running of household and estate is less visible in the sources. Oral tradition attributes considerable power to the one-eyed Mairghread MacLeod, wife of Domhnall Gorm Mór MacDonald of Sleat and sister to his great rival Ruairidh Mór of Harris, even to the extent of having the chief's poet, Niall Mór, of the great MacMhuirich bardic family, exiled for his insolence towards her.[35] Domhnall Gorm Mór's idiosyncratic method of divorcing her – sending her back to her brother on a one-eyed horse led by a one-eyed groom with a one-eyed dog – should perhaps be read as an oblique comment upon the miserable dowry she had brought into his household.[36]

The assistance that well-connected wives could give their husbands is suggested by Ruairidh Mór's own wife Iseabail Mhór MacDonald, whose apparent experience as a maid of honour to Anna of Denmark, wife of James VI, was surely one of the reasons why the wily chief was able to win the king's approval, and indeed a knighthood.[37] Again, the odium excited by the wife of Sir Domhnall Gorm Òg MacDonald of Sleat, Seònaid Mackenzie, might indicate that she was no mere marriage pawn of her family. Seònaid was actively involved in supporting Mackenzie interests and helping reorganise her husband's estate along commercial lines. This impression is strengthened by her attempts in 1639 to rally her relatives to defend the Sleat estates against a possible attack by Gilleasbaig Campbell seventh earl of Argyll, Gilleasbaig Fiar-Shùileach.[38] Later in the century, again in Skye, Seònaid MacLeod, daughter of Alexander of Greshornish, appears to have been the driving force in her marriages to two of the most powerful men in the island, firstly to John MacLeod of Talisker, then to James MacDonald of Oronsay, who eventually succeeded to the Sleat estates as sixth baronet.[39]

Despite the lack of early modern female diaries, autobiographies or funeral sermons, surviving letters can give us some insight into how upper-class women lived, thought and felt, especially during the latter half of the period. Although no such sources exist for women of the *tuath* (peasantry), we are lucky to have the *luinneagan* (choral work songs). Most of these have survived to the present in the form of waulking songs to keep time for fulling cloth. Although they were at one time sung throughout the Gàidhealtachd,[40] the surviving corpus is concentrated in the Uists and Barra, and among the descendants of emigrants from these islands in the Maritime region of Canada, especially Cape Breton. In John MacInnes' words, 'the choral songs are essentially the women's contribution to Gaelic literature, and in this poetry we view through their eyes the order of society'.[41] At best, these songs, despite their ostensibly formulaic composition, are intensely personal, possessed of a passionate beauty and power quite without parallel in Scottish, or even British, literature. What makes them interesting to a social historian, however, is that they were composed in a space forbidden to men.[42] To women, a waulking was not only a focus for private recreation, but an opportunity to create and voice a 'female public opinion' on neighbourhood matters and beyond.[43]

As we might expect, many songs are taken up with themes of the panegyric code, although the praise is transformed and personalised through the erotic strain which pervades the genre.[44] A surprisingly common theme is nostalgia for a distant – or even not so distant – birthplace, and the anguish of being separated from one's kindred.[45] Again, waulking songs can function as artistic gossip, for example in defending sexual reputation. One early seventeenth-century song, possibly from Morar, goes further: the singer, in tradition one Nighean Aonghais Bhàin 'ic Dhomhnaill Òig, complains to the aforementioned Raghnall MacDonald of Benbecula, that she has been raped by a MacMhuirich and demands justice.[46] It is noteworthy, however, that other songs quite clearly imply that no shame was attached to bearing a nobleman's child, a fact also mentioned by later travellers such as the morally scandalous Rev. John Lane Buchanan.[47]

The *luinneagan* do not just deal with neighbourhood matters alone. As well as inter-clan flyting, certain of the songs deal with more overtly political matters, particularly those composed during the chaotic years following the 1609 Statutes of Iona when the clans of the western seaboard were riven between those, usually of the chief's party, who recommended accommodation with the Edinburgh authorities, and others, often brothers, younger sons, and minor gentry, who advocated outright resistance. A song from the Clan Ranald territories seems tacitly to support the rebellious Raghnall MacDonald of Benbecula against his nephew the young chief Iain Mùideartach.[48] On the contrary, another song from the estates of MacDonald of Sleat appears to back Domhnall Gorm Òg in his attempt to reach an understanding with central government.[49] Such examples demonstrate that some women, at that particular time and in these areas, were involved to some extent in public debates and in shaping political opinions among their people.

Finally, in dealing with family relations in the Scottish Gàidhealtachd, one might note the vast number of lullabies surviving in the tradition and the universal popularity of stories about *tàcharan-sìthe* (changelings), indicating a widespread anxiety over the loss of children which transcends purely economic reasons for grief. In the absence of any ecclesiastical framework in the western Gàidhealtachd for much of the early modern era, parents were determined to have their children baptised, even if only by godparents.[50] It thus seems somewhat unlikely that a 'low-affect' society, typified by parental severity and psychological coolness towards children, was the norm at any level of Scottish Gàidhealtachd society during this period.

In general, Raymond Gillespie's comments upon women and crime in contemporary Ireland hold true for the Scottish Gàidhealtachd as well.[51] Although the area underwent extraordinary socio-economic changes during the early modern period, cohesion within community and clan, suspicion of outsiders – many of who were only too ready to criminalise the whole society – and, above all, the lack of powerful independent centralised ecclesiastical and legislative power structures meant that, unlike in England, the tensions resulting from the transformation did not generate a culture of litigation, or full-scale witch hunts.[52] In the records of heritable jurisdictions, there are none of the depositions, testimonies and petitions that are so enlightening for English historians of the period. Social control, through community norms, was informal and evidently effective.[53] Surviving criminal evidence is sparse, suggesting that women were prosecuted, as might be expected, mainly for theft of small, though not necessarily cheap, goods, for receivership of stolen property, and, occasionally, for violence against other women and infanticide.[54]

The spiritual side of women's life – of which witchcraft is an extreme manifestation – must not be overlooked. For example, the vast majority of the myriad charms and prayers recorded by Alexander Carmichael were collected from women.[55] Women's involvement with the spiritual is perhaps epitomised by the *bean-tuirim* (professional mourning woman), apparently kept by the township for keening the *coronach* at local burials.[56]

The devotional books filling the library of Lilias Murray, Lady Grant, or Lachlann MacKinnon of Coire Chatachain's request to an Edinburgh friend on behalf of his wife, who was 'curious to have Thomas a Kempis', testify that, as elsewhere, personal piety was an area of activity in which many women of the clan élite found emotional fulfilment and spiritual satisfaction.[57] It was in actively aiding and sustaining Roman Catholicism, however, that women in the Gàidhealtachd achieved most prominence. Indeed, for much of the seventeenth century chiefs' wives had a crucial part to play in supporting a faith that would be extremely unwise for their husbands to support openly.[58] This was especially the case with noblewomen who had married into the region, whose faith had been forged in staunch, and wealthy, English recusant or even continental backgrounds. Such women were able to exert a profound influence behind the scenes over their household and husbands. Lady Anna Cornwallis, wife of Gilleasbaig Campbell, Gilleasbaig Fiar-shùileach, seventh earl of Argyll, was surely instrumental in the astonishing conversion of her husband to Catholicism in 1618.[59] Lady Katherine Villiers, widow of George Villiers, duke of Buckingham, was to a large extent the power behind her second husband Raghnall MacDonnell, second earl of Antrim.[60] Early in the following century, Lady Francis Herbert, daughter of the marquess of Powys and widow of Coinneach MacKenzie, Coinneach Mór, fourth earl of Seaforth, virtually ran the estate herself, sending her son Uilleam Dubh to be educated in France rather than be brought up a Protestant at home.[61] The exotic Penelope, daughter of Colin MacKenzie governor of Tangiers, and wife of Ailean MacDonald of Clan Ranald, Ailean Dearg, controlled the family interest after her husband's death at Sheriffmuir, and was instrumental in having the forfeited estate restored to the MacDonalds in 1727.[62] The support and protection given by the Clan Ranald estate under her leadership to the Catholic clergy was vital in sustaining the faith in the western Gàidhealtachd.[63]

Women of all classes played a crucial rôle in aiding the Irish Franciscan missionaries from the early seventeenth century onwards, when Catholicism remained a 'fortress faith' sustained by sporadic, badly-funded missions, or even by individual priests. In such straits, the protection and patronage of noblewomen, especially widows, proved of fundamental importance. Widows in Kintyre sheltered Cornelius Ward and Paul O'Neill when they arrived from Ulster in 1624; the following year, visions reported by local women were instrumental in converting many in Uist and Barra, which was to be the heartland of Catholicism in the area.[64] In the mid-1650s, the strongly Catholic and by then extremely aged Iseabail Mhór, widow of Ruairidh Mór MacLeod of Harris, effectively starved the Protestant minister out of Glenelg, by refusing to pay his stipend – much to the disgust of the Synod of Argyll.[65] The synod's excommunication of Anna nic Dhomhnaill of Kintyre earlier in the same decade suggests that they may have been using her as a scapegoat to intimidate other Catholics.[66] This is undoubtedly the case with the dogged persecution of Iseabail Robertson of Kinmylies by the Presbytery of Inverness during the 1670s. Iseabail was a servant of Robert Byers of Coats, the Catholic governor of Inverness Castle, and his wife Lilias Grant. In venting their spleen on her, the local ministers were prosecuting a long vendetta against His Majesty's representative in the north.[67]

Perhaps the most immediately effective of the series of measures forced upon the chiefs of the western Gàidhealtachd in 1609 and 1616 by the Edinburgh authorities, was the requirement that eldest sons of the clan élite, or, failing that, daughters, be educated in the Lowlands.[68] It is clear from the conduct of a new generation of chiefs that this upbringing involved not only the inculcation of an alien culture and ideology, but also Protestantism. In this connection, it is rather interesting to see how, during the 1630s, the Catholic Sir Domhnall Gorm Òg MacDonald of Sleat apparently tried to circumvent this state of affairs by hiring the classical Gaelic poet Cathal MacMhuirich to tutor his daughters Catrìona and Seònaid, and probably his younger son Gilleasbaig as well. Catrìona, married to Coinneach MacKenzie of Gairloch, died young; Cathal's elegy *Leasg leinn gabháil gu Geárrloch* commemorates her great learning.[69] The religion of Seònaid, later wife of Aonghas Òg MacDonald, Lord Glengarry and Àros, and Gilleasbaig, better known as the poet Àn Ciaran Mabach, suggest that counter-reformation Catholicism which Cathal had imbued during his own bardic education in Ireland was transmitted to his pupils as well.[70] Possibly Iain Mùideartach II, Captain of Clan Ranald, was following Domhnall Gorm Òg's example in having one of the MacMhuirichs – it is unclear which one – educate his own daughter Anna, probably in the following decade.[71]

Even after the general relaxation of persecution in the early eighteenth century women still played an important rôle in promoting Catholicism, none more so than Jacobite poet Sìleas na Ceapaich (*c.*1660–*c.*1729), daughter of Gilleasbaig MacDonald of Keppoch and wife of Alexander Gordon of Camdell in Gaelic Banffshire. Sìleas was probably taught her craft by her father, himself a poet of some distinction. Her non-political songs constitute a valuable source for women's social history: for example, in *Comhairle air na Nigheanan Òga* (Advice to Young Girls), seemingly based on contemporary conduct-book literature, her listeners are warned through a series of vignettes to avoid the wiles of young men trying to entrap them.[72] This, and the song *An Aghaidh na h-Obair Nodha* (Against the New Work), appear to have been composed in reaction to the rise in openly risqué Gaelic poetry during this time.[73]

In oral tradition, however, it is Sìleas' hymns that are her most popular work, revealing a depth of piety strengthened by her isolation from her kindred in Lochaber. This was precipitated by a lengthy and debilitating illness, and tested to the limits by the death of her husband and daughter in the space of one week.[74] Intriguingly, a church report in 1714 for Glenlivet and Strathavon parishes states that women were instructed by priests, who 'send them through the Country to propagat their delusions'. It is likely that their teaching involved Sìleas' poems, such as *'S e do bheatha, Mhoire Mhaighdean* (Hail to thee, Virgin Mary), a versified life of Christ.[75]

It is probable that women played just as vital a rôle in supporting early evangelical Protestantism in the Gàidhealtachd. Barbara MacKay, wife of John, second Lord Reay, appears to have influenced his toleration of Presbyterians after the Restoration, a crucial development in the forging of a Gaelic Protestantism in Dùthaich MhicAoidh (Mackay country).[76] Also notable is the petition by Margaret MacDonald, Lady Clan Ranald, and Lady Boisdale to the Presbytery of Long Island, asking for a Protestant minister to be sent to Catholic South Uist, apparently immediately after the death of the Catholic Penelope MacKenzie.[77]

During the latter half of the seventeenth century, ecclesiastical authority was being asserted across all levels of society in the Gàidhealtachd. The success of the Episcopalian ministry is most visible in the marked decline in illegitimacy rates following the Restoration, a trend which continued until the 1690s, a decade of social, not to mention clerical, dislocation and famine throughout the region.[78] The outlawing of trial marriages certainly benefited women of the clan élite. This strengthened their legal position as they were now entitled to a secure jointure after their husband's death. Widows such as Lady Francis Herbert and Penelope Mackenzie were thus able to exert influence over their property by ensuring strict payment of their settlement, though the law caused considerable financial problems for their heirs. However, Lowland women rarely married into Gaelic nobility or gentry at this time, probably because of the comparative niggardliness of Highland jointures, and the isolation of the country.[79]

In addition to contemporary socio-economic and religious developments in the Gàidhealtachd, new cultural mores were spreading from the south. By the end of the seventeenth century women had largely abandoned the traditional *earasaid* (female plaid), in favour of garments of the

Lowland pattern.[80] In songs of the period by both men and women there is a new emphasis upon consumer goods, especially fashionable clothes as tokens of status, as objects of praise, or satire.[81] The increasing number of letters written by women attests to growing female literacy in Lowland Scots and in English. A new emphasis on female education – not to mention the increased privacy afforded by rebuilt mansions – is also suggested by a series of notorious scandals at the end of the seventeenth century resulting from illicit liaisons between noblewomen and their tutors.[82]

Family histories suggest that more freedom was being allowed to young people of the clan élites in choosing their husbands.[83] The era of the great clan marriage networks was over. Perhaps an extreme example of women's freedom is seen by the scandalous behaviour of two, or maybe three, daughters of Domhnall Breac MacDonald of Sleat, who eloped and bore their lovers' children.[84] According to their brother, Domhnall a'Chogaidh, 'it seems god has determin'd that the last generation of daughters in this house should give their family little (if any) contentment'; these misfortunes must have been behind the almost obsessive care he took over the upbringing of his own children in Edinburgh.[85] Martin Martin was doubtless alluding to these and other scandals with his dry comment that 'women were anciently denied the use of writing in the islands to prevent love-intrigues'.[86]

Central to the new cultural mores introduced from the south was the strongly gendered concept of civility, being ideal codes of behaviour for men and women based upon supposed psycho perceptual differences between them. Of course, it is very much to be doubted whether male paradigms of innate feminine sentimentality, domesticity and submissiveness had much direct effect on Gaelic women outwith the clan élite.[87] Nevertheless, socio-economic circumstances inevitably led to their increasing exclusion from public life. If women's horizons expanded during the early eighteenth century, men's broadened considerably more. Male clan gentry and peasantry alike were able to participate in and profit from the new educational, commercial and professional opportunities offered by the British state at home and abroad. Even among the *tuath*, between two and three times as many boys as girls learnt English – the most important tool in the new commercialism – in the SSPCK charity schools.[88] Certainly, some younger, unmarried women were able to take advantage of new freedoms: the shearing bands from the Small Isles whose spending-power so scandalised the local minister serve as a good example.[89] Nevertheless, new cultural and economic barriers stood between most women in the western Gàidhealtachd, no matter how resourceful, and participation in the driving forces then transforming their culture and society.

NOTES

1. 'The Gàidhealtachd' is preferred to 'the Highlands' for the Gaelic-speaking area of Scotland for the late medieval period until the twentieth century, insofar as the former term, used by the inhabitants themselves, is not merely geographic, but highlights the linguistic and cultural unity of the region.
2. J. MacInnes, 'The Panegyric Code in Gaelic Tradition and its Historical Background', *Transactions of the Gaelic Society of Inverness* [*TGSI*], 50 (1976–8), 447–8; see also 435, 454–5; cf. S. D. Amussen, '"The part of a Christian man": the cultural politics of manhood in early modern England' in S. D. Amussen & M. A. Kishlansky, eds. *Political culture and cultural politics in early modern England* (Manchester, 1995), 214–15.
3. MacInnes, 'Panegyric Code', 495.
4. Cf. J. Wormald, 'Bloodfeud, Kindred and Government in Early Modern Scotland', *Past and Present*, 88 (1980), 54–97; K. M. Brown, *Bloodfeud in Scotland, 1573–1625* (Edinburgh, 1986), 23–31, 76–80, 266–7, 271–2.
5. Niall Mór MacMhuirich's famous *Soraidh slán don oidhche a-réir*. See Derick S. Thomson 'Niall Mór MacMhuirich', *TGSI*, 49 (1974–6), 15–18.
6. W. Gillies 'Courtly and Satiric Poems in the Book of the Dean of Lismore', *Scottish Studies*, 21 (1977), 35–53; cf. Helen J. T. O'Sullivan, 'Developments in Love Poetry in Irish, Welsh, and Scottish Gaelic, before 1650' (University of Glasgow, B.Litt. thesis, 1971), 95–101, 109–11, 136, 137–8, 140, 142–3, 235 n.85; M. S. Mac Craith, *Lorg na hIasachta ar na Dánta Grá* (Dublin, 1989) & 'Gaelic courtly love poetry: a window on the Renaissance', in C. Byrne et al eds. *Celtic Languages and Celtic Peoples* (Halifax, Nova Scotia, 1992); S. Ó Tuama, *An Grá i bhFilíocht na nUaisle* (Dublin, 1988), 18, 41, 57.
7. P. Mac Cana, 'Notes on the Early Irish Concepts of Unity', in M. P. Herman & R. Kearney, eds. *The Crane Bag Book of Irish Studies 1977–81* (Dublin, 1982), 205–19; T. Ó Dúshláine, *An Eoraip agus Litríocht na Gaeilge 1600–1650* (Dublin, 1987), 13, 157–61; G. Neville, 'Medieval Irish Courtly Love Poetry: An Exercise in Power-Struggle?', *Ètudes Irlandais* vii (1982), 19–30, 'Les Dánta Grádha et la Poésie des Troubadours: un Genre Littéraire Paradoxal' in J-M Picard, ed. *Aquitaine and Ireland in the Middle Ages* (Dublin, 1995), 161–72, '"All these pleasant verses"?: Grá, Ciapadh agus Céasadh sna Dánta Grádha' in M. Ní Dhonnchadha ed., *Nua-Léamha: Gnéithe de Chultúr, Stair agus Polaitíochţ na hèireann c.1600–c.1900* (Dublin, 1996), 72–88. See also Ó Tuama, *An Grá i bhFilíocht*, 22, 25–6, 33, 63.
8. I disagree with the interpretations advanced in J. Dawson, 'Calvinism and the Gàidhealtachd in Scotland' in A. Pettegree, A. Duke & G. Lewis, eds. *Calvinism in Europe 1540–1620* (Cambridge, 1994), 231–53, J. Kirk, 'The Jacobean Church in the Highlands 1567–1625' in *The Seventeenth Century in the Highlands* (Inverness, 1986), 24–51 and his 'The Kirk and the Highlands at the Reformation', *Northern Scotland,* 7 (1986), 1–22.
9. Cf. J. Bannerman, *The Beatons: a medical kindred in the classical Gaelic tradition* (Edinburgh, 1986), 120–33; also M. Kidd, 'An edition of folios

72v-73r, National Library of Scotland [NLS] Adv. MS 72.1.2' (University of Edinburgh, MA Thesis, 1997).

10. A. Fletcher, *Gender, Sex and Subordination in England 1500–1800* (London, 1995), 27; cf. S. D. Amussen, *An Ordered Society: Gender and Class in Early Modern England* (Oxford, 1988), 122–3, 181–2; D. Underdown, 'The Taming of the Scold: The Enforcement of Patriarchal Authority in Early Modern England' in A. Fletcher & J. Stevenson, eds., *Order and Disorder in Early Modern England* (Cambridge, 1985), 116–36. See also M. Ingram, '"Scolding Women Cucked or Washed": A Crisis in Gender Relations in Early Modern England?' in J. Kermode & G. Walker, eds. *Women, Crime and the Courts in Early Modern England* (London, 1994), 48–80.

11. A. I. Macinnes, *Clanship, Commerce and the House of Stuart, 1603–1788* (East Linton, 1996), 14–22.

12. I. F. Grant, *Highland Folk Ways* (London, 1977), 76, 77, 107, 112, 115–16, 128–9, 178, 198–9, 211–12, 221, 222–7, 228–37, 280–1, 297–302; E. Burt, *Letters from the North of Scotland,* 2 vols (Edinburgh, 1876) ii, 147–50, 152–3; T. Pennant, *A Tour in Scotland and Voyage to the Hebrides MDCCLXXII,* 2 vols (London, 1790) i, 332; A. Allardyce, ed. *Scotland and Scotsmen in the Eighteenth Century: MSS of John Ramsay of Ochtertyre* (2 vols, Edinburgh, 1888) ii, 408; cf. R. A. Houston, 'Women in the economy . . .' 120–1; A. Clark, *Working Life of Women in the Seventeenth Century* (London, 1982), 42–64 *passim*; H. Graham, '"A woman's work . . .": Labour and Gender in the Late Medieval Countryside' in P. J. P. Goldberg, ed. *Woman is a Worthy Wight: Women in English Society c.1200–1500* (Stroud, 1992), 126–9; B. A. Hanawalt, 'Peasant Women's Contribution to the Home Economy in Late Medieval England' in Hanawault, ed. *Women and work in preindustrial Europe* (Bloomington, 1986), 3–19.

13. O. Hufton, *The Prospect Before Her* (London, 1995), 154.

14. *The Statistical Account of Scotland* [OSA], (21 vols, Edinburgh 1791–99), xx, 251–2 (Small Isles), 307 (Kilfinichen, Mull); J. Knox, *A Tour through the Highlands of Scotland and the Hebride Isles, in MDCCLXXXVI* (London, 1787), 60; cf. J. L. Campbell & F. Collinson, eds., *Hebridean Folksongs* [HF] (3 vols, Oxford, 1969–81), iii, ll.1037–52. T. M. Devine 'Temporary Migration and the Scottish Highlands in the Nineteenth Century' *Economic History Review*, 2nd ser., 32 (1979), 348–51.

15. C. W. J. Withers, *Gaelic Scotland: The Transformation of a Culture Region* (London, 1988), 289–98; Pennant, T. A. *Tour in Scotland MDCCLXIX*, (London, 1790) 219.

16. J. Leyden, ed. James Sinton, *Tour in the Highlands & Western Islands, 1800* (Edinburgh, 1903), 35; L. A. Necker de Saussure, *Voyage en Ècosse et aux Iles Hébrides* (Paris, 1821) i, 384; iii, 12; H. Miller, *My Schools and Schoolmasters or The Story of my Education* (Edinburgh, 1858), 266–7, 285–6.

17. A. G. Macpherson, 'An Old Highland Genealogy and the Evolution of a Scottish Clan', *Scottish Studies,* 10 (1966), 17, 18–21; 'An Old Highland Parish Register: Survivals of Clanship and Social Change in Laggan, Inverness-shire, 1775–1854 II', *Scottish Studies,* 12 (1968), 81–98, 108 and his

'Migration fields in a traditional Highland community, 1350–1850', *Journal of Historical Geography,* 10 (1984), 1–14, especially 7–9.

18. Scottish Record Office [SRO], RH 15/14/121; D. Graham-Campbell, 'The Younger Generation in Argyll at the beginning of the Eighteenth Century', *Scottish Studies,* 18 (1974), 91. See also R. Reddington-Wilde in this volume.

19. NLS, MS 1277 fos 317, 319; MS 1320 fos 83–4, 85, 86, 88–9, 90–1, 93; MS 1351 fos 232–3; MS 1389 fos 79–80, 81, 83; Alexander Mackenzie, *History of the Clan Mackenzie* (Inverness, 1879), 448–9.

20. Macinnes, *Clanship,* 9.

21. SRO GD 201/1/81 & 162. T. Pennant, *Tour in Scotland* MDCCLXXII, i, 348; ii, 435; cf. K. W. Nicholls, 'Irishwomen and Property in the Sixteenth Century' in M. MacCurtain and M. O'Dowd, eds. *Women in Early Modern Ireland* (Edinburgh, 1991), 20–25.

22. Cf. NLS MS 1311 fos 2–7; Burt, *Letters* I, 253–5.

23. M. W. Flinn, *Scottish population history from the 17th century to the 1930s* (Cambridge, 1977), 37, 274, 279, 329–31; R. Mitchison & L. Leneman, *Sexuality and Social Control: Scotland 1660–1780* (Oxford, 1989), 84. Also *OSA* xx, 38 (Stornoway), 44 (Uig, Lewis), 91 (Harris), 113n. (North Uist), 239 (Small Isles), 266 (Tiree), 300n. (Kilfinichen, Mull), 395 (Kilchoman, Islay), 436 (Gigha); Allardyce, ed., *Scotland and Scotsmen* ii, 420; J. Walker, *An Economical History of the Hebrides and Highlands of Scotland* (2 vols, Edinburgh, 1812) i, 32; cf. R. A. Houston, 'Age at marriage of Scottish women, circa 1660–1770', *Local Population Studies,* 43 (1987), 63–6. See also the paper by I & K. Whyte in this volume.

24. Buchanan, *Travels,* 47, 72, 102–3.

25. NLS Adv. 33.3.20 fo 22. M. Martin, *A Description of the Western Isles of Scotland c. 1695* (Edinburgh, 1994), 438; R. Pococke, *Tours in Scotland 1747, 1750, 1760* (Scottish History Society [SHS], 1887), 94.

26. Allardyce, *Scotland and Scotsmen,* ii, 420; Mitchison & Leneman, *Sexuality and Social Control,* 186.

27. W. D. H. Sellar, 'Marriage, Divorce and Concubinage in Gaelic Scotland', *TGSI,* 51 (1979–80), 464–95, especially 473, 478–88; K. W. Nicholls, *Gaelic and Gaelicised Ireland in the Middle Ages* (Dublin, 1972), 5, 10–11, 59, 73–7; cf. I. F. MacLeod, *The MacLeods: The History of a Clan* (Edinburgh, 1981), 145; C. Giblin, ed. *Irish Franciscan Mission to Scotland 1619–1646: Documents from Roman Archives* (Dublin, 1964), 58; D. C. MacTavish, ed. *Minutes of the Synod of Argyll,* (2 vols, SHS, 1943–4) i, 45; Martin, *Description,* 175; Pennant, *Tour in Scotland* MDCCLXXII, ii, 434.

28. A. Cameron, ed. *Reliquiæ Celticæ* (2 vols, Inverness, 1892–4) ii, 172; Macinnes, *Clanship,* 86n.46.

29. SRO, GD 201/1/98 &186, 201/4/23; J. L. Campbell, *Canna: The Story of a Hebridean Island* (Oxford, 1984), 77–83; C. Ó Baoill & D. MacAulay, eds. *Scottish Gaelic Vernacular Verse to 1730: A Checklist* [*ÓBMA*] (Aberdeen, 1988) nos 291 & 156; cf. *HF* i, l.143–96, ibid iii, ll.348–53; A. A. Whyte, 'Scottish Gaelic Folksong 1500–1800' (University of Glasgow, B.Litt. thesis 1971), 281–3.

30. A. G. Macpherson, 'An Old Highland Parish Register I', *Scottish Studies,* 11

(1967), 151; 'An Old Highland Parish Register II', *Scottish Studies,* 12 (1968), 102–8; cf. J. L. Buchanan, *Travels in the Western Hebrides from 1782 to 1790* (Waternish, 1997), 89, 103.

31. Grant, *The MacLeods,* 116–26; D. MacKinnon & A. Morrison, *The MacLeods – The Genealogy of a Clan* (5 vols, Edinburgh, 1968–76) i, 16–18.

32. School of Scottish Studies, Edinburgh, D. J. MacDonald MSS, i, 31–8; D. I. MacDhomhnaill, *Uibhist-a-Deas* (Stornoway, 1981), 37; *ÓBMA,* 287; Morrison, *The MacLeods,* iv, 36.

33. Nicholls, 'Irishwomen and Property', 22.

34. K. Simms, 'Women in Gaelic Society during the Age of Transition' in MacCurtain & O'Dowd, eds. *Women in Early Modern Ireland,* 35, 38–9; C. Brady, 'Political Women and Reform in Tudor Ireland' in ibid. 78–9.

35. Edinburgh University Library, Carmichael Watson Papers 112, fos 89v.-90.

36. Grant, *The MacLeods,* 196; cf. *ÓBMA* 407; Whyte, 'Scottish Gaelic Folk-song 1500–1800', 271–4.

37. *The Register of the Privy Council of Scotland* [*RPC*] eds. J. H. Burton et al (Edinburgh, 1877–) ix, 187, 442; x, 291, 692; Grant, *The MacLeods,* 186; MacKinnon and Morrison, *The MacLeods,* i, 23; A. & A. MacDonald, *The Clan Donald,* (3 vols, Inverness, 1896–1904) iii, 310–11;R. C. MacLeod ed. *The Book of Dunvegan* (2 vols, Third Spalding Club, Aberdeen, 1938–9) i, 140–1.

38. *HF,* iii, ll.249–55, 272–8. C. Fraser-Mackintosh, *Letters of Four Centuries* (Inverness, 1890), 375–6.

39. NLS, MS 1307 fos 202, 203, 273. MacKinnon & Morrison, *The MacLeods,* iv, 117–18.

40. Allardyce, ed. *Scotland and Scotsmen,* ii, 415–16.

41. MacInnes, 'Panegyric Code', 482. See also A. Bruford, 'Workers, weepers and witches: the status of the female singer in Gaelic society', *Scottish Gaelic Studies,* 17 (1996), 64–5.

42. J. MacInnes, 'The Choral Tradition in Scottish Gaelic Poetry', *TGSI,* 46 (1969–70), 63–4; cf. *HF,* i, 13.

43. See B. Capp, 'Separate Domains? Women and Authority in Early Modern England' in P. Griffiths, A. Fox & S. Hindle, eds. *The Experience of Authority in Early Modern England* (Basingstoke, 1996), especially 129–31.

44. Cf. Amussen, 'The part of a Christian man', 214, 217–20.

45. *HF,* iii, 19.

46. Ibid. i, ll.678–746; cf. iii, 22.

47. Ibid. iii, 24–5; Burt, *Letters* ii, 195–6; Pennant, *Tour in Scotland* MDCCLXXII, ii, 426–7; cf. Mitchison & Leneman, *Sexuality and Social Control,* 224–8; J. L. Buchanan, *Travels,* vii-viii, 47, 72.

48. *HF,* i, ll.568–96.

49. NLS, MS 14876 fo 32v; cf. *ÓBMA* 412, 433; *HF,* ii, ll.525–92

50. NLS, MS 1389 fo 66; Scottish Catholic Archives [SCA], BL 1/99/1; Burt, *Letters* i, 130–1; cf. MacTavish, *Synod of Argyll,* ii, 28; A. Buchan, *A Description of St. Kilda, the Most remote Western Isle of Scotland* (Edinburgh, 1727), 34–5.

51. R. Gillespie, 'Women and Crime in Seventeenth-Century Ireland' in Mac-Curtain & O'Dowd, *Women in Early Modern Ireland,* 43–52.

52. Ibid. 45–7. For witches in the Gàidhealtachd, see Alan Bruford, 'Scottish Gaelic Witch Stories: A Provisional Type-List', *Scottish Studies*, 11 (1967), 149–92.
53. *OSA* xx, 174; also 123–4, 275–6, 314–15, 322.
54. Cf. SRO RH11/34/1; *The Justiciary Records of Argyll and the Isles*, (2 vols, Stair Society, Edinburgh 1949 & 1969). See also Garthine Walker, 'Women, theft and the world of stolen goods' in Kermode and Walker, *Women, Crime and the Courts*, 81–105.
55. A. Carmichael, *Carmina Gadelica*, (6 vols, Edinburgh, 1900–71).
56. Ibid. v, 338–9, 345. cf. Bruford, 'Workers', 63–4.
57. NLS MS 1331 fo 172v. W. Fraser, ed. *The Chiefs of Grant* (Edinburgh, 1883) ii, 54.
58. C. Giblin, 'St. Oliver Plunkett, Francis MacDonnell, O.F.M., and the Mission to the Hebrides', *Collectanea Hibernica*, 17 (1974–5), 100; W. J. Anderson, ed. 'Narratives of the Scottish Reformation: Prefect Ballentine's Report, *c.*1660', *The Innes Review* [IR], 8 (1957), 127. Cf. M. B. Rowlands, 'Recusant Women 1560–1640' in M. Prior, ed. *Women in English Society 1500–1800* (London, 1985), 160–2, 174–5; M. MacCurtain, 'Women, Education and Learning in Early Modern Ireland' in MacCurtain & O'Dowd, *Women in Early Modern Ireland*, 165–6, 167–9; P. J. Corish, 'Women and Religious Practice' in ibid. 212–15.
59. D. U. Stiùbhart, 'An Gàidheal, A'Ghàidhlig agus A'Ghàidhealtachd anns an t-seachdamh linn deug', (University of Edinburgh, PhD thesis, 1997), 98.
60. J. H. Ohlmeyer, *Civil War and Restoration in the three Stuart Kingdoms: The Career of Randal MacDonnell, marquis of Antrim, 1609–1683* (Cambridge, 1993), 29–32.
61. Mackenzie, *History of the Clan Mackenzie*, 215, 216, 232–3, 243; A. C. MacWilliam, 'A Highland Mission: Strathglass, 1671–1777', *IR*, 24 (1973), 86–7, 94.
62. NLS, MS 1303 fos 81–126. SRO GD 201/1/98 & 219. See also K. van den Steinen in this volume.
63. Cf. J. A. Stewart Jr., 'The Clan Ranald and Catholic Mission Successes, 1715–1745', *IR*, 45 (1994), 29–46, especially 32–5.
64. Giblin, *Irish Franciscan Mission*, 51–2, 84, 86, 87–8.
65. MacTavish, *Synod of Argyll, 1639–61*, i, 60–1; ii, 126–7; cf. Martin, *Description*, 237.
66. MacTavish, *Synod of Argyll*, ii, 5, 17, 26–7, 69.
67. W. Mackay, ed. *Records of the Presbytery of Inverness and Dingwall 1643–1688* (SHS, 1896), 47, 57, 59, 69–70, 92.
68. *RPC*, x, 777–8.
69. Stiùbhart, 'An Gàidheal, A'Ghàidhlig agus A'Ghàidhealtachd', 153–4; R. Black, 'The Genius of Cathal MacMhuirich', *TGSI*, 50 (1976–78), 332–3; W. J. Watson, 'Classical Gaelic Poetry of Panegyric in Scotland', ibid. 29 (1914–19), 225, 226, 227; A. Matheson, 'Poems from a Manuscript of Cathal Mac Muireadhaigh', *Èigse*, 11 (1964–6), 7–10.
70. Cf. A. M. Mackenzie, ed. *Òrain Iain Luim* (Edinburgh, 1964), ll, 1650–61.
71. Cf. note 32.

72. C. Ó Baoill, ed. *Bàrdachd Shìlis na Ceapaich: Poems and Songs by Sìleas MacDonald* (Edinburgh, 1972), 6–10, 125–6.
73. Ibid. 76–82, 165–8, 253–4. See also the paper by A. Frater in this volume.
74. Ibid. xlv-xlvi, lxiii-lxiv, 54–68, 108–112, 156–63, 175–80.
75. N. MacDonald Wilby, 'The 'Encreasce of Popery' in the Highlands, 1714–47', *IR*, 27 (1966), 94. Ó Baoill, *Bàrdachd Shìlis*, 94–100, 170–3.
76. W. R. Mackay, 'Early evangelical religion in the far north: a *Kulturkampf*', *Records of the Scottish Church History Society*, 26 (1997), 108, 113–14, 116, 119.
77. SRO, CH 1/2/72 fo 23; 1/2/73 fos 259, 268, 274, 275.
78. Mitchison & Leneman, *Sexuality and Social Control*, 140–1, 142–3, 146, 165, 168; Macinnes, *Clanship*, 78; *HF*, iii, 29. See also L. Stone, *The Road to Divorce: England 1530–1987* (Oxford, 1990), 64–5.
79. NLS, MS 1307 fos 136, 219. Burt, *Letters* ii, 214–18 (cf. NLS MS 1285 fo 186).
80. Martin, *Description*, 154, 247–8; W. Sacheverell, *An Account of the Isle of Man with a Voyage to I-Collumb-Kill* (Douglas, 1859), 99; F. J. Shaw, *The Northern and Western Islands of Scotland: Their Economy and Society in the Seventeenth Century* (Edinburgh, 1980), 196; Grant, *Highland Folk Ways*, 326–30; cf. M. Dunlevy, *Dress in Ireland* (London, 1989), 68–9, 79–81, 83–4, 96.
81. Stiùbhart, 'An Gàidheal, A'Ghàidhlig agus A'Ghàidhealtachd', 292–5. *HF*, ii, ll.879–81, 885–91; ibid. iii, 22–3, ll.727–736; *ÓBMA*, 243, 459; Martin, *Description*, 461.
82. SCA, BL 1/63/80, 1/120/13; P. Hopkins, *Glencoe and the End of the Highland War* (Edinburgh, 1986), 105, 233, 465, 484n.151; MacKinnon & Morrison, *The MacLeods*, ii, 47, 50–1; cf. D. MacRoberts, 'The Death of Father Francis White', *IR*, 27 (1966), 186–8; *ÓBMA*, 243, also 304.
83. Cf. NLS, MS 1303 fo 3; MS 1307 fo 219. R. Marshall, *Virgins and Viragos* (London, 1983), 71, 73–4. See also MacTavish, *Synod of Argyll*, ii, 62, 69.
84. Clan Donald Centre, Skye, MacDonald of Sleat Papers, 5288/7. NLS MS 1307 fo 245; MacDonald & MacDonald, *Clan Donald*, iii, 255; see also, although possibly a mistake for a daughter of MacLeod of Dunvegan, D. MacLeod, *Memoirs of the life and gallant exploits of the Old Highlander, Donald MacLeod* (London, 1791), 3–7.
85. NLS, MS 1307 fo 158. J. Dunlop, 'A Chief and his Lawyer', *TGSI*, 45 (1967–68), 268–70.
86. Martin, *Description*, 176.
87. In this respect, one might look forward to the signal, and occasionally violent, role they played in resisting clearance in various crofting riots and deforcements throughout the nienteenth century.
88. Withers, *Gaelic Scotland*, 130, 135.
89. *OSA*, xx, 251–2.

Contributors

PRISCILLA BAWCUTT is an Honorary Professor in the Department of English Language and Literature, University of Liverpool. She has published widely on early Scottish Literature, including *Gavin Douglas: a Critical Study* (1976) and *Dunbar the Makar* (1990).

WINIFRED COUTTS is a doctoral student in the Department of Scottish History at the University of Edinburgh. Her thesis is on 'The Work of the College of Justice in 1600'. She is the author of 'Women, Children and Domestic Servants in Dumfries in the Seventeenth Century', *Transactions of the Dumfriesshire and Galloway Natural History and Antiquarian Society*, 61 (1986).

GORDON DESBRISAY is an Associate Professor of History at the University of Saskatchewan. He is working on a study of seventeenth-century Aberdeen. His most recent publications include 'Catholics, Quakers and Religious Persecution in Restoration Aberdeen' *The Innes Review*, 47 (1996) and 'City Limits: Female Philanthropists and Unwed Wet Nurses in Seventeenth-Century Scottish Towns' *Journal of the Canadian Historical Association*, new series, 8 (1997).

HELEN DINGWALL is a Lecturer in History at the University of Stirling. She is the author of *Late Seventeenth-Century Edinburgh: a Demographic Study* (1994) and *Physicians, Surgeons and Apothecaries: Medical Practice in Seventeenth-Century Edinburgh* (1995).

ELIZABETH EWAN is Associate Professor of History/Scottish Studies at the University of Guelph, Ontario. She is the author of *Townlife in Fourteenth-century Scotland* (1990) and several articles on Scottish medieval women. She is also writing a book on women in late medieval Scottish towns.

JOHN FINLAY is a lecturer in the School of Law at the University of Glasgow. He completed his PhD thesis 'Men of Law before the Lords of Council, c.1500–c.1550' at the University of Edinburgh.

AUDREY-BETH FITCH is Assistant Professor of History at the California University of Pennsylvania. She is author of *The Search for Salvation in Late Medieval Scotland* (forthcoming).

ANNE C. FRATER is a Gaelic poet and works at BBC Scotland. Her PhD thesis, 'Gaelic Women's Poetry before 1750', was completed at the University of Glasgow in 1994. She is the author of 'The Gaelic Tradition up to 1750', in D. Gifford and D. McMillan, eds. *A History of Scottish Women's Writing* (1997).

MICHAEL F. GRAHAM is Associate Professor of History at the University of Akron, Ohio. His book *The Uses of Reform: 'Godly Discipline' and Popular Behaviour in Scotland and Beyond* (1996) was awarded the Roland Bainton Prize for History and Theology in 1997. He has also published several articles in British and French history.

RUTH GRANT is Educational Development Advisor in the Centre for Learning and Professional Development at the University of Aberdeen. She is currently working towards a University of Edinburgh PhD thesis – 'George Gordon, sixth earl of Huntly: a case study in Counter-Reformation politique, c.1576–1617'.

BRIDGET HENISCH is an independent scholar, who works in medieval studies and the history of photography. She is the author of *Fast and Feast: Food in Medieval Society* (1976) and a forthcoming study of the illuminations in books of hours.

R. ANDREW MCDONALD is Assistant Professor of History at University College of Cape Breton. He is the author of *The Kingdom of the Isles: Scotland's Western Seaboard, c. 1100–c. 1336* (1997) and has contributed to *A New History of the Isle of Man, volume 3: The Medieval Period, 1000–1400* (forthcoming).

ALASTAIR J. MANN is a Research Fellow (Scottish Parliament Project) at the University of St Andrews. He is the author of a forthcoming monograph, *The Scottish Book Trade, 1500–1720*.

MAUREEN M. MEIKLE is a Senior Lecturer in History at the University of Sunderland. She is working on a biography of Anna of Denmark as queen consort of Scotland, 1589–1603 and as well as publishing several articles on the Borders, has completed a monograph on Landed Society in the Eastern Anglo-Scottish Borders, 1540–1603.

DAVID G. MULLAN is Associate Professor of History and Religious Studies at the University College of Cape Breton. He is the author of *Episcopacy in Scotland* (1986) and the forthcoming *Scottish Puritanism, 1575–1636* and *Religious Controversy in Scotland, 1575–1636*.

EVELYN S. NEWLYN is Associate Professor of English at the State University of New York at Brockport. She has published articles on Middle Cornish literature as well as Middle Scots poetry. She is currently studying women's voices in early Scottish literary manuscripts.

ROXANNE REDDINGTON-WILDE has worked at Harvard's Peabody Museum of Archaeology and Ethnology and is currently teaching critical thinking through anthropology and archaeology at Cambridge College, Massachusetts. Her University of Harvard PhD thesis is now published as *The Power of Place: Spatial Analysis and Social Organisation of the Campbells in Early Modern Argyll, Scotland* (1995).

DOMHNALL UILLEAM STIÙBHART completed his PhD thesis 'An Gàidheal, A'Ghàidhlig agus A'Ghàidhealtachd anns an t-seachdamh linn deug' (Gael, Gaelic and Gàidhealtachd in the seventeenth century) at the University of Edinburgh in 1997. He is an actor, playwright and researcher in Gaelic history.

ANDREA THOMAS was Head of History at Chigwell School in Essex. She is the author of a forthcoming monograph, *Princelie Majestie: The Court of James V of Scotland, 1528–42.*

KARL VON DEN STEINEN is Professor of History at California State University, Sacramento. His publications include 'The Discovery of Women in 18th Century English Political Life', in *The Women Of England*, ed. S. B. Kanner (1979).

IAN D. WHYTE is Professor of Historical Geography at the University of Lancaster. KATHLEEN A. WHYTE is the Academic Registrar of the University of Salford. They have co-authored many articles and books, including *Exploring Scotland's Historic Landscapes* (1987). Ian's recent publications are *Scotland Before the Industrial Revolution* (1995) and *Scotland's Society & Economy in Transition, c. 1500–1760* (1997).

Index